Trauma and Grief Component Therapy for Adolescents

Trauma and Grief Component Therapy for Adolescents

A Modular Approach to Treating Traumatized and Bereaved Youth

William Saltzman
California State University at Long Beach

Christopher M. Layne
University of California at Los Angeles

Robert Pynoos
University of California at Los Angeles

Erna Olafson
University of Cincinnati College of Medicine

Julie Kaplow
Baylor College of Medicine

Barbara Boat
University of Cincinnati College of Medicine

CAMBRIDGE
UNIVERSITY PRESS

CAMBRIDGE
UNIVERSITY PRESS

University Printing House, Cambridge CB2 8BS, United Kingdom

One Liberty Plaza, 20th Floor, New York, NY 10006, USA

477 Williamstown Road, Port Melbourne, VIC 3207, Australia

314–321, 3rd Floor, Plot 3, Splendor Forum, Jasola District Centre, New Delhi – 110025, India

79 Anson Road, #06–04/06, Singapore 079906

Cambridge University Press is part of the University of Cambridge.

It furthers the University's mission by disseminating knowledge in the pursuit of
education, learning, and research at the highest international levels of excellence.

www.cambridge.org
Information on this title: www.cambridge.org/9781107579040
DOI: 10.1017/9781316443132

First published 2017
3rd printing 2018

Printed in the United Kingdom by TJ International Ltd. Padstow Cornwall

A catalog record for this publication is available from the British Library.

Library of Congress Cataloging-in-Publication Data
Names: Saltzman, William (Clinical psychologist), author.
Title: Trauma and grief component therapy for adolescents : a modular
approach to treating traumatized and bereaved youth / William Saltzman,
Christopher M. Layne, Robert Pynoos, Erna Olafson, Julie Kaplow, Barbara Boat.
Description: Cambridge, United Kingdom ; New York, NY : Cambridge University
Press, 2017.
Identifiers: LCCN 2017018748 | ISBN 9781107579040 (paperback)
Subjects: | MESH: Psychological Trauma – therapy | Psychotherapy – methods |
Counseling – methods | Bereavement | Adolescent | Counselors
Classification: LCC RC480.5 | NLM WM 172.5 | DDC 616.89/14–dc23
LC record available at https://lccn.loc.gov/2017018748

ISBN 978-1-107-57904-0 Paperback

Cambridge University Press has no responsibility for the persistence or accuracy
of URLs for external or third-party internet websites referred to in this publication
and does not guarantee that any content on such websites is, or will remain,
accurate or appropriate.

Every effort has been made in preparing this book to provide accurate and
up-to-date information that is in accord with accepted standards and practice
at the time of publication. Although case histories are drawn from actual cases,
every effort has been made to disguise the identities of the individuals involved.
Nevertheless, the authors, editors, and publishers can make no warranties that the
information contained herein is totally free from error, not least because clinical
standards are constantly changing through research and regulation. The authors,
editors, and publishers therefore disclaim all liability for direct or consequential
damages resulting from the use of material contained in this book. Readers are
strongly advised to pay careful attention to information provided by the
manufacturer of any drugs or equipment that they plan to use.

Contents

Module 4 Preparing for the Future   261

Introduction

What is Trauma and Grief Component Therapy for Adolescents (TGCTA)?

Why Does TGCTA Focus on Adolescents and Adolescence?

Adolescence is, in many ways, the best of times and the worst of times. It is a developmental period of *maximum risk* – with (along with young adulthood) the highest rates of exposure of any age group to many types of violent crime, traumatic injury, and traumatic death (Layne et al., in press). Adolescence is also a highly favorable time in which to intervene, presenting a *window of opportunity* to reduce severe distress, risky behavior, functional impairment, and the risk for developmental derailment prior to early adulthood. Adolescence is a time of growth, promise, hope, and opportunity – a period in which many quasi-adult capacities emerge and quasi-adult privileges are bestowed. These include physical growth and maturation; enhanced physical and cognitive abilities; increased self-control, self-direction, and self-protection; increased autonomy; and increased participation in society. Developmental neuroscience teaches us that adolescence is a second critical period of heightened brain plasticity (a restricted developmental period during which the nervous system is especially sensitive to the effects of experience, the first being 0–3 years). Steinberg (2014) describes this increased malleability of the adolescent brain as a two-edged sword, in which adolescents are not only more adept at acquiring new information and abilities through observation and experimentation, but also more vulnerable to the effects of physical and psychological harms, including drugs, toxins, stress, and trauma. The developmental tasks of adolescence form a window of neural "re-wiring" in which brain systems that manage rewards, relationships, self-regulation, and planning for the future each mature and are highly susceptible to disruptions. These emerging strengths and privileges both set the stage for healthy developmental progression into adulthood, yet also create new risks for developmental disruption. We (the authors) find our work with adolescents – especially youth contending with trauma and bereavement – to be an endlessly challenging, stimulating, and rewarding experience.

This manual represents both a distillation of our clinical insights and research efforts, and a personal invitation to join us in this deeply fulfilling and much-needed work.

Aspects of Adolescent Development that Inform TGCTA

Increased capacity to self-regulate and develop adaptive coping strategies. Adolescence is a developmental period in which a growing sense of self-efficacy in the face of danger arises in conjunction with major gains in brain cortex maturation and reorganization, cognitive abilities, and motor development. Nevertheless, adolescence is a period of increased sensation-seeking and risk-taking behavior, coupled with immature self-regulation (Steinberg, 2017). As such, adolescents – especially youth with histories of trauma and loss – benefit from adult supervision and assistance with appraising and developing appropriate responses to dangerous situations. As reflected by the fascination that many youth have with horror movies and their increase in thrill-seeking behaviors, adolescents strive to achieve two key developmental tasks: (1) *To strengthen their capacity to self-regulate their fear responses when confronting danger in the absence of adult protection*, and (2) *to build a repertoire of effective preventive and intervention strategies to cope with dangerous situations*. As they strive for independence, adolescents increasingly rely on their inexperienced peers to appraise and respond to danger, while typically depending on the guidance of parents and other mature caregivers to judge longer-term consequences and weigh important life decisions.

Increased ability to engage in complex causal reasoning. Adolescents' cognitive maturation enables them to engage in more sophisticated forms of causal reasoning. For example, they understand that *multiple converging causes* can collectively produce an outcome (e.g. "My buddy was in the wrong place at the wrong time"). Adolescents can also engage in *counterfactual reasoning* by constructing "if–then" hypothetical scenarios of an event, mentally altering its presumed causes, and evaluating the effects on the outcome (e.g. "If I had been there, then my friend would still be alive"). These more advanced causal reasoning skills help adolescents to develop a more sophisticated and nuanced view of the world that can accommodate complexity, ambiguity, multiple "if–then" possibilities, and competing explanations for events. Similarly, these same reasoning skills can increase the risk that some youth will become deeply preoccupied with the belief that terrible events that *have* occurred *could and should have been prevented*. These beliefs often evoke intense negative emotions including guilt, shame, remorse, bitterness, or rage at those they perceive to be responsible, whether through acts of commission or omission.

Evolving capacity to make complex moral judgments. Adolescent moral development is also evolving beyond the capacity to make simple judgments between "good" versus "bad" behavior, towards more complex and sophisticated considerations that involve weighing the likely consequences and merits of different courses of action. Adolescents possess an increased capacity to regulate their impulses to retaliate and take revenge and, instead, to rely on social institutions (including parents, schools, community leaders, and legal and law enforcement systems) to uphold the *social contract* (a typically unspoken agreement among members of society that defines the rights and duties of each member and forms a common social bond) to ensure that justice is served. Adolescents have a deepening understanding of the social contract and its attendant considerations of the rule of law, fairness, justice, safety, the protection of individual liberties, and the rights and duties of citizens, parents and other caregivers, and social institutions. Adolescents also have an increased capacity to recognize the presence and contributions of human error, negligence, greed, and malevolence to adverse life events. Such attributions often arise in a search for meaning after the *adult protective shield* has failed and resulted in traumatic events – including deaths characterized by the "Three V's": *violence*, the *violation* of laws and of the social contract, and *volition* or malevolent intent (Rynearson, 2001).

Encountering and making judgments about different social systems. Society views adolescents as falling increasingly under the broader social contract as manifest by its extension of "semi-adult" privileges and responsibilities. For example, in some cultures, youths can earn a driver's license and are granted opportunities to spend unsupervised time with friends, join the work force, and actively participate in social and civic events. At the same time, adolescents are making judgments about the legitimacy, fairness, and protective efficacy of social, governmental, and legal institutions, including schools, law enforcement, the justice system, and the child welfare system. Adolescents' experiences with these social systems, and their judgments regarding whether these systems protect them and their loved ones from danger (and effectively address the harmful consequences when the adult protective shield fails), can powerfully shape their values, expectations, conscience formation, and actions, and carry serious repercussions for their life choices, future aspirations, and preparation for the future. Inconsistent or ineffective institutional responses to sexual and interpersonal violence may pose a special risk for adolescent girls, given that these events can further undermine their expectations of safety and equal protection under the law.

When adults fail to uphold the social contract. Adolescent moral development involves becoming more aware that one *has* a conscience (knowing the difference between right and wrong), and developing the willpower to *act* on one's conscience (having the courage and determination to do what is right). Moral development can be severely disrupted when laws are violated, people are harmed, and efforts to repair and uphold the social contract are ineffectual, inconsistent, or absent. Such failures of the "adult" world can undermine a sense of predictability and safety. Further, they can erode adolescents' capacity and motivation to regulate their vengeful desires, relegate the task of enforcing the law and upholding the social contract to the proper societal institutions, and obey the law. Conversely, failures to uphold the social contract can also increase the risk that adolescents may seek to take matters into their own hands, or enlist the help of powerful others (e.g. join a gang, take on a gang-member boyfriend) to feel safer and more secure and to avenge perceived wrongs. More broadly, major failures by the adult world to protect and nurture adolescents increases the risk of producing a "lost generation" – a cohort of youth who view the privileges and responsibilities of citizenship, work, and home life with cynicism and disillusionment, treat the social contract with skepticism or indifference, and invest little in society and in their own future (Layne et al., 2008).

Overview of TGCTA

Consistent with its assessment-driven approach, TGCTA is divided into a pre-treatment assessment interview and four flexibly tailored treatment modules. Each module begins with an overview describing its theoretical underpinnings and overarching aims. A session-by-session guide then follows, which contains specific procedures, exercises, and suggested "adolescent" language for implementing each session. Although TGCTA is designed for small groups, each module includes an appendix that contains guidelines for adapting the sessions for individual clients, as well as "copy-friendly" handouts that can be used in either group or individual settings.

The Pre-Treatment Assessment Interview

The *pre-treatment assessment interview* is preferably conducted on an *individual* basis by a clinician who will be facilitating the TGCTA sessions. Its primary goals are to determine whether TGCTA is an appropriate intervention for the adolescent and to provide sufficient information about the program and the perceived needs of the youth so that he or she can make an informed decision about whether participation would be beneficial. During such interviews, it is helpful to remain keenly aware that the adolescent may well have undergone profoundly disempowering and deeply unsettling experiences involving such themes as extreme danger; horrific violence; innocent misjudgments gone terribly awry; extreme helplessness; disturbing encounters with human malice; violated expectations regarding the adult protective shield and the legitimacy of the social contract; powerfully contradicted assumptions about the safety, predictability, controllability, and benevolence of the world; extreme helplessness; and catastrophic loss. The clinician should also carry the realization that he or she acts as a representative of the adult world and can be a powerful force for good in helping to restore the protective shield, repair the social contract, facilitate supportive connections with others, and promote adaptive developmental progression.

To assist in these joint decisions, the clinician administers selected measures (or relies solely on the clinical interview) to gather information regarding the adolescent's functioning across a range of developmentally important life domains. Depending on the culture and setting, these typically include: current distress, role functioning (academic performance, school behavior, peer relationships, family life, and, as appropriate, romantic relationships, workforce participation, leisure), developmental progression as benchmarked against culturally appropriate developmental tasks and milestones, civic involvement, life satisfaction, risky behavior, and aspirations for the future (see the *pre-treatment assessment interview* for recommended measures). The clinician then reviews the (quickly/rough-scored) assessment results with the adolescent and uses clinical judgment in making recommendations for intervention. These recommendations may include the number and sequence of TGCTA modules to administer, and treatment modality (group, individual, or classroom-based), depending on the youth's specific needs, strengths, life circumstances, and informed personal wishes. The clinician also has an opportunity to assess for immediate risks and, as needed, provide appropriate referrals or safeguards.

The Treatment Modules

Module 1 has six primary objectives: (1) Increase understanding of common reactions to trauma and bereavement. (2) Increase understanding of what trauma reminders and loss reminders *are* and *how* they evoke posttraumatic stress and grief reactions, respectively. (3) Increase insight into personal posttraumatic stress, grief, and other reactions, especially as evoked by their personal trauma reminders and loss reminders. (4) Strengthen emotional self-regulation skills, especially skills needed to manage members' reactivity to trauma and loss reminders. (5) Improve members' abilities to problem-solve

difficult or challenging situations, especially hardships created or worsened by traumatic or bereavement-related experiences (*secondary adversities*), as well as developmental challenges and daily hassles. And (6) enhance abilities to appraise stressful situations and recruit appropriate types and sources of social support to help them cope with those situations.

Module 2 is dedicated to more intensive working through of members' self-selected traumatic experiences or the traumatic circumstances of the death of a loved one. Primary objectives include: (1) Select a primary traumatic experience for therapeutic work and briefly share it with the group. (2) Construct a detailed and coherent trauma narrative of that experience that weaves together *what was happening outside of me* with *what was happening inside of me*. This includes identifying one or more *traumatic moments* (moments of experiencing or witnessing imminent threat, actual harm, terror, horror, or extreme helplessness) within each members' experience and clarifying their respective links to trauma reminders or loss reminders. (3) Identify and process the *worst moments* of each member's experiences, which consist of the parts of the experience or its aftermath that were most difficult to bear and are typically the most painful to be reminded of. (4) Identify and process *intervention fantasies* (what they wish would have happened) and accompanying intense negative emotions including extreme fear, guilt, shame, rage, and desires for revenge. TGCTA can also accommodate (especially in individual "pull-out" sessions), traumatic events in which members perpetrated violent acts that harmed others and over which they feel remorse (Kerig et al., 2015). (5) Identify *traumatic expectations*, which consist of pessimistic "lessons learned" that youths' traumatic experiences have taught them about themselves, others, and the world, and which can powerfully influence their worldview, relationship with society, and preparations for adulthood. (6) Strengthen adolescent impulse control by increasing insight into how reactions to traumatic moments, often as evoked by trauma reminders, can lead to risky and destructive behaviors (Steinberg & Chein, 2015; van den Bos et al., 2015).

Module 3 addresses bereavement (often due to violent or tragic death) and its aftermath. Primary objectives include: (1) Identify personal loss reminders and understand their role in evoking grief and other reactions. (2) Identify personal grief reactions and mourning rituals. (3) Explain how grief is a beneficial process that facilitates adjustment to bereavement, but under some conditions can go awry (lead to severe persisting distress, functional impairment, risky behavior, developmental disruption) in any of three primary domains. These domains include *separation distress, existential/identity distress*, and *distress over the circumstances of the death*. (4) Reduce maladaptive grief reactions using exercises that are specifically tailored for each of the three grief domains. And (5) promote healthy grieving and mourning within each of the three primary grief domains.

Module 4 is designed to promote adaptive developmental progression and to help youth prepare for the roles and responsibilities of young adulthood and full citizenship. Its activities focus on helping youth contemplate, plan, and actively prepare for their futures. Objectives include: (1) Revisit *traumatic expectations* that continue to undermine adolescents' hopes, motivation, and potential, and choose in their place more constructive basic beliefs and moral principles by which to guide their lives. (2) Strengthen adolescents' capacity to problem-solve and cope with current and anticipated future life adversities. This includes developing plans to appropriately disclose their trauma- and bereavement-related experiences to important and trusted people in their lives. (3) Form positive yet realistic life ambitions and professional aspirations, and problem-solve concrete strategies to achieve those ambitions in ways that renew and promote adaptive developmental progression. And (4) promote constructive engagement in pro-social activities and investment in the social contract through such activities as public advocacy, community service, helping vulnerable others, random acts of kindness, and acting on intervention thoughts (fantasies about what they *wish* could have happened to prevent or mitigate the outcome) in positive and proactive ways. This includes reducing impulsive revenge-taking behavior by encouraging pro-social responses to traumatic events and losses (e.g. making their communities safer by taking steps to prevent future trauma; suicide prevention) (Steinberg & Chein, 2015; van den Bos et al., 2015; Layne et al., in press).

The Developmental History of TGCTA

A prototype of TGCTA was first field-tested in school settings following a devastating 1988 earthquake in Armenia. A follow-up evaluation found that treatment gains with respect to posttraumatic stress reactions, depressive symptoms, moral functioning, and adaptive behavior were retained five years later (Goenjian et al., 1997). Expanded pilot versions were subsequently implemented throughout the 1990s in diverse field settings, including underserved inner-city youth exposed to high rates of community violence (Layne et al., 2001a; Saltzman et al., 2001b). The first manualized version of TGCTA was implemented after the 1992–1995 Bosnian civil war in the first UNICEF-sponsored post-war psychosocial program for youth. TGCTA was rigorously implemented, evaluated, and refined in this post-war setting between 1997 and 2002, producing an open trial (Layne et al., 2001b), a conceptual model for multi-tiered intervention (Saltzman et al., 2003), a qualitative field evaluation (Cox et al., 2007), and a randomized controlled trial (Layne et al., 2008). Collectively, these studies produced consistent evidence of the effectiveness of TGCTA in reducing posttraumatic stress and maladaptive grief reactions, and in improving academic performance and peer relationships.

Following the September 11, 2001 terrorist attacks on the World Trade Center, TGCTA was selected by the State of New York as the primary intervention for traumatized and traumatically bereaved adolescents for the Child and Adolescent Trauma Treatments and Services Consortium (CATTS) in New York City. The intervention showed good evidence of effectiveness, producing outcomes in adolescents that were on par with those observed in children who received trauma-focused cognitive behavioral therapy (TF-CBT), the companion CATTS intervention for children (Hoagwood et al., 2007; Saltzman et al., 2006). Adaptations of TGCTA were also effectively employed with youth following major disasters, including hurricanes Katrina and Rita.

The current version of TGCTA was field-tested in an open trial with high-risk high-school students in Delaware, USA, where it showed evidence of effectiveness in reducing both posttraumatic stress and maladaptive grief reactions. The use of *grief*-focused treatment components was linked to greater decreases in maladaptive grief reactions compared to posttraumatic stress reactions (Grassetti et al., 2014). This study also found that group cohesion grew during Module 1 and increased as members engaged in trauma and grief processing work using Module 2 and Module 3 components. This finding underscores the galvanizing effects that trauma and grief work can have on group cohesion in adolescents, including youth with complex trauma histories. A follow-up study (Herres et al., in press) found that students who reported higher rates of *externalizing* symptoms improved more rapidly during the *skills-building* (Module 1 components) phase of treatment, whereas students with higher *internalizing* symptoms improved more during the *trauma and grief processing* (Modules 2 and 3) phase.

A current version of TGCTA, in combination with a trauma-informed staff training (*Think Trauma*), was tested in an open multi-year field study conducted in four residential juvenile justice facilities with traumatized youth incarcerated for felony-level offenses. Data showed that the mostly male youth in this study averaged between 10 and 11 different kinds of traumas and adverse events in their lifetimes, with well over half reporting exposure to community violence and violence in their homes as well as unexpected deaths of persons close to them. A comparison of pre- and post-treatment assessment scores found significant reductions in posttraumatic stress, depression, dissociation, and anger, but not in anxiety or sexual concerns. Further, incarcerated youth who completed all modules of group-based TGCTA reported greater reductions in posttraumatic stress symptoms compared to incarcerated youth who completed an abbreviated version. Facilities also reported large reductions in incident reports. Facility staff and leadership stated during monthly clinical conference calls with developers that trauma treatment for youth, coupled with trauma-informed training for staff, led to changes in organizational culture that made facilities safer and calmer for both youth and staff. This study also found no evidence that in-depth trauma and grief processing components of TGCTA had a destabilizing effect on these polytraumatized youth. No incidents were reported by clinicians for youth who did intensive trauma- and loss-focused narrative work when Modules 2 and 3 were implemented (Olafson et al., 2016).

Taken together, results of these studies point to four general conclusions. First, adolescents with histories of trauma and bereavement are best served when clinicians are properly trained and equipped to distinguish between and assess trauma exposure versus bereavement, posttraumatic stress reactions versus grief reactions, and internalizing versus externalizing problems (Layne et al., in press). Second, treatment for multiply traumatized and bereaved youth can be effectively tailored by matching specific intervention components (e.g. grief- versus posttraumatic stress-focused exercises) to clients' specific needs (e.g. elevations in grief versus posttraumatic stress reactions) as identified in their assessment profiles. Third, TGCTA can be successfully implemented in both school and juvenile justice systems and produce even greater improvements in key domains of symptoms and functioning when accompanied by trauma-informed staff training; TGCTA can also promote facility safety. Fourth, TGCTA treatment outcomes generally exhibit a dose–response effect such that youth who receive the *full* treatment (especially Modules 2 and 3) show greater benefit than youth who receive an *abbreviated* treatment (skills components from Modules 1 and 4 only).

As of this publication, TGCTA is being widely disseminated in juvenile justice, school-based, and community-based mental health sites across the USA through learning collaboratives and communities, and other initiatives sponsored by the National Child Traumatic Stress Network (NCTSN). TGCTA is now being implemented in multiple state-wide juvenile justice systems, which are developing sustainable platforms using on-site trained trainers. Additional basic research and field evaluation studies are underway.

What Makes TGCTA Unique? Six Primary Strengths

TGCTA has six built-in strengths that set it apart as a cutting-edge intervention for traumatized adolescents, bereaved adolescents, or traumatically bereaved adolescents.

1. Specialized focus on adolescence. TGCTA specifically addresses the developmental needs, strengths, risks, challenges, tasks, and life circumstances of adolescents. Adolescence is characterized by increased sensation-seeking, immature self-regulation, and at times, immature appraisals of risky situations (often *downplaying* the level of danger) that can result in reckless behavior. TGCTA approaches adolescence as a brief yet highly consequential developmental period in which clusters of both beneficial resources (called *resource caravans*) and risk factors (called *risk factor caravans*) can accumulate in number, accrue in their effects, and cascade forward in ways that can powerfully influence the entire life course (Layne et al., 2014a). A primary aim of TGCTA is to prevent causal risk factors, vulnerabilities, and the risks they pose from further accumulating and cascading forward (Layne et al., 2014b). A related aim is to help youth create, preserve, and grow *resource caravans* (collections of beneficial resources including knowledge, skills, optimism, self-esteem, self-efficacy, and healthy relationships) that can continue to meet their evolving needs and sustain them in the future (Hobfoll, 2014). TGCTA is designed to help adolescents adopt a more constructive, forward-looking set of expectations and aspirations, and to acquire the knowledge and skills needed to promote their transition through the remaining years of adolescence and into young adulthood.

TGCTA also reflects the understanding that *recognizing gender differences* is essential to developmentally informed intervention with adolescents and should be an integral part of risk screening, assessment, case formulation, treatment planning, and treatment delivery. For example, girls are exposed to higher rates of sexual victimization and interpersonal trauma within the family than are boys (Finkelhor et al., 2013). Further, studies of youth involved in the juvenile justice system and in gangs report that girls experience higher rates of every form of sexual victimization and more interpersonal trauma exposure in the family and with close others than do boys, whereas boys tend to experience more exposure to community violence (Resnick et al., 2004; Kerig and Becker, 2012; Kerig & Schindler, 2013; Kerig et al., 2015). More broadly, these gender differences in trauma exposure are similar to those reported in a large US survey of youth in the general population (Finkelhor et al., 2013). Boys reported significantly higher lifetime physical assault and exposure to community violence, whereas girls reported higher levels of dating violence and higher levels of all forms of sexual victimization, including rape and sexual assault by adults and peers. Girls also reported higher levels of sexual harassment, including Internet and cell-phone harassment, and higher rates of unwanted Internet sex talk.

Studies of gender differences in posttraumatic stress reactions have long reported disproportionately more internalizing responses in females, and disproportionately more externalizing responses, including aggression, in males (Gorman-Smith & Tolan, 1998) although some recent research indicates that rates of violence perpetration by girls may be increasing (Kerig & Becker, 2012). Rates of posttraumatic stress disorder (PTSD) and complex PTSD are also higher for girls (Kerig & Becker, 2012). These gender differences may reflect, in part, findings that girls experience higher rates of sexual abuse and sexual assault than boys and are sexually victimized by trusted others more often than boys. These transgressions of the social contract may fuel a deep sense of betrayal and contribute to long-term difficulties with trusting others. Further, the stigma of sexual victimization can instill female victims with a sense of being permanently damaged and shamed (Kerig & Becker, 2012). Clinicians can draw on these insights to make better-informed decisions about whether to form TGCTA groups – including gender-specific groups – that share a common theme such as interpersonal betrayal or loss.

TGCTA also takes adolescent risky behavior and risky situations very seriously. It provides repeated opportunities to screen for and therapeutically address current and ongoing risks, especially risks for self-harm, suicide, and exposure to dangerous circumstances in the home and community. This is done in the pre-treatment assessment interview, during Modules 1–3 as different types of risk and exposure are explored, and during Module 4 in activities that focus on helping youth to discriminate between safe versus unsafe situations and address ongoing life and developmental adversities (e.g. living with a parent with an alcohol problem).

2. Interplay between trauma and bereavement. A second strength of TGCTA is its integrative focus on trauma, bereavement, and the interplay that can arise between posttraumatic stress and grief reactions following traumatic bereavement (Layne et al., in press). Several authors of TGCTA were invited to serve as members of the *Diagnostic and Statistical Manual of Mental Disorders, Fifth Edition* (DSM-5) Posttraumatic Stress Disorder, Trauma, and Dissociative Disorders Sub-Work Group, in which capacity they provided age-specific expert recommendations for both PTSD criteria and newly proposed persistent complex bereavement disorder (PCBD) criteria (Kaplow et al., 2012b). TGCTA aligns with the latest diagnostic and treatment considerations for these particular trauma- and bereavement-related outcomes.

Whereas most interventions are designed to address *either* trauma *or* bereavement (or treat "loss" as simply another form of trauma), TGCTA approaches *both* trauma *and* bereavement as separate and distinct yet related entities. The design of TGCTA reflects a clear conceptual understanding of the interplay between *trauma* and *bereavement* as causal risk factors, and *posttraumatic stress reactions* and *grief reactions* as their respective primary causal consequences (Layne et al., 2014b; in press). Trauma and bereavement may occur in different configurations in adolescents' lives. For example, they may co-occur *simultaneously*, as in the case of *traumatic bereavement* – in which the death occurs under traumatic circumstances. Alternatively, bereaved youth may also be directly exposed to imminent life threat or serious injury (e.g. being involved in a car accident in which a loved one is killed). As a third example, trauma and bereavement may occur *separately*, in either closely or widely spaced life events (e.g. a youth experiences sexual assault followed by the death of a grandma). Regardless of their particular configuration, co-occurring trauma and bereavement each exert their own effects on distress and functioning. Their accumulation carries a risk for forming constellations of life events that accrue in their adverse effects and cascade forward across development. The resulting *risk factor caravans* can gain momentum over time, creating *resource loss cycles* that can accelerate and spiral downwards if not altered through timely and effective intervention (Hobfoll, 2014; Layne et al., 2014a).

Clinicians who use TGCTA will gain a clear conceptual understanding of key elements that make up traumatic and bereavement experiences from an adolescent perspective (Layne et al., 2001b), as well as different dimensions and aspects of bereavement, grief, and mourning as these evolve across adolescence (Kaplow et al., 2012a; Kaplow et al., 2013). The design of Modules 2 and 3 reflects the recognition that trauma and bereavement often co-occur in adolescents' lives, yet typically lead to different primary consequences (posttraumatic stress versus grief reactions, respectively), that each carry different risks, require different assessment tools, such as the University of California at Los Angeles (UCLA) Reaction Index and for DSM-5 (Ri-5; Pynoos & Steinberg, 2014) and the PCBD Checklist (Layne et al., 2014a) and call for different intervention components. TGCTA treatment planning emphasizes clarifying the respective intervention objectives for *trauma-focused* versus *bereavement-focused* therapeutic work, given that maladaptive grief reactions are theorized to have an *adaptive* "good grief" counterpart that should be recognized and facilitated (Kaplow et al., 2012a). In contrast, posttraumatic stress reactions largely lack an adaptive counterpart (although some degree of hypervigilance and arousal may be adaptive if the adolescent continues to live in a dangerous environment).

The difference between trauma-focused versus bereavement-focused therapeutic work with adolescents is reflected in the treatment objectives of each approach. The primary objective when working with traumatized adolescents is to *help posttraumatic stress reactions recede* in their frequency, intensity, duration, and disruptive impact on adolescents' daily lives and functioning. In contrast, the dual primary objectives in working with bereaved adolescents are to *help maladaptive grief reactions recede* (e.g. reducing distressing preoccupations over how the person died) and to also *facilitate adaptive grieving and mourning* (e.g. reminiscing in comforting ways and finding constructive ways to honor the memory of the deceased). TGCTA reflects the understanding that both posttraumatic stress reactions and grief reactions can each exert enormous demands on the inner resources of adolescents (Pynoos, 1992). Further, the demands of each set of reactions can reduce and intersect in complex ways with the social, physical, psychological, and spiritual resources available to cope with the other set of reactions (Layne et al., 2009).

3. Modularized, assessment-driven format. A third strength of TGCTA is its modularized format, which supports assessment-driven, flexibly tailored intervention (Layne et al., 2017). When paired with evidence-based assessment methods, TGCTA helps practitioners to carry out a central task of evidence-based practice: *to gather and use the best available evidence to tailor intervention in accordance with clients' specific needs, strengths, life circumstances, values, informed wishes, and the practitioners' clinical wisdom and expert judgment* (Layne et al., 2014c). TGCTA can be "customized" in various ways (DeRosa et al., 2013). Group-based assessment tools can be used to guide the selection of group members (Burlingame et al., 2011a). Based on assessment information gathered in the pre-session interview, the clinician can also determine whether trauma and/or bereavement are presenting issues and the degree to which posttraumatic stress and/or grief reactions currently interfere with the youth's life. This information can be used to select which TGCTA modules will be relevant and beneficial for the youth. The interview and assessment data may also be used to develop an *individual assessment profile* that summarizes each member's degree of distress along specific dimensions of posttraumatic stress and grief reactions. This assessment profile can further inform how specific modules and sessions within those modules are selected, prioritized, and tailored. This capacity to strategically "customize" TGCTA for the needs of each group or individual client is especially helpful in settings (such as schools or juvenile justice) with severe time limits, to ensure that treatment focuses on youth's most pressing priorities and needs.

The individual assessment profile also helps to identify key benchmarks of functioning, risky behavior, and developmental progression versus derailment that can be used to evaluate *clinically significant impairment* at baseline and monitor *clinically significant improvement* as treatment progresses (Layne et al., 2010). Both the pre-treatment interview and clinician-administered measures can be used to build a working clinical theory and intervention plan that address the experiences, needs, and strengths of youths in both group (Davies et al., 2006) and individual settings (Hoagwood et al., 2007; Hoagwood and Layne, 2010; Layne et al., 2001a, 2008; Saltzman et al., 2001a, b).

4. Multi-tiered intervention framework. A fourth strength of TGCTA, also derived from its flexibly-tailored format, is its capacity to support *multi-tiered mental health and wellness interventions.* Multi-tiered interventions are especially valuable in high-risk, high-need, low-resource settings because they help service providers to balance both *program effectiveness* and *program efficiency.* TGCTA is built on a three-tiered conceptual framework (Saltzman et al., 2003) that allows practitioners to flexibly provide services ranging from general wellness promotion to specialized mental health therapeutic services (Cox et al., 2007). This conceptual framework draws on public mental health principles to help practitioners flexibly implement interventions that reach many beneficiaries while conserving and concentrating specialized services for those in greatest need. These tiers consist of *widely disseminated classroom-based psychoeducation and skills-building* (Tier 1), *specialized group-based treatment for youth with complex trauma and/or loss histories* (Tier 2), and *referral to intensive specialized psychiatric/mental health treatment* (only as needed, either as stand-alone treatment or a supplement to Tier-2 treatment) *for youth at severe risk* (Tier 3).

A randomized controlled trial with war-exposed Bosnian adolescents found that although the Tier 1 classroom-based intervention (derived from TGCTA Module 1 and Module 4 components only) produced good evidence of effectiveness and very few reliably worsened cases, the Tier 2 group-based intervention (comprising Modules 1–4) produced significantly higher rates of reliable improvement in posttraumatic stress and grief reactions and no reliably worsened cases (Layne et al., 2008). More broadly, TGCTA components can be tailored for high-risk adolescents (Olafson et al., 2016). These include youth with histories of *complex trauma exposure* – a profile characterized by multiple types of interpersonal trauma and losses (e.g. domestic violence, physical abuse, sexual abuse) during vulnerable developmental periods that increases the risk for severe emotional dysregulation, disrupted interpersonal relationships, and other forms of severe dysfunction (Cloitre et al., 2009).

5. Group-based format. A fifth strength of TGCTA is its *group-based format,* which is uniquely suited to treat groups of adolescents with significant trauma and loss histories. These include youth in such settings as school-based health clinics, juvenile justice group homes, residential care, diversion programs, and community-based mental health centers (Grassetti et al., 2014). In contrast to other treatments that originated as individual or classroom-based modalities and were later *adapted* for a group modality, TGCTA was *originally* designed for use with teens in a school-based therapeutic group setting (Layne et al., 2001a). A sizeable literature documents that groups are generally as effective as, and are more efficient than, individual treatment for many problems (Davies et al., 2006). A group-based modality can also improve access to care, especially in underserved youth, who may not receive mental health services elsewhere.

TGCTA contains field-tested recommendations for selecting appropriate group members and for facilitating beneficial group processes during adolescence. TGCTA approaches the group setting as a potent crucible for therapeutic change. Great care is taken to make the group a safe haven where adolescents work together to build cohesion, create a sense of belonging, exchange experiences, make self-enhancing comparisons, and learn how to cope with trauma, bereavement, and their aftermath. Early sessions are also vital for establishing positive group norms, clarifying group goals, and promoting group cohesion by fostering a sense of "we're all in this together" sense of solidarity, common identity, and purpose (Davies et al., 2006).

TGCTA is specifically designed to therapeutically harness three potent forces. (a) *Adolescence,* a developmental window of maximum susceptibility to peer influences. (b) *A group modality,* in recognition that *peer groups* are the self-help setting to which adolescents naturally gravitate to confront danger, mourn losses, explore the unfamiliar, make comparisons, encourage one another, and work on developmental tasks (Steinberg, 2014). Groups are an optimal setting in which to treat many adolescent problems given that the beneficial effect of group cohesion is generally *more* therapeutically potent among youth than among adults (Burlingame et al., 2011b), and skillfully facilitated *group member-to-member exchanges* generally produce more potent therapeutic effects than *group leader-to-member exchanges* (Davies et al., 2006). And (c) *confronting trauma and bereavement* – two of the most powerful and impactful experiences human beings can undergo, which naturally draw survivors together to exchange support and recover (Gottlieb, 1996; La Greca et al., 2002; Layne et al., 2001a). Groups are also potent tools for reducing loneliness – a risk factor linked to the health of the developing brain (Cole et al., 2015).

6. Grounded in cutting-edge theoretical and empirical developments. A sixth strength of TGCTA is that it *draws on recent clinical and scientific advances in the fields of child and adolescent trauma and bereavement.* The narrative construction procedures used in Modules 2 and 3 are based on recent advances in cognitive neuroscience, including findings of potent links between memory, expectations, plans of action, and reminders. Module 1 components draw on advances in the study of *trauma reminders* and *loss reminders* and ways in which they differentially evoke posttraumatic stress and grief reactions. Module 1 and Module 4 components also draw on the study of *secondary adversities* (hardships caused or worsened by traumatic events or losses) and ways in which they generate their own consequences, thereby worsening the effects of the original trauma or loss (Layne et al., 2006). Modules 1 and 4 thus focus on coping with secondary adversities and *developmental adversities* (barriers to carrying out developmental tasks, achieving developmental milestones, and negotiating developmental transitions) with the aim of preventing accumulations of risk factors over time. Module 1 and Module 4 components also focus on cultivating *resource gain cycles* and promoting their continued growth, maturation, and forward momentum across development, by strengthening adaptive coping skills, reinforcing realistic yet optimistic expectations, and strengthening connections to healthy people and social institutions (Hobfoll, 2014; Layne et al., 2014a).

Moreover, TGCTA draws on *multidimensional grief theory* (Kaplow et al., 2012a, 2013; Layne et al., 2012, in press) to guide assessment, case formulation, treatment planning and tailoring, monitoring treatment progress, and treatment outcome evaluation. A core assumption of multidimensional grief theory is that *grief is an inherently beneficial yet often taxing process of responding to, and making ongoing efforts to adjust to, a world in which the deceased person is no longer physically present.* The theory proposes that, although primarily adaptive, grief reactions can go awry and increase the risk for prolonged severe distress, functional impairment, risky behavior, and developmental derailment. Discussions of grief reactions in Modules 1 (basic psychoeducation) and 3 (grief processing) thus emphasize *both* adaptive *and* maladaptive grief reactions with the aim of avoiding the "over-pathologizing" of normal grief reactions while also promoting positive adjustment to bereavement.

Module 3 can be tailored to address a range of theorized maladaptive and adaptive grief reactions. These include three primary dimensions proposed by multidimensional grief theory (Layne et al., 2012; Kaplow et al., 2013) consisting of *separation distress, existential/identity distress*, and **circumstance-related distress** (Kaplow et al., 2012a, 2013); as well as PCBD reactions proposed in DSM-5 (Kaplow et al., 2012b; Kaplow et al., 2014; Claycomb et al., 2016). Module 3 is enhanced when paired with an assessment tool – such as the *PCBD Checklist* (Layne et al., 2014d) – that can be scored in accordance with multidimensional grief theory. Understanding which specific grief dimensions are current sources of distress enables the clinician to

tailor treatment according to the specific needs of bereaved youth. This is done by selecting or emphasizing therapeutic exercises (e.g. specific sketches or scenarios) that address those dimensions of grief that are elevated in the youth's assessment profile (Kaplow et al., in press). A detailed overview of multidimensional grief theory and of each session is provided in the introduction to Module 3.

Using TGCTA Modules Flexibly, to Create Multi-tiered Intervention Programs

How can I strategically use TGCTA's modularized design to promote both treatment effectiveness and treatment efficiency? The modular architecture of TGCTA enables clinicians to customize intervention for different levels and types of youths' needs, settings (e.g. school-based versus community clinic), and the intervention modality (e.g. group versus individual versus classroom-based). TGCTA's highly adaptable design allows it to be used as both a broad-spectrum tool to promote hardiness and strengthen stress resistance, or facilitate resilient recovery following large-scale events in the *general population* (e.g. providing classroom-based services to the entire student body) while also concentrating specialized services for a smaller proportion of *high-risk students* (e.g. providing highly distressed students with group or individual treatment). In particular, different combinations of TGCTA modules can be varyingly used to provide *general skills-building supportive intervention*, as well as *specialized treatment* focusing on trauma, bereavement, trauma *and* bereavement, or traumatic bereavement (Saltzman et al., 2003). Although commencing with Module 1 is always recommended, field evaluations suggest that beneficial outcomes can be obtained using a variety of different configurations of TGCTA modules depending on youth's specific needs, goals, and the time available (Cox et al., 2007; Layne et al., 2001b; Layne et al., 2008; Saltzman et al., 2001a). Table P1 presents six such options.

As shown in the table, TGCTA modules are designed to support at least five different options for intervention ranging from *general population-based intervention* consisting of basic psychoeducation and coping skills (Tier 1), to *specialized therapeutic treatment* focusing on trauma, bereavement, and the interplay between posttraumatic stress symptoms and grief reactions (Tier 2).

Tier 1 intervention. TGCTA can be configured to deliver a *general support* intervention, as implemented in a group- or classroom-based modality for the general population. The modularized design of TGCTA provides clinicians with the flexibility to implement only Modules 1 and 4 – an approach that was field-tested with war-exposed youth in a classroom setting and produced strong results (Layne et al., 2008). This (Module 1 and 4) approach efficiently furnishes youth with both a *coping skills toolkit* and a *developmental progression* toolkit, and can be used with moderately distressed youth who do not require more

Table P1 Using TGCTA modules flexibly, to tailor intervention for specific clients and settings

Tier 1: Trauma/bereavement-informed general supportive *intervention*

Option	Intervention aim	Module sequence	Modality
1.	Psychoeducational and skills-building supportive intervention, plus promoting positive adjustment and adaptive development progression	1, 4	Group, classroom, or individual (e.g. teach and practice one coping skill per therapy or class session)

Tier 2: Trauma/bereavement-focused specialized *treatment*

Option	Therapeutic aim	Module sequence	Modality
2.	Trauma-focused treatment	1, 2, 4	Group or individual
3.	Bereavement-focused treatment	1, 3, 4	Group or individual
4.	Integrative treatment focusing on trauma, bereavement, and their interplay; reduce posttraumatic stress reactions before addressing grief reactions (recommended "default" procedure)	1, 2, 3, 4	Group or individual
5.	Integrative treatment focusing on trauma, bereavement, and their interplay; access and construct positive memories of deceased, therapeutically harness memories to help work through traumatic experiences	1, 3, 2, 4	Group or individual

Tier 3: Referral for specialized intensive treatment for high-risk youth

	Therapeutic aim
6.	Referral of high-risk youth with severe problems (e.g. severe depression, severe substance abuse, suicidal ideation, intent to harm self or others) to specialized clinical services (e.g. individual treatment focusing on severe depression or anxiety; substance abuse; pharmacotherapy; inpatient or outpatient psychiatric services). These clinical services may either *replace* or *supplement* TGCTA, depending on the client's specific needs and life circumstances.

specialized trauma- and grief-focused treatment components (contained in Modules 2 and 3, respectively). Tier 1 intervention can be delivered within a comparatively short interval (e.g. delivering Modules 1 and 4 to the student body in a classroom setting). Tier 1 intervention can also be spaced by "unpacking" Modules 1 and 4 (e.g. delivering Module 1 in the Fall of the school year to promote adaptive coping, Module 4 in the following Spring to promote developmental progression).

Tier 2 intervention. TGCTA can also be configured to provide Tier 2 intervention, which provides specialized therapeutic services in a community-based setting (e.g. school-based, juvenile justice group home, private practice, community clinic). TGCTA modules are designed and sequenced to build on one another beginning with foundational knowledge and skills (*Module 1*), working through traumatic experiences (*Module 2*), grieving losses in constructive ways (*Module 3*), and consolidating treatment gains and promoting developmental progression (*Module 4*). Evaluation studies to date placed Module 2 (trauma processing) *before* Module 3 (grief processing); this sequence

thus carries the best current evidence for the treatment of youth with histories of both trauma and bereavement. Nevertheless, some youth may respond better to trauma work after they have been helped to access and/or construct a positive image of the deceased (especially if the death involved gruesome or disturbing images) that can serve as a source of comfort and support. We have also seen the benefits of sequencing Module 3 before Module 2 if youth are experiencing extremely high levels of separation distress – a grief reaction. Module 3 exercises designed to help youth strengthen healthy psychological connections to the deceased can then be therapeutically leveraged to assist the youth in conducting subsequent Module 2 trauma-focused work. Decisions regarding the sequencing of Modules 2 and 3 are thus left to the discretion of the clinician.

Notably, both general supportive intervention (Tier 1) and specialized therapeutic treatment (Tier 2) configurations of TGCTA (as implemented in *classroom- or group-based* modalities) can also be combined with *individual pull-out sessions* when needed. For example, pull-out sessions may be appropriate when working with content that

(a) is very distressing (e.g. exposure to rape, torture, gruesome details) and could vicariously distress other members, (b) is deeply private (e.g. sexual concerns, pharmacotherapy), or (c) could otherwise adversely affect vulnerable group members (e.g. suicidal ideation, sharing retaliatory fantasies).

Tier 3 intervention. TGCTA can also be used to create an interlinking *three-tiered risk screening and referral system* (Saltzman et al., 2003). Tier 1 services can be combined with risk screening to refer moderately to severely traumatized or bereaved youth to specialized (Tier 2) services, as implemented in a group or individual modality. Further, both Tier 1 and Tier 2 services can refer high risk youth to specialized and intensive (Tier 3) inpatient or outpatient psychiatric/mental health services, including youth struggling with severe psychopathology, suicide risk, or substance abuse (King et al., 2013). Our field research to date (e.g. Layne et al., 2008) suggests that cases in need of Tier 3 referral are rarely found in school settings. Nevertheless, referral networks that link Tier 1 (e.g. Modules 1 *and* 4), Tier 2 (e.g. Modules 1 *through* 4), and Tier 3 (e.g. intensive individual, outpatient, or inpatient services) levels of intervention and treatment may carry strong advantages. These include (a) providing a safety net for schools, (b) increasing school counselor confidence in screening for and working with difficult cases, (c) creating the option of continuing Tier 1 or Tier 2 services in conjunction with services provided by the Tier 3 provider (Cox et al., 2007), (d) forging ties between schools and community mental health agencies, and (e) enhancing continuity of care across multiple service systems (Ko et al., 2008).

Deciding Between a Group or Individual Treatment Modality

As noted previously, the group modality has a number of advantages over individual-based work. These advantages include greater efficiency (moderate-sized groups of five to nine members tend to benefit more from group cohesion than either smaller or larger groups) (Burlingame et al., 2011), therapeutically leveraging an increased susceptibility to peer influences during adolescence, and the potency of group cohesion and collective support in helping youth to open up and engage in meaningful psychological work. A group setting also facilitates *social referencing* as members compare themselves, their life experiences and challenges, and ways of coping, thereby helping members to reassure, teach, encourage, challenge, motivate, and inspire one another.

In contrast, *individual* treatment carries different advantages. First, it does not require clinicians to access and identify a group of youths prior to beginning treatment, as a "closed enrollment" group-based intervention like TGCTA does. Even in school settings, conducting the risk screening and pre-treatment assessment interviews needed to assemble a promising list of candidates can require considerable time and effort before group sessions begin (e.g. Saltzman et al., 2001b). Second, individual treatment provides more

opportunities for in-depth therapeutic processing of the youth's traumatic and loss-related experiences, thereby allowing for a greater dose of direct exposure. Third, individual treatment helps the clinician to tailor treatment to the specific needs, strengths, life circumstances, and informed wishes of each youth. For example, individual sessions offer additional freedom to deal with sensitive or provocative content as it arises and do not require special "pull-out" sessions for group members dealing with difficult experiences (e.g. sexual assault) that are contraindicated for in-depth work in the group. Notwithstanding these potential advantages, the critical importance of the peer group in adolescence underscores the need to give special therapeutic attention in individual treatment (during coping skills exercises, social support recruitment exercises, regular session check-ins, etc.) to the status and quality of the youth's peer relationships.

Concluding Comments

Having provided our best information regarding the underlying theory, design, history, and application of TGCTA, we now conclude this introduction with our best wishes for your work with traumatized and bereaved adolescents. We hope these materials are useful tools, although we remain keenly aware that the primary resource and intervention is **you** – your compassion, commitment, good humor, optimism, and sincere desire to help the youth around you. In that same spirit, we hope you take good care of yourself and continue to seek out the help, support, and guidance *you* need in order to sustain your valuable and much- needed efforts.

References

Burlingame, G. M., Cox, J. C., Davies, D., Layne, C. M., & Gleave, R. (2011a). The Group Selection Questionnaire: Further refinements in group member selection. *Group Dynamics*, 15, 60–74.

Burlingame, G. M., McClendon, D. T., & Alonso, J. (2011b). Cohesion in group therapy. *Psychotherapy*, 48, 34–42.

Claycomb, M., Charak, R., Kaplow, J. B., et al. (2016). Persistent complex bereavement disorder symptom domains relate differentially to PTSD and depression: A study of war-exposed Bosnian adolescents. *Journal of Abnormal Child Psychology*, 44, 1361–1373.

Cloitre, M., Stolbach, B. C., Herman, J. L., et al. (2009). A developmental approach to complex PTSD: Childhood and adult cumulative trauma as predictors of symptom complexity. *Journal of Traumatic Stress*, 22, 399–408.

Cole, S. W., Capitanio, J. P., Chun, K., et al. (2015). Myeloid differentiation architecture of leukocyte transcriptome dynamics in perceived social isolation. *Proceedings of the National Academy of Sciences*, 112, 15142–15147.

Cox, J., Davies, D. R., Burlingame, G. M., et al. (2007). Effectiveness of a trauma/grief-focused group intervention: A qualitative study with war-exposed Bosnian adolescents. *International Journal of Group Psychotherapy*, 57, 319–345.

Davies, D. R., Burlingame, G. M., & Layne, C. M. (2006). *Integrating Small Process Principles into Trauma-focused*

Group Psychosocial: What Should a Group Trauma Therapist Know? New York: Haworth Press.

DeRosa, R. R., Amaya-Jackson, L. & Layne, C. M. (2013). From rifts to riffs: Evidence-based principles to guide critical thinking about next-generation child trauma treatments and training. *Training and Education in Professional Psychology*, 7, 195–204.

Finkelhor, D., Turner, H. A., Shattuck, A., & Hamby, S. L. (2013). Violence, crime, and abuse exposure in a national sample of children and youth: An update. *Journal of the American Medical Association Pediatrics*, 167, 614–621. Published online May 13, 2013. Updated corrected version January 15, 2014.

Goenjian, A., Karayan, I., Pynoos, R., et al. (1997) Outcome of psychotherapy among early adolescents after trauma. *American Journal of Psychiatry*, 154, 536–542.

Gorman-Smith, D. & Tolan, P. (1998). The role of exposure to community violence and developmental problems among inner-city youth. *Development and Psychopathology*, 10, 101–116.

Gottlieb, B. H. (1996). Theories and practices of mobilizing support in stressful circumstances. In C. L. Cooper (ed.), *Handbook of Stress, Medicine, and Health* (pp. 339–356). Boca Raton, FL: CRC Press.

Grassetti, S. N., Herres, J., Williamson, A., et al. (2014). Narrative focus moderates symptom change trajectories in group treatment for traumatized and bereaved adolescents. *Journal of Clinical Child and Adolescent Psychology*, 44, 933–941.

Herres, J., Williamson, A. A., Kobak, R., et al. (in press). Internalizing and externalizing symptoms moderate treatment response to school-based Trauma and Grief Component Therapy for Adolescents. *School Mental Health*.

Hoagwood, K. E. & Layne, C. M. (2010). Child and Adolescent Trauma Treatment and Services Consortium. Implementation of CBT for children and adolescents affected by the World Trade Center disaster: Outcomes in reducing trauma symptoms. *Journal of Traumatic Stress*, 23, 699–707.

Hoagwood, K. E., Saltzman, W. R., & Layne, C. M., Child and Adolescent Trauma Treatment and Services Consortium (2007). Implementing CBT for children and adolescents after September 11th: Lessons from the Child and Adolescent Trauma Treatments and Services (CATS) Project. *Journal of Clinical Child and Adolescent Psychology*, 36, 581–592.

Hobfoll, S. (2014). Resource caravans and resource caravan passageways: A new paradigm for trauma responding. *Intervention*, 12, S21–32.

Kaplow, J., Layne, C., Howell, K., et al. (2012a). Evidence-based assessment of bereaved children and adolescents: Psychometric properties and correlates of the Multidimensional Grief Reactions Scale. In C. M. Layne (Chair), *Integrating Developmentally-Informed Theory, Evidence-Based Assessment, and Evidence-Based Treatment of Childhood Maladaptive Grief.* Symposium presented at the Annual Meeting of the International Society for Traumatic Stress Studies, Los Angeles, CA, November, 2012.

Kaplow, J. B., Layne, C. M., Pynoos, R. S., Cohen, J., & Lieberman, A. (2012b). DSM-5 diagnostic criteria for bereavement-related disorders in children and adolescents: Developmental considerations. *Psychiatry*, 75, 243–266.

Kaplow, J. B., Layne, C. M., Saltzman, W. R., Cozza, S. J., & Pynoos, R. S. (2013). Using multidimensional grief theory to explore effects of deployment, reintegration, and death on military youth and families. *Clinical Child and Family Psychology Review*, 16, 322–340.

Kaplow, J. B., Layne, C. M., & Pynoos, R. S. (2014). Persistent Complex Bereavement Disorder as a call to action: Using a proposed DSM-5 diagnosis to advance the field of childhood grief. *Stress Points* (published online by the International Society for Traumatic Stress Studies); see: www.istss.org/education-research/traumatic-stresspoints/2014-january/persistent-complex-bereavement-disorder-as-a-call.aspx l.

Kaplow, J. B., Layne, C. M., Pynoos, R. S., & Saltzman, W. (in press). *Multidimensional Grief Therapy: A Flexible Approach to Assessing and Supporting Bereaved Youth.* Cambridge: Cambridge University Press.

Kerig, P. K. & Becker, S. P. (2012). Trauma and girls' delinquency. In S. Miller, L. D. Leve, & P. K. Kerig (eds.), *Delinquent Girls: Context, Relationships, and Adaptations.* New York: Springer + Business Media.

Kerig, P. K. & Schindler, S. R. (2013). Engendering the evidence base: A critical review of the conceptual and empirical foundations of gender-responsive interventions for girls' delinquency. *Laws*, 2, 244–282. doi:10.3390/laws2030244.

Kerig, P. K., Chaplo, S., Bennett, D. C., & Modrowski, C. A. (2015). "Harm as harm": Gang membership, perpetration trauma, and posttraumatic stress symptoms among youth in the juvenile justice system. *Criminal Justice and Behavior*, 43, 635–652.

King, C., Ewell-Foster, C., & Rogalski, K. (2013). *Teen Suicide Risk: A Practitioner Guide to Screening, Assessment, and Management.* New York: Guilford Press.

Ko, S. J., Ford, J. D., Kassam-Adams, N., et al. (2008). Creating trauma-informed systems: Child welfare, education, first responders, health care, juvenile justice. *Professional Psychology: Research and Practice*, 39, 396–404.

La Greca, A. M., Silverman, W. K., Vernberg, E. M., & Roberts, M. C. (2002). *Helping Children Cope with Disasters and Terrorism.* Washington, DC: American Psychological Association.

Layne, C. M., Pynoos, R. S., & Cardenas, J. (2001a). Wounded adolescence: School-based group psychotherapy for adolescents who have sustained or witnessed violent interpersonal injury. In M. Shafii & S. Shafii (eds.), *School Violence: Contributing Factors, Management, and Prevention* (pp. 163–186). Washington, DC: American Psychiatric Press.

Layne, C. M., Saltzman, W. R., Arslanagic, B., et al. (2001b). Trauma/grief-focused group treatment for war-exposed Bosnian adolescents: Preliminary results from a school-based post-war program. *Group Dynamics: Theory, Research, and Practice*, 5(4), 277–290.

Layne, C. M., Warren, J. S., Saltzman, W. R., et al. (2006). Contextual influences on post-traumatic adjustment: Retraumatization and the roles of distressing reminders, secondary adversities, and revictimization. In Schein, L. A., Spitz, H. I., Burlingame, G. M., & Muskin, P. R., (eds.), *Group Approaches for the Psychological Effects of Terrorist Disasters*. New York: Haworth, pp. 235–286.

Layne, C. M., Saltzman, W. R., Poppleton, L., et al. (2008). Effectiveness of a school-based group psychotherapy program for war-exposed adolescents: A randomized controlled trial. *Journal of the American Academy of Child and Adolescent Psychiatry*, 47, 1048–1062. DOI: http://dx.doi.org/10.1097/CHI.0b013e31817eecae

Layne, C. M., Beck, C. J., Rimmasch, H., et al. (2009). Promoting "resilient" posttraumatic adjustment in childhood and beyond: "Unpacking" life events, adjustment trajectories, resources, and interventions. In D. Brom, R. Pat-Horenczyk, & J. Ford (eds.), *Treating Traumatized Children: Risk, Resilience, and Recovery* (pp. 13–47). New York: Routledge.

Layne, C. M., Ostrowski, S. A., Greeson, J. K. P., Briggs-King, E., & Olsen, J. A. (2010). Beyond statistical significance: Evaluating clinically significant change in child and adolescent trauma treatment. In E. B. King (Chair), *Cumulative Risk of Adverse Childhood Experiences and PTSD Symptoms: Findings from the National Child Traumatic Stress Network*. Symposium presented at the Annual Meeting of the International Society of Traumatic Stress Studies, Montreal, Canada, November, 2010.

Layne, C. M., Kaplow, J. B., & Pynoos, R. S. (2012). Using developmentally-informed theory and evidence-based assessment to guide intervention with bereaved youth and families. In C. M. Layne (Chair), *Integrating Developmentally-Informed Theory, Evidence-Based Assessment, and Evidence-Based Treatment of Childhood Maladaptive Grief*. Symposium presented at the Annual Meeting of the International Society for Traumatic Stress Studies, Los Angeles, CA, November, 2012.

Layne, C. M., Briggs-King, E., & Courtois, C. (2014a). Introduction to the Special Section: Unpacking risk factor caravans across development: Findings from the NCTSN core data set. *Psychological Trauma Theory Research Practice and Policy*, 6, S1–S8.

Layne, C. M., Steinberg, J. R., & Steinberg, A. M. (2014b). Causal reasoning skills training for mental health practitioners: Promoting sound clinical judgment in evidence-based practice. *Training and Education in Professional Psychology*, 8, 292–302.

Layne, C. M., Strand, V., Popescu, M., et al. (2014c). Using the core curriculum on childhood trauma to strengthen clinical knowledge in evidence-based practitioners. *Journal of Clinical Child and Adolescent Psychology*, 43, 286–300.

Layne, C. M., Kaplow, J. B., & Pynoos, R. S. (2014d). *Persistent Complex Bereavement Disorder (PCBD) Checklist – Youth Version: Test and Administration Manual*. Los Angeles: UCLA Office of Intellectual Property.

Layne, C. M., Kaplow, J. B., & Youngstrom, E. A. (2017). Applying evidence-based assessment to childhood trauma and bereavement: Concepts, principles, and practices. In M. A. Landholt, M. Cloitre, & U. Schnyder (eds), *Evidence-Based Treatments for Trauma-Related Disorders in Children and Adolescents*. Cham: Springer International Publishing AG, pp. 67–96.

Layne, C. M., Kaplow, J. B., Oosterhoff, B., Hill, R., & Pynoos, R. S. (in press). The interplay between posttraumatic stress and grief reactions in traumatically bereaved adolescents: When trauma, bereavement, and adolescence converge. *Adolescent Psychiatry*.

Olafson, E., Boat, B. W., Putnam, K. T., et al. (2016). Implementing Trauma and Grief Component Therapy for Adolescents and Think Trauma for traumatized youth in secure juvenile justice settings. *Journal of Interpersonal Violence*, February, 1–21. DOI: 10.1177/0886260516628287,

Pynoos, R. S. (1992). Grief and trauma in children and adolescents. *Bereavement Care*, 11, 2–10.

Pynoos, R. S. & Steinberg, A. M. (2014). *The UCLA PTSD Reaction Index for DSM-5*. University of California, Los Angeles.

Resnick, M. D., Ireland, M., & Borowsky, I. (2004). Youth violence perpetration: What protects? What predicts? Findings from the National Longitudinal Study of Adolescent Health. *Journal of Adolescent Health*, 35, 424.e–424.e10.

Rynearson, E. K. (2001). *Retelling Violent Death*. Philadelphia: Brunner/Routledge.

Saltzman, W. R., Pynoos, R. S., Layne, C. M., Steinberg, A., & Aisenberg, E. (2001a). School-based trauma/grief focused group psychotherapy program for youth exposed to community violence. *Group Dynamics: Theory, Research, and Practice*, 5, 291–303.

Saltzman, W. R., Steinberg, A., Layne, C. M., Aisenberg, E., & Pynoos, R. S. (2001b). A developmental approach to school-based treatment of adolescents exposed to trauma and traumatic loss. *Journal of Child and Adolescent Group Therapy*, 11, 43–56.

Saltzman, W. R., Layne, C. M., Steinberg, A. M., Arslanagic, B., & Pynoos, R. S. (2003). Developing a culturally-ecologically sound intervention program for youth exposed to war and terrorism. *Child and Adolescent Psychiatric Clinics of North America*, 12, 319–342.

Saltzman, W. R., Layne, C. M., Steinberg, A. M., & Pynoos, R. S. (2006). Trauma/grief-focused group psychotherapy with adolescents. In L. Schein, H. Spitz, G. Burlingame, & P. Muskin, (eds.), *Group Approaches for the Psychological Effects of Terrorist Disasters*. New York: Haworth Press, pp. 669–729.

Steinberg, L. (2010). A behavioral scientist looks at the science of adolescent brain development. *Brain and Cognition*, 72, 160–164.

Steinberg, L. (2014). *Age of Opportunity: Lessons from the New Science of Adolescence*. New York: Houghton Mifflin Harcourt.

Steinberg, L. & Chein, J. M. (2015). Multiple accounts of adolescent impulsivity. *Proceedings of the National Academy of Sciences*, 112, 8807–8808.

van den Bos, W., Rodriguez, C. A., Schweitzer, J. B., & McClure, S. M. (2015). Adolescent impatience decreases with increased frontostriatal connectivity. *Proceedings of the National Academy of Sciences*, 112, E3765–E3774.

TGCTA Pre-Treatment Assessment Interview

Introduction, Assessment, and Goal Setting for Individual or Group Participation

Note: The pre-treatment assessment interview (hereafter *assessment interview*) is usually conducted on an individual basis between a TGCTA clinician who will be facilitating the group or individual sessions, and a prospective youth participant. Primary aims of this interview include the following: (1) Gathering information needed to determine whether TGCTA is an appropriate treatment for this particular youth, or whether a referral for other services is appropriate. If TGCTA is indicated, then: (2) Gathering information relevant to deciding which modality (group versus individual) is most appropriate. (3) Gathering information regarding traumatic experiences and/or losses, and ranking them according to their severity/current impact to decide which will be a primary focus of treatment. (4) Beginning to build an "adolescent-friendly" shared vocabulary for describing traumatic experiences, losses, and their consequences. (5) Building trust, therapeutic rapport, and teamwork, which you will draw on in subsequent sessions.

Selecting Appropriate Participants

Inclusion/Exclusion Criteria

Participants should meet the following criteria:

Age: 12 or older

Mental age: 11 or higher

Inclusion criteria: (1) A history of exposure to trauma or bereavement, accompanied by (2) significant distress (especially posttraumatic stress and/or maladaptive grief reactions), and evidence of (3) impaired role functioning in important life domains (e.g. truancy, interpersonal estrangements with friends or family), risky behavior (e.g. fighting), or developmental derailment (e.g. failing a grade, dropping out of school).

Exclusion criteria: Generally speaking, youth who show signs of psychosis, severe psychopathology, or significant suicidal ideation should be referred for more intensive and targeted services.

Clinical Decision-Making Considerations for Selecting Group- or Individually-Based TGCTA

- Youth with *moderately* severe psychopathology may potentially be treated in *individual* TGCTA treatment, which is easier to tailor to meet their needs. In such cases, consider offering individual treatment as an adjunct to other targeted services or case management to which you will refer the youth.
- To be considered appropriate for *group work*, the youth must have the behavioral control and interpersonal skills needed to avoid significantly disrupting the group process.
- When working with youth exposed to *sexual trauma*, the group leader may choose to offer individual TGCTA services. A second option is to form a group in which all members choose to work on sexual trauma. A third option is to include a member with sexual trauma in a general-trauma/loss group if the member can nevertheless profit from focusing on other stressors, traumas, or losses, and reserve the sexual trauma work for individual sessions.
- Youth who have undergone *extremely difficult experiences* that may be vicariously distressing to other group members (e.g. witnessing a gruesome death or rape) can be treated individually. A second option is to invite the youth to work on less distressing experiences in the group and reserve the highly distressing experience for individual sessions. A third option is to invite such youth to share only *subjective* aspects of their experiences (focusing on what was going on *inside* of me, not *outside* of me) in the group to receive its support, and instead work on the full narrative in individual sessions.
- Youth who see themselves as having played a role as a potential *perpetrator, instigator,* or *contributor* to a

traumatic experience or death (e.g. driving provocatively led to a "road rage" incident in which a friend was killed; being pressed into service as a child soldier; gang initiations involving harm to others) may also be traumatized by these experiences. Nevertheless, they may feel reluctant to join the group out of concern that they will be rejected, stigmatized, or marginalized. In such cases, individual treatment can be offered. A second option (consider only if you decide that the youth would benefit from the group) is to clarify and therapeutically address expectations about "What do you think might happen if you shared this experience in the group?" A third option is to form a group of youth who share such experiences in common (e.g. child soldiers, trafficking victims). Such groups can be especially challenging to manage and require two very skilled leaders.

- In all cases, therapists should consider their own degree of competence and comfort in working with individuals with specific trauma and loss histories. Clinicians whose own children or family members share the same age or other similarities with those affected may be especially susceptible to secondary traumatic stress reactions and should make appropriate referrals or engage in appropriate self-care.

Structure

Form groups of five to nine members to maximize group cohesion, with minimal differences in age; or offer individual counseling.

- Consider starting with up to 10–11 members to manage potential attrition.
- *Homogeneous* groups can be formed regarding types of trauma or loss (e.g. all members have physical abuse or bereavement as a primary issue) and can quickly develop group cohesion; however, members of more *heterogeneous* groups (e.g, combining youth with different types of primary trauma) often learn more from one another due to the greater variety of perspectives and experiences they bring.
- *Single-gender* groups are generally recommended for younger youth, youth who have undergone very difficult experiences (e.g. sexual abuse, sexual assault), or youth who are difficult to manage (e.g. juvenile justice boys or girls). Combining genders in any of these three subtypes is more challenging and requires two very skilled group leaders. This decision is left to the judgment of the group leaders.

Preparation Before Meeting

- Review the introductory information about TGCTA and the content of this session so that you can explain it briefly and clearly.
- Have the selected assessment materials available, including measures you have chosen from those listed below.

- Have pens, pencils, or slim markers ready.
- Have copies of Handout P1, the Personal Timeline Worksheet, as well as Handout P2, the Personal Goals Worksheet, Handout P3, the Trauma Goals Worksheet, and Handout P4, the Interview Summary Worksheet.

Overview of the Assessment Interview

Procedure

To complete all of the steps described below, the procedure could take between one and two hours. If you have significantly less time available, you may do a streamlined version of the interview that should take less than one hour. For this you would skip over steps 1–3 in the "formal assessment" described on pages 16 and 17. While it is very useful to do those steps, it is not critical. Those steps that may be skipped in the formal assessment will have the words "suggested yet optional" next to the heading.

1. If you do not know the youth, introduce yourself and begin to build rapport.

2. Determine whether this youth is appropriate for the group.

3. Describe the purpose of the group and build motivation to participate.

4. Complete the assessments and Handout P1, the Personal Timeline Worksheet.

5. Clarify possible connections between the youth's past trauma or loss experiences and current difficulties.

6. If you judge the youth to be appropriate for treatment, extend an invitation to participate in group-based or individual treatment.

7. If possible, help the youth select an initial *goal* for participating in the group and a central trauma or loss *experience* to work on in the group. (Both goals and experiences can be changed during the course of treatment.)

8. If a youth is not appropriate for the group, have other treatment options available (e.g. individual therapy). If the youth is appropriate for the program, obtain his or her commitment to participate in group or individual treatment.

Meeting with the Adolescent

1. Engagement

Greet the youth and, if the youth was not self-referred, inquire what he/she knows about the group and/or the program and how and why she/he was referred. Be as transparent and open as possible regarding the referral and what you already know about the youth. Present the interview as an opportunity to learn about the youth, describe the program, answer any questions, and work together to decide whether the program might be helpful and is a good fit at the present time.

Explain the limits of confidentiality with the youth, as you would with any client in your setting. (Consider all content confidential unless you identify a threat to self or other.)

2. Explain the Purpose of the Group

Using the information below, talk about the program in your own words, emphasizing how TGCTA has helped many other young people with similar histories. Feel free to shorten and personalize these comments.

- *This is a group for adolescents who have lived through some very difficult experiences and losses that might still be causing them problems.*
- *The group is a place where young people who have been through tough times get together, learn new things, share ideas, and support one another. Every member has something unique and valuable to add. The stories we choose to share are confidential – they don't leave the group.*
- *Of course, this group won't* **solve all** *of the difficulties you face. But it is all about opening up* **new choices**, *trying out new ways of dealing with problems, and working to create a future where you have the skills and knowledge you need to cope without being overwhelmed by the memories of everything you've gone through.*

THIS GROUP CAN HELP YOU IN FOUR IMPORTANT WAYS:
- **First: provide support**. *The group is a place where members can talk with other teens who have lived through similar experiences. There is a special kind of support that only you can give one another, because only you really know what it's like to go through these things. The group is a safe place where members deal with painful memories and feelings connected to their traumatic experiences and losses, so those feelings don't interfere so much with their lives.*
- **Second: learn new skills**. *The group is a place where members learn how to deal with their problems better, like learning how to* **calm yourself down** *when you get upset, and choosing how you want to respond rather than just reacting automatically. These kinds of skills will give you a greater sense of control over your feelings, your body, and your life. Group members also help one another deal with feelings of grief over the loss of someone close to them.*
- **Third: feel better**. *The things we do in the group have a proven track record for helping young people like you. They have helped youth who have lived through earthquakes, wars, terrorist attacks, and severe community violence. The group may help you in practical ways, like being able to sleep better, not being bothered so much by memories of what has happened, feeling calmer*

and not so angry or sad or scared, getting along better with people, doing better in school, and keeping out of trouble.
- **Fourth: create a better future**. *Group members learn to deal with changes in their lives that these traumas and losses have created and work to create a better future for themselves.*

3. Collect Information and Extend an Invitation to Appropriate Youth

A number of measures may be useful for risk screening, to help customize the treatment plan for group or individual work, monitor treatment response over time, and evaluate change at post-treatment. Below is a list of *suggested* measures that have proven useful in different settings where TGCTA has been implemented. Each measure is accompanied by a brief description and information on how to obtain it (the final choice of measures is left to your judgment, and a more extensive list of measures is available from the National Child Traumatic Stress Network website (nctsn.org)).

We recommend not fully scoring the measures during the interview, because doing so can lengthen the interview, create awkward moments of silence, make the youth feel very self-conscious, and detract from rapport-building. Instead, *quickly* glean basic information regarding trauma exposure, posttraumatic stress symptoms, grief reactions, and other difficulties, so that you can incorporate this information into your feedback at the end of this interview and (if appropriate) explain how the program can help and extend an invitation to participate. Try to set aside time to completely score the measures *after* the interview (or carefully review the scores if tests are scored electronically). Capturing a pre-treatment baseline allows you to monitor each adolescent's change over time. Carefully reviewing your test scores will also prepare you for future sessions by gathering details about different traumatic experiences and losses, specific types of distress, current life adversities, and current trauma reminders and loss reminders. This information will help you to personalize your upcoming psychoeducational discussions, set the stage for in-depth processing of trauma and loss experiences, and help you identify areas of developmental disruption that require attention.

THE UCLA REACTION INDEX
The University of California at Los Angeles (UCLA) Reaction Index for Children and Adolescents (Pynoos & Steinberg, 2014) assesses *Diagnostic and Statistical Manual of Mental Disorders, Fifth Edition* (DSM-5) posttraumatic stress disorder (PTSD) symptoms. For determining whether clinically significant trauma exposure and posttraumatic stress symptoms are present, you need fill out only the last two of the three sections that comprise the measure. A license to use the UCLA Reaction Index can be purchased through the UCLA Office of Intellectual Property at http://oip.ucla.edu/ptsd-reaction-index-instrument-licenses.

THE PCBD CHECKLIST

The PCBD Checklist (Layne et al., 2014) assesses persistent complex bereavement disorder (PCBD), the first (proposed) bereavement-related diagnosis of its kind, currently listed in the appendix of DSM-5. The PCBD Checklist includes a screening item inquiring whether the youth has experienced the death of someone close and (if yes) the relationship and circumstances of the death. Subsequent items assess the frequency with which the youth has experienced symptoms of PCBD, including those that capture information about the three domains of grief outlined in multidimensional grief theory (see the introduction to Module 3), during the last month. A license can be purchased through the UCLA Office of Intellectual Property at http://oip.ucla.edu/pcbd-checklist-test-license.

BEGIN THE FORMAL ASSESSMENT

Step 1: Fill Out the "Personal Timeline" Chart (*Suggested Yet Optional*) First use Handout P1, the Personal Timeline Worksheet, to learn about the range of experiences that the youth identifies as having been important or formative. This will include stressful, traumatic, and loss experiences as well as important positive and successful experiences that denote the youth's strengths and resources. Keep in mind that this is a brief initial mapping of these experiences that will inform the interview process. Hold back from in-depth exploration – there will be opportunities for this later in the program. Right now your job is to use this task as a way to further engage with the youth and determine if there is a trauma or loss history that is pertinent to the proposed treatment.

- Have on hand Figure P1, an example of a personal timeline for reference. When filling in Handout P1, it can be helpful to color in the quadrants of the thermometers with green, yellow, orange, and red markers in ascending order. The lowest "green zone" indicates experiences that were comfortable with minimal stress; the "yellow zone," experiences that were somewhat stressful; "orange zone," very stressful; and "red zone," experiences that were extremely stressful and uncomfortable. Along the horizontal axis will be placed the events identified by the youth in approximate chronological order.

- Introduce the timeline task as a way to identify and put in order important experiences in the youth's life. This should include both positive and negative or painful experiences that were formative for the youth and which he or she still thinks about. Explain that you will invite the youth to briefly describe the experiences, locate them on the timeline horizontally (approximate chronology) and vertically in terms of level of stress or discomfort associated with the experience. Events can include births, deaths, moves, separations, and traumas such as accidents, assaults, and witnessing of domestic or community violence.

- Place some anchor points on the horizontal axis that you may know about, such as starting at a new school, divorce, or death of a parent. As you elicit experiences, you may note key expressions or phrases used to describe the experiences and write these on the timeline as well. You may also hand a marker to the youth and have him or her collaborate by drawing in where the experience should be placed.

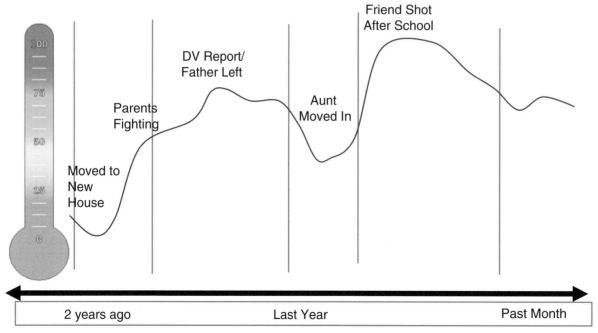

Figure P1: Example of personal timeline

- Remember that the timeline need not be exhaustive. Focus only on formative life events identified by the youth.
- Reserve the last portion of the timeline (on the far right of the horizontal line) to ask about positive and negative experiences during the past month.
- Once the timeline is complete, summarize the key events, capturing positive and negative experiences and highlighting past successes in coping with stress and strengths evidenced by the youth. Ask the youth which of the highly stressful events designated as peaks on the timeline he or she continues to think about, have reactions to when reminded of, or exert problematic influences on daily life. In this way you may rank order the current prominence of past difficult experiences. Top experiences should be included in the interview summary worksheet as prospective foci for the youth's work in the program.
- As you elicit the youth's timeline, you may list some of the positive and negative experiences that you want to include on the appropriate sections of Handout P4, the Interview Summary Worksheet. This worksheet is designed to help you summarize to the youth his or her primary issues and potential reasons for participating in the treatment. Make sure to describe the current difficulties and issues in that section of the worksheet

Step 2: Administer UCLA Reaction Index and PCBD Checklist (*Suggested Yet Optional*)

Administer the UCLA Reaction Index

- For an *in-depth* trauma and loss assessment, you may complete section one of the UCLA Reaction Index which will guide you in gathering information regarding exposure to 20 different types of trauma and loss across childhood and adolescence. This can help you to identify and visually depict *risk factor caravans* (if present) as they accumulate and cascade forward across development.
- For a *standard* (more brief) trauma and loss assessment, skip over section one and begin with the self report trauma history on page 4 of the measure and continue through page 7.
- Quickly scan the completed pages, looking for which trauma items were endorsed and which trauma was selected as the greatest source of distress on page 5.
- Note the number of items endorsed at the level of "3" (much of the time) and "4" (most of the time) on pages 6–7. These are PTSD symptoms that the youth experiences fairly regularly.
- Summarize these frequent items on Handout P4, the Interview Summary Worksheet, to use when you offer your summary of the assessment to the youth.

Administer the PCBD Checklist

- Fill out the first part of the checklist with the youth by sensitively exploring whether the youth has experienced the death of someone close, and if so, who. (If the youth

has not experienced the death of a significant life figure, discontinue and move to the next assessment measure or step.)

- If the youth reports experiencing at least one significant death, then ask him or her to fill out the remaining questions regarding the frequency of specific grief reactions.
- Be sure to note the "cause of death" as described by the youth, as this is often an important part of his/her trauma narrative work.
- Quickly scan the sheet to see whether any checklist items are endorsed at the level of a "3" (a lot of the time) or "4" (all of the time). Briefly summarize these items on the interview summary worksheet (Handout P4) and use this information when you offer your summary of the assessment.

Step 3: Summarize Basic Findings (*Suggested Yet Optional*) Review Handout P4, the Interview Summary Worksheet, with the youth.

- Summarize the picture that has emerged of the youth's trauma- and loss-related experiences, as well as current strengths and positive experiences. Interpret the results to show possible connections between past trauma or loss experiences and current life difficulties.
- When present, note current posttraumatic or grief reactions and how they may be interfering with the youth's ability to enjoy life and to do the things he or she wants to do.
- Also note that posttraumatic stress and grief reactions are different in that they can lead to different types of feelings and have different types of challenges associated with each of them, which is why we split them into two separate modules – one for trauma and one for grief.
- When possible, highlight strengths and resilience, including times when the youth showed courage or achieved success despite challenges. For example, note a few of the youth's stressful and traumatic experiences and express admiration by saying something like "I'm impressed at how you've been able to …."
- Validate and normalize current difficulties, and express realistic hope and confidence that, especially if provided with the right kinds of support (like we provide in the group), the youth can successfully deal with a history of hardships like this and still have a good/great life.

Step 4: Extend an Invitation to Participate or Make a Referral If, in your judgment, the youth is appropriate for TGCTA, extend an invitation to participate.

- Provide details for the group or individual setting, including the frequency and length of the sessions, when and where meetings will take place, the number of members in the group, etc.
- Address any concerns or questions they have, including confidentiality, reluctance stemming from the fear that past socially undesirable experiences or behavior will lead to rejection or marginalization, or concerns that

their experiences are too sad or horrible for you or others to hear.

- Ask whether the youth has any questions.
- Obtain a commitment to participate, or give time to decide if she or he wants to think it over.

If the youth is not appropriate for TGCTA yet could benefit from some form of therapy you may provide a referral at this time. It is best to have a list of possible referrals available going into the interview so these may be readily provided. If you think the severity or urgency of the presenting issues warrants a parent contact, discuss this with the youth. In some cases you may determine that a youth may benefit from TGCTA treatment, although he or she lacks the behavioral or interpersonal skills for participating in a group. In these instances, you may choose to offer individual TGCTA treatment, or refer to a basic coping skills/behavioral management group (if available) as a first step.

Step 5: Select a Trauma or Loss on Which to Focus in the Program During the program, the youth will focus on a primary trauma or loss experience. The selected experience should be one that continues to exert a negative influence on the youth:

- Keep in mind that TGCTA allows you to flexibly address *primary trauma* (e.g. accidents, assaults, witnessing violence), *primary bereavement* (e.g. loss of a loved one to death such as old age), *or primary traumatic bereavement* (e.g. murder, suicide, accidental death, slow death with potentially traumatic elements such as witnessing extreme distress or intense suffering). In most cases, this primary trauma or loss will be the experience that the youth has identified on the UCLAA Reaction Index as "what bothers me the most." You may also refer to other trauma or loss experiences acknowledged on Handout P1, the Personal Timeline Worksheet. Explore these, trying to strike a balance between selecting an experience that is both a significant source of distress, and something the youth can remember, describe, and share in the group (or with you individually).
- Examples of *trauma-related distress* include intrusive thoughts or images, nightmares, strong negative emotions/behaviors or physiological reactivity when encountering a trauma reminder, etc.
- Examples of *bereavement-related distress* include intense sorrow upon encountering a loss reminder, yearning for the deceased to return or to be reunited with the deceased in an afterlife, or intense fear that the youth will forget important aspects of the deceased (i.e. separation distress); feeling lost without the deceased, feeling like the best part of the youth died with him/her, feeling like the youth has no future without him/her (i.e. existential distress); or intense anger, confusion, terror, horror, revulsion, or sorrow over how the person died (i.e. circumstance-related distress).
- Examples of *traumatic bereavement-related distress* may include both of the above elements in connection to how the person died, as well as their interplay (e.g.

exposure to a loss reminder, such as hearing the person's name or seeing his photo, evokes highly distressing images or memories of the way he/she died that makes it hard to reminisce.)

- Youth who have had *multiple* traumatic events or losses, or experienced *chronic* trauma or abuse, may have difficulty identifying a single experience. Considerations for selecting a therapeutically useful event include:
- You do not have to select the youth's most traumatic or evocative experience. It may be appropriate to select an experience that is of lesser severity for the initial work and then build on the skills acquired to work on the more difficult experience (such as conducting a second trauma narrative featuring the more difficult experience).
- If the primary experience involves sexual trauma, consider its appropriateness for the group. It is sometimes appropriate for the youth to select a secondary trauma to focus on, as noted earlier, and instead work with you individually on the primary trauma (see Introduction).
- For youth who report hazy memories of chronic or recurrent traumatic events, work with them to see if they can remember a single instance or representative example.
- Reassure the youth that there will be opportunities to focus on other experiences later.

Step 6: Develop One or Two Goals for Participating in the Program A primary aim of TGCTA is for the youth to select, work on, and achieve one or two personally meaningful goals relating to his or her trauma or loss history and its present consequences. These are to be noted on the Handout P2, the Personal Goals Worksheet. You may also choose to use Handout P3, the Trauma Goals Worksheet for specific goals related to posttraumatic stress symptoms. Earlier, you elicited and summarized salient trauma and loss experiences, linked these to current posttraumatic or grief reactions, and began exploring how these reactions may be linked to things the youth is unhappy about in his or her life. Mapping out cause–effect connections between *past* traumatic experiences and losses and *current* symptoms and problems is a motivational interviewing strategy that increases youth insight, gives TGCTA greater traction, and helps to identify key benchmarks for measuring clinically significant change over time. Connections between prior trauma and loss and current difficulties that the youth feels motivated to change should be pointed out in clear and concrete ways – a recurrent process that begins in this interview and continues throughout the program.

Youth should be encouraged to select goals that: (a) are related to trauma or loss experiences, (b) focus on a current problem the youth is motivated to address, (c) are concrete and specific, and (d) are realistically achievable within the allotted time span. Youths can also choose to work on goals that can be practiced both *within* and *outside* the group or individual sessions (see Mendelsohn et al., 2011). Prompts for guiding the selection of appropriate treatment goals include:

- *Do you see a connection between this problem and your history of trauma (or loss)?* (Trauma- or loss-related)
- *In what ways is your life still affected by your trauma (or loss)? What would you want to change in this area of your life?* (Focus on current problem)
- *How would you know if you had accomplished that goal? How would your daily life look different?* (Concrete and specific)
- *Is there a particular area of your life in which you experience this problem the most? How is it affecting you in this area?* (Concrete and specific)
- *That sounds like an important but very large goal. What piece of that might be achievable within the next few months?* (Realistically achievable)
- *What part of your goal can you practice in the group/ individual session? What part of your goal can you practice outside of the group/individual session?*

To identify a personally meaningful goal, start with a clear description of a real problem in daily living that the youth cares about. Work to assemble a good *problem statement* by using good active listening skills (e.g. listen closely, paraphrase, reflect feelings, use clients words, check it out with client) to distil a clear statement of what the youth finds most distressing at this time. Use any of the prompts above to refine the problem statement. Once you arrive at a problem statement that resonates with the youth, work to create a positively framed goal statement that addresses the problem. At each step, check in with the youth to make sure the problem and goal statements reflect their concerns and motivations.

Example of a problem statement: "So it sounds like you really hate it when people at school ask you about the shooting, or when you are in the locker room and other kids see your scar and make comments. These things get you feeling angry and down, and you end up either getting in arguments or pulling back and feeling distant and quiet for hours or even days on end. Does that sound right?"

Example of a possible goal statement: "Tell me if this makes sense for one of your goals for participating in the group: Learning how to respond to peoples' questions and comments about the shooting without getting really angry, shutting down, or getting into arguments with your friends?"

Examples of making this goal concrete, specific and realistic, with a part to be achieved within the group or individual session and a part outside of the group or session:

Within the group or individual session: "By the end of the program I want to be able to talk about the shooting during the session and stay present, without shutting down, or getting angry and out of control."

Outside of the group or individual session: "By the end of the program I want to be able to talk about the shooting when asked at school or other social settings in ways that don't leave me feeling bad or get me to act out in ways that create problems."

Be sure to write down the problem and goal statements as accepted by the youth, and refer to them throughout the program. Reassure the youth that he or she will have multiple opportunities to change the problem and goal statements throughout the program. As youth continue to learn about trauma and loss and become more aware of their past history and current difficulties, they often get better at selecting appropriate experiences to focus on. The problem and goal statements should keep pace with this evolution.

4. Conclude the Session

Conclude the session, check in with the youth regarding any remaining questions, share the date for the first meeting, arrange for parental signing of any necessary consent forms, and express your enthusiasm for seeing the youth again at the first meeting.

References

Layne, C. M., Kaplow, J. B., & Pynoos, R. S. (2014). *Persistent Complex Bereavement Disorder (PCBD) Checklist – Youth Version: Test and Administration Manual.* Los Angeles: UCLA Office of Intellectual Property.

Mendelsohn, M., Herman, J. L., Schatzow, E., et al. (2011). *The Trauma Recovery Group: A Guide for Practitioners.* New York, NY: Guilford Press.

Pynoos, R. S. & Steinberg, A. M. (2014). *The UCLA PTSD Reaction Index for DSM-5.* University of California, Los Angeles.

Personal Timeline Worksheet

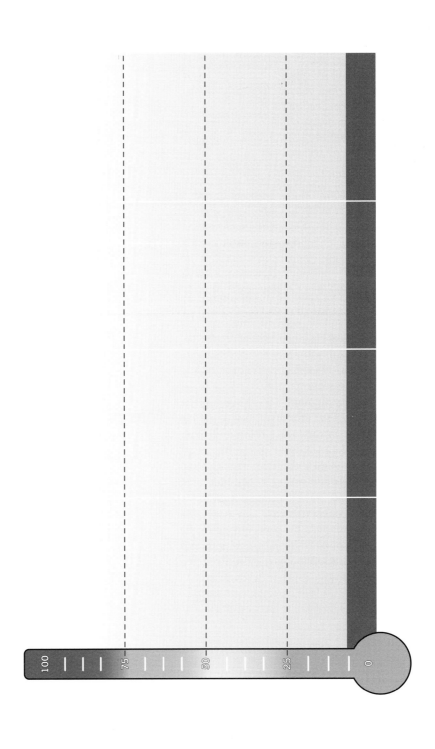

HANDOUT P2

Personal Goals Worksheet

Problem statement

Goal statement

Problem statement

Goal statement

Problem statement

Goal statement

HANDOUT P3

Trauma Goals Worksheet

By the end of this intervention:				
I want to feel *LESS*: *(please circle all that apply)*				
Nervous	Scared	Angry	Upset	Sad
I want to feel *MORE*: *(please circle all that apply)*				
Happy	Calm	Excited	Relaxed	
I want to change the way I do things and think about things: *(please check ✓ all that apply)*				
❏	Calm myself down when I feel upset.			
❏	Think about things that happened without feeling upset.			
❏	Talk about things that happened without feeling upset.			
❏	Stop avoiding things that made me nervous.			
❏	Do more of the things that I used to do.			
❏	Think more about things before I do them.			
❏	Make better decisions.			
❏	Have fewer problems with my family.			
❏	Have fewer problems with my friends.			
I also want to change:				

HANDOUT P4

Interview Summary Worksheet

Strengths and past successes

Trauma and high stress exposure (from personal timeline and reaction index)

Frequent posttraumatic stress symptoms (from reaction index)

Death of significant other (who, when, how) (from PCBD Checklist)

Frequent complex bereavement symptoms (from PCBD Checklist)

1

Foundational Knowledge and Skills

Introduction

Laying the Foundation for Treatment

Module 1 sessions are designed to establish foundational knowledge and skills that adolescents build on in subsequent modules. A primary aim of Module 1 is to create the conditions necessary for *group cohesion* to develop. Group members come to value and rely on this spirit of mutual support and camaraderie as the therapeutic work progresses. Group cohesion builds as members share and recognize important commonalities in their experiences, reactions, and circumstances, while also respecting the unique features of each individual's experiences and responses. Adolescents are social creatures who are well-accustomed to being in groups and striving to fit in. Nevertheless, the demands of trauma- and bereavement-focused work in a group setting are challenging. Members' active participation in the group requires a degree of self-awareness and self-disclosure that can, at times, evoke self-consciousness and intense feelings of vulnerability. Group sharing and disclosure exercises also evoke curiosity and concern about how each youth is perceived and accepted by others. The often-emotionally draining work of managing reminders and addressing trauma- and loss-related experiences also places demands on adolescents' maturing self-regulatory capacities and self-concept. Daily hassles, developmental tasks, and developmental transitions (e.g. finishing school) also compete for attention and need to be managed without derailing the sessions.

Building the Group

Adolescents generally have a good working grasp of the "ins and outs" of groups, including an appreciation for ways in which groups can be both helpful and destructive. *Session 1* harnesses this developmental competency by engaging group members in forming and "owning" their own *group rules, norms*, and *procedures* so that they have a place to feel safe, understood, and supported. Each session begins with a *Today's Highlights* overview to provide the sense of predictability, structure, and security needed to help adolescents regulate their emotions. The *check-in* procedure focuses on positive events in ways that build on members' capacity to share their interests, experiences, and day-to-day lives with peers. This procedure also encourages a more positive outlook and self-confidence (by celebrating achievements) while identifying concerns that may distract from full participation. Next, an *introductory exercise and discussion* helps to challenge pessimistic assumptions that members' symptoms and circumstances can't or won't get better, while also building realistic expectations about what treatment can deliver. *Ongoing monitoring* of each member's perceptions regarding how the group is doing (using either formal or informal assessment tools), including group cohesion and the working alliance between fellow members and the group leaders, provides each member with a voice in monitoring the group's health and performance.

Group leaders call upon a variety of skills to guide TGCTA groups. Leaders encourage optimistic yet realistic expectations, and *tell it like it is* by explaining that the road to getting better will pass through the ups and downs of confronting distressing thoughts and painful emotions, and learning to deal with them. Module 1 activities focus on both acknowledging *unique* aspects of individual members' experiences and inner lives, while calling attention to important *commonalities* among members' experiences in ways that challenge self-isolating expectations such as "No one can relate to what I've been through" (Layne et al., 2001). The art of facilitating adolescent groups often feels like a juggling act, with its dynamic balance between acknowledging current concerns while attending to the planned tasks of each session; identifying comforting commonalities across members' experiences while creating room for unique and private experiences; and keeping members within a productive range of emotional intensity and engagement.

Employing a Therapeutic Focus on Distressing Reminders

TGCTA has shown high rates of treatment compliance and completion in field evaluations, including the demanding trauma and grief work of Modules 2 and 3 (Cox et al., 2007; Layne et al., 2008). One factor contributing to these low drop-out rates is the careful attention given in Module 1 to trauma reminders, loss reminders, and social support. Adolescents learn to identify reminders, understand the ways in which reminders may be affecting their everyday lives, and develop skills needed to anticipate and cope with reminders – both while reminders are occurring and by implementing a recovery plan afterwards. Acquiring these insights and skills can increase adolescents' preparation and motivation for forthcoming work. This work may include coping with temporary increases in posttraumatic stress reactions that can accompany trauma processing in Module 2, and increases in grief reactions that can accompany grief processing in Module 3. It is important to distinguish between posttraumatic stress and grief reactions given evidence that these two sets of reactions respond differently to trauma-focused versus loss-focused TGCTA components (Grassetti et al., 2015). It is especially important to use both trauma-focused and bereavement-focused assessment tools when assessing youth with histories of both trauma and bereavement, because these youth may need assistance in learning to identify and manage both trauma reminders and loss reminders, and the different types of reactions they evoke (Layne et al., in press). Module 1 helps adolescents to understand how trauma narrative work can help them recognize their personal trauma reminders, clarify how trauma reminders are connected to their traumatic experiences, and increase their ability to manage distressing reminders in their daily lives.

It is important to focus on what adolescents can reasonably expect to gain from treatment. Put plainly, there is no "magic" therapeutic wand that removes all reactivity to reminders. Neurobiological studies suggest that certain cues (reminders) can evoke reactive responses long into the future. Even thorough trauma narrative work will not necessarily identify and work through *all* trauma reminders that may be embedded within a given experience. Indeed, some reminders may emerge over time – even years later – and point to moments of a traumatic experience that were not fully understood and therapeutically addressed before. Instead, a realistic and achievable aim of TGCTA is to furnish adolescents with lifelong skills that they can use to recognize and effectively manage their present and future reminders – both expected and unexpected. These skills for managing reminders, combined with other emotional regulation and social support recruitment skills taught in Module 1, provide adolescents with a robust and portable *coping toolkit* that they can incorporate into their personal resource caravans. They can use these skills in the future to cope with stressful life events and developmental challenges, as well as in the present as they engage in the trauma- and loss-processing work of Modules 2 and 3.

Reframing Posttraumatic Stress Reactions

Posttraumatic stress reactions can pose a significant developmental challenge to adolescents. Adolescents are especially prone to interpret their distress reactions as regressive and as a sign of weakness, with possible fears that there is something wrong with them (e.g. that they are "weird" or "going crazy"). self-reflective experiences that produce. Adolescents may come to hate certain posttraumatic stress symptoms (e.g. nightmares), or use bluster to mask embarrassing reactions, such as bouts of fear, or exaggerated physiological responses such as startling at loud noises. Some youth may cope by attempting to hide their reactions from themselves and others by doing their best to put on a brave face and looking cool and indifferent. Adolescents may also harbor the belief that they are unique and alone in their hardships and personal suffering, even when surrounded by hundreds of others who are facing a similar plight.

Adolescents' distress reactions, and the ways in which they perceive and interpret them, can contribute to changes in self-concept (e.g. "I'm weak or cowardly" or "There's something really wrong with me, because I haven't gotten over this"). Such fears can be amplified by the "invisible audience" – self-conscious adolescents sense that others are watching as a judgmental eye towards how well they are measuring up and fitting in. In contrast to grief reactions, which – although often painful – may be more socially acceptable (and even a source of pride among tough gang members), posttraumatic stress reactions are often more difficult for adolescents to fully acknowledge and address. Thus, a key intervention objective in both the pre-treatment assessment interview and in Module 1 is to *reframe posttraumatic reactions as expectable responses that make sense given what they have been through, and that can be reduced and managed using this intervention* (Layne et al., 2001; Saltzman et al., 2001).

Adolescents often possess insight into how their traumatic experiences and losses are affecting their development. Building on this developmental capacity, Module 1 contains a variety of activities designed to increase members' awareness of ways in which trauma reminders and posttraumatic stress reactions, as well as loss reminders and grief reactions, may continue to affect their mood and behavior, even years after the experience. Module 1 psychoeducational exercises describe the fluctuating course of posttraumatic stress and grief reactions and explain how these fluctuations are linked to trauma and loss reminders. Adolescents also learn about similarities and differences between trauma and loss reminders, begin to examine their own pattern of responses to trauma and loss reminders, and explore ways in which reminders may be influencing their day-to-day lives.

Adolescents learn that *trauma reminders* consist of exposures to trauma-related cues that can exacerbate and prolong posttraumatic stress reactions. Trauma reminders can evoke irritability and mood changes that affect interpersonal life, disrupt sleep, interfere with learning, and prompt avoidant or reckless behavior. Similarly, adolescents learn that *loss reminders* primarily evoke grief reactions and are often made up of simple, everyday cues that remind you that the person is physically absent, such as the person's name, belongings, family and friends, favorite music, or empty chair. Common grief reactions include missing the person, as well as sadness, yearning for the deceased to return, protest over the unfairness of the loss, and anger over the way they died (Layne et al., 2006, in press). Adolescents learn to monitor their mood and behaviour, and to track how they are connected to personal trauma reminders and loss reminders.

Developing Coping Strategies

A key aim of Module 1 sessions is to help adolescents convert their unpredictable, reactive exposures to reminders into self-reflective experiences that produce new learning and alleviate distress. To help achieve this objective, adolescents practice *coping strategies* that they can use to anticipate, prevent where appropriate, confront, and recover from exposure to reminders. They learn how timely *social support* can help reduce their arousal and fear responses. Adolescents also learn to discriminate between current reminder-laden situations and their original traumatic experiences (e.g. "that was then, this is now") in ways that reduce fear reactions. Members also learn how to *relax* and *soothe* themselves in ways that reduce their arousal before they confront anticipated reminders. Adolescents also reflect on distressing situations they encounter, recognize unforeseen or previously undetected reminders, and practice recruiting social support to help them recover after encountering a reminder.

Identifying Undetected Trauma and Loss Reminders

Module 1 gives special attention to identifying adolescent *avoidance* of reminders. Session activities explore how avoiding reminders may restrict adolescents' daily lives and impede their ability to work on developmental tasks and take advantage of developmental opportunities. For example, a 13-year-old client who witnessed his friend being shot and killed after playing soccer at a park began to avoid both the park and playing sports. Helping adolescents become aware of how reminders negatively affect their lives – including depriving them of growth-inducing developmental opportunities and impeding their strivings for independence – can increase their motivation to participate in treatment. This knowledge and skill will serve as a valuable foundation for Module 2 work, as the in-depth exploration of traumatic experiences will inevitably serve as a trauma reminder or loss reminder.

Addressing Danger, Protection, and Safety as an Adolescent Developmental Task

As they strive for greater independence, adolescents face the developmental task of learning to rely on themselves and their peers to accurately appraise and effectively respond to danger. Adolescents are often fascinated with thrill-seeking, in which they confront situations that typically involve "tolerable" levels of threat and risk, while striving to regulate their arousal. Adolescents practice, in various ways, their capacity to self-regulate fear responses when confronting danger in the absence of an effective adult protective shield. An innocuous example includes viewing horror movies whose plots center around the failure of the adult protective shield (typically portrayed as absent or inadequate adult oversight and protection, despite repeated adolescent warnings), leaving the teen protagonists to rely on their own wits and courage to contend with evil villains and imminent danger. These "self-exposures" help adolescents build a repertoire of skills and strategies for anticipating, appraising, preventing, tolerating, and contending with danger in responsible ways. In contrast, youth who enter adolescence with minimal coping strategies or prior histories of trauma exposure may be more likely to engage in risky or reckless behaviors, immature and inaccurate appraisals, and highly reactive responses to danger. Trauma-exposed youths may also react strongly to *trauma reminders*, either through recklessness or marked avoidance, in ways that impair functioning and disrupt developmental progression (Pynoos et al., 1995). Thus, a major aim of Module 1 is to help adolescents use their increased capacity for insight and self-regulation to counter "reactive" thoughts, moods, and risky behavior that can get them into serious trouble. This is done using a variety of group exercises that encourage skills acquisition, reflection and insight, mutual understanding, and member-to-member sharing, challenging, and encouragement.

Establishing and Leveraging Group Norms to Strengthen Adolescent Competencies

Positive group norms are best established early in treatment. Beginning in the pre-group interview, the therapists work consistently (especially in early sessions; Davies et al., 2006) to establish group norms of safety, acceptance, and reciprocity in which members both help – and are helped by – one another in a spirit of "we're all in this together" mutual support (Gottlieb, 1996). Fluidly exchanging roles between help-giver and help-receiver helps group members to experience and see themselves as empowered individuals who are capable of helping one another recover from the most difficult experiences of their lives. These supportive exchanges also help to challenge adolescent negative self-perceptions and "secret" fears, including common adolescent fears of being inadequate, incompetent, useless, not fitting in, isolated, rejected, unimportant, defective, "damaged goods," childishly regressed, a "needy" burden on others, or a "drag" to be around.

The initial sessions of Module 1 are designed to establish positive group norms that will allow clinicians to strategically leverage adolescents' growing competencies, desires for independence, drive to learn how to handle danger, and susceptibility to peer influence to achieve five developmentally important objectives (see Layne et al., 2001): (1)

Group leaders assume a somewhat deferential posture by presenting the group as an exclusive, supportive forum in which the *adolescents themselves are experts* in what it feels like to live through and survive the worst kinds of experiences. This empowering stance helps to counteract negative attitudes adolescents may carry that the group is a place where they send "defective" kids, or that group therapy is a second-class "watered-down" treatment compared to individual therapy. (2) TGCTA activities establish *fellow group members as an appropriate reference group* against which to evaluate how they are doing, rather than comparing themselves to others outside the group. This process encourages *self-enhancing social comparisons* that can reassure (e.g. "Maybe I'm not crazy or alone after all – other kids are jumpy too" or "Maybe my problems aren't as bad and unfixable as I thought") as well as motivate youth to learn from one another's challenges and successes (e.g. "Other kids have got through this, so I can too"). (3) Reframing adolescents as experts also helps to evoke and therapeutically harness the *trauma membrane* (e.g. "You can't possibly understand what it's like to go through this unless you've been through it yourself") in the service of building group cohesion. The group is presented as an exclusive place where "wounded adolescent" experts draw on their life experiences, knowledge, skills, and courage as they work together (with adult oversight) to heal themselves. (4) Reframing adolescents as experts also invites constructive exchanges during a developmental window of *maximum susceptibility to peer influences*. Evidence that the beneficial effect of group cohesion on treatment outcomes is more potent in youth than adults (Burlingame et al., 2011) underscores the importance of using effective cohesion-building strategies, including pairing praise with constructive criticism, and interrupting harsh criticism and excessive self-disclosure (Davies et al., 2006). (5) Reframing adolescents as experts invites them to *take personal initiative* in regulating their emotions, managing their behavior, planning for their future, and engaging in constructive social action.

In adopting this "adolescent expert" reframe, clinicians should adjust to and accommodate adolescents' growing knowledge, skill, and confidence by increasingly playing the role of a "supporting cast" member as treatment progresses. This supporting role includes (a) facilitating member-to-member sharing of knowledge, skills, support, and constructive feedback; (b) expressing therapeutic surprise and admiration at members' resilience and resourcefulness, and sincere appreciation for their generosity towards each other; (c) sympathetic listening and bearing witness to members' trauma or loss narratives and other personal disclosures; (d) cheerleading effort and achievements, both large and small; and (e) modelling and coaching. This supporting role, including stepping in to intervene as needed, and offering consistent empathic support to vulnerable members, reassures adolescents that the adult protective shield is firmly in place and operating effectively in the therapeutic background. Creating this safe and supportive space

helps to create the secure base adolescents need to nurture hope, experiment, practice, make mistakes and acknowledge them, problem-solve, share ideas, and strengthen their skills in preparation for the developmental transition to young adulthood.

Accessing Social Support within the Group and Beyond

A primary coping skill emphasized in Module 1 is the *ability to recruit social support to deal with distressing reminders*. Understanding how trauma reminders evoke distress helps adolescents learn how to use their social networks to provide the support they need. The aim is to build adolescents' capacity to recruit the *types* of support they need (so it matches the type of challenge they face), *when* they need it (so it is timely), *as much as* they need it (so the amount is sufficient), at the level of *quality* they need (so it is truly helpful), for *as long as* they need it (so its duration matches the need) (Gottlieb, 1996). Evidence that social support may act as both a *protective factor* when sufficient (buffering the harmful effects of trauma exposure) or *vulnerability factor* when insufficient (increasing the risk for PTSD) underscores the value of this skill (Charuvastra & Cloitre, 2008; Layne et al., 2009). For youth with depopulated or poorly functioning support networks, building supportive relationships among group members that can endure after group termination may be especially valuable and assist in sustaining treatment gains. Exchanges of mutual support *within* the group (and eventual engagement in constructive social action such as acts of service and advocacy *outside* the group) also foster the growth of a positive adolescent self-concept of being *capable, caring, connected, creative, consistent, courageous,* and *committed* citizens and survivors. The principle of "It is more blessed to give than to receive" truly applies to group treatment with traumatized and bereaved adolescents.

Module 1 also helps youth to recognize and begin to address potential barriers to recruiting support, including *bridging estrangements* in interpersonal relationships that have arisen from trauma- or loss-related experiences. For example, close friends may avoid one another or have bitter exchanges after a traumatic event because they serve as trauma reminders to one another. Helping adolescents understand how trauma and loss can strain their relationships, and working to bridge those estrangements when appropriate, can often bring relief. Attention can also be given to helping youths whose support networks are insufficient for their current needs to better meet those needs by deepening existing relationships (such as by making an acquaintance a friend) or by forming healthy new relationships. Collectively, this skill-building, reparative, and insight-focused work helps to lay the foundation for the challenging work of Module 2.

Guide for Moving Quickly through the Sessions When Time Is Limited

Certain treatment settings, such as schools, have significant limitations on how long sessions may be and how many sessions overall are possible. In these circumstances sessions may be limited to 50–60 minutes and, perhaps, only 15–20 sessions overall are possible. Since a number of the sessions in Module 1 require approximately 75 minutes to complete, Appendix 1 (at the end of the manual) provides guidance on how to select the most essential activities in each session when time is very limited.

Module 1 Indicators of Therapeutic Progress and Readiness to Transition to the Next Module

Clinicians should monitor various indicators of therapeutic process that signal a readiness to proceed to the next module. We recommend that by the end of Module 1, the adolescent should:

1. Show improved ability to manage two to three distressing trauma reminders or loss reminders. Examples of these skills include: (a) identifying personal reminders and predicting when they will arise; (b) using effective coping strategies to manage reminders; (c) reporting a reduced *frequency* of being reminded in distressing/dysregulating ways; (d) reporting reduced *reactivity* to reminders after being exposed, such that they are less intense and/or disruptive; and (e) demonstrating an improved ability to *recover* following exposure to a reminder, so that one is able to resume adaptive functioning sooner than before.
2. Demonstrate improved use of social support in two ways: (a) successfully recruiting support from someone to help before, during or after a distressing reminder; and (b) selecting an appropriate person outside the group, such as a family member or close friend, to turn to for social support during the upcoming trauma or loss narrative work.

References

Burlingame, G. M., McClendon, D. T., & Alonso, J. (2011). Cohesion in group therapy. *Psychotherapy*, 48, 34–42.

Charuvastra A., & Cloitre, M. (2008). Social bonds and posttraumatic stress disorder. *Annual Review of Psychology*, 2008, 59, 301–328.

Cox, J., Davies D. R., Burlingame, G. M., et al. (2007). Effectiveness of a trauma/grief-focused group intervention: a qualitative study with war-exposed Bosnian adolescents.

International Journal of Group Psychotherapy, 57, 319–345.

Davies, D. R., Burlingame, G. M., & Layne, C. M. (2006). Integrating small group process principles into trauma-focused group psychotherapy: What should a group trauma therapist know? In L. A. Schein, H. I. Spitz, G. Burlingame, & P. R. Muskin (eds.), *Psychological Effects of Catastrophic Disasters: Group Approaches to Treatment*. New York: Haworth.

Grassetti, S. N., Herres, J., Williamson, A. A., et al. (2015). Narrative focus predicts symptom change trajectories in group treatment for traumatized and bereaved adolescents. *Journal of Clinical Child & Adolescent Psychology*, 44, 933–941.

Gottlieb, B. (1996). Theories and practices of mobilizing support in stressful circumstances. In C. L. Cooper (ed.), *Handbook of Stress, Medicine, and Health*. New York: CRC Press.

Layne, C. M., Pynoos, R. S., & Cardenas, J. (2001). *Wounded Adolescence: School-Based Group Psychotherapy for Adolescents Who Sustained or Witnessed Violent Injury*. Washington, DC: American Psychiatric Association.

Layne, C. M., Warren, J. S., Saltzman, W. R. et al. (2006). Contextual influences on post-traumatic adjustment: Retraumatization and the roles of distressing reminders, secondary adversities, and revictimization. In L. A. Schein, H. I. Spitz, G. M. Burlingame, & P. R. Muskin (eds.), *Group Approaches for the Psychological Effects of Terrorist Disasters*. New York: Haworth, pp. 235–286.

Layne, C. M., Saltzman, W. R., Poppleton, L., et al. (2008). Effectiveness of a school-based group psychotherapy program for war-exposed adolescents: A randomized controlled trial. *Journal of the American Academy of Child and Adolescent Psychiatry of Child and Adolescent Psychiatry*, 47, 1048–1062.

Layne, C. M., Warren, J. S., Hilton, S., et al. (2009). Measuring adolescent perceived support amidst war and disaster: The Multi-Sector Social Support Inventory. In B. K. Barber (ed.), *Adolescents and War: How Youth Deal with Political Violence*. Oxford: Oxford University Press, pp. 145–176.

Pynoos, R., Steinberg, A., Wraith, R. (1995). A developmental psychopathology model of childhood traumatic stress. In D. Cicchetti & D. J. Cohen (eds.), *Manual of Developmental Psychopathology, Volume 2*. New York: John Wiley, pp. 72–95.

Saltzman W. R., Pynoos R. S., Layne C. M., Steinberg A. M., & Aisenberg E. (2001). Trauma/Grief-Focused Intervention for adolescents exposed to community violence: Results of a School-Based Screening and Group Treatment Protocol. *Group Dynamics: Theory, Research, and Practice*, 5, 290–303.

1.1 Welcome and Introduction

Session Objectives

1. Describe program content and session format.
2. Begin building group cohesion.
3. Begin exploring current coping strategies and possible supports.

Note: Individual therapy guide on last page of session.

Preparation

- Review each member's traumatic experiences, reported reactions, and current living circumstances noted in their screening surveys and pre-group clinical interviews.
- Review information in Session 2 about posttraumatic and grief reactions so you can answer any questions.
- Download the Participant Workbook from www.tgcta.com and provide a copy to each participant. **Have group members' workbooks available for each session.**
- **Note**: Some youth or groups may have a strong negative reaction to doing written work in a "workbook." If it seems to be a significant obstacle, you may decide to not use Participant Workbooks and, instead, selectively present handouts in the group, especially the illustrations, and convert all written exercises to interactive discussions or activities.
- If conducting individual therapy, consult the individual therapy guide on the last page of the session.

Section number	Session overview
I	Greet group members and review group highlights
II	Develop a group contract
III	Do introductory activities

Section number	Session overview
IV	Current coping strategies
V	Overview of program
VI	Review of session format
VII	Transitional activity and check-out

Supplies

Every session	This session
• Flipchart	• TGCTA workbooks for each member
• Large paper or easel pad	• Name tags (optional)
• Colored markers or crayons	
• Pencils/pens	
• Kleenex	
• Tape	

Handouts in Workbook

Handout 1.01	Sample Contract
Handout 1.02	Trauma Goals Worksheet
Handout 1.03	Personal Goals Worksheet
Handout 1.04	Check-Out Feedback Form

Flipcharts

1.1a Today's Highlights

1. Greetings
2. Group contract
3. Introductory activity
4. Current coping strategies
5. Overview of program and session format
6. Transitional activity
7. Check-out and Check-Out Feedback Form

1.1b What This Group Can Do for You

1. Make special types of friends
   - Develop supportive friendships based on trust, understanding, and helping each other.
2. Learn special skills to deal with:
   - Past stressful or traumatic experiences and things that still remind you about them.
   - The loss of people or things you love.
   - Current problems related to the stress or trauma.

1.1c Overview of the Program

Module	Topic
1	Coping skills
2	Trauma processing
3	Grief processing
4	Preparing for the future

Session 1.1: Welcome and Introduction

I. Greet Group Members and Review Group Highlights

Gather the youth in a circle with the group leaders sitting at different parts of the circle.

- Greet the group members warmly and tell them that it is a pleasure to see them again.
- Introduce yourselves (group leaders only) and describe your professional role at the facility.
- Go around the circle and ask group members to briefly introduce themselves to each other by saying their names.
- Say that you have already met with each member and you are looking forward to working with them together as a group.
- Describe the group in general terms (e.g. "a special group for young people who have been affected by severe stress, trauma, or the loss of someone close to them. This is something that you all have in common.").
- Use Today's Highlights (Flipchart 1.1a) to briefly review the activities that the group will be doing today.

II. Develop a Group Contract

Activity: Group Contract

The facilitator should review Handout 1.01 prior to the group. You need not share it with the group as you will be developing your own. It is a sample of a group contract that you may pattern yours on.

Before we go on, we need to establish the group rules around confidentiality, respect, and listening.

What kind of rules should we have for this group to make sure everybody feels comfortable, safe, and supported?

Elicit the rules from the group. Get a volunteer from the group to write down the rules on a blank flip chart. Either make a typed copy for each member to sign in Session 2 or have group members sign the flip chart. Display the flip chart with the rules at every future session.

If group members do not spontaneously include rules about confidentiality and sufficient guidelines to insure respectful and appropriate interactions within the group, you may explore with the group possible additional rules based on the items below:

1. I will keep confidentiality at all times.
   *What goes on in the group stays in the group. This includes not talking about **who** attends the group.*
2. I will treat other group members as I would wish to be treated.
3. I will do my best to encourage and support the other group members.
4. I will express myself without hurting others in the group.
   This means no teasing or put-downs, no talking when someone else is talking, and no interrupting.
5. I will push myself beyond my comfort zone by trying out the new things I have learned and by working hard on the practice assignments.
6. I will let a group leader know if I am having trouble with my goals or if serious personal problems come up (including having thoughts of hurting myself or someone else).

III. Do Introductory Activities with Goals Worksheet

Activity: Getting to Know You Group Rounds

Because we'll be spending time together each week, let's get to know one another better. We'll go around the circle several times and tell something new about ourselves each time.

Group leaders can begin by sharing something not too personal about themselves in response to these questions.

Round 1: Personal Sharing

On this first go-around, tell us your name again and two things about yourself:

- *What is your favorite food?*
- *What is something you are good at?*

After Round 1 is completed, transition to Rounds 2 and 3.

Round 2: Briefly Describe Your Trauma or Loss

Briefly describe the traumatic or stressful experience or loss you have come here to work on and tell us how old you were when it happened.

This is a quick review of 30 seconds to 1 minute, so have youth focus only on WHAT happened to WHOM, WHEN, and HOW. Do not probe for details.

Round 3: Complete and Share Goals Worksheet

Make sure each group member has a copy of the goal worksheets filled out in the pre-session interview. This can include Handout 1.02, the Trauma Goals Worksheet, and/or Handout 1.03, the Personal Goals Worksheet. If you do not have a filled-out form, have the youth fill out Handout 1.02. With at least one of the worksheets complete, go around the group and have group members share something they would like to get out of the program.

Tell us something you would like to get out of the group or something that you would like to change in your life as a result of being in the group. You may share what you filled out on the worksheet or any other ways you would like your life to be better or different as a result of being in the group.

Thank the group. *Thank you all for sharing your experiences. There will be plenty of time in our future sessions to talk about your experiences with the depth and attention that they deserve. As everyone can see, each of you has lived through some very tough experiences. This group is designed to help you deal with the memories and current problems that have resulted from these stresses, traumas, and losses.*

If a group member becomes very upset, calmly and quickly move them through the event to the present. Reassure them that the group will help them to deal with these difficult feelings.

I can see that what happened still affects you very deeply. Thank you for being so honest with us – that takes courage. We're confident that you'll find that this group will be a supportive place where you can talk about these things in a way that will help you feel better. How are you feeling now?

IV. Invite Group Members to Share their Current Coping Strategies

Activity: Sharing Current Coping

For this activity you will need a large piece of paper on an easel or taped to a wall on which you will write group member's coping strategies. You will save the completed list for use in a later session.

Let's talk about how you cope with everything you've been through. How do you deal with bad or painful memories and things that remind you of what happened? How do you cope when you feel overwhelmed with strong feelings like anger, sadness, worry, fear, and hopelessness?

Note: As an option, you may choose to ask the students more generally how other youth their age cope with stress rather than asking them to report on themselves.

- Ask for a volunteer to write down on the flipchart or paper all the ways group members say they cope. **Important**: Write down these strategies along the *left* side the paper and leave an open space along the right side of the paper.
- Encourage group members to list both positive and more problematic ways of coping (i.e. smoking, weed, drinking, self-injury, risk-taking).
- Check to see if group members have someone they can go to when they need to talk about difficult feelings.
- Discuss the importance of having someone to talk to for support, especially during difficult times.
- Let them know that throughout the group, the group leaders will be helping them explore and find supports both within the group and elsewhere.
- Focus on group members' openness about the positive and negative coping strategies they have tried. Reinforce positive coping, and help them identify supports (some group members may have very few).
- **Remember to praise current attempts to cope.** Emphasize that they are not "crazy" and that many of the coping strategies they describe are strategies others have used. They have been coping the best that they can, and the group will teach more skills.

V. Provide an Overview of the Program

Before presenting Flipchart 1.1b, on what this group can do for you, ask group members to recall what you presented to them in the pre-session about the four major ways the group can be helpful. Adapt your message to the unique experiences and needs of the group.

1. *Provide help and support* that only you can give each other because you really know what it's like to go through these things.
2. *Be a safe place* to deal with painful memories and feelings connected to your traumatic experiences so that they don't interfere so much with your lives. You might have fewer nightmares, for example, or find that you don't get angry so easily.
3. *Learn new skills* to calm yourself down in a safe way when you get upset (instead of fighting with someone or doing drugs) to have a greater sense of control over your memories, bodies, and lives. This group can also help you cope with grief and loss.
4. *Create a better future* by dealing with the ways your life has changed because of these traumas and losses.

Supplement this discussion with reference to Flipchart 1.1b. Keep it brief.

*We know that this group won't solve **all** of the difficulties you face. But it is about opening up some hope for the future. We'd like you to leave this group with the skills and knowledge to cope with your current challenges without being overwhelmed by the memories of everything you've gone through.*

VI. Review the Session Format

Using Flipchart 1.1c, an overview of the program, focus especially on Module 1. Tell them that you will bring out this flipchart again to refresh their memories when you start a new module.

Explain that the sessions will have common features, including:

1. Check-in:
Each session will begin with a check-in.
- *First, you will rate your distress level on your Feeling Thermometer (we will talk more about this next session).*
- *Next, we will ask what happened or what you did since we last met that you feel good about.*

2. Group activities:
Each session will have an activity to help you learn something new and put it into practice. There will also be some time to talk about important things that have come up during that week.

3. Practice assignments:
Each week you will have the chance to practice a skill outside of the group. Practice is essential if you really want to master a skill so that it is yours to use whenever you need it, just like when you learn a new sport or how to play music. We'll review the practice exercises right after check-in.

4. Transitional activity/check-out and Check-Out Feedback Form:
We want to make sure everyone is doing okay before they leave the group. Sometimes we'll have an activity at the end of the group to help you calm your body and mind. Then you will fill out a check-out feedback form. We need your ideas

about each group session so we can know how you are doing and how we can make the program better.

VII. Provide Transitional Activity and Do Check-Out

- Bring closure to the group and make sure that group members are ready to return to their settings.
- *What did you learn about yourself today?*
- *Please fill out the Check-Out Feedback Form (Handout 1.04). The title of today's session was "Welcome and Introduction."*

If any group members are visibly agitated or troubled, keep them after the group and determine an appropriate way to help them transition back to their settings.

Implementing Module 1, Session 1.1 with Individual Clients

Preparation: Review the group highlights for this session and be comfortable with how you will adapt the activities for your individual client. Have the necessary handouts available. You may want to have available a single-page version of Flipchart 1.1c to help you provide an overview of the program.

I. **Engage with the client**. Greet your client as you normally would, provide introductions as necessary and check in what the client might know about the program. Clarify any misperceptions and describe the program in general terms.

II. **Develop program contract**. Depending on your standard practice, you may do this in an informal or more formal manner as described in the group guidelines. The heart of this is to clarify expectations for attendance, confidentiality, and participation in the program. Review the types of rules listed on the group contract and select or adapt any that you think may be pertinent. You may choose to actually develop a written individual contract, or not depending on your practice.

III. **Introductory activity and goals worksheet**. Review the group activity and see which aspects of this may be adapted for use with your individual client. Many clinicians use the same or similar prompts with individual clients. Go over the personal goals worksheet and facilitate a discussion to help your client select personal goals for participating in the program.

IV. **Invite client to share his/her current coping strategies**. You may do this as described in the group guideline.

V. **Give an overview of the program as described in Section V.**

VI. **Review the session format**. You may do this as described in Section VI.

VII. **Provide transitional activity and do check-out**. You may do this as described in the group guideline.

1.2 Posttraumatic Stress Reactions, Grief Reactions, and Introduction to Coping Strategies

Session Objectives

1. Learn how to use the Feeling Thermometer for check-in and check-out.
2. Discuss posttraumatic and grief reactions.
3. Model empathetic listening skills.
4. Introduce and practice deep (abdominal) breathing as a coping strategy.

Note: Individual therapy guide on last page of session.

Section number	Session overview
I	Check-in and introduction of the Feeling Thermometer
II	Stress reduction exercise
III	Normalizing posttraumatic and grief reactions
IV	Practice deep (abdominal) breathing
V	Practice assignment
VI	Check-out

Supplies

Every session	This session
• Flipchart	• Copies of the group contract for group members to review and sign
• Large paper or easel pad	

Every session	This session
• Colored markers or crayons	
• Pencils/pens	
• Kleenex	
• Tape	
• Workbooks	

Handouts in Workbook

Handout 1.05	Feeling Thermometer
Handout 1.06	Instructions for Deep (Abdominal) Breathing
Handout 1.07	Using the Breathing Technique Every Day
Handout 1.08	Checklist: Re-Experiencing
Handout 1.09	Checklist: Avoidance and Numbing
Handout 1.10	Checklist: Persistent Negative Mood
Handout 1.11	Checklist: Hyperarousal
Handout 1.12	Checklist: Grief
Handout 1.13	Monitoring Changes in My Mood and Feelings
Handout 1.14	Check-Out Feedback Form

Flipcharts

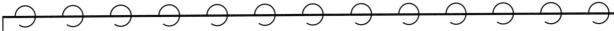

> *1.2 Today's Highlights*
> 1. *Check-in: one good thing that happened since last session*
> 2. *Introduction of Feeling Thermometer*
> 3. *Explain and practice deep (abdominal) breathing*
> 4. *Discuss posttraumatic and grief reactions*
> 5. *Practice deep (abdominal) breathing again*
> 6. *Practice assignment*
> 7. *Check-out with the Feeling Thermometer and Check-Out Feedback Form*

Session 1.2: Posttraumatic Stress and Grief Reactions, and Introduction to Coping Strategies

I. Check-In and Introduction of Feeling Thermometer

- Go around the room and ask group members about something they did or something that happened since the group last met that they feel good about. Although many will report positive events, some group members will report failures or losses ("I failed the GED" or "My uncle was killed"). In such cases, follow up with prompts such as "Tell me more about what happened," and express empathy and interest.
- Use Handout 1.05, the Feeling Thermometer, and train youth to use it to report how they are feeling right now. The number 0 represents totally relaxed and not distressed, 5 represents moderately distressed, and 10 is the most extreme level of distress they've ever felt. These distressing emotions can include feelings like anxious, scared, terrified, sad, ashamed, hysterical, hopeless, angry, enraged, or helpless.

II. Stress Reduction Exercise

Traumatic or very stressful events can cause one to feel "on edge" or nervous. In this session we will learn more about posttraumatic stress reactions. These include some level of hyperarousal or nervousness that at times can take over your entire body. Throughout this group we will be showing you a number of ways to feel better when this happens. One way that many experts have found works best is deep breathing. We will learn this today and practice it each week.

A Quick Biology Lesson about Breathing

*When we are afraid or anxious, our nervous system causes our heart to beat fast, muscles to tense, and breathing to become rapid and shallow. This causes us to have **too much** oxygen in our bodies. Too much oxygen over a long period of time causes a lot of physical problems such as swelling, high blood pressure, and muscle pain. Slowing our breathing and making it deeper normalizes our oxygen levels and turns on the calming nervous system. Deep breathing slows our heartbeat, decreases sweating, and helps us calm down.*

Activity: Practice Relaxation Breathing

Note: The full instructions for deep breathing are in the youth handouts. Ask youth to look at this page as you go over the following.

Have group members sit comfortably in their chairs with both feet on the floor, or if the group has space and feels comfortable doing so, they may lie on the floor. Either way will work. Tell them to make sure their belts are not too tight.

- Show them how to place one hand on their chest and one hand on their abdomen, and demonstrate deep (abdominal) breathing in which the upper hand hardly moves and the lower hand rises and falls with each breath. Refer to Handout 1.06, Instructions for Deep (Abdominal) Breathing, in group members' workbooks, and point out that it is available for future use and practice. Closing their eyes is optional, as it may not feel safe and relaxing to some group members.
- After people finish, you may show them Handout 1.07, Using the Breathing Technique Every Day. Explain that with practice you can use the technique whenever you wish without people even knowing you are doing it.

III. Normalizing Posttraumatic Stress and Grief Reactions

The goals for normalizing posttraumatic stress and grief reactions can be summarized as follows:

- Help the group understand posttraumatic and grief reactions as normal reactions to highly stressful events. Help them view their reactions as automatic coping responses that make perfect sense at the time of the event, but may now be causing problems in their lives.

- Help group members discover ways in which their reactions may be interfering in their lives.
- Use your own words to cover the information provided in the sample remarks. DO NOT LECTURE. Instead, facilitate a discussion in which group members can talk about their own personal reactions and the problems they create (e.g. losing sleep).
- As appropriate, incorporate information gathered in the pre-group interviews to increase the personal relevance of this discussion. Speak in general summary terms about the *types* of reactions and problems group members have experienced, but allow individual group members the choice of whether to disclose their specific reactions and associated problems.

Introduce Posttraumatic Stress and Grief Reactions

Before giving this explanation, ask group members whether they have heard about posttraumatic stress disorder or PTSD and what they know about it. Make the following presentation an interactive discussion, and keep group members engaged. Have group members refer to the handouts in their workbooks.

- *We know from scientific studies that very stressful or traumatic events can produce reactions in almost anyone. It doesn't matter how strong or emotionally healthy you are – when something terrible shakes you to the core, it can affect how you feel, think, and act in many parts of your life. A traumatic experience can change the way you look at yourself, other people, and the world.*
- *We learned this when soldiers came back from the wars in Vietnam, Afghanistan, and Iraq with posttraumatic stress disorder (PTSD). Ask if group members know any veterans or others with PTSD. Take time to discuss what they know about PTSD from personal experience or the media.*
- *From what you all have told us, many of you have lived in places a lot like war zones. Some of you have told us that you have been threatened with death or serious injury, have witnessed others die or get seriously hurt, have learned about violence done to close family members or friends, or have experienced or seen sexual violence. You have seen the police officers and ambulances, heard the sirens, and have witnessed the horrified reactions of those around you.*
- *You may have wondered what was wrong with you because you couldn't "get over it." You may have felt tremendous pressure from family members and friends to appear OK, to "be cool," to forget about it, and to just "put it all behind you." You may even feel that you have been permanently changed by what happened to you. You may think that no one really understands how bad it was and the hopeless thoughts you may have, such as, "I will never get over this."*
- *We are going to start by understanding what these reactions are, what they are called, and where they come from. We also want to help you take a look at the lessons you took away from your traumatic experiences, and how well they are working for you now.*

Introduce the four categories of posttraumatic reactions and grief and direct youth to the handouts for each in their workbooks.

- Handout 1.08 (Re-Experiencing): "Upsetting Thoughts, Images, and Memories Pop Into My Mind"
- Handout 1.09 (Avoidance and Numbing): "I Am Avoiding People, Situations, and Feelings that Upset or Stress Me Out"
- Handout 1.10 (Persistent Negative Mood): "I Am Having Persistent Negative Thoughts and Feelings"
- Handout 1.11 (Hyperarousal): "I Am Feeling Jumpy, Irritable, and On Guard"
- Handout 1.12 (Grief): "I Am Feeling Sad, Hopeless, Lost or Angry About the Death"

Explain that you will review each category and group members should put a check next to each reaction they currently experience using the checklists in their workbooks for today's session. After each category, have group members give examples of their reactions.

Re-experiencing (Handout 1.08): "Upsetting Thoughts, Images, and Memories Pop Into My Mind"

Re-experiencing occurs when thoughts or images of a very stressful or traumatic event come back into your mind against your will when you are not even focusing on them. Re-experiencing reactions are often the most common type of reaction that people have. They can make you feel upset, tense, scared, and on edge.

Read aloud the contents of the following box and have youth

Common Signs of Re-Experiencing

- **Intrusive, involuntary memories**: *You may have repeated, distressing memories of the traumatic event(s) that just pop into your head when you don't want them to.*
- **Nightmares**: *You may have nightmares about what happened.*
- **Dissociative reactions (flashbacks)**: *You may suddenly feel and act as if the trauma were happening again, and it can be so severe that you are not aware of where you are or what day it is.*
- **Sudden changes in how you are feeling**: *When you are reminded of what happened or of someone you have lost, you may suddenly get sad, scared, angry, irritable, or numb.*
- **Changes in how your body feels**: *Your body may react to cues or reminders about the traumatic event.*

check off items that they have experienced as you do so. After youth have filled out this box, ask them: *How many of you experience one or more of these reactions?* Have volunteers share their reactions.

As appropriate, provide the following information:

- *Re-experiencing or intrusive reactions often come after something reminds you of what happened. These are called* "trauma or loss reminders."

- These reactions often focus on the **worst moments** of what happened – the parts when you felt the most scared, grossed out, horrified, helpless, or in pain, or when you realized there was nothing you could do to stop what was happening. By "playing over" our worst experiences, our minds also show us how much we wish that things could have turned out differently, with a happier ending.
- Re-experiencing these terrible moments can cause intense negative emotions and bodily reactions that are hard for anyone to deal with.
- During the next few weeks, we will work together as a group to help each of you learn how to **recognize** your own personal trauma and loss reminders, and practice ways to cope with the thoughts and feelings that they bring up.

Avoidance and Numbing (Handout 1.09): "I Am Avoiding People, Situations, and Feelings That Upset or Stress Me Out"

Avoidance and numbing occur when you attempt to avoid things that would remind you of the trauma or loss. You may even seem at times to have no feelings at all.

Common Signs of Avoidance

- You **avoid people, places, activities**, or things that remind you of what happened.
- You **feel emotionally "flat,"** as if you are trying to avoid having any feelings at all.
- You **avoid thoughts, memories, feelings**, or conversations about the traumatic event(s).

Read aloud the contents of the following box and have youth check off items that they have experienced as you do so.
After youth have filled out this box, ask them: *How many of you experience one or more of these reactions?* Have volunteers share their reactions.

As appropriate explain why avoidance or numbing occurs:

- After being on "high alert" for so long there comes a point at which your body and brain say, "Enough!" To protect you they start to "turn down the volume." Your body and your brain become less sensitive to things outside and inside and prompt you to avoid anything that will cause painful memories and feelings. Sometimes it feels like you create a barrier or a glass wall between yourself and the world.
- All of these reactions are natural responses to extreme stress. They are automatic coping responses built into human biology to protect and stabilize us when we are living with extreme stress or trauma. But when these reactions become your normal way of responding, they interfere with your life, your ability to learn, and your whole development.

Persistent Negative Mood (Handout 1.10): "I Am Having Persistent Negative Thoughts and Feelings"

When terrible things have happened to you, they change how you think about everything including yourself, other people, and

the whole world around you. Some people blame themselves, or they blame others and want to get even. Your emotions can change too, so that you feel stuck in strong feelings such as rage or shame, or you can feel cut off so that nothing interests you and you can't feel anything positive. You may feel very separate from the people around you, as if you were seeing them through a glass wall.

Read aloud the contents of the following box and have youth

Common Signs of Persistent Negative Mood

- **Memory loss:** You may be unable to recall important parts of what happened.
- **Persistent negative beliefs**: You may have developed hurtful thoughts about yourself, other people, and the world because of what happened.
- **Blame**: You may be stuck in blaming yourself or others about what happened.
- **Negative emotions**: You may feel afraid, angry, horrified, or ashamed most of the time.
- **No interests**: You may feel like you don't want to do anything that you used to like doing.
- **Cut off**: You may feel detached, estranged, and cut off from other people
- **No joy**: You may feel that you can't feel any happy, satisfied, or loving feelings.

check off items that they have experienced as you do so.
After youth have filled out this box, ask them: *How many of you experience one or more of these reactions?* Have volunteers share their reactions.

Hyperarousal (Handout 1.11): "I Am Feeling Jumpy, Irritable, and On Guard"

Hyperarousal is the sensation of always being on guard, feeling nervous or jumpy because your body may be constantly scanning (on the lookout) for signs of danger. It is your body's way of trying to keep you safe.

Common Signs of Hyperarousal

- You may feel **irritable**, aggressive, or "on edge" much of the time.
- You may start to do **reckless** or self-destructive things.
- You may feel constantly **on guard and hypervigilant**, as if danger is lurking everywhere.
- You may **startle** easily, feel jumpy.
- You may **find it hard to pay attention** in school, concentrate on homework, or remember what you have learned.
- You may have a **difficult time falling or staying asleep**.

Read aloud the contents of the following box and have youth check off items that they have experienced as you do so. As appropriate, explain why hyperarousal occurs:

- *Once you have an experience that forces you to face the fact that you are not totally safe, that terrible things can happen to you and other people like you, and that sometimes you can't predict or control what happens, your feelings about what is safe and what is dangerous can be changed and even distorted.*
- *Your body's survival mechanisms go into overdrive and you go on "high alert." For many people after one or more severe traumas or stressors, that "switch" does not turn off even though the actual threats of danger are over and they are now safe.*
- *When that alarm bell in your body works overtime, you can overreact to small, safe things, such as a sudden noise or someone's facial expression, as if they were dangerous.*

Grief (Handout 1.12): "I Am Feeling Sad, Hopeless, Lost, or Angry About the Death"

Last, there are grief reactions after you have lost someone close to you.

Common Signs of Grief

- *You may **miss** the person who died.*
- *You may **feel sad** whenever you are reminded that they are gone and not in your life anymore.*
- *You may **feel angry** that they are gone.*
- *You may **feel regret** about things you did or didn't do at the time of their death.*
- *You may **have both strong negative** and **strong positive feelings (ambivalence)** about the person who died.*
- *You may **feel lost or hopeless**.*
- *You may **wonder who you are** without this person in your life.*

Read aloud the contents of the following box and have youth check off items that they have experienced as you do so.

After youth have filled out this box, ask them: *How many of you experience one or more of these reactions?* Have volunteers share their reactions.

Grieving itself can be very hard, but it can be made worse when someone dies in a violent or tragic way. When someone you care about dies suddenly and horribly, it can make it harder to think about and remember them in comforting ways.

- *These reactions can include: Finding it difficult to think about them because thoughts or pictures of how they died pop into your mind.*
- *Feeling very angry at the way they died, including at people you think were responsible.*
- *Feeling bad that you are alive and they aren't.*

- *Feeling like you can't bear to hear their name or think about them because it brings up a bunch of upsetting memories or feelings.*

Trauma and Grief Reactions Summary

*All of these reactions (re-experiencing, avoidance, persistent negative mood and feelings, hyperarousal, and grief reactions) are natural consequences of experiencing extreme stress and loss. They are automatic coping mechanisms that protect and stabilize you. They help you keep a sense of control, make sure you don't get overwhelmed by painful thoughts and feelings, and help you to carry on with your daily life. **But these reactions can become a habit and last longer than is good for you.** They can interfere with your life and development in important ways.*

IV. Practice Relaxation Breathing

Refer back to Section II, the stress reduction exercise, and have youth practice abdominal breathing again, as the preceding discussion may have evoked stressful reactions.

V. Practice Assignment

Explain how to use Handout 1.13, Monitoring Changes in My Mood and Feelings.

During this session we talked about re-experiencing, avoidance and numbing, changes in thinking and mood, hyperarousal, and grief/loss feelings. In order to work on skills to help you with these reactions, it will be important for you to pay attention to when these reactions happen.

Directions: *Pick one to three times this week in which you noticed a sudden change for the worse in your mood, such as times in which you start to feel very distressed or times when you sense that you have NO feelings. Note strong feelings such as sadness, anxiety, fear, shame, helplessness, guilt, or anger. These strong feelings may be signs that you are having a reaction triggered by a reminder of your trauma or loss experiences. For each time, write a brief description of what was happening **outside** of you. Then, describe one or two emotions that you felt most strongly **inside** of you.*

VI. Check-Out

Have group members rate themselves on their Feeling Thermometer and share with the group.

- Refer group members to the Check-Out Feedback Form (Handout 1.14) and have group members fill it out. The title of today's session was, "Posttraumatic and Grief Reactions and Introduction to Coping Strategies."
- The group leader may either send workbooks with the youth or keep them for the next session.
- Have each member answer the following questions:
  - *How are you feeling now?*
  - *What did you learn about yourself today?*

If any group members are visibly agitated or troubled or report a high level of distress on the Feeling Thermometer, keep them after the group and determine an appropriate way to transition them back to their settings.

Implementing Module 1, Session 1.2 with Individual Clients

Preparation: Make a printed copy of Today's Highlights (Flipchart 1.2) that would be on a flipchart if done in a group, so that youth has a copy of today's agenda.

I. **Check-in and introduction of the Feeling Thermometer**. Ask your client about something good that happened in the past week, as described in the first bullet. You may also break the ice by sharing something good that happened to you this week. Then introduce and describe the Feeling Thermometer, which is in the youth workbook and your manual.

II. **Stress reduction exercise**. Do this breathing exercise as described with appropriate adaptations for working with an individual.

III. **Normalizing posttraumatic and grief reactions**. In order to avoid "lecturing," first have the client fill out the forms in the workbook, and then engage in a conversation about posttraumatic and grief reactions, so that you cover the content in the manual and the youth's workbook while making it personal for this individual.

IV. **Practice deep (abdominal) breathing**. Do this together for five or ten breaths, as appropriate.

V. **Practice assignment**. This can be delivered without adaptations.

VI. **Check-out**. In order to level the playing field with an individual client, you may wish to rate yourself on the Feeling Thermometer as well as the client.

Note: Individual therapy guide on last page of session.

1.3 Monitoring and Managing Strong Feelings

Session Objectives

1. Increase ability to track emotions by becoming aware of how emotions are experienced in the body.
2. Increase ability to experience emotions in the moderate ranges of intensity, rather than bouncing between 0 and 10 on the feeling thermometer.
3. Increase ability to become aware of emotions expressed by others through facial expression, posture, and tone of voice.
4. Increase vocabulary for describing feelings and emotions.
5. Practice sharing these feelings with the group, especially during Module 2 (working through traumatic experiences), when trauma stories are told and shared.
6. Increasingly tolerate (rather than avoid) the experience of painful emotions.

Note: individual therapy guide on last page of session.

Section number	Session overview
I	Check-in and Feeling Thermometer
II	Review last session and practice assignment
III	Step one: "*What* am I feeling?"
IV	Step two: "*Why* am I feeling this way?"
V	Practice assignment
VI	Check-out

Supplies

Every Session	This Session
• Flipchart	
• Large paper or easel pad	
• Several sets of colored markers or crayons	
• Pencils/pens	
• Kleenex	
• Tape	
• Workbooks	

Handouts in Workbook

Handout 1.15	Three Steps to Taking Charge of Your Feelings
Handout 1.16	Feelings Selfie
Handout 1.17	Feeling Faces
Handout 1.18	What's Behind Your Anger?
Handout 1.19	Check-Out Feedback Form

Flipcharts

1.3a Today's Highlights

1. Check-in: one good thing that happened and the Feeling Thermometer

2. Review practice assignment: deep (abdominal) breathing and monitoring changes in my mood and feelings (if assigned)

3. Step one: "What am I feeling?"

4. Color your body

5. Reading emotions in others

6. Step two: "Why am I feeling this way?"

7. Practice assignment

8. Check-out with the Feeling Thermometer and Check-Out Feedback Form

---

1.3b Three Steps to Taking Charge of Your Feelings

Step One: "What am I feeling?"
Step Two: "Why am I feeling this way?"
Step Three: "How can I feel better?"

Session 1.3: Emotions and Feelings

I. Check-In and Feeling Thermometer

- *How are you feeling right now?* (Use Handout 1.05, the Feeling Thermometer.)
- Practice with the group doing five to ten abdominal breaths.
- *What happened or what did you do since we last met that you feel good about?*
- *Is anything going on that may make it difficult for you to keep your mind on the group today?*
- Briefly review (or have a group member review) Today's Highlights (Flipchart 1.3a).

II. Review Last Session and Practice Assignment

Review Last Session

- Customize your review of the last session to reflect what actually went on in your group. Try to include some of the content as well. This is a good opportunity to reinforce their learning.
- Use visual cues. Bring out last week's flipchart or refer them to the information in their workbooks about trauma and loss.
- *Last session we talked about posttraumatic and grief reactions as natural human coping responses to extreme stress and loss. Posttraumatic feelings and behaviors fall into four categories. Do any of you remember what they are?* Pause to let youth look back at the handouts for Session 2 if they would like and discuss posttraumatic reactions.

- *We discussed reactions that might fall into those four categories and how these reactions can interfere with people's lives. We spoke about the pressures people often feel to "get over it" and avoid talking or thinking about how scared, angry, or numb they still feel. It takes a lot of courage to face these difficulties and to actually try to do something about them – like being in this group.*

Review Practice Assignment

Ask group members to look at their filled in Handout 1.13, Monitoring Changes in My Mood and Feelings, and talk about times last week when they reacted to something that had happened and what they felt. If group members did not fill this form out, have them do so now. It is not required that every member participate in the verbal sharing. If group members do report strong reactions, have them describe what they think prompted their reactions, including specifics in the situation, how they may have interpreted the situation, or what they may have said to themselves. You can also inquire how they coped with these strong feelings. Use this discussion to transition to the next topic.

III: Present Step One: *"What* Am I Feeling?"

Today we are going to focus on feelings and emotions. When people have had a lot of stressful and traumatic things happen to them, it can change how they experience emotions.
- *Some people numb out and try to "stay cool" so as not to feel anything.*
- *Others seem overwhelmed with strong, angry, or sad feelings all the time.*
- *Many people bounce back and forth between high and low levels of emotion.*

Ask group members to share with each other how they experience emotions.

During this group, you'll learn to live in the middle range of feelings rather than feeling numbed out sometimes and feeling too much at others. You will learn ways to take charge of your emotions. Today we'll focus first on Step One, "What am I feeling?"

- Teach and practice Step One skills that include being aware of changes in one's mood or feelings, experiencing and tolerating emotions, and giving feelings a name.
- Help youth to understand why people may avoid or block their strong emotions.

Refer to Handout 1.15 (shown below).

The first step in this new skill is to ask yourself, *"What am I feeling?" Having a strong feeling or emotion is often your first clue that a reminder of a painful memory is bothering you.*

For example, you may feel suddenly sad, scared, or angry and have no clue why you feel that way because nothing is going on right now to cause that feeling. It may be a reminder of something dangerous or hurtful from the past that suddenly bubbles up into your mind.

At other times, you may feel suddenly happy because something – a particular song or the smell of pizza – reminds you of a happy time in the past.

*When we ask people how they are feeling, they usually respond with a word or two: "good," "not bad," "I'm cool," "nervous," "great," "could be worse," and so forth. Actually, people are often feeling **more** than one emotion at a given time.*

Note: The activities presented next are all fun but you may need to select only two or three depending on time available. Choose the activities that meet the needs of each group.

Activity: Feelings Selfie (Handout 1.16)

The purpose of this activity is to increase understanding of specific emotions and that many different emotions can be experienced at the same time. Emotions can be experienced strongly, moderately, or faintly. Pass out colored markers and/or crayons and introduce the "emotional snapshot" exercise as a fun warm-up that will give the group practice in identifying and naming feelings.

The next activity is kind of like taking an "emotional snapshot" of all the emotions you feel right now. Pick two to four emotions that you feel right now. Assign a color to each emotion and write the name of that emotion in that color on the blank lines of Handout 1.16, *the Feelings Selfie. Refer to* Handout 1.17, *Feeling Faces, if you need ideas. Then color in the Feelings Selfie showing how much you are feeling each emotion. So if you are half hopeful, a quarter sad, and a quarter anxious, then color half the circle with the color you chose for hopeful, and a quarter each with the colors you chose for sad and anxious.*

Go around the group and invite group members to share their personal emotional snapshots with the group. Validate and normalize as appropriate. Emphasize the following points:

- *Different group members have different emotions.*
- *Even when group members feel the same emotions, they feel them differently. One person feels the emotion strongly, another medium, another only faintly.*
- *Our emotional snapshots change from moment to moment and from one situation to the next.*
- *When we develop an understanding of our emotions and expand the vocabulary to talk about them, this can help us feel close to others. It helps us understand ourselves and each other better, helps clarify misunderstandings, and helps us support each other.*

Activity: What's Behind Your Anger? (Handout 1.18)

The purpose of this exercise is to understand that anger is often a surface emotion that shields the vulnerable feelings underneath. View Handout 1.18 with the group and ask them what emotions are shielded by anger.

If they say that they need to hold onto their anger to feel safe in their neighborhoods, acknowledge that you understand that. Then tell them that in this room, where they may feel safer, they can let themselves become aware of, and share with others, some of the more vulnerable feelings that may lie hidden underneath their anger, such as worry, sadness, shame, or fear. See if they wish to share some of these shielded feelings.

Activity: Color your Body, Part 1 (The Color of Emotions)

Draw a gingerbread figure on the flipchart. Ask group members to name, one at a time, four to six different emotions. As you are discussing each emotion, ask them to discuss and decide what color should represent each emotion, and then write (or have a group member write) on the flipchart each emotion in its chosen color. If group members cannot agree about the colors, the group leader should make the decision. Be sure that anger, sadness, happiness, and fear are listed. Example: red = anger, blue = sadness, yellow = happiness, purple = fear, etc.

Activity: Color your Body, Part 2 (Locating Emotions in the Body)

Sudden distressing changes in how you feel are often the first signs that something has reminded you of a past danger, trauma, or loss. Learning to track these shifts in feeling will help you manage

posttraumatic or depressive reactions early on, before they become habits and more difficult to change. Our bodies broadcast messages all the time about how and what we are feeling. If you learn to "tune in" to your body's special signals, you can decode them to understand what you are feeling. In later sessions you'll learn how to take charge of emotions so that you can change how you feel.

Take one emotion at a time and ask each group member to tell you where in his or her body each one feels that emotion. Have a group member fill in the color on the gingerbread figure as group members call out where they feel different emotions in their bodies.

For example,

- *You may get a "knot" in your stomach, cold hands, or weak legs when you are feeling anxious or afraid. This is **your** body's unique way of responding to stress or threat.*
- *You may feel anger in your jaw, or your fists, or your forehead.*
- *When you are feeling sad, you may feel emptiness down in the pit of your stomach, or your heart might hurt.*
- *When you are feeling happy, your face may feel energetic around your eyes and your mouth.*
- *An important thing to keep in mind is that everybody's body is different and broadcasts different types of signals.*

Have group members share their "body messages" for the various emotions. It helps if you ask them to imagine a time, either now or in the past, when they felt each emotion; have them recall it vividly and try to feel where they feel it in their bodies.

Note: As this exercise covers several emotions, the gingerbread figure will most likely end up layered with many colors in certain parts of the body, such as the face or heart areas.

Activity: What Are You Feeling? (Reading Emotional Expressions in Others)

It can be easy to misread facial expressions in others, especially if we are already upset or expect people to be angry at us or hurt us. Learning to pay attention to others' faces is important because we cannot always tell what another person is thinking or feeling. Fortunately, we can always ask: "Are you feeling angry? Sad?" Checking in with a person about their feelings saves us the trouble of misreading facial expressions.

Guess What I'm Feeling

Give each member a 3×5 card. Tell them to select a feeling they will demonstrate using only their facial expression and have them write that feeling on the card. Tell them to not let anyone see what they have written. Group leaders should also choose a feeling and be the first to demonstrate this activity. Group members take turns expressing the feeling written on their card.

Others try to guess the feeling by saying, "You are looking …. Is that how you are feeling?" The member who guesses the correct feeling is given the card. You can be creative and award points, etc., to the member who gets the most cards.

Summarize Step One: "*What* Am I Feeling?"

Our feelings and moods change throughout the day. Practice paying attention to what you are feeling, especially emotions like fear, sadness, or anger. Frequently, people try to "stuff" or ignore strong negative feelings. It is important to stay with these bad feelings long enough so you can name them. All emotions are OK; it is what you do with these emotions that matters. Remember, when people are under pressure and stressed out, they sometimes forget to pay attention to the good things they are feeling. So try to be open to your good feelings as well.

IV: Present Step Two: *Why* Am I Feeling This Way?

Introduce Step Two skills to answer, "WHY am I feeling this way?" Look outside to the immediate situation, which may be provoking the response, and inside to the thoughts, feelings, or images that may be contributing to the experience of painful emotions.

Refer to Handout 1.15, Three Steps to Taking Charge of Your Feelings, and use this to introduce Step Two in the model.

*After you can answer the first question, "**What am I feeling?**" (Step One), you are ready to begin to consider the second question: "**Why am I feeling this way?**" (Step Two). There are two important ways to do this:*

- *Look **outside** of yourself – that is, pay attention to what is going on around you.*
- *Look **inside** of yourself – that is, pay attention what you might be saying to yourself in your mind.*

Refer to their responses to the homework assignment in which they identified situations that evoke strong emotions. Elicit more examples of their experience during the week of how things outside of them led to strong emotional or behavioral reactions. Through your prompts, also try to elicit examples of things they thought or said to themselves (inside of them) that may have contributed to their reactions.

Introduce the Topic of Trauma and Loss Reminders

Many different types of things – both inside of us and outside of us – can cause trauma and loss reactions.

- ***Trauma and loss reminders:*** *External events that are connected to past traumas, dangers, or losses are called trauma or loss reminders. Things that we see, hear, smell, taste, or feel can remind us of past dangers or losses. What are some examples you can think of? Ask a group member to write examples on the flipchart under the heading "External Events" or "Outside of Me."*
- *Examples can include the sound of an ambulance or police siren, the smell of smoke, or a scared or angry expression on someone's face.*

- *Another example is a person who has been repeatedly whipped by a parent or beaten up by another student. When someone bumps into him/her by accident or startles him/her, he/she lashes out and punches.*
- *A girl who has been sexually assaulted in the past reacts to a friendly greeting or a pat on the shoulder as a threat.*
- ***Trauma and loss reactions:*** *Internal events such as thoughts, emotions, or images can trigger trauma and loss reactions. What are some examples you can think of? Ask a group member to write examples on the flipchart under the heading "Internal Events" or "Inside of Me."*
- *Examples include feeling lonely and being reminded of a time after the sudden death of a special person.*
- *Your heart racing after a game or jogging remind you of a time when you felt terrified and your heart was racing. For this reason, many people with trauma histories avoid exercising.*

*Step One was "**What** am I feeling?" By paying attention to changes in your feelings and mood and using "body messages," you can give feelings names, such as angry, sad, scared, guilty, ashamed, etc. We will be helping with managing these feelings in later sessions.*

*Step Two was "**Why** am I feeling this way?" Look outside of yourselves for possible trauma or loss reminders, and look inside of yourselves for automatic thoughts or images (trauma and loss reactions) that may be contributing to how you are feeling.*

Capturing these thoughts or images can be difficult because they happen so fast. But you can learn to go into slow motion and change the way you think at each moment to become more in charge of your feelings.

Next session we will continue to talk about Step Two, "WHY am I feeling this way," and learn more about trauma and loss reminders. In the sessions after that, we will talk about Step Three, "HOW can I feel better?" and learn and practice many coping skills and different ways to think.

For this week, try to tune into the feelings and emotions you experience and where in your body you feel them. You need these skills because next session we will look at trauma and loss reminders and how you feel when you have them.

V. Practice Assignment

Use Handout 1.13, Monitoring Changes in My Mood and Feelings. This essential exercise was assigned at the end of Session 2, reviewed at the beginning of this session, and is repeated here to give youth additional practice.

During this session we talked about re-experiencing, hyperarousal, avoidance/numbing, and some grief/loss feelings. In order to work on skills to help you with these reactions, it will be important for you to pay attention to when these reactions are happening.

Directions: *Pick one to three times this week in which you noticed a sudden change for the worse in your mood, such as times in which you start to feel worse or times when you sense* *that you have NO feelings. Note strong feelings such as sadness, anxiety, fear, guilt, or anger. These strong feelings may be signs that you are having a reaction related to your trauma or loss experience, such as hyperarousal, re-experiencing, numbing/avoidance, or grief.*

For each time, write a brief description of what was happening OUTSIDE of you. Then, describe one or two emotions that you felt most strongly INSIDE of you.

VI. Check-Out

- *How are you feeling now?* (Use the Feeling Thermometer ratings.)
- *What did you learn about yourself today?*
- *Please fill out the Check-Out Feedback Form* (Handout 1.19). *The title of today's session was "Emotions and Feelings."*

If any group members are visibly agitated or troubled or report high levels of distress on the feeling thermometer, keep them after the group and determine an appropriate way to transition back to their settings.

Implementing Module 1, Session 1.3 with Individual Clients

Preparation: Make printed copies of Today's Highlights (Flipchart 1.3a), and Three Steps to Taking Charge of your Feelings (Flipchart 1.3b), if that is easier instead of using flipcharts.

I. **Check-in**. Ask your client about something good that happened in the past week, as described in the first bullet. You may also break the ice by sharing something good that happened to you this week.

II. **Review last session and practice assignment**. Deliver the exercise as written but omit references to the group.

III. **Present Step One: "What am I feeling?"** Select activities that you think will be most effective with your client, though you may not have time to do both of the activities in this section. The "feelings snapshot" is good with most individuals. If anger is a presenting issue, make sure you use the What's Behind Your Anger? activity (Handout 1.18).

IV. **Color your body**. Although this is listed as a group activity, Color Your Body is often done with individual children, adolescents, and adults. It can be done as a light hearted exercise during later sessions as well; most people enjoy it.

V. **What are you feeling?** This is done as a group game, so it cannot be done as written during solo sessions. However, to assess and teach the skill of accurately reading facial expressions, many clinicians with internet access during sessions use the Emotions Color Wheel.

VI. **Present Step Two: Why am I feeling this way?** This can be delivered as written.

VII. **Practice assignment**. This can be delivered as written.

VIII. **Check-out**. This can be delivered as written.

1.4 Learning to Cope with Trauma and Loss Reminders

Session Objectives

1. Learn about trauma and loss reminders.
2. Identify and share personal reminders.
3. Identify ways that posttraumatic reactions interfere with youth's lives.
4. Model empathetic listening skills.

Pre-Session Preparation

- Review each member's pre-session responses on the University of California at Los Angeles Reaction Index to posttraumatic stress disorder (PTSD).
- Review each member's group Trauma Goals Worksheet (Handout 1.02) as filled out in Session 1.1.

Section number	Session overview
I	Check-in and Feeling Thermometer
II	Review practice assignment
III	Trauma and loss reminders
IV	Reacting to and coping with distressing reminders
V	Present the "SLOW down" technique
VI	Provide a calming activity
VII	Practice assignment
VIII	Check-out

Supplies

Every Session	This Session
Flipchart	
Large paper or easel pad	
Colored markers or crayons	
Pencils/pens	
Kleenex	
Tape	
Workbooks	

Handouts in Workbook

Handout 1.20	Trauma Reminders Worksheet
Handout 1.21	Loss Reminders Worksheet
Handout 1.22	How I React to and Cope with Distressing Reminders
Handout 1.23	SLOW Down
Handout 1.24	Check-Out Feedback Form

Flipcharts

1.4a Today's Highlights

1. Check-in: one good thing that happened and Feeling Thermometer
2. Review practice assignment: deep breathing and monitoring changes in my mood and feelings
3. Learn about trauma and loss reminders
4. How people react to and cope with distressing reminders
5. Calming activity
6. Check-out with Feeling Thermometer and feedback form

1.4b Distressing Reminders (Trauma Reminders)

1. Outside of me:
   - A person, place, or situation
   - A sound, smell, or sight
   - A time or date
   - A change in routine
   - An activity
   - The media
2. Inside of me:
   - A bodily sensation
   - An emotion
   - A thought

1.4c Loss Reminders

1. "Missing" reminders:
   - Empty situations
   - Shared activities
   - Rituals
2. "Changed life" reminders

Session 1.4: Learning to Cope with Trauma and Loss Reminders

I. Check-In and Feeling Thermometer

- *How are you feeling right now?* (Use the Feeling Thermometer.)
- *What happened or what did you do since we last met that you feel good about?*
- *Is anything going on that may make it difficult for you to keep your mind on the group today?*
- Briefly review (or have a group member review) Today's Highlights (Flipchart 1.4a).

II. Review Previous Sessions and Practice Assignment

Review Previous Sessions

- It is important to summarize the major content up to this point because you are incrementally building skills to manage emotions.
- Touch upon just the main points and focus on Steps One and Two of the model.
- Refer to Handout 1.15, Three Steps to Taking Charge of Your Feelings, and review the model.

In the second session, we talked about posttraumatic and grief reactions as natural coping responses to danger, trauma, and loss. Do you recall some of what we talked about?

Stop and ask the group what they recall, and suggest that they look back at the handouts for Session 2 to review that content.

We discussed the strong emotions that trauma and loss can cause and how these reactions can interfere with people's lives. We spoke about the pressures people often feel to "get over it" and avoid talking or thinking about how scared or angry or numb they still feel. It takes courage to acknowledge these difficulties and to actually do something about them – like being in this group.

In the third session, we focused on emotions, the way we feel emotions in our bodies and the things inside and outside of us that can trigger emotions.

*Today we are going to learn about how understanding trauma and loss reminders can help you with Step Two: "**Why** am I feeling this way?" because reminders often bring up strong feelings, such as anger, fear, or sadness.*

*In later sessions, we will be practicing Step Three: "**How** Can I Feel Better?" by learning coping skills and different ways to think about things.*

Review Practice Assignment

Ask group members to look at their filled-in Handout 1.13, Monitoring Changes in My Mood and Feelings. If group members did not fill this form out since the last session, have them do so now. If they wish, they may talk about times this week when they reacted to something that had happened and what they felt. It is not required that every member participate in the verbal sharing. If group members **do** report strong reactions, ask them what prompted these reactions and whether they were caused by trauma and loss reminders. Then ask what they did to cope. Use this discussion to transition to the next topic.

III. Trauma and Loss Reminders

Refer to either the Trauma Goals Worksheet (Handout 1.02) or the Personal Goals Worksheet (Handout 1.03) filled out in Session 1.1 and explain how this group can help them with their goals.

Elicit discussion on the youth's personal reminders.

Trauma Reminders

A **trauma reminder** is something that brings up distressing memories, sensations, or feelings related to a past trauma. Trauma reminders trigger strong posttraumatic reactions, such as unpleasant memories of what you went through. These memories can be so strong and seem so real that it almost feels in your body like dangerous or traumatic things are happening **right now**.

Trauma reminders can be things **outside** of you (use Flipchart 1.4b) such as:

- A familiar sight
- A person
- A smell
- A specific time or date
- A sound
- A facial expression

Trauma reminders can also be things **inside** of you, such as:

- A bodily sensation (like your heart pounding)
- An emotion
- A thought

Loss Reminders

A **loss reminder** is something that reminds people of the person or thing that was lost and what it feels like to be without them. Loss reminders make people feel grief, sadness, anger, or longing to be with the person or thing that they love. (Use Flipchart 1.4c and get input from the group.)

Loss reminders can be about missing the person:

- Empty situations
- Shared activities
- Rituals

Loss reminders can also be about how your life has changed since the death:

- Moving to a new place
- Separation from loved ones
- Difficulty adjusting to a new household, school, or neighborhood
- Difficulty making new friends
- Loss of income, worry about money

Activity: Trauma and Loss Reminders Worksheets

Note: This exercise can bring up strong memories and reactions, so be sure to stop at least 10 minutes before the end to do a calming activity with group members.

- Refer to Flipcharts 1.4b and 1.4c and to the trauma and loss reminder handouts in their workbooks. Tell group members to think about traumas and losses they have experienced in order to identify their current reminders.
- Have group members fill out Handouts 1.20 *and* 1.21 that focus on personal trauma and loss reminders. This will take 10–15 minutes.
- Have group members share with the group selected items from their worksheets, and encourage group discussion and mutual support. Group leaders may, when appropriate, also share one of their own trauma or loss reminders, to model for the group that we all have them to some degree.

Last session, we focused on reminders that can trigger a traumatic stress or grief reaction.

Because these reactions are often very upsetting, we all naturally develop strategies to reduce or get rid of the painful feelings, thoughts, and memories that can flood us when we are reminded of bad experiences. You have all learned ways to try to keep going despite often having trauma reminders and the distressing reactions that follow.

When you encounter a reminder and have a distressing reaction, your ability to cope and control your emotions and actions may be affected. You may have trouble concentrating on schoolwork, or want to hit somebody, or fall asleep at school, or find you can't sleep at night. Usually you manage to do something to bring yourself back to the present moment so that you don't get into trouble. In this section and during the week, you will be taking a look at your coping responses.

We will be going over what you can do to take care of yourself when you are upset by a trauma or loss reminder. We will practice ways to manage your trauma and loss reminders without getting into trouble.

*To be clear about the difference between **automatic survival responses** to trauma reminders and **good coping responses**, let's take a look at the practice sheet for this week.*

IV. Reacting to and Coping with Distressing Reminders

Note to group leaders: This practice exercise may be optional or you may choose to do only Part One if there is not enough time to learn the subsequent calming skill before the session ends. Use your judgment. You may also choose to have the group members take these practice sheets home to complete. If you are not doing Section 4.4, move directly to Section 4.5.

Activity: How I React to and Cope with Distressing Reminders Worksheet (Handout 1.22)

[This exercise will take 15–20 minutes]

Part One

Refer to Handout 1.22. Have group members fill out page 1. Then read aloud each page 2 category and have group members fill in their worksheets. Ask group members which posttraumatic stress reactions or grief reactions they experience most often. Next, read aloud page 3 on coping strategies, and have group members fill in their sheets and share which strategies they use most often. Then, have them discuss as a group which of the strategies may be considered "positive" (adaptive) or "negative" (non-adaptive). Finally, ask youth the following and have the group discuss it: *Which of these strategies are **automatic survival responses** (things we do without thinking)?*

(Optional) Part Two

Have group members review their trauma and loss reminder worksheets again and pick out one of their "A" or most distressing reminders. Take the group through the following steps (some group members may choose to listen without sharing, and this is OK):

1. Have group members describe one personal trauma or loss reminder and the situations in which it might occur.
2. Ask them to describe their emotional and physical reactions when encountering this reminder.
3. Have them check Part 1 of the worksheet, "My reactions to being reminded," and ask them to identify the primary reactions they experience with each reminder.
4. Ask them to then describe what kind of coping response they could use.
5. Have them consult the list on Part 3 of the worksheet and identify the strategies that are most like their own. Discuss both positive and negative ways of coping.
6. Tell group members to become aware of their coping responses to trauma and loss reminders in the days until the next session, making use of the practice sheet.

V. Present the "SLOW Down" Technique

Because trauma reminders can make you feel as if you have to fight or run away in order to protect yourself even though you are actually safe, we are going to teach you a way to slow down your automatic reactions that can get you into trouble. Learning to slow down your reactions may help you with your group goals. When you feel yourself suddenly overwhelmed by a trauma reminder, you can slow down instead of fighting, freezing, or running. Although automatic survival responses probably helped many of you stay alive in the past when you were really in danger on the street or at home, these reactions now can interfere with your functioning and your relationships with other people.

Activity: SLOW Down Group Cohesion

Have youth look at Handout 1.23, the SLOW Down Technique, and go over it with them. SLOW down stands for the following steps:

- Scan/Stop
- Look
- Orient
- Wise mind*

Read the top two sentences of the SLOW down handout and then select four group members to read the four steps that follow. Invite a discussion about how effective they think SLOW down will be to help them achieve their group goals.

SLOW down is especially helpful when people are having an overwhelming reaction to a trauma reminder and when they get stuck in "alarm mode." The next time they feel themselves getting triggered by a known trauma reminder or a "hidden" reminder, tell them to practice SLOW down. Future work will help group members SLOW down to examine their *automatic survival responses* and generate adaptive coping responses.

VI. Provide a Calming Activity

Calming Activity

Because this session focused on memories of trauma and loss, it may be helpful for group members to have at least ten minutes of calming and enjoyable time together before transitioning back to their classrooms or residences. Group leaders should plan an activity that is emotionally and physically calming and enjoyable.

Suggested activities:

- Share a favorite food or "comfort food"
- Discuss favorite music
- Share happiest memories
- Play charades in which people guess the emotion portrayed
- Abdominal breathing

*Note for Group Leaders: "Wise Mind" comes from Dialectical Behavior Therapy, but youth may understand it in this context as learning to calm down and think before they act.

VII. Practice Assignment

Assign the usual Handout 1.13, Monitoring Changes in My Mood and Feelings, and ask youth to try using SLOW down as needed for any strong reactions to trauma reminders.

VIII. Check-Out

- *How are you feeling now? (Use the Feeling Thermometer ratings.)*
- *What did you learn about yourself today?*
- *Please fill out the Check-Out Feedback Form (Handout 1.24). The title of today's session was "Trauma and Loss Reminders."*

If any group members are visibly agitated or troubled or report high levels of distress on the Feeling Thermometer, keep them after the group and determine an appropriate way to transition them back to their settings. For those in residential treatment, you may need to alert line staff that a particular youth may need some TLC that evening.

Implementing Module 1, Session 1.4 with Individual Clients

Preparation: Make printed copies of Today's Highlights (Flipchart 1.4a), Distressing Reminders (Flipchart 1.4b), and Loss Reminders (Flipchart 1.4c) if that is easier than using flipcharts.

I. **Check-in and Feeling Thermometer**. Ask your client about something good that happened in the past week, as described in the first bullet. You may also break the ice by sharing something good that happened to you this week.

II. **Review practice assignment and previous sessions**. Deliver the exercise as written but omit references to the group.

III. **Present trauma and loss reminders**. Deliver the content as written, but because this is a solo session, deliver this conversationally rather than as a lecture. You may also wish to describe trauma and loss reminders (not too personal) of your own in order to level the playing field.

IV. **Reacting to and coping with distressing reminders**. This activity is optional, so use your judgment about your client's attention span for the day before deciding whether to include it.

V. **Present the SLOW down technique**. This activity is NOT optional; it provides youth with a powerful means to recognize and respond early and effectively when triggered by a trauma or loss reminder. Omit references to the group as you learn and practice this exercise together.

VI. **Provide a calming activity**. Because this session focuses on memories of trauma and loss, it is essential to take time for a calming and enjoyable conversation or activity before ending the session.

VII. **Practice assignment**. Deliver this step as written.

VIII. **Check-out**. Deliver this step as written.

1.5 Learning Coping Skills

Session Objectives

1. Discuss the pros and cons of coping strategies.
2. Generate a list of coping strategies that "mess you up" (MUPS).
3. Learn about getting stuck in alarm mode.
4. Develop a personal toolkit of positive coping strategies.
5. Learn to apply positive coping strategies to use *before, during*, or *after* a trauma or loss reminder or other very stressful situation.
6. Practice using helpful coping strategies.

Preparation

Read over Section V on coping strategies so you are prepared to explain Handout 1.26, Developing a Positive Personal Coping Toolkit. Have available the list of coping strategies generated by the youth in Session 1.1.

Section number	Session overview
I	Check-in and Feeling Thermometer
II	Review practice assignment and last session
III	Getting stuck in alarm mode
IV	Positive and negative coping strategies for trauma and loss reminders
V	Help youth develop a positive personal coping toolkit
VI	Practice assignment
VII	Check-out

Supplies

Every Session	This Session
• Flipchart	• Summary of group goals worksheet
• Large paper or easel pad	• List of coping strategies developed by youth from Session 1.1
• Colored markers or crayons	
• Pencils/pens	
• Kleenex	
• Tape	
• Workbooks	

Handouts in Workbook

Handout 1.25	MUPS: Survival Coping Responses That "Mess You Up"
Handout 1.26	Developing a Positive Personal Coping Toolkit
Handout 1.27	Disrupting Negative Self-Talk and Rules for Writing Self-Calming Phrases
Handout 1.28	Using a Positive Personal Coping Toolkit
Handout 1.29	Check-Out Feedback Form

Flipcharts

1.5a Today's Highlights

1. Check-in: one good thing that happened and Feeling Thermometer
2. Review practice assignment: deep (abdominal) breathing and how I react to and cope with distressing reminders
3. Learn about getting stuck in alarm mode
4. Discuss coping strategies
5. Practice coping techniques
6. Develop a positive personal coping toolkit
7. Practice assignment: using a positive personal coping toolkit
8. Feeling Thermometer and Check-Out Feedback Form

1.5b Coping Strategies

1. Review SLOW down technique
2. Disrupt negative self-talk
3. Calming self-talk
4. Remind yourself that was then and it is not happening now
5. Reduce unnecessary reminders
6. Prepare reminders
7. Do calming exercises
8. Build resilience by staying in touch and active
9. Distract yourself through positive activities
10. Seek support
11. Take a time-out
12. Do workbook writing

Session 1.5: Learning Coping Skills

I. Do Check-In and Feeling Thermometer

- *How are you feeling right now?* (Use Handout 1.05, the Feeling Thermometer.)
- Practice with the group doing five to ten deep breaths.
- *Is anything going on that may make it difficult for you to keep your mind on the group today?*
- Briefly review (or have a group member review) Today's Highlights (Flipchart 1.5a).

II. Review Last Session and Practice Assignment

Review Last Session

Customize a brief review of the last session to reflect what actually happened. Have group members share with you and the group what they recall. Refer to Handout 1.15, Three Steps to Taking Charge of Your Feelings.

*We've been learning about dealing with feelings in three steps: Step One, "**What** am I feeling?" And Step Two, "**Why** am I feeling this way?" Last time we learned about how trauma and loss reminders help you understand more about Step Two. Today and next time, we will practice Step Three, "HOW can I feel better?" We will learn and practice coping skills today. Next time we will focus on how to recognize and challenge hurtful thoughts. The more strategies you have to manage reminders, the better. This will help you so that you don't have to try to numb yourself out by using drugs, acting recklessly, or getting into trouble.*

Refer to your summary of the Group Goals Worksheet and say.

These skills will help you achieve the goals you set in Session 1, such as feeling less angry or learning to make better decisions or having fewer problems with other people. (Refer to the goals group members actually selected during Session 1.1.)

Review Practice Assignment

Praise group members who did the assignment, and take time to have others fill out the practice forms before proceeding. Handout 1.22, How I React to and Cope with Distressing Reminders, asks group members to:

- Identify the most distressing trauma or loss reminder they encountered
- Indicate their reactions to the reminders
- Describe the coping strategies they used.

If some group members did not know why they were upset, explain briefly about "hidden triggers" as follows:

We've spent time talking about trauma reminders and our reactions to them. However, it sometimes happens that people who have experienced traumas have strong emotional and physical reactions without knowing exactly what trauma reminder caused these reactions.

III. Getting Stuck in "Alarm Mode"

It is important to take some time to explain fully what happens when people who have survived many hardships and traumas get "stuck" in alarm mode, so try to make this little lecture lively. As you explain this, stop from time to time to make sure youth are "getting" it. You can use Handout 1.11 to graphically illustrate getting stuck in alarm mode.

Scientists tell us that when humans are in danger, the brain goes immediately into overdrive to help us quickly "size up" situations in order to survive. We all do one of three things:

1. *First, we can **turn to the danger, to take it on directly**. This is sometimes called the "**fight**" response.*
2. *Second, we can **try to get away from the danger to a safe place**. This is called the "**flight**" response.*
3. *Third, we can try to **keep still and hope the danger passes us by**, even while our mind may be racing as we try to size up the situation and any options available to us. This is called the "**freeze**" response.*

These different "fight–flight–freeze" responses to danger can each happen in a split second – even faster than we consciously think and react. This "survival coping" has helped many of you survive the traumas you've told us about. These automatic, strong reactions may have saved your life in the past when you were in danger.

- *But when the life and death situations are over and people are safe again, the human brain sometimes fails to reset itself out of "survival coping." The brain reacts as if small things are dangerous even when you are perfectly safe. People's brains get stuck in **alarm mode**, like a car alarm that keeps jangling and drives you nuts.*
- *When the brain and body are locked into alarm mode, many people feel jumpy, irritable, and super alert. They overreact to little things as if they were very dangerous. Thus, when you are stuck in alarm mode and someone drops a book with a loud bang in class, or looks at you funny, or brushes against you in the hallway, you react by jumping, or lashing out violently, or becoming numb and withdrawing.*
- *When this happens, your parents or teachers tell you to "calm down" or "stop overreacting," and it can make you feel bad about yourself. All this can cause you problems in school, at work, or when you are with family or friends. Remember, this survival system keeps humans safe in dangerous situations, but if it constantly stays locked on it makes the usual tasks of normal life very difficult.*
- *Being jumpy and hyper-alert, as if you have a chip on your shoulder, can even make it hard for you to get along with other people. It can also interfere with your ability to rest or sleep. You never feel safe.*
- *The good news is that you can rewire your brain so it can turn down the alarm reactions, and that's what we'll be working on here.*

IV. Positive and Negative Coping Strategies for Trauma and Loss Reminders

Activity: Positive and Negative Coping Strategies for Trauma and Loss Reminders

- Review the saved list of coping strategies that the group filled out in Session 1.1 and add any additional coping strategies they suggest.

- On the right side of the flipchart, add a grid with columns for "short-term consequences" and "long-term consequences." Next to each strategy, put a + or a – after each item as group members tell you whether a strategy is negative or positive in the short term and negative or positive in the long term.
- Take enough time to do this exercise completely; it is one that really engages young people as they think through the short- and long-term consequences of their actions.
- Once this list has been completed, have youth refer to the MUPS handout about negative coping strategies. MUPS are the things people do when stressed out that "mess you up." Ask group members to study this list for negative coping strategies and evaluate their short- and long-term consequences. This can be done with the whole group as a cohesion-building activity.

Examples of MUPS or coping strategies that can "mess you up":* Use this chart to have youth evaluate the short- and long-term consequences of MUPS. (Refer to Handout 1.25.)

MUPS	Consequences	
	Short-term	Long-term
1. Avoiding all people and places that make you feel bad		
2. Withdrawing from friends and family		
3. Withdrawing from activities		
4. Not asking for help (when you need or want it)		
5. Denying to people close to you that you have a problem		
6. Dropping out of the group		
7. Drinking alcohol/taking drugs		
8. Over-eating		
9. Excessive TV or video games		
10. Doing risky or dangerous things		
11. Acting angry and aggressive/ getting into fights		
12. Blaming others/overreacting to little things		
13. Feeling super guilty or responsible for what happened		
14. Not taking care of yourself (sleep, diet, exercise, grooming)		

MUPS	Consequences	
	Short-term	Long-term
15. Getting sick		
16. Numbing out, going into "I don't care" mode		
17. Cutting yourself		

* The concept of MUPS originated with SPARCS: *Structured Psychotherapy for Adolescents Responding to Chronic Stress: A Trauma-Focused Guide*, by Ruth DeRosa, Mandy Habib, David Pelcovitz, et al., North Shore Long Island Jewish Health System, Manhasset, NY, 2005–2008, Session 1.

V. Help Youth Develop a Positive Personal Coping Toolkit

- Help group members understand the need for a personal coping strategy to calm emotions and control behaviors when they feel triggered or overwhelmed.
- Provide a basic understanding of each coping strategy.
- Provide an opportunity for group members to determine which strategies suit them best.
- Help group members decide which strategies are most helpful before, during, and after trauma reminders and stressors.
- This should be an interactive exercise, not a lecture.

Have participants refer to Handout 1.26, Developing a Positive Personal Coping Toolkit, in their workbooks. Have them keep this form out while going through the exercise below. Tell group members that they have done amazingly well given what they have been through and that they have already identified a lot of very positive personal coping responses. Now each member can put these together with some additional coping techniques and create their own personal coping toolkit, to be used for before, during, or after trauma or loss reminders, and for "hidden triggers," when they don't know exactly what set them off.

All of you already employ a number of very good coping strategies and we have learned a few new ones like deep breathing and the "SLOW down" technique.

Today we will go over some additional coping strategies that might be useful to you. The idea is to have a number of strategies that you can choose from to deal with the different situations that may come up.

Some of these will work better for you than others.

We will start by reviewing the SLOW down technique and then go onto some new ones. As we go through each, I would like you to think whether this would work for you and what kind of situations might it be useful for.

Note: After each strategy, ask whether group members have used this before and who might want to include it in their Handout 1.26, Developing a Positive Personal Coping Toolkit. You can ask how they might use the coping strategy and in which situations.

1. Review SLOW down technique (Handout 1.23)

SLOW down stands for the following steps:
- Scan/Stop
- Look
- Orient
- Wise mind

Have group members refer to the "SLOW down" handout in their workbooks and go over it with them again. SLOW down is especially helpful when people are having an overwhelming reaction to a trauma reminder so that they are stuck in alarm mode. The next time they feel themselves getting triggered by a known trauma reminder or a hidden reminder, have them practice SLOW down.

2. Disrupt Negative Self-Talk (Handout 1.27)

Do not read every word. Many youth may already have experiences with thought-stopping, so if that is the case, you can do this exercise briefly.

You can also change how you think. Most people are not aware of the fact that they have an automatic running commentary going on in their head throughout the day. We talk to ourselves all day long, but these can be like conversations we don't hear, even though the things we tell ourselves can affect how we feel and what we do.

When we catch ourselves overreacting to a situation or feeling worried, angry, scared, or sad, we often make automatic negative statements to ourselves, such as "What's the matter with me?" "I must be 'crazy,' 'weak,' 'babyish,' or 'screwed up'." Other thoughts can be, "He made a fool of me," "I've got to get even," or "They are laughing at me." If you are aware of the reminders and situations that trigger these thoughts, you can avoid these automatic hurtful thoughts. You can replace them with positive thoughts. However, this is not always easy. Here are the steps you can take:

a. *Notice that when you feel worried, angry, depressed, or scared, you are often engaging in negative self-talk.*

b. *Stop and ask yourself:*

- *"What am I telling myself that is making me feel this way?"*
- *"Do I really want to do this to myself?"*
- *"Do I really want to stay upset?"*

c. *Relax or distract yourself so that you can "switch gears" by using deep breathing, exercise, chatting with friends, sports, or dance.*

d. *Thought-stopping.*

You can stop a thought by saying "Stop!" to yourself and imagining a new thought such as "Relax," "Calm," "I'm safe." It is also very effective to imagine that you are using a remote control to change the channel in your brain to a new, peaceful channel. For your new channel, think about times and places where you feel relaxed and safe, whether this is spending time with friends, eating pizza, watching sports on television, funny clips on YouTube, listening to music, or fishing. Visualize this new channel in full detail.

Note: you may ask group members whether they think changing their thinking channels will work, and have them share with each other what their peaceful channels will be like.

3. Calming Self-Talk (Handout 1.27)

This is helpful before, during, and after exposure to reminders. Refer group members to the handout.

Guidelines for Creating Self-Calming Phrases

- Avoid writing *negatives* in your phrase. Instead of saying "I'm not going to get nervous when I go into the … ….," try "I am cool, calm, and confident about going into the … …."
- Keep your phrase in the *present tense*.
- Keep each phrase in the *first person*. Begin what you tell yourself with "I" or refer to "I" somewhere in the statement.
- Don't choose something just because it is positive; it's got to be right for you!
- The phrase, "That was then, this is now. I'm safe now," is very effective, almost like a mantra to repeat for calming you when you are having a flashback.

Activity: Examples of Self-Calming Phrases

Ask the group to give you examples of calming self-talk and write them on a large piece of paper or easel pad. Then go over the following examples if they have not mentioned them.

Examples of self-calming phrases can include

- "I can get through this."
- "It's just a feeling."
- "This feeling will pass."
- "I can handle this."
- "This will pass."
- "These are just thoughts, and I can let them go."
- "This situation is different from when I was beaten up."
- "That was then, this is now. I'm safe now."

Have group members select a trauma or loss reminder scenario from their list and practice using their personal calming self-talk phrase.

4. Remind yourself that was then and it is not happening now

Clarify in your head all the ways in which the current situation is different from the past traumatic situation. When people are triggered, they respond to current situations as if they were right back in the past when the trauma was happening. So if you hear a police or ambulance siren, for example, your body and mind may react with all the horror and fear and helplessness you felt when the trauma happened.

When group members experience a posttraumatic reaction that involves fear, anxiety, or anger, have them mentally make a list of ways the current situation is similar to the past and ways it is different.

Activity: That Was Then, This Is Now

Demonstrate "That was then, this is now" with one or two examples drawn from group members. You may use either exaggerated fear/danger reactions from the previous discussion, or more general reactive situations, such as anger or revenge reactions.

Additional Coping Strategies

Ask youth what else they do to take care of themselves before, during, or after being exposed to trauma reminders and triggers. If youth do not mention some of the items from points 5 to 12 below, bring them up for discussion. Make sure they have Handout 1.26, Developing a Positive Personal Toolkit, in front of them and are filling it out. Lead a brief group discussion of additional coping strategies to use before, during, and after a trauma or loss reminder or a "hidden" trigger.

Do not read every word of points 5 to 12. Instead, read the titles for each strategy and discuss with group members which strategies they have used or would like to try. Then go over the content briefly. The lengthy explanations are included to help group leaders guide the discussions.

5. Reduce unnecessary reminders

Limit exposure to reminders and distressing situations in a commonsense fashion, especially right after a trauma. For example, after someone has seen someone die in a street shooting or in the hospital, it might be best for a while to avoid television or radio programs with similar themes, such as police or hospital dramas that include the sounds of sirens or the beeping of life support machines. (Use examples the group has generated of trauma reminders if appropriate here, or ask for discussion.)

This temporary choice to reduce exposure to stressful reminders should not be confused with avoidance, where people isolate and numb themselves by trying to stay away from any reminder of what happened, sometimes never even leaving their homes.

6. Prepare for reminders

Some reminders can't be avoided. How can you be proactive and get support when you know that next week is the anniversary of your cousin's death, or a holiday that you always spent together? Think about how you might feel on that day (sad, angry, lonely). Planning ahead gives you some sense of control. Plan to get support such as arranging to spend time with a close friend or family member, tell a teacher or counselor how you feel, or arrange to be alone if that is what you need. If there is a reminder that you might have to face daily (such as a street corner near your home where you were in a terrible accident), being guided and supported through telling the story of the trauma will reduce your reactions to that trigger and will be covered in subsequent sessions or in individual work with your clinician.

7.   Do calming exercises

Specific *calming* activities may be used before, during, and after exposure to reminders or distressing situations to manage your reactions. Key techniques include abdominal breathing and progressive muscle relaxation by tensing and relaxing muscles from head to toe. Once you realize that you are not in real danger, slowed breathing will decrease the oxygen in your body and help decrease your body's stress response. Learning to tense and relax muscle groups voluntarily can make you reduce tension in your jaw, neck, shoulder muscles, and elsewhere in your body when you are frightened or angry. Other calming activities include sports and other vigorous exercise, listening to music, singing, rocking, swaddling yourself in a blanket, or another calming activity of your choosing.

8.   Build resilience by staying in touch and active

Build resilience by staying in touch and active. Healthy lifestyles that build resilience before, during, and after exposure include appropriate sleep, eating, and exercise routines. Especially after you have been through a trauma or loss, it is important to take care of your health by eating and sleeping well and getting daily exercise. Stay connected to your network of support.

9.   Distract yourself through positive activities

Exercise, sports, hobbies, projects, and work are all positive activities. Regular exercise through active sports can be especially calming. Once the body has gone into alarm mode, it can take over an hour to calm down, but some people find that jogging, basketball, or some active sport seems to help them when they feel this way. While the body is in alarm mode, many people are tempted to use alcohol or drugs to "medicate" themselves, so it is important to find a safe replacement activity (such as vigorous exercise, a hot shower, or talking to a trusted person) to take care of yourself while the body calms itself down.

10.   Seek support

Many people who have been through a lot of trauma and loss tend to withdraw from other people, and this often makes them feel worse. We recommend going out of your way to keep in touch with family, friends, and teachers, even if you don't feel like it at first. These contacts will help you manage your posttraumatic reactions. Do continue as best you can to keep active and sociable. It helps to share your concerns by talking with a trusted friend or family member before, during, and after getting hit with a trauma or loss reminder. This support can help prevent an outsize reaction to a reminder. Even when you feel yourself beginning to react to something more strongly than you wish, telling someone you trust about what you are going through can help diminish the intensity of your reaction. It is also supportive to "debrief" afterwards, even if you were unable to seek support before or during the reminder. We will have an entire session on seeking support at the end of this module.

11.   Take a time-out

You can calm yourself down sometimes by simply taking yourself out of a stressful situation, by quietly leaving and taking a walk or going to a quiet place.

12.   Do workbook writing

Many teenagers and adults who have experienced trauma or traumatic loss have found benefit in keeping a workbook. Reflecting back on your day or on past events can be calming, and it helps many people find meaning as they write down the things they remember, think, and feel.

VI. Practice Assignment

Go over Handout 1.28, Using a Positive Personal Coping Toolkit, with group members and tell them to use it this week to identify one reminder or stressful situation they encounter, describe it briefly on the lines provided, and then use at least one coping strategy from each category they used before, during, or after a reminder. Ask them to note how useful it was and how skillful they were in applying it. Group members should bring the completed sheet back with them next week, but if they do not, have them fill it out at the start of the next session.

VII. Check-Out

- *How are you feeling now?* (Use the Feeling Thermometer ratings.)
- *What did you learn about yourself today?*
- *Please fill out the Check-Out Feedback Form* (Handout 1.29). *The title of today's session was "Learning Coping Skills."*

If any group members are visibly agitated or troubled or report high levels of distress on the Feeling Thermometer, keep them after the group and determine an appropriate way to transition back to their settings.

Implementing Module 1, Session 1.5 with Individual Clients

Preparation: Make printed copies of Today's Highlights (Flipchart 1.5a) and the coping strategies (Flipchart 1.5b) if that is easier than using flipcharts. Bring the list of coping strategies that the client generated on a flip chart or a piece of paper during Session 1.

I. **Check-in and Feeling Thermometer**. Ask your client about something good that happened in the past week, as described in the first bullet. You may also break the ice by sharing something good that happened to you this week.

II. **Review practice assignment and previous sessions**. Deliver the exercise as written but omit references to the group.

III. **Getting stuck in** "**alarm mode**." This important content can be delivered conversationally. Take time to see that your client understands, and invite her or him to offer examples from their own experiences.

IV. **Positive and negative coping strategies for trauma and loss reminders**. If your client made a list of the coping strategies she or he most often uses, make sure you have saved it and bring it out to work with the client to discuss and rate commonly used coping strategies. The client may also wish to work with the MUPS list that is in your manual and the youth workbook.

V. **Help youth develop a positive personal coping toolkit**. This activity is one that is more easily and thoroughly completed in individual rather than group sessions. Review and discuss the detailed list of 12 coping strategies for a discussion of which positive coping strategies suit this client best. You may also wish to share which coping strategies you commonly use and find effective. This levels the playing field and helps youth understand that we all have stressors and inconveniences with which we have to deal on a daily basis.

VI. **Toolkit**. Adapt the language for this assignment for use with an individual. Make sure to practice the delivery before the session.

VII. **Check-out**. Deliver this step as written.

1.6 Sizing Up a Situation

Session Objectives

1. Learn to distinguish thoughts, feelings, and behaviors.
2. Understand the link between thoughts, feelings, and behaviors, using the Cognitive Triangle.
3. Differentiate and learn to be aware of one's own helpful and hurtful thoughts.
4. Present the three steps to taking charge of your feelings.
5. Practice the Three-Step Model using scenarios and drawings

Section number	Session overview
I	Check-in and Feeling Thermometer
II	Review last session and practice assignment
III	Explain "Sizing Up a Situation"
IV	Identifying hurtful thoughts
V	Practice replacing hurtful thoughts
VI	Summarize and assign practice assignment
VII	Check-out

Supplies

Every session	This session
• Flipchart	
• Large paper or easel pad	
• Colored markers or crayons	
• Pencils/pens	
• Kleenex	
• Tape	
• Workbooks (if group leaders keep them between sessions)	

Handouts in Workbook

Handout 1.30	Sizing Up a Situation
Handouts 1.31–1.34	Illustrations
Handouts 1.35 and 1.36	Hurtful Thoughts and Helpful Thoughts Checklists
Handouts 1.37 and 1.38	Illustrations
Handout 1.39	Three Steps to Taking Charge of Your Thoughts and Feelings
Handout 1.40	Check-Out Feedback Form

Flipcharts

1.6a Today's Highlights

1. Check-in: one good thing that happened this week and the Feeling Thermometer
2. Review practice assignment: breathing and developing a personal coping strategy
3. Sizing Up a Situation
4. Identifying hurtful thoughts
5. Identifying and replacing hurtful thoughts
6. Do summary and practice assignment: helpful and hurtful thoughts
7. Check-out with the Feeling Thermometer and feedback form

1.6b Three Steps to Take Charge of Your Thoughts and Feelings

Answer these questions:

1. "What am I feeling?"
2. "Why am I feeling this way?"
   - Look outside
   - Look inside – "What am I thinking?"
3. "How can I feel better by thinking better?"

1.6c Questions for Catching Your Thoughts

1. "What is going through my mind right now?" Or "What am I saying to myself right now?"
2. "Is this a helpful thought or a hurtful thought?"

Situation	Trauma/ loss reminders	What do you think?	What do you feel?	What do you do?

Session 1.6: Sizing Up a Situation

I. Do Check-In and Feeling Thermometer

- How are you feeling right now? (Use the Feeling Thermometer ratings.)
- Practice with the group doing five to ten deep breaths, then recheck Thermometer ratings.
- Is anything going on that may make it difficult for you to keep your mind on the group today?
- Briefly review Today's Highlights (Flipchart 1.6a).

II. Review Last Session and Practice Assignment

Provide a brief review of key points from last session. Go over the homework practice sheet (Handout 1.26) on developing a personal coping strategy. If group members did not fill it out during the week, have group members fill it out now. Provide assistance to those with limited literacy.

Invite each group member to share his/her practice assignment. Use the large paper or easel pad to write down what each group member reports.

Describe the situations during the week when you noticed your mood or feelings become distressing or painful. Ask some of the following questions.

- *Was there a **trauma reminder**, a **loss reminder**, or something else? Was it a reminder of a situation you recall, or was it a **hidden trigger** (one that you can't connect to a past situation)?*
- *What thought was going through your mind just before your feelings changed? Can you put the thought into words?*
- *What were your emotional reactions? What did you feel?*
- *Which emotion did you feel the most strongly?*
- *What did you do to cope?*
- *Did you use one of the coping strategies we reviewed last week, such as practicing SLOW down, deep breathing, positive self-talk, taking a time-out, talking to someone you trust, or distracting through a positive activity (sports, music, dancing)?*

Some group members may report having used a MUPS coping response (coping strategies that "mess you up"). If they did, listen empathetically, and ask how that made them feel and what the consequences were. Then ask whether they would like to try a different response the next time they encounter a trauma reminder or stressful situation.

III. Explain Sizing Up a Situation: Changing Feelings and Behaviors by Changing Thoughts

Sizing Up a Situation

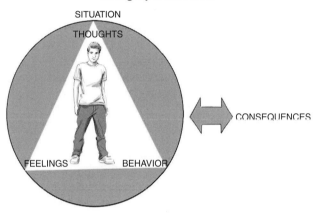

Refer to Handout 1.30.

Today we are going to teach you a skill that will help you expand your list of coping strategies by focusing on **how thoughts change what you feel and then what you do.** *When you have experienced one dangerous situation after another throughout your life, it becomes automatic to see new situations as threatening or dangerous, even when they are not.*

When people try to figure out a new situation – including what's going on and what to do, they act based on what they **believe** *they have learned from their past experiences (like believing that no one can ever be trusted).*

There are close and very rapid connections between how you see a situation, how you feel, and how you behave. For example, the thought that "the world is always dangerous" is not always true, but if you believe it this can lead to feelings of always being "on edge." You can then fall into risky behaviors that get you into real trouble, such as starting fights with people you believe have it in for you and might hurt you. These reactions often happen very quickly.

However, when people understand the connections between how they think and feel and what they do, they can take steps to improve the way they feel and the things they do in new situations by slowing down the process and learning to think through what is happening and how best to react.

As a way to practice this reappraisal skill, we will start by focusing on thoughts, so that you can learn to tell the difference between situations that are really dangerous and those that you may mistakenly think are dangerous because you have faced so many dangers in the past.

People talk to themselves (in their thoughts) all day. Do you ever catch yourself doing that? Pause to listen to responses. Everybody does it, but most of the time we don't even know we are doing it. But whether or not we are aware of them, our thoughts affect how we feel and how we act.

When we have had a lot of traumas and losses, we can develop patterns of always expecting the worst, and these "traumatic expectations" can color everything we think, do, and feel.

Let's start by sorting out the differences between situations, thoughts, feelings, and your own behaviors.

Activity: Distinguishing Thoughts, Feelings, and Behaviors

Situation–Thought–Feeling–Your Behavior Quiz

Teens frequently have difficulty differentiating *external situations, thoughts, feelings,* and their own *behaviors.* This quiz is a light-hearted way to practice. Tell the group that you will read items from the list below and they are to shout out whether it is a situation, thought, feeling, or behavior.

S = Situation T = Thought F = Feeling B = Your behavior

1. Irritated	F
2. Someone knocks at the door	S
3. You work hard on homework	B
4. I can't do it	T
5. Frustrated	F
6. You hit someone	B
7. I've got to get even	T
8. Someone hits you	S
9. A teacher yells at you	S
10. Scared	F
11. A police car passes with siren	S
12. I'll always be alone	T
13. Surprised	F
14. I can do it	T
15. It's my fault	T
16. My sister is the favorite	T
17. A teacher praises you	S
18. You yell at someone	B
19. You share a treat with someone	B
20. Happy	F

Activity: Practice Sizing Up a Situation

Now let's look at a couple of examples showing how thoughts can change how you feel and what you do.

Have group members refer to Handout 1.30, the Sizing Up a Situation diagram, and then illustrations on the handouts specified below. You also can make a drawing of the basic diagram on a flipchart in order to walk the youth through each illustration highlighting the situation, thoughts, feelings, behaviors, and consequences.

Step 1: View Handout 1.31 and use Handout 1.30, the Sizing Up a Situation diagram, to explore situation, thought, feelings, etc.: *Let's say Joe bumps into Mike and knocks his books down. Mike might think to himself, "He did that on purpose!" How would Mike feel if he had this thought? What would he do as a result? What are the consequences likely to be if he does that?*

Lead them through the *situation* (Joe knocks down Mike's books), the *thought* (Mike thinks Joe did that on purpose), how Mike is *feeling* (most group members will name strong anger as a response, especially because there are girls in the picture who may have seen Mike being humiliated or "dissed"), Mike's next *behavior* (many youth suggest that Mike will attack Joe), and the likely *consequences* (school suspension/expulsion, lost weekend visiting privileges, someone gets injured).

Step 2: View Handout 1.32 and use Handout 1.30, the Sizing Up a Situation diagram, to explore situation, thought, feelings, etc.: *But what if Mike thinks instead, "I guess he wasn't watching where he was going." How might Mike feel if he had this thought? What might he do as a result? What will the consequences be if he does that?"*

Many still say that Mike will be irritated but not at a 9 or 10 on the Feeling Thermometer, more like a 2 or 3, so Mike is unlikely to attack Joe and get into trouble. Emphasize here that even if Mike *is* angry, he should not hit Joe, but changing his thoughts will also help him control his angry reactions.

Several of you stated that your group goals were to learn to control your anger or make better choices about how to react. Challenging and changing your automatic thoughts can help you do that.

Step 3: View Handout 1.33 **and use Handout 1.30, the Sizing Up a Situation diagram:** Trace the feelings, behaviors, and consequences the three students are likely to have when they respond with three different thoughts to the same test.

What is Erica likely to be feeling when she tells herself that she is stupid and can't do the test? What will she do? What about Andy in the back, who thinks the teacher can't expect him to know all this? What about Bill, who tells himself, "If I take my time, I should be OK?" How will their behaviors and the consequences differ?

Step 4: View Handout 1.34 and use Handout 1.30, the Sizing Up a Situation diagram, to explore situation, thought, feelings, etc.: *Let's say that Monica tells Angie that they are all going to Michael's party and asks her, "Didn't he invite you?" What thoughts would Angie have that would make her feel angry? What might she do if she's angry? What thoughts would she have that would make her feel sad? What will she do if she feels sad? What thoughts would make her feel OK, and what is she likely to do if she feels OK?*

Allow students time to use the Sizing Up a Situation diagram to get them to think about their own *helpful* or *hurtful thoughts*, *strong reactions*, and quick *behaviors* in similar unclear situations (such as those pictured in the illustrations in Handouts 1.31–1.34). This exercise is a powerful way to help them replace posttraumatic reactions with mindful, modulated emotions and behaviors and modify embedded patterns of traumatic expectations.

Note: This is not just about an automatic flight or fight response. We all have expectations that govern our responses. If we give ourselves enough time in a new situation, we can discriminate whether a situation is dangerous or not.

The important issue is, "How do I tell the difference between a true danger and a trauma reminder that feels dangerous but isn't?"

Summary and Introduction of Step Three

Remind group members that learning to modulate and control their emotions and actions by changing these automatic thoughts and expectations will help many group members with their personal goals, such as to get out of residential treatment or the juvenile justice facility, to earn a weekend pass, to get along better with their teachers and peers, to find and keep a job, to finish school, to have a happy family life.

Turn back to Flipchart 1.6b, Three Steps to Taking Charge of Your Thoughts and Feelings and have group members refer to Handouts 1.15 and 1.30.

Step One was "*What am I feeling?*" *By paying attention to changes in your feelings and mood and using "body messages," you can give feelings names (happy, angry, sad, scared, ashamed, etc.).*
Step Two was "*Why am I feeling this way?*" *Look outside of yourselves for possible trauma or loss reminders, and look inside of yourselves for automatic thoughts or images that may change how you are feeling.*
Step Three is the work we are learning to do today, which is, "*How can I feel better?*" *We are focusing on HOW you can feel better by changing how you think. We all get into bad habits about how we think, and habits can be changed when they are hurting us.*

Capturing these thoughts or images can be difficult because they happen so fast. But **in order to change the way you feel, you can learn to go into slow motion and change the way you think at each moment and with each new situation you face.** *Then you can become more in charge of what you feel and how you act. We learned this with "SLOW down."*

Because thoughts are often automatic, they are hard to detect.

• *Thoughts are like breathing. Think about your breathing; it goes on automatically, so that you don't consciously think about each breath. However, if you pay attention, you become aware of each breath, and you can control your breathing. You can make yourself breathe faster or slower, for example.*

- *The same goes with thinking. If you pay attention to what you are thinking and how each thought makes you feel, you can actually change and control your thoughts. If you have a thought that makes you feel terrible, you can replace it with a different thought.*

- *To study your thoughts, ask yourself these questions:*
- *"What is going through my mind right now?"*
- *"What did I just say to myself?"*

After you have identified the thoughts that are making you feel bad, you can replace them with better thoughts. You replace **hurtful thoughts** *(thoughts that can lead to MUPS coping) with* **helpful thoughts***.*

IV. Identifying Hurtful Thoughts

Have students refer to Handout 1.35, the Hurtful Thoughts Checklist, in their workbooks, and check off which ones bother them. Ask for volunteers to share their "most frequent" hurtful thoughts, and ask some or all of the following questions:

- *How many of the thoughts on this list seem like they can't be changed?*
- *When these thoughts go through your mind, how do you feel?*
- *What do you want to do when you think and feel this way?*
- *What do you do?*
- *What are the consequences?* (Refer to Handout 1.30, the Sizing Up a Situation diagram, to help with these questions.)

The tricky thing about automatic hurtful thoughts is that they seem completely and obviously true. They seem permanent. When they pop into our minds, we rarely question them. We all tend to do this to some extent, and people who have been through a lot of trauma tend to do it more.

- ***Examples:*** *When we feel depressed or sad, it feels like we will ALWAYS be depressed, and we tell ourselves that nothing will ever change.*
- *When a student calls himself "stupid" because he got a bad grade on a math test, he may be forgetting that he did well on other tests or in other subjects.*
- *When a student tells herself people are ALWAYS mean to her, she is overlooking all the times just in the past week when the people around her were neutral or friendly to her.*

Hurtful thoughts, therefore, often are based on inaccurate or incomplete information. People make themselves feel worse when they tell themselves that whatever is going wrong will never change. These hurtful thoughts make people feel hopeless. They can make people stop trying and give up.

The idea is to catch yourself when you are engaging in hurtful thoughts and replace these with thoughts that are more accurate, truthful, and helpful. This does not just mean to try and force yourself to think "happy thoughts." Instead, the intent is to identify thoughts that are more true and that you can honestly believe.

Some possible candidates are covered in Handout 1.35, the Hurtful Thoughts Checklist. Review these with participants and see if they can even add to the options with their own helpful thoughts.

[Do the following exercise only if there is enough time. If there is not, go directly to the summary and then do the check-out. Session 1.7 will also have practice exercises about replacing hurtful thoughts.]

V. Replacing Hurtful Thoughts

Optional Activity: Replacing Hurtful Thoughts

If this is a group with girls, have them turn to Handout 1.37 in their workbooks. For boys, use Handout 1.38.

Write two column headings on the flipchart or paper: *hurtful thoughts* and *helpful thoughts*. As group members identify the hurtful thoughts in the illustration, write them in the hurtful-thought column. Then have them come up with one or more helpful thoughts to replace the hurtful thought from the illustration. Write these in the helpful-thought column.

- If using Handout 1.37, say: *Let's look at what this girl is thinking. What thought could she have instead?*
- If using Handout 1.38, say: *Let's look at what this boy is thinking. What thought could he have instead?*

The following examples of replacement thoughts may be helpful if group members cannot think of examples.

Hurtful thought		Helpful thought
(hopeless and negative)		(hopeful and positive)
Handout 1.37		
"They're laughing at me".	→	"They may have just heard a funny joke."
"They think I'm weird. Nobody likes me."	→	"Maybe some people don't like me, but I know that some people do."
Handout 1.38		
"My life is already over and I won't live long."	→	"I've had a lot of tough challenges, but there are people who will know how to help me."

Elicit responses and discuss. For each hurtful thought, use Handout 1.30, Sizing Up a Situation, to have group members determine:

- What feeling does this hurtful thought generate?
- What is he/she likely to do next when he or she has that thought and feeling?
- What will the consequences be if they behave that way?

Then have them discuss helpful thoughts that can replace the hurtful thoughts mentioned above. (See examples below: this will be hard for some group members, so you can help by reading these aloud.)

- What feeling does this replacement thought generate?
- What is the person likely to do next when they have that thought and feeling?
- What will the consequences be if they behave that way?

After group members have worked to find more helpful thoughts for each cartoon, have them refer to the Hurtful Thoughts Checklist (Handout 1.35) in their workbooks for additional ideas about replacement thoughts. If there is time, have the group members generate the feelings, acts, and consequences that each replacement thought will generate.

VI. Summary and Practice Assignment

Briefly summarize the major points presented today and explain the practice assignment. Ask group members to observe their thoughts this week and fill out the questionnaire to bring back next week.

Walk the youth through Handout 1.39, a practice sheet for using the Three-Step Model and replacing hurtful with helpful thoughts. Ask group members what they thought were the most important topics or points covered in today's session. As necessary, make the following points:

- *Hurtful thoughts make us feel bad and can lead to MUPS coping.*
- *Hurtful thoughts often imply that things can never change and are usually inaccurate.*
- *We can study, catch, and change our hurtful thoughts.*
- *When we replace a hurtful thought with a helpful thought, we usually feel better.*
- *When we feel better, we do better.*
- *When we do better, the consequences are usually better.*

Review Handout 1.39 with youth as the practice assignment for the week.

VII. Check-Out

- *How are you feeling now? (Use the Feeling Thermometer rating.)*
- *What did you learn about yourself today?*
- *Please fill out the Check-Out Feedback Form (Handout 1.40). The title of today's session is "Sizing Up a Situation".*

If any group members report high levels of stress on the Feeling Thermometer, take time to process with them before returning them to their classrooms or residences.

Implementing Module 1, Session 1.6 with Individual Clients

Preparation: Make printed copies of Today's Highlights (Flipchart 1.6a), Three Steps to Taking Charge of your Thoughts and Feelings (Flipchart 1.6b), and Questions for Catching your Thoughts (Flipchart 1.6c), if that is easier than using flipcharts.

I. **Check-in and Feeling Thermometer**: Ask your client about something good that happened in the past week, as described in the first bullet. You may also break the ice by sharing something good that happened to you this week.

II. **Review practice assignment and previous sessions**. Deliver as written but omit references to the group.

III. **Explain Sizing Up a Situation: changing feelings and behaviors by changing thoughts.** Deliver as written, and omit any references to the group. This content can easily be delivered to an individual.

IV. **Identifying hurtful thoughts.** Consider sharing one of your own hurtful thoughts that is not too personal, in order to level the playing field, before asking the client to share hers or his.

V. **Replacing hurtful thoughts**. Although this is listed as optional for group delivery, there may be enough time in an individual session, depending on the attention span of your client. Deliver as written while omitting references to the group.

VI. **Summary and practice assignment**. Ask the client what he or she thought were the most important topics covered.

VII. **Check-out**. Deliver as written.

1.7

Identifying and Replacing Hurtful Thoughts

Session Objectives

1. Practice identifying hurtful and helpful thoughts.
2. Identify the categories of hurtful thoughts.
3. Perform skits replacing hurtful thoughts with helpful thoughts.
4. Learn the final steps of taking charge of your thoughts and feelings.
5. Increase ability to share thoughts and feelings with other group members.

Section number	Session overview
I	Check-in and Feeling Thermometer
II	Review last session and practice assignment
III	Generating alternative interpretations
IV	Replacing hurtful thoughts
V	Practice three steps to take charge of your thoughts and feelings
VI	Summary and practice assignment
VII	Check-out

Supplies

Every Session	This Session
• Flipchart	
• Large paper or easel pad	
• Colored markers or crayons	
• Pencils/pens	
• Kleenex	
• Tape	
• Workbook	

Handouts in Workbook

Handout 1.41	Common Thinking Errors Checklist
Handout 1.42	Common Errors in Thinking
Handouts 1.43–1.45	Practice Illustrations
Handout 1.46	Skits
Handout 1.47	Three Steps to Taking Charge of Your Thoughts and Feelings
Handout 1.48	Check-Out Feedback Form

Flipcharts

1.7a Today's Highlights

1. Check-in: one good thing that happened this week and Feeling Thermometer
2. Review practice assignment: breathing and identifying hurtful and helpful thoughts
3. Practice generating alternative interpretations
4. Activity: replacing hurtful thoughts skits
5. Practice on Three Steps to Take Charge of Your Thoughts and Feelings
6. Check-out with the Feeling Thermometer and Check-Out Feedback Form

1.7b Three Steps to Take Charge of Your Thoughts and Feelings

Answer these questions:

1. "What am I feeling?"
2. "Why am I feeling this way?"
   - Look outside
   - Look inside – "What am I thinking?"
3. "How can I feel better by thinking better?"

Situation	Hurtful thought	Emotional reaction	Thinking error

Session 1.7: Identifying and Replacing Hurtful Thoughts

I. Do Check-In and Feeling Thermometer

- *How are you feeling right now?* (Use the Feeling Thermometer ratings.)
- Practice with the group doing five to ten calming abdominal breaths.
- *Is anything going on that may make it difficult for you to keep your mind on the group?*
- Briefly review Today's Highlights (Flipchart 1.7a).

II. Review Last Session and Practice Assignment

Review Last Session

We learned during our last session that our feelings don't just happen to us, like the weather. Of course, many things, such as being tired or hungry, can affect how we feel, but very often **thoughts** *generate* **feelings***. When you change how you think, you can often change how you feel.*

Changing how you feel can change what you do. This may help you control your life better and achieve your goals.

Last session you learned to identify **hurtful thoughts** *and replace them with* **helpful thoughts***. Today we will focus on identifying and challenging specific* **thinking errors***. We'll use your responses on Handout 1.35, the Hurtful Thoughts Checklist, to do this.*

Review Practice Assignment

Have group members bring out their completed Handouts 1.35 and 1.36, the Hurtful and Helpful Thoughts checklists. If they did not do this between sessions, have them fill it out now. Point out the general categories of hurtful thoughts:

Feeling unloved and unwanted	Hopeless thoughts
Helpless thoughts	Preoccupation with danger
Self-critical thoughts	Self-blaming
Distrusting everyone	

Ask group members to add categories that are not listed on this checklist. Additional categories could include:

Revenge fantasies	Blaming others
Making excuses for yourself	Catastrophizing

Ask group members for any hurtful thoughts they have in addition to those on the checklist. Ask them how their hurtful thoughts affect their feelings and their actions. Normalize and validate these thoughts as common reactions to traumas and losses.

Help each group member identify one hurtful thought that he or she finds especially distressing and point out similarities and differences among group members' chosen hurtful thoughts. Then ask group members to locate helpful thoughts on Handout 1.36, the Helpful Thoughts Checklist, that are the opposite of feeling unloved, hopeless, helpless, preoccupied with danger or revenge, and so on.

Ask them what helpful thoughts they have in addition to those on the checklist. Help group members to identify one helpful thought that they found particularly beneficial and point out similarities and differences among group members' favorite helpful thoughts.

III. Generating Alternative Interpretations

The general goal in this section is to gain practice in identifying hurtful thoughts and generating alternative helpful interpretations. Hurtful thoughts are often caused by "negative thinking errors." These errors can become so habitual that they become automatic, but we can learn to spot them and change them so that we will feel better.

*Simply by answering the questions posed by Steps One and Two ("**What** am I feeling?" and "**Why** am I feeling this way?") from our Three-Step Model, you have come a long way toward taking control of your emotions.*

Step Three tells you *how* to feel better. Here is how you do it:

1. You **challenge** the **hurtful thought** by finding evidence that it is false.
2. You **replace it** with a more realistic **helpful thought**.

Activity: Challenging Common Thinking Errors

Review common thinking errors by going through Handout 1.41. You can also refer to Handout 1.42 for a more detailed explanation and examples of thinking errors. With the list of thinking errors in hand, use the following prompts to evaluate the thinking of youth portrayed in the following illustrations.

Use all of the illustrations or as many for which you have time. These include illustrations of a youth blaming himself for parents' fighting (Handout 1.43), a youth misinterpreting a teacher's attentions (Handout 1.44), and a youth self-criticizing for posttraumatic reactions (Handout 1.45).

- *What's going on in this picture?*
- *What hurtful thought(s) is the boy/girl having?*
- *How do you think she/he is feeling?*
- *What common thinking errors might she/he be making in the way he/she is thinking?*
- *What is she/he likely to do if she/he feels this way?*

You may refer to this list to help students recognize the errors in thinking that are present in the illustrations.

Common Thinking Errors

1.	Filtering and discounting
2.	Shoulds and musts
3.	All-or-none thinking
4.	*Then* is *now*
5.	Self-blame
6.	If it *feels* true it *is true*
7.	Self put-downs
8.	Permanent thoughts
9.	Foretelling the future
10.	Mind-reading
11.	Catastrophizing

For each picture used, ask group members to suggest alternative interpretations that may be more accurate and realistic. Then ask them to guess how the youth might feel with those thoughts. What might she/he do?

- *What are some more realistic and helpful ways she/he can think about this situation?*
- *How might she/he feel if she/he had those alternate thoughts? What is she/he likely to do?*

IV. Replacing Hurtful Thoughts

Activity: Replacing Hurtful Thoughts Skits

Refer to Handouts 1.35 and 1.36. Divide the group into pairs and assign each a skit from those shown below (the skits are described on Handout 1.46 for group members to look at in their dyads). Each skit involves a character responding to a situation by generating a negative thought either about the situation or about oneself. Each skit covers a common trauma-related hurtful thought.

- When the group members are divided into pairs and you have given each pair a skit, have them identify all of the negative thinking errors they find in their skit.
- Second, have each pair generate alternative, more helpful thoughts for their skits. The group members will re-write their skits so that the teenager has more realistic, helpful thoughts.
- After 5–10 minutes, regroup and have volunteers act out both versions of their skits. First have them act out the original skit and share the thinking errors in their skit. Discuss as a group the consequences of these thoughts. Then, have each pair perform their new version with helpful thoughts. Ask what the consequences of these helpful thoughts might be.
- Group members may also generate their own hurtful thoughts skits in consultation with the group leader.

Skit 1: Mother and Teen Talk about Money

Mother:	"I'm sorry I can't get you those new shoes. We just can't afford it."
Teen:	(*Angrily*) "We can't afford anything!"
	(*Thinking to self*) "I can't remember the last time she got me anything. I'm never going to have anything new or that doesn't look all ratty. Everybody is going to be looking at my shoes and making comments."

Skit 2: Two Friends Talk about Sports

Matt	"Hey, they're having tryouts for the football team next week. Let's practice and we'll both get on the team. That will be awesome!"

David:	"It won't happen. I never get chosen for teams, plays, or anything."
	"Anyway, the coach just picks his local favorite boys to play."

Skit 3: Two Friends at School Discuss Grades

Sarah	"Hey David. What did you get?"
David:	"A 'D!' That must be the lowest grade in the class. I am so stupid! I won't pass this class."
Sarah:	"I didn't do that well either. Maybe we could study together."
David	"Forget it. I'll never understand this stuff."

Skit 4: Parent with Teen Discuss an Accident

Mother	(Comes into teenager's room) "Did you hear about your cousin? He got in a bad accident coming home from that dance club last night."
Teen	(Thinking to self) "I told him not to go without me. I should have been the one driving. I always hurt the people around me."

Skit 5: Teen Vows to Get Even With Abusive Stepfather

(Teen comes home from school to find his little brother Andy with bruises on his face and arms.)

Andy	"Our stepdad beat me up this morning."
Teen	(Thinking to self) "I'm going to find that guy and kill him."

Skit 6: Parent Tells Teen She Lost Her Job

Mom	"I just lost my job. I don't know what we are going to do."
Teen	(Thinking to self) "I'll quit school and start dealing so that my mom and my little sisters will have something to live on."

Skit 7: Girl Sees Teacher in the Hallway

(Sarah's male teacher walks toward her in the hallway smiling.)

Teacher	"Hello, Sarah."
Sarah	(Thinking to self) "He's looking at me funny. I bet he wants to screw me. All men want from me is sex."

V. Practice Three Steps to Take Charge of Your Thoughts and Feelings

This activity is designed to help group members select situations from their own lives during which they struggle with trauma-related errors in thinking. It will help them expand their recognition of these automatic hurtful thoughts as they go through their daily lives and ways to generate alternative, more helpful thoughts, in these daily situations.

Activity: Taking Charge of Your Thoughts and Feelings

Have group members fill out Handout 1.47, Three Steps to Taking Charge of Your Thoughts and Feelings.

Think about a time you felt distressed or unhappy within the past few days, or even about the current moment.

- *Was your thought linked to one of the traumas or losses you wrote about in the handout?*
- *Take time to write down the thought or image in the blank space on your worksheet.*

The group leader should review how to complete the remainder of the worksheet and help those that need help. (Allow 15 minutes to complete.)

- ***What** am I feeling?*
- ***Why** am I feeling this way?*
  - *What is happening outside?*
  - *What is happening inside?*
- ***How** can I feel better?*
- *What facts support the hurtful thought?*
- *What facts do not support the hurtful thought?*
- *What thinking error might I be making?*
- *Is there a more helpful thought I can have?*

Once members have completed this individually, using the handout, say the following:

We now invite you to share with the group this hurtful thought so that you can get help looking at the evidence for it and determining helpful thoughts you can use to replace it. Each of you will have an opportunity to describe your thought, and to receive the group's help.

If group members are reluctant to share, you may break the ice and help group members open up if one or both group leaders share a (not too personal) hurtful thought they have had recently that has generated negative emotions. "I'll never learn to be on time," or "I'm hopelessly messy," or "I'll never learn to do this right," might be examples.

Draw four columns on the flipchart. Use Flipchart 1.7b. The first column is entitled "Situation", the second "Hurtful thought," the third "Emotional reaction," and the fourth "Thinking error."

Help each member, in turn, to fill out all four columns with the group's support.

- *Describe a recent situation in which you experienced this hurtful thought. What was going on **outside** of you? What were you doing?*

67

- *Now, tell us what was going on **inside** of you. What was your hurtful thought?*
- *Can you put it into words (Was it a word? A sentence? If it was an image, can you describe what it looked like in your mind?)?*
- *Next, please describe your emotional reaction to this thought (Were you sad? Scared? Hurt? Angry? Hopeless?).*
- *Now, let's work together as a group to evaluate this hurtful thought or image. Can you see any potential weaknesses in it? Any thinking errors? Does it seem like a fair and balanced way of interpreting the situation, or does it seem to be one-sided or excessively negative? Feel free to look at your handouts if you want some hints.*
- *What's a more positive thought you could have about this situation?*

VI. Summary and Practice Assignment

Briefly summarize the major points presented today and explain the homework. Refer group members to Handout 1.27, Disrupting Negative Self-Talk and Rules for Writing Self-Calming Phrases, and Handout 1.47, Three Steps to Take Charge of Your Thoughts and Feelings.

*For practice this week, please select a situation in which you can practice all three steps of the model. During a situation where you feel bad, study your thoughts and find your hurtful thought. Use the handout to write "**What** am I feeling?," "**Why** am I feeling this way?," and "**How** can I feel better?"*

VII. Check-Out

- *How are you feeling now?* (Use the Feeling Thermometer ratings.)
- *What did you learn about yourself today?*
- *Please fill out the Check-Out Feedback Form (Handout 1.48). The title of today's session was "Identifying and Challenging Hurtful Thoughts."*

If any group members are visibly agitated or troubled or report high levels of distress on the Feeling Thermometer, keep them after the group and determine an appropriate way to transition back to their settings.

Implementing Module 1, Session 1.7 with Individual Clients

Because at least half of this session involves group activities that are not easily adapted for individual sessions, this entire session can be omitted if the cognitive training in Session 6 was sufficient.

Preparation: Make printed copies of Today's Highlights (Flipchart 1.7a) and Three Steps to Take Charge of your Thoughts and Feelings (Flipchart 1.7b), if that is easier than using flipcharts.

I. **Check-in and Feeling Thermometer**. Ask your client about something good that happened in the past week, as described in the first bullet. You may also break the ice by sharing something good that happened to you this week.

II. **Review practice assignment and previous sessions**. Deliver as written but omit references to the group.

III. **Generating alternative interpretations**. Deliver this session as written. Because you will not be doing the replacing hurtful thoughts skits activity, you may take time with this.

IV. **Replacing hurtful thoughts skits**. This activity can be omitted or modified, as time permits. For an individual session, you can take each skit and use the chart in Flipchart 1.7b to analyze and generate a replacement thought.

V. **Practice**. This is also a group exercise that can be omitted or combined with the replacing hurtful thoughts skits activity.

VI. **Summary and practice assignment**. Deliver as written.

VII. **Check-out**. Deliver as written.

1.8 Recruiting Effective Support

Session Objectives

1. Practice appropriate self-disclosure.
2. Practice replacing hurtful thoughts with helpful thoughts.
3. Identify barriers to good communication.
4. Present a five-step model for getting support and practice with "I" message.
5. Review what has been learned in Module 1.

Hints: This session is about recruiting effective support, so encourage group members to interact with each other. Help the group become a resource, a "think tank" for generating new ideas to make the skills they are learning work for them.

Section number	Session overview
I	Check-in
II	Review last session and practice assignment
III	Discussion on aids and barriers to communication
V	Five Steps to Getting Support
VI	Go over the personal coping toolkit
VII	Do practice exercise: Module 1 feedback
VIII	Check-out

Supplies

Every Session	This Session
• Flipchart	
• Large paper or easel pad	
• Colored markers or crayons	
• Pencils/pens	
• Kleenex	
• Tape	
• Workbooks	

Handouts in Workbook

Handout 1.49	Five Steps to Getting Support
Handout 1.50	"I" Message for Sharing
Handout 1.51	Things That *I* Can Do: My Personal Coping Toolkit
Handout 1.52	Group Goals Worksheet
Handout 1.53	Check-Out Feedback Form

Flipcharts

1.8a Today's Highlights

1. Check-in: one good thing that happened and the Feeling Thermometer
2. Review practice assignment: breathing and three steps to take charge of your thoughts and feelings
3. Aids and barriers to communication
4. Five steps to getting support
5. Sharing feelings using an "I" message
6. My personal coping toolkit
7. Module I feedback
8. Check-out with Feeling Thermometer and Check-Out Feedback Form

1.8b Three Steps to Take Charge of Your Thoughts and Feelings

Answer these questions:
1. "What am I feeling?"
2. "Why am I feeling this way?"
   • Look outside
   • Look inside – "What am I thinking?"
3. "How can I feel better?"

1.8c Aids and Barriers to Communication

• Aids: "helpful"
• Barriers: "unhelpful"

1.8d Five Steps to Getting Support

1. "What do I want?"
2. "Whom should I ask?"
3. Find the right time
4. Request with an "I" message
5. Express sincere appreciation

1.8e Using an "I" Message for Communicating

Tell others:
1. What I am feeling
2. What happened:
   • Outside of me
   • Inside of me
3. What I want them to do?

Session 1.8: Recruiting Effective Support

I. Do Check-In and Feeling Thermometer

- *How are you feeling right now?* (Use the Feeling Thermometer ratings.)
- Practice with the group doing five to ten deep breaths.
- *Is anything going on that may make it difficult for you to keep your mind on the group today?*
- Briefly review (or have a group member review) Today's Highlights (Flipchart 1.8a).

II. Review Last Session and Practice Assignment

Provide a brief summary of key points from last session.

Review the practice assignment

The purpose of this exercise is to:
- Teach and reinforce the appropriate use of the three-step method.
- Strengthen the group members' confidence that these skills can really work for them.

Invite group members to ask questions of each other and to provide advice on how to use helpful thoughts. As needed, supplement this with your own questions, observations, and suggestions.

Present Three Steps to Take Charge of your Thoughts and Feelings (Flipchart 1.8b).

*Let's start by reviewing your practice assignment. You worked on trying out the three-step method for replacing distressing or **hurtful thoughts** with **helpful thoughts**, to see if that worked with stressful situations.*

- Go around the group and invite each member to share his/her assignment.
- Make a summary statement in which you praise group members for the progress they are showing, and call attention to the need for continued practice.

III. Discussion on Aids and Barriers to Communication

- Discuss the benefits of good communication with our families and others.
- Identify and explore barriers to good communication.
- The goal is to encourage group members to open up and share everyday events, feelings, and concerns and to be more consistently involved in each other's lives.
- Do not press group members to share their intimate feelings on personal topics that teenagers typically do not share openly with others. Keep the focus on the communication *process* that makes day-to-day communication go well or poorly. WHAT they talk about is less important than HOW they talk about it.

Purpose of Communication Focus

*So far, we have been working on things that **you** can do to help you feel better, like replacing hurtful thoughts with helpful thoughts. Today we focus on the ways in which **other** people can help you to feel better. Actually, being in this group is a way in which you have already recruited social support. We emphasize good communication right now because as you continue to think and talk about the traumas and losses you have experienced, there will probably be times when you will want the support and understanding of others.*

Ask the group to give examples of how we react when communication goes well and we get what we want. Examples include that we:

- Believe we are understood and cared for
- Believe we fit in and belong
- Believe we are needed and wanted
- Gain reassurance that we can handle problems
- Gain reassurance that others will be there for us if we need them
- Obtain guidance and advice

Now ask for examples of what we feel when communication does not go well and we do **not** get what we want. Examples include that we:

- Feel misunderstood
- Feel isolated
- Feel angry
- Feel sad
- Feel lonely

Activity: Aids and Barriers to Communication

You can each take about two minutes to:

- *Describe a time when you talked to a parent, friend, teacher, or other adult, and you felt GOOD about how it went*
- *Describe a time when you talked and you felt BAD about how it went.*

Use Flipchart 1.8c.

- *We will write the things that made the communication go well in the "Aids" column and the things that made the communication go badly in the "Barriers" column.*

Ask:

- *What did the **other person** do that made it go well?*
- *What did **you** do that made it go well?*
- *What did the **other person** do that made it go badly?*
- *What did **you** do that made it go badly?*

Using Flipchart 1.8c, write down why the communication felt GOOD in the Aids column and why it felt BAD in the Barriers column.

Give special attention to the skills that will be focused on this session. Barriers may include being too busy, not paying attention, not understanding, blaming, and lecturing instead of listening. Aids may include listening, caring, and understanding. This exercise will take 10–15 minutes.

IV. Discuss Five Steps to Getting Support

This five-step model of getting support helps to avoid some barriers that we've just talked about.

Present Five Steps to Getting Support (Flipchart 1.8d), and have group members refer to Handout 1.49 in their workbooks.

1. "**What do I want**?" *The first part of getting support is taking the time to figure out what you really want. For example, sometimes we want to be understood, and sometimes we want advice. Things group members may want are listed below and on Handout 1.49, Five Steps to Getting Support.*

Here are some ideas of things you may want. (Group leaders: select items as appropriate)

- *Someone to just listen and try to understand without giving advice?*
- *A hug?*
- *Companionship?*
- *Encouragement that I can handle a difficult situation?*
- *Reassurance that people will be there for me in case I need them?*

- *Advice?*
- *Practical help to solve a problem?*
- *Things (material support)?*

2. **"Whom should I ask?"** *The second step is to think about your relationships with the people you know. Who has been, or could be, a good source of support for what you want? Your parents or caregivers may be important sources of many types of support, but there are usually others as well, such as siblings, relatives, close friends your age, or an adult mentor. (The following questions are listed on the handout.)*

- *Which of my relationships has been a good source of this type of support in the past (e.g. parent, grandparent, friend, relative, teacher, social worker)?*
- *Are there others who might give me this type of support? For example, even if I have never gone to him or her to talk before, do I have an aunt or uncle whom I think would be a good listener? What about an adult friend or mentor?*
- *Can I look for additional people to meet a need? For example, if I want someone to talk to, are there people I know whom I could start spending more time with? Is there a group or organization that would provide support?*

3. **Find the right time**. *Because you'll be talking to the person about something that matters to you, you want them to take the time to listen. So you need to find a time when they will have enough time and energy to be a good listener. How do you find a good time to talk? (Emphasize that asking is one of the best ways to find the right time.)*

- *"Do you have the time to talk right now?"*
- *"When would you have the time to talk?"*

4. **Request with an "I" message**. *Once you have decided what you want, whom to ask, and have found a good time to talk, then you talk to them. A good way to do this is with an "I" message. In an "I" message you communicate three things (These bullets are on the handout.):*

- *You tell them how you're feeling.*
- *You tell them about your situation, what led you to feel the way you do.*
- *You tell them specifically what you want them to do. For example, you might say, "I'm really upset (angry) about what happened in school today, and I just want to tell you about it. And I would just like for you to listen and let me vent."*

5. **Express sincere appreciation**. *Finally, end the conversation by sincerely thanking them for listening. This is very important. Being a good listener is not easy, and giving your listeners positive feedback will encourage them to keep trying, even if they don't "get it" completely right this time. Thanking them will also strengthen your relationship. If you can, tell them specifically HOW they have helped you so they will know how to help you in the future.*

For example, you might say, "Thank you for letting me vent. I'm feeling much better now."

V. Demonstrate Communicating by Using an "I" Message

The goal of this section is to train group members how to use "I" messages. This is the focus of Step 4 of the Five Steps to Getting Support. Have group members refer to their Handout 1.50, the "I" Message for Sharing, as you go over the following points.

When someone is really listening to you, they pay attention and listen carefully. They show you by what they do and say that they are really interested in you and care about your life, your feelings, and your ideas. They don't judge you or try to give you quick solutions. They understand that you just want to be heard, and that you will ask for advice if you want it.

A good way to get people to listen instead of giving advice is by using an "I" message that lets them know what you want. As we explained, when you give an "I" message, you say three things:

Refer to Flipchart 1.8e, Using an "I" Message for Communicating.

1. What I am feeling?

Feelings are probably the most important thing that you're sharing. Lots of communication problems develop because someone assumes that they know how another person is feeling. Therefore, don't assume that people automatically know how you feel – tell them! The first step is to say how you are feeling in a clear, straightforward way. For example, you could say, "I'm feeling worried about an exam I'll be taking on Tuesday."

2. What happened (outside and inside)?

Second, tell them what has happened that led you to feel this way. Tell them what happened both outside and inside you:

Outside you: *Tell them about the stressful situation. Who? What? Where? When? (Sometimes talking about what happened will help you to understand the situation more clearly.)*

Inside you: *Tell them about your thoughts and feelings. Did you have a hurtful thought? A helpful thought? What emotions did you feel?*

3. What do I want them to do?

*Third, let them know that you want them to listen and try to understand without telling you what to do. (We say **try** because really understanding someone is very hard to do, and if someone is trying that's important, too, even if they don't quite get there.) For example, you can say, "I just want you to know about this. I don't want you to try to fix it right now."*

Example: *"I'm feeling angry because of something that happened today. Can I just tell you about it without you giving me advice?"*

Activity: Communication Role Play (Listening Without Giving Advice)

We're now going to do a role-play activity to help you practice these communication skills.

The two group leaders can role-play first, as an example.

Instructions to group: *Think of one thing that you would like to talk to someone else about. It doesn't need to be something big – just something that you care about. It could be something that happened today, a conversation that you had with a friend – anything you have some feelings about. Use Handout 1.50 to write down information about the situation.* (Give participants a few minutes to do this)

Select two volunteers: *I need two volunteers. One person will present an "I" message, and the other person (parent, teacher, mentor, friend) will listen. One way to let a person know you are really listening is to repeat back what you hear them say to you – this is called "reflective listening."*

Instructions to volunteers: Have the youth do the role play and then ask volunteers and group members to discuss things that were done well and things that may need improvement. Group leaders should acknowledge these and try to include two strengths (things done well) and one area where the youth could develop further.

Summarize: *As you can see, good communication isn't easy. It takes practice to give "I" messages. It also takes practice for parents and other people to just listen instead of giving advice.* **"Just"** listening isn't as easy as it sounds. Ask for the reactions of the "listeners" to underscore how difficult it can be to be a good listener.

VI. Go over My Personal Coping Toolkit

Have group members refer to Handout 1.51, My Personal Coping Toolkit. This list summarizes the coping strategies they have worked on as a group for the past weeks. If group members wish, they can take this handout out of their workbook to keep with them in their rooms.

VII. Do Practice Exercise: Module 1 Feedback

Practice Exercise: Group Goals Worksheet

The practice exercise is designed to show you how your thinking, feelings, and behavior have changed or remained the same since the beginning of the group. Please look at Handout 1.03, the Personal Goals Worksheet you filled out in Session 1.1. Check off on the new Group Goals Worksheet (Handout 1.52) only the goals that you need to continue to work on. You might want to add new goals as well.

What goals remain for you to work on? (Group leaders should help group members who have limited literacy.)

VIII. Check-Out

- *How are you feeling now?* (Use the Feeling Thermometer ratings.)
- *What did you learn about yourself today?*
- *Please fill out the Check-Out Feedback Form* (Handout 1.53). *The title of today's session was "Recruiting Effective Support".*

If any group members are visibly agitated or troubled or report high levels of distress on the Feeling Thermometer, keep them after the group and determine an appropriate way to transition them back to their settings.

Implementing Module 1, Session 1.8 with Individual Clients

Preparation: Make printed copies of Today's Highlights (Flipchart 1.8a), Three Steps to Take Charge of your Thoughts and Feelings (Flipchart 1.8b), Aids and Barriers to Communication (Flipchart 1.8c), Five Steps to Getting Support (Flipchart 1.8d), and Using an "I" Message for Communicating (Flipchart 1.8e), if that is easier than using flipcharts.

I. **Check-in and Feeling Thermometer.** Ask your client about something good that happened in the past week, as described in the first bullet. You may also break the ice by sharing something good that happened to you this week.

II. **Review practice assignment and previous sessions**. Deliver as written but omit references to the group.

III. **Aids and barriers to communication**. Adapt this for an individual session by participating in the discussion with (not too personal) examples from your own life. Omit references to the group.

IV. **Discuss Five Steps to Getting Support**. This is easily adapted for an individual session.

V. **Demonstrate communicating by using an "I" message**. This is essentially a group exercise and can be omitted or adapted for a two-person role-play.

VI. **Go over my personal coping toolkit**. Clients may or may not remember to bring their toolkit to sessions with them, so be sure you have a copy of this client's toolkit with you.

This is an important summary of all that has been covered in Module 1.

VII. Module 1 **feedback**. This is easily adapted for an individual session. Have the client review the goals set in Session 1 (make sure you have a copy) and have the client create a second goals worksheet. Do not refer to this as a "group goals worksheet."

VIII. **Check-out**. Deliver as written.

MODULE 1 HANDOUTS

HANDOUT 1.01 (SAMPLE)

SAMPLE CONTRACT

Note: This is *not a youth handout*. It is provided to the leaders as a sample.

To do my part to make this group a safe, supportive, and helpful place for everyone, I agree to comply with the following rules:

1. I will keep confidentiality at all times.

2. I will treat other group members as I would wish to be treated.

3. I will do my best to encourage and support the other group members.

4. I will express myself without hurting others in the group.

5. I will not read personal materials, smoke, or eat food in the group (group treats excepted).

6. I will come, on time, to each session whenever possible. If I cannot attend a session, I will do my best to let a group leader know beforehand.

7. I will attend sessions drug- and alcohol-free.

8. I will work diligently on my personal goals. I will push myself beyond my "zone of comfort" by trying out the new things I have learned and by doing the practice exercises.

9. I will let a group leader know if I am having trouble with my goals or if I have serious personal problems (including having strong thoughts of hurting myself or someone else).

10. Other rules to make the group a safe and helpful place:

    _____

    _____

11. The group leaders agree to work with me to help me get the most I can out of the group.

Signatures:

My signature: _____ Date: _____

Group leader: _____ Date: _____

Group leader: _____ Date: _____

HANDOUT 1.02

Trauma Goals Worksheet

By the end of this intervention:				
I want to feel _LESS_: *(please circle all that apply)*				
Nervous	Scared	Angry	Upset	Sad
I want to feel _MORE_: *(please circle all that apply)*				
Happy	Calm	Excited	Relaxed	
I want to change the way I do things and think about things: *(please check all that apply)*				
☐	Calm myself down when I feel upset.			
☐	Think about things that happened without feeling upset.			
☐	Talk about things that happened without feeling upset.			
☐	Stop avoiding things that make me nervous.			
☐	Do more of the things that I used to do.			
☐	Think more about things before I do them.			
☐	Make better decisions.			
☐	Have fewer problems with my family.			
☐	Have fewer problems with my friends.			
I also want to change:				

HANDOUT 1.03

Personal Goals Worksheet

Problem statement	Date:
Goal statement	

Problem statement	Date:
Goal statement	

HANDOUT 1.04

Check-Out Feedback Form

Session topic: Welcome and Introduction

Your date of birth: _____

Today's date: _____

Facility: _____

What about today's session was most useful to you? Which activities and materials were the most helpful?

_____

_____

_____

What specific suggestions do you have for how to make the group better?

_____

_____

_____

How comfortable were you about today's topic? (Please circle a number.)

1	2	3	4	5
Extremely uncomfortable	Fairly uncomfortable	Somewhat comfortable	Fairly comfortable	Very comfortable

What were you thinking and feeling during today's group?

_____

_____

_____

_____

How are you feeling now?

_____

_____

_____

_____

HANDOUT 1.05

Feeling Thermometer

What emotion do you feel right now? Name the feeling you are having and rate how strong or weak it is on this thermometer: 10 means extremely strong, 5 means medium, and 1 means you have the feeling just a little bit.

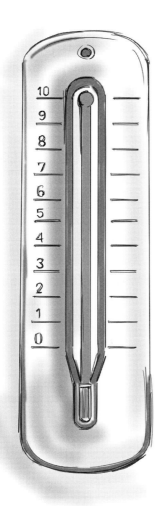

What distressing feelings do you have right now? Rate the strength of these feelings from 1 to 10.

HANDOUT 1.06

Instructions for Deep (Abdominal) Breathing

Inhale slowly and deeply though your nose into the "bottom" of your lungs. In other words, send the air as low down as you can. If you're breathing from your abdomen, your lower hand should actually rise. Your chest should move only slightly. It helps to imagine that you are blowing up a balloon in your abdomen.

When you've taken in a full breath, pause for a moment and then exhale slowly through your nose or mouth, depending on your preference. Be sure to exhale fully, so that breathing out takes longer than breathing in. As you exhale, allow your whole body to just let go (you might visualize your arms and legs going loose and limp, like a rag doll). As you exhale, think of a soothing word or phrase, such as, "Calm," "I'm OK," or "Peace."

Do ten slow, full abdominal breaths. Try to keep your breathing smooth and regular, without gulping in a big breath or letting your breath out all at once. Remember to pause briefly at the end of each inhalation. Count to ten, progressing with each exhalation. The process should go like this:

Slow inhale … Pause … Slow exhale (count "one") Slow inhale … Pause … Slow exhale (count "two") Slow inhale … Pause … Slow exhale (count "three")

… and so on.

If you start to feel light-headed while practicing the breathing, breathe normally for thirty seconds, and then start up again.

Upon completing the exercise, have participants re-rate their anxiety/distress level on the Feeling Thermometer. Note changes, if any.

Tell group members to try doing 10 breaths early in the morning, at midday, and as they are falling asleep. For those who awaken in the night, the breathing can help them relax and fall back to sleep.

HANDOUT 1.07

Using the Breathing Technique Every Day

HANDOUT 1.08

Posttraumatic Stress and Grief Checklist:
Re-Experiencing ("Upsetting Thoughts, Images and Memories Pop Into My Mind")

Put a check next to the reactions that you currently experience.

	Distressing memories pop into my mind when I don't want them to
	Nightmares
	Flashbacks
	Sudden changes in how I am feeling
	Sudden changes in how my body feels

HANDOUT 1.09

Posttraumatic Stress and Grief Checklist:
Avoidance and Numbing ("I am Avoiding People, Situations, and Feelings That Upset or Stress Me Out")

Put a check next to the reactions that you *currently* experience.

	Avoid people, places, activities or things that remind me of what happened
	Feel emotionally "flat," as if I am trying to avoid having any feelings at all
	Avoid thoughts, memories, feelings, or conversations about the traumatic event(s)

HANDOUT 1.10

Posttraumatic Stress and Grief Checklist:
Persistent Negative Mood ("I Am Having Persistent Negative Thoughts and Feelings")

Put a check next to the reactions that you *currently* experience.

	Memory loss
	Persistent negative beliefs
	Blame
	Negative emotions
	No interests
	Cut off
	No joy

HANDOUT 1.11

Posttraumatic Stress and Grief Checklist:
Hyperarousal ("I Am Feeling Jumpy, Irritable, and On Guard")

Put a check next to the reactions that you *currently* experience.

	I feel irritable, aggressive, or "on edge" much of the time
	I may start to do reckless or self-destructive things
	I may feel constantly on guard and hypervigilant, as if danger is lurking everywhere
	I may startle easily, feel jumpy
	I may find it hard to pay attention in school, concentrate on homework or remember what I have learned
	I may have a difficult time falling or staying asleep

HANDOUT 1.12

Posttraumatic Stress and Grief Checklist:
Grief ("I Am Feeling Sad, Hopeless, Lost, or Angry About the Death")

Put a check next to the reactions that you *currently* experience.

	I miss the person who died
	I feel sad whenever I am reminded that they are gone and not in my life anymore
	I feel angry that they are gone
	I feel regret about things I did or didn't do at the time of their death
	I have both strong negative and strong positive feelings (ambivalence) about the person who died
	I feel lost or hopeless
	I wonder who I am without this person in my life

HANDOUT 1.13

Monitoring Changes in My Mood and Feelings

Directions: Pick one to three times this week when you noticed your mood change for the worse. Be especially alert for strong feelings such as sadness, anxiety, fear, guilt, or anger. All of these may be signs that you might be having a reaction triggered by a reminder of your trauma or loss experiences.

For each occasion, write a brief description of what was happening *outside* of you.

Then, describe one or two emotions that you felt most strongly *inside*. Rate each emotion on a "thermometer" from 0 to 10.

Situation 1:

What's happening *outside* of you?

_____

_____

_____

What's happening *inside* of you?

| Emotion | _____ | Intensity (0–10) |
| Emotion | _____ | Intensity (0–10) |

Situation 2:

What's happening *outside* of you?

_____

_____

What's happening *inside* of you?

| Emotion | _____ | Intensity (0–10) |
| Emotion | _____ | Intensity (0–10) |

Situation 3:

What's happening *outside* of you?

_____

_____

What's happening *inside* of you?

| Emotion | _____ | Intensity (0–10) |
| Emotion | _____ | Intensity (0–10) |

HANDOUT 1.14

Check-Out Feedback Form

Session topic: Posttraumatic Stress Reactions, Grief Reactions, and Introduction to Coping Strategies

Your date of birth: _____

Today's date: _____

Facility: _____

What about today's session was most useful to you? Which activities and materials were the most helpful?

_____

_____

_____

What specific suggestions do you have for how to make the group better?

_____

_____

_____

How comfortable were you about today's topic? (Please circle a number.)

1	2	3	4	5
Extremely uncomfortable	Fairly uncomfortable	Somewhat comfortable	Fairly comfortable	Very comfortable

What were you thinking and feeling during today's group?

_____

_____

_____

_____

How are you feeling now?

_____

_____

_____

HANDOUT 1.15

Three Steps to Taking Charge of Your Feelings

HANDOUT 1.16

Feelings Selfie

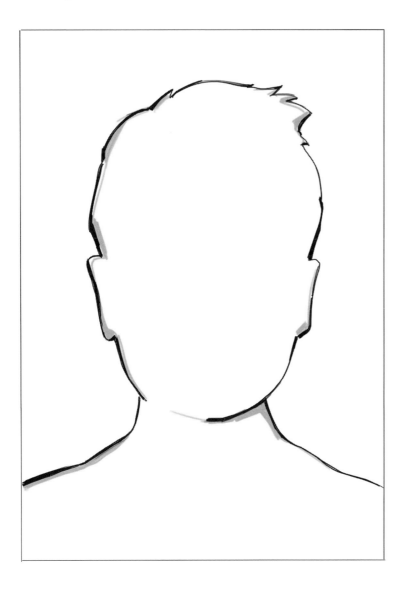

Color	Feeling

HANDOUT 1.17

Feelings Faces

HANDOUT 1.18

What's Behind Your Anger?

HANDOUT 1.19

Check-Out Feedback Form

Session topic: Monitoring and Managing Strong Feelings

Your date of birth: _____

Today's date: _____

Facility: _____

What about today's session was most useful to you? Which activities and materials were the most helpful?

_____

_____

_____

What specific suggestions do you have for how to make the group better?

_____

_____

_____

How comfortable were you about today's topic? (Please circle a number.)

1	2	3	4	5
Extremely uncomfortable	Fairly uncomfortable	Somewhat comfortable	Fairly comfortable	Very comfortable

What were you thinking and feeling during today's group?

_____

_____

_____

_____

How are you feeling now?

_____

_____

_____

_____

HANDOUT 1.20

Trauma Reminders Worksheet

"Outside" trauma reminders	Personal trauma reminders
Person, place, or situation • Friend or family member who was with you when it happened • The house, room, school where it occurred or similar places • Being in traffic, watching a movie about family	
Sound, smell, or sight • Loud noises, footsteps, male/female voices, school bell, heavy breathing, groaning, gunshots • Food cooking, hospital smell, burning smell, perfume • A person who resembles person who hurt you, police officers, police car, a color	
Time or date • Holiday, birthday, date of death, time we always did something together, bed time, dinner time	
• Changes in routine • Moving to a new home/community • Changing schools • Entering foster care • Therapy • New rules at home	
• Doing what you were doing when the trauma occurred • Running • Sleeping or preparing to go to sleep	
Media • News or TV shows come on that remind you of what happened, violent TV shows, shows about abuse, prison, hospitals, courtrooms	
"Inside" trauma reminders	**Personal trauma reminders**
Bodily sensations • Heart pounding fast, breathing quickly, shaky muscles, stomach ache	
An emotion • Feeling scared, sad, angry, guilty, embarrassed, vulnerable, anxious, ashamed, or even happy, in love, contented, if that is how you were feeling just before the terrible thing happened	
A thought • Thinking about what happened • Thinking of a similar situation • Thinking it was your fault • Worrying about someone who was there • Thinking you have to get even	

HANDOUT 1.21

Loss Reminders Worksheet

"Missing" reminders	Personal loss reminders
Empty situations Situations in which the person used to be present, such as in certain classes or rooms, their bedroom, favorite chair, clothes, or place at the table	
Shared activities Activities that we used to do together, such as playing games, going for walks, doing homework together, sports, listening to music, and eating meals together	
Rituals Activities such as graduations, birthdays, holidays, school activities, family reunions, award ceremonies, and weddings and other celebrations	
"Changed life" reminders	Personal "changed life" reminders
• Taking on added responsibilities, more chores • Losing privacy • Having less money than before • Moving to a new neighborhood or school • Having to make new friends • Not having someone to help with schoolwork • Having a surviving parent or relative less available than before • Not having anyone who listens to me the way that person did	

HANDOUT 1.22

How I React to and Cope with Distressing Reminders, Page1

Pick a specific time during the week when you were reminded of a distressing past experience. It may be a trauma reminder or a loss reminder.

If you encountered many types of reminders this week, pick the most upsetting one.

First, describe the reminder you experienced.

_____

_____

_____

Second, describe what the reminder involved. (Check all that apply.)

Things outside of me	Things inside of me
____ Something you **saw?**	____ Something you were **thinking?**
____ Something you **heard?**	____ An **emotion** you felt?
____ Something you **smelled?**	____ A **bodily sensation?** (tight muscles, fast heartbeat, dizzy, stomach ache)
____ Something you **tasted?**	
____ Something you **touched?**	____ Other (describe) _____

Third, describe briefly what the past distressing experience was.

_____

_____

_____

_____

How I React to and Cope with Distressing Reminders, Page 2

Fourth, describe your reactions to being reminded:

My reactions to being reminded:	Yes	No
Posttraumatic stress:		
1. Upsetting thoughts or pictures of a trauma or severe stress came into my mind when I did not want them to		
2. I got very upset, afraid, or sad when I was reminded of a stress or trauma		
3. I tried to stay away from the people, places, or things that reminded me of my stress or trauma		
4. I felt different and isolated from other people		
5. I had trouble concentrating or paying attention		
6. I had strong feelings in my body when I was reminded of what happened (heart beating fast, headache, stomach ache		
7. I felt jumpy or got startled (spooked) easily		
8. I was "on the lookout" for danger or things that I am afraid of		
9. I felt irritable or was easily angered		
10. It was hard for me to have normal feelings, such as pleasure, happiness, or sadness		
Grief (due to death, separation, or disappearance) of a cherished person or possession:		
1. I missed someone or something dear to me		
2. I felt lonely or sad when I was reminded of the absence of someone I care about		
3. I thought I wasn't getting what I needed because the person I care about wasn't there		
4. I felt angry or resentful about the loss		
5. I avoided talking or thinking about the person/possession because it was too painful		
6. I didn't do positive things I wanted or needed to do because they reminded me of what I lost		
Depression:		
1. I felt helpless, out of control		
2. My thoughts were discouraging or hopeless		
3. I felt worthless, like I couldn't do anything right		
4. I didn't feel pleasure or enjoy things		
5. I felt sad or "down" in my emotions		
6. I felt guilty, like things were my fault		
Anxiety:		
1. I felt nervous or anxious		
2. I felt frightened or scared		
3. I worried about things over and over		
4. I felt tense or "on edge"		
5. I feared that something bad will happen		

How I React to and Cope with Distressing Reminders, Page 3

Fifth, describe how you coped with the reminder:

Coping strategy	Yes	No
1. I thought about something else, tried to forget it, and/or went and did something else like watched TV or played a game to get if off my mind (Distraction)		
2. I stayed away from people, kept my feelings to myself, and just handled the situation on my own (Social withdrawal)		
3. I tried to see the good side of things and/or concentrated on something good that could come out of the situation (Optimism)		
4. I believed that I brought the problem onto myself and blamed myself for causing it. (Self-blame)		
5. I believed that someone else caused the problem and blamed them for making me go through this (Other-blame)		
6. I thought of ways to solve the problem, talked to others to get more facts and information about what to do, and/or tried to solve the problem (Problem-solving)		
7. I complained, yelled, screamed, or hit something (Venting)		
8. I tried to calm myself by talking to myself, praying, taking a walk, listening to music, or trying to relax (Calming oneself)		
9. I kept thinking and wishing this had never happened, and/or that I could change what had happened (Regret)		
10. I just accepted the problem because I knew I could not do anything about it (Acceptance)		
11. I tried to NOT have any emotional reactions by blocking off my feelings (Emotional suppression)		
12. I talked to someone about how I was feeling (Seeking emotional support)		
13. I turned to my family, friends, or other adults to help me feel better (Support-seeking)		

HANDOUT 1.23

If your heart is racing, palms sweating, stomach queasy, or muscles tight, remind yourself that this is just your body's automatic alarm system reacting strongly to keep you safe. Help it get "unstuck."

---

1. *Scan* the environment to make sure that you are safe.

- If you are safe, then *stop*, take some deep breaths, and slow down your thoughts. You are safe.

---

2. *Look* inside to your thoughts, emotions, and senses.

- What can you see, hear, feel, smell, and taste?
- How does your body feel?
- What are you thinking?
- What emotions do you feel?

---

3. *Orient* yourself.

- Look around you to see where you are, what time it is, who is there with you.
- Feel the floor under your feet, where you are sitting, and familiar objects you are touching.

---

4. Find your *wise* mind.

- You are not in danger.
- Thank your body for trying to keep you safe.
- Tell yourself that you will feel calmer soon.
- Find one main feeling.
- Find one main thought.
- Choose to stay in control by continuing to breathe slowly while your body calms down.
- Choose a coping response to use to keep yourself safe and out of trouble, such as asking for a time-out, talking with someone, journaling, or getting some exercise.

HANDOUT 1.24

Check-Out Feedback Form

Session topic: Learning to Cope with Trauma and Loss Reminders

Your date of birth: _____

Today's date: _____

Facility: _____

What about today's session was most useful to you? Which activities and materials were the most helpful?

_____

_____

_____

What specific suggestions do you have for how to make the group better?

_____

_____

_____

How comfortable were you about today's topic? (Please circle a number.)

1	2	3	4	5
Extremely uncomfortable	Fairly uncomfortable	Somewhat comfortable	Fairly comfortable	Very comfortable

What were you thinking and feeling during today's group?

_____

_____

_____

_____

How are you feeling now?

_____

_____

_____

_____

HANDOUT 1.25

MUPS: Survival Coping Responses That "Mess You Up"

MUPS	Consequences	
	Short-term	Long-term
1. Avoiding all people and places that make you feel bad		
2. Withdrawing from friends and family		
3. Withdrawing from activities		
4. Not asking for help when you need it		
5. Denying to people close to you that you have a problem		
6. Dropping out of the group		
7. Drinking alcohol/taking drugs		
8. Over-eating		
9. Excessive TV or video games		
10. Doing risky or dangerous things		
11. Acting angry and aggressive/getting into fights		
12. Blaming others/overreacting to little things		
13. Feeling super guilty or responsible for what happened		
14. Not taking care of yourself (sleep, diet, exercise, grooming, etc.)		
15. Getting sick		
16. Numbing out, going into "I don't care" mode		
17. Cutting yourself		

HANDOUT 1.26

Developing a Positive Personal Coping Toolkit

	How helpful?		
	Not	**Maybe**	**Yes**
SLOW down: Scan/Stop, Look inside, Orient, Wise mind			
Self-talk:			
Disrupting negative thoughts			
Thought-stopping			
Calming self-talk			
Difference between *then* and *now*			
Reduce unnecessary reminders			
Prepare (self-talk, planning, support) for reminders			
Relax (breathing, muscle relaxation)			
Build resilience (eat well, stay active, exercise, build self-esteem, etc.)			
Distraction through positive activities (sports, exercise, hobbies, reading)			
Seek support (from friends, family, counselor, etc.)			
Time-out			
Journal			
(Other):			

HANDOUT 1.27

Disrupting Negative Self-Talk and Rules for Writing Self-Calming Phrases

Rules for Writing Self-Calming Phrases

- Avoid writing *negatives* in your phrase. Instead of saying "I'm not going to get nervous when I go into the lunchroom" try saying, "I am calm and confident about going into the lunchroom."
- Keep your phrase in the *present tense*.
- Keep them in the *first person*. Begin them with "I" or refer to "I" somewhere in the statement.
- It's important that you have some belief in your positive self-talk.
- Don't choose something just because it is positive; it's got to be right for you!
- Tell yourself, "That was then. This is now. I'm safe now."

Disrupting Negative Self-Talk

1. *Notice* that you are engaging in negative self-talk.
2. *Stop* and ask yourself any or all of the following questions:
    - "What am I telling myself that is making me feel this way?"
    - "Do I really want to do this to myself?"
    - "Do I really want to stay upset?"
3. *Relax* or *distract*
4. *Counter* negative self-talk by repeating a positive coping statement or affirmation over and over again.

HANDOUT 1.28

Using a Positive Personal Coping Toolkit

List your trauma reminders here and decide how helpful the following coping strategies will be before, during, or after a time when you are reminded.

_____

_____

_____

_____

	How helpful?		
	Not	**Maybe**	**Yes**
SLOW down: Scan/Stop, Look inside, Orient, Wise mind			
Self-talk:			
Disrupting negative thoughts			
Thought stopping			
Calming self-talk			
Difference between _then_ and _now_			
Reduce unnecessary reminders			
Prepare (self-talk, planning, support) for reminders			
Relax (breathing, muscle relaxation)			
Build resilience (eat well, stay active, exercise, build self-esteem, etc.)			
Distraction through positive activities (sports, exercise, hobbies, reading)			
Seek support (from friends, family, counselor, etc.)			
Time-out			
Journal			
(Other):			

HANDOUT 1.29

Check-Out Feedback Form

Session topic: Learning Coping Skills

Your date of birth: _____

Today's date: _____

Facility: _____

What about today's session was most useful to you? Which activities and materials were the most helpful?

_____

_____

_____

What specific suggestions do you have for how to make the group better?

_____

_____

_____

How comfortable were you about today's topic? (Please circle a number.)

1	2	3	4	5
Extremely uncomfortable	Fairly uncomfortable	Somewhat comfortable	Fairly comfortable	Very comfortable

What were you thinking and feeling during today's group?

_____

_____

_____

_____

How are you feeling now?

_____

_____

_____

_____

HANDOUT 1.30

Sizing Up a Situation

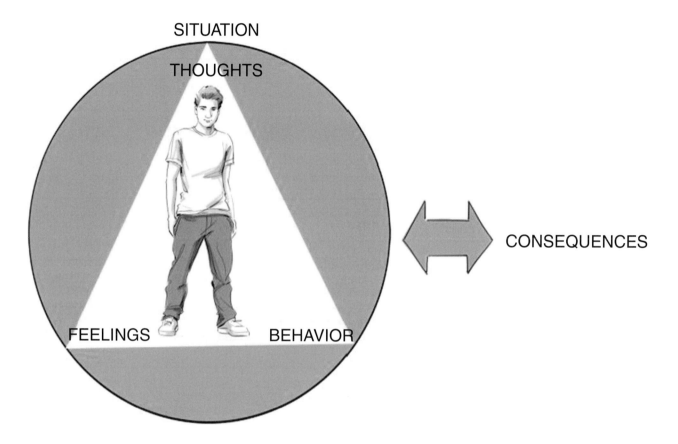

HANDOUT 1.31

Sizing Up a Situation: "He Did That On Purpose!"

HANDOUT 1.32

Sizing Up a Situation: "I Guess He Wasn't Watching Where He Was Going."

HANDOUT 1.33

Sizing Up a Situation: Taking a Test

HANDOUT 1.34

Sizing Up a Situation: Invitation

THOUGHT	EMOTION
	Angry
	Sad
	OK

HANDOUT 1.35

Hurtful Thoughts Checklist

Which distressing thoughts am I likely to have?	
Feeling unloved and unwanted	**Self-criticism**
___No one understands me	___I'm weird
___No one cares about me	___I'm ugly
___No one likes me	___I'm weak
___No one wants me	___I'm stupid
___I'll never fit in	___I'm a loser
___I'll always be alone	___I'm trapped
___No one needs me	___I'm inferior
___If I shared how I feel with others, they wouldn't care	___I'm deficient (I'm not good enough)
	___I'm defective (there's something really wrong with me)
Hopelessness	___I'm too needy
___Things will always be like this	___I don't like myself (I hate myself)
___Things will never get better	___I'm worthless (I can't do anything right; I have nothing to offer)
___My future is hopeless	
___Nothing ever goes right for me	___I can't get along with anybody
Helplessness	**Distrust**
___I'm helpless (I'm powerless)	___No one should be trusted
___I have no one to turn to if I need help	___I always expect the worst from people
___My problems are so bad that nothing can help	___If I opened up to people, they would hurt me
___Things will never get better, so it's no use trying	___If I shared how I feel, people wouldn't like me
___I'm out of control	___I must not burden people with my problems
___I can't take it anymore; I can't handle this	
Preoccupation with danger	**Other hurtful thoughts**
___I always expect the worst will happen	___(describe) _____
___I must always be ready for the worst	___(describe) _____
___I can never allow myself to feel safe or to relax	___(describe) _____
Self-blame	___(describe) _____
___Bad things always happen to me (I have bad luck; I'm cursed; I'm jinxed)	___(describe) _____
	___(describe) _____
___I don't deserve to be happy	___(describe) _____
___I did something bad to deserve this	___(describe) _____
___This is all my fault	

HANDOUT 1.36

Helpful Thoughts Checklist

Which helpful thoughts can I use to challenge hurtful thoughts?	
Feeling loved or lovable (emotional closeness)	**Having confidence in my abilities**
__Someone understands me __Someone loves me __Some people can be trusted __I'm a good person __There' nothing wrong with me (I'm OK) __It's not my fault that bad things happen __I deserve to be happy __I'm as good as other kids __I can connect with people	__I have what it takes—I can do this __I'm smart __I'm a winner __There are some problems right now but I know I can handle them __I can do things as well as other kids __People respect me
Feeling liked or likeable (social connection)	**Having confidence in others**
__People like me __I'm a good friend __I fit in __I'm fun to be around __I'm cute	__There are people I can depend on if I need help __I'm not alone in this – other people have been through this and they will understand and know how to help me
Feeling needed	**Guidance and advice**
__People appreciate me __People need me __I'm important __The world is a better place because I'm here	__There are people I can go to who will know how to help
Other helpful thoughts	
___(describe) —————————————— ___(describe) —————————————— ___(describe) —————————————— ___(describe) —————————————— ___(describe) ——————————————	

HANDOUT 1.37

Replacing Hurtful Thoughts: "They Think I'm Weird"

HANDOUT 1.38

Replacing Hurtful Thoughts: "It Doesn't Matter"

HANDOUT 1.39

Three Steps to Taking Charge of Your Thoughts and Feelings

1. *"What am I feeling?"*

   Label your emotion(s) _____

   Rate its intensity (0–10): _____

2. *"Why am I feeling this way?"*

   What's happening **outside** of me? (Describe the situation):

   _____

   _____

   What's happening **inside** of me? (The hurtful thought or image – put it into words):

   _____

   _____

3. *"How can I feel better?"*

   (a) What are the problems with looking at the situation in this negative way? (what doesn't make sense or is counterproductive?)

   _____

   _____

   _____

   (b) What's a more positive and constructive way of looking at the situation?

   _____

   _____

   _____

   _____

   Re-rate the intensity of the emotion(s) you are feeling (0–10)

HANDOUT 1.40

Check-Out Feedback Form

Session Topic: Sizing Up a Situation

Your date of birth: _____

Today's date: _____

Facility: _____

What about today's session was most useful to you? Which activities and materials were the most helpful?

_____

_____

_____

What specific suggestions do you have for how to make the group better?

_____

_____

_____

How comfortable were you about today's topic? (Please circle a number.)

1	2	3	4	5
Extremely uncomfortable	Fairly uncomfortable	Somewhat comfortable	Fairly comfortable	Very comfortable

What were you thinking and feeling during today's group?

_____

_____

_____

_____

How are you feeling now?

_____

_____

_____

_____

HANDOUT 1.41

Common Thinking Errors Checklist

Think of a *hurtful thought* that often bothers you. Write the hurtful thought on the lines below. Does the hurtful thought contain any *errors in thinking*? Check all that apply. The next pages give more information about each thinking error.

____ **Filtering and discounting** (focusing on the negative, discounting the positive)

____ **Shoulds and musts** (having high and inflexible rules for how things "should" be)

____ **All-or-none thinking** (seeing things in black and white/either–or terms)

____ **Then is now** (responding to the present as if it is the traumatic past)

____ **Self-blame** (things are your fault when you actually have little influence over what happens)

____ **If it *feels* true it *is* true** (taking feelings as proof that something is really true)

____ **Self put-downs** (you put negative labels like "loser" on yourself and tear yourself down.)

____ **Permanent thoughts** (drawing big conclusions from small bits of information: if something is true once, it is always true; if something goes wrong, it always will.)

____ **Foretelling the future** (playing "fortune teller" by assuming that you can accurately predict future events)

____ **Mind-reading** (assuming you know what others are thinking)

____ **Catastrophizing** (thinking that things are much worse than they really are)

HANDOUT 1.42

Common Errors in Thinking, Page 1

Error in thinking	Description	Hurtful-thought examples
Filtering out and discounting	You focus on the negative aspects of a situation while "filtering out" its positive aspects by ignoring or minimizing them.	Who cares if Sandra likes me? Veronica doesn't! • It doesn't matter that I did well in *almost* all my classes. I didn't do well in *all* of them. • Nothing I do turns out right. • My parents' compliments don't matter. They *have* to say that.
Shoulds and musts	You have rigid and sometimes unrealistic expectations for yourself, others, and the world. If these expectations are not met you become upset.	• I shouldn't feel this way. • I must get an "A!" • I must never show any weakness. • I must never rely on others, because they might disappoint me and that would be awful. • I must never allow myself to get attached to someone again, because I might lose them too.
All-or-none thinking	Seeing things in black and white/either–or terms (I have to be perfect or I am a failure. There is no middle ground.)	• Because I didn't get an "A," it means I failed the class. • If talking about what happened makes me feel worse at first, then the program is not working. • If I can't forget what happened, my life will be ruined. • Because I have lost someone or something I dearly loved, I can never be happy again.
Then is *now*	You respond to a current situation as if it were a traumatic situation from your past.	• I can't trust anyone. • I must focus on day-to-day survival, not my future. • I must not get too close to anyone, because they or I could be gone tomorrow. • I can participate in risky behavior, because I probably won't live long anyway. • I should avoid going out at night, because that's when it happened. • I don't need to prepare for the future, because there's no guarantee there will even be one. • Whether I live or die is a matter of fate (whatever I try to do won't make any difference to what happens). • Danger is everywhere.

Common Errors in Thinking, Page 2

Error in thinking	Description	Hurtful-thought examples
Self-blame (it's my fault)	You see yourself as the cause of something bad that has happened when you actually had little or no influence over what took place. Or, you assume excessive responsibility for others' feelings or lives and then blame yourself for not fixing their problems yourself.	• If it weren't for me, this never would have happened. • If I were stronger, I wouldn't be having these problems. • If I can't make mom feel better, then it will mean I don't love her enough. • Mom is sad because of something I did. • It's my fault that … my father was killed; my parents got divorced; my mom is unemployed.
If it *feels* true it *is* true (emotional reasoning)	You take your feelings as proof that something is true.	• I feel like my sadness will never end (so it won't). • I have desires for revenge, so I must act on them. • I feel helpless, so I am. • I feel hopeless, so I should end it all. • I feel guilty, so I must have done something bad. • I feel scared, so I must be in danger. • I feel angry, so I must have been wronged.
Self put-downs	You put negative labels on yourself and tear yourself down.	• I feel worthless, so I am. • I feel unneeded, so I am. • I'm a loser. • I'm stupid. • I'm ugly. • I can't do anything right. • I'm worthless. • I'm unlovable. • I'm a victim. • There's something seriously wrong with me. • I'm irreparably damaged. • I'm helpless. • Bad things happen to me because I deserve it. • No one will want me after this has happened to me. • Sandra was late to our lunch date because she doesn't respect me.
Permanent thoughts	Drawing big, sweeping conclusions from very limited evidence. If something is true once, it will *always* be true; if things are bad now, they will *always* be bad. • (Look for "extreme" words like *always, never, everything, nothing, everyone, no one, completely, totally,* and *absolutely*.)	• Marco invited me to his party just because he feels sorry for me. • I'm *no* good at anything. • *No one* cares. • If talking about what happened makes me feel worse at first, then it will *always* make me feel worse. • If I haven't been able to figure out a way to solve my problems, then *no one* else can either. • *No one* can be trusted. • Because I feel bad now, then I'll *always* feel this way. • Things will *never* get better. • If Laurel turned me down for a date, it means that *every* girl I like will turn me down.

Common Errors in Thinking, Page 3

Error in thinking	Description	Hurtful-thought examples
Foretelling the future (playing "fortune-teller")	You assume that you can predict the future and treat your prediction as an established fact. Examples include: • Predicting that something will turn out badly, and acting accordingly (thus setting yourself up for failure). • You blame yourself for not preventing something terrible that happened.	• I just know I'll fail this test (so why even try to study?). • I know what my brother will do (so why waste the effort?). • I just know I won't be able to handle this group work (so why not just give up now?). • Things will *always* be this way. • If I start crying, I'll never stop. • I should have noticed *something* (a bad omen?) that would have told me what was about to happen that day. • I shouldn't have allowed my brother to be outside that day. • I should have known this was going to happen. • I just know we'll have to move again (and I won't be able to stand it!). • I can't forgive myself for not being there to save my friend. • It's my fault my brother died because I wasn't there to protect him. • (Even though they've never said it), I just know my family blames me for what happened.
Mind-reading	You assume that you know what other people think or know (especially about you!), and treat your *guess* as an established fact.	• I just know what Grandma will say, so why try to talk to her? • No one can understand what I've been through. • Unless this has happened to you, you won't know how to help me. • People don't really want to help me. • If I told the group how I really feel, or what really happened, they would reject me. • No one really cares about how I feel. • Everyone thinks this is my fault. • If I don't pass this test, I won't ever graduate. • I just know I'll totally bomb this test.
Catastrophizing	You predict that the worst outcome will happen; OR, When something bad *does* happen, you tell yourself that it is unbearably awful and catastrophic.	• If I can't forget this experience, then I'll never be happy. • Nothing matters after what I've lost. • Because my life will never be the same, my life is forever ruined. • Because my life won't go as I had planned and hoped, I can never have a good life.

HANDOUT 1.43

Youth Blaming Self for Parents' Fighting

HANDOUT 1.44

Youth Misinterpreting a Teacher's Attentions

HANDOUT 1.45

Youth Self-Criticizing for Grief Reactions

HANDOUT 1.46

SKITS

Skit 1 – Mother and Teen Talk About Money

Mother: "I'm sorry I can't get you those new shoes. We just can't afford it."

Teen: (Angrily) "We can't afford anything!"

(Thinking to self) I can't remember the last time she got me anything. I'm never going to have anything new or that doesn't look all ratty. Everybody is going to be looking at my shoes and making comments.

Skit 2 – Two Friends Talk About Sports

Matt: "Hey, they're having tryouts for the football team next week. Let's practice and we'll both get on the team. That will be awesome!"

David: "It won't happen. I never get chosen for teams, plays, or anything.   Anyway, the coach just picks his local favorite boys to play."

Skit 3 – Two Friends at School Discuss Grades

(Sarah and David pick up their math tests at the end of class.)

Sarah: "Hey David. What did you get?"

David: "A 'D!' That must be the lowest grade in the class. I am so stupid! I won't pass this class."

Sarah: "I didn't do that well either. Maybe we could study together."

David: "Forget it. I'll never understand this stuff."

Skit 4 – Parent with Teen Discuss an Accident

Mother: (comes into teenager's room) "Did you hear about your cousin? He got in a bad accident coming home from that dance club last night."

Teen: (Thinking to self) "I told him not to go without me. I should have been driving. I always hurt the people around me."

Skit 5 – Teen Vows to Get Even With Abusive Stepfather

(Teen comes home from school to find his little brother Andy with bruises on his face and arms.)

Andy: "Our stepdad beat me up this morning."

Teen: (Thinking to self) "I'm going to find that guy and kill him."

Skit 6 – Parent Tells Teen She Lost Her Job

Mom: "I just lost my job. I don't know what we are going to do."

Teen: (Thinking to self) "I'll quit school and start dealing drugs so that my mom and my little sisters will have something to live on."

Skit 7 – Girl Sees Teacher in the Hallway

(Sarah's male teacher walks toward her in the hallway smiling.)

Teacher: "Hello, Sarah."

Sarah: (Thinking to self) "He's looking at me funny. I bet he wants to screw me. All men want from me is sex."

HANDOUT 1.47

Three Steps to Taking Charge of your Thoughts and Feelings

1. **"What am I feeling?"**

   Label your emotion(s) _____

   Rate its intensity (0–10): _____

2. **"Why am I feeling this way?"**

   What's happening **outside** of me? (Describe the situation):

   _____

   _____

   What's happening **inside** of me? (Put the hurtful thought or image into words):

   _____

   _____

3. **"HOW can I feel better?"**

   (a) Does the hurtful thought contain **errors in thinking**? (check all that apply):

   ____ **Filtering and discounting** (focusing on the negative, discounting the positive)

   ____ **Shoulds and musts** (having high and inflexible rules for how things "should" be)

   ____ **All-or-none thinking** (seeing things in black and white/either–or terms)

   ____ **Then is now** (responding to the present as if it is the traumatic past)

   ____ **Self-blame** (things are your fault when you actually have little influence over what happens)

   ____ **If it feels true it is true** (taking feelings as proof that something is really true)

   ____ **Self put-downs** (You put negative labels like "loser" on yourself and tear yourself down)

   ____ **Permanent thoughts** (drawing big conclusions from small bits of information: if something is true once, it is always true; if something goes wrong, it always will)

   ____ **Foretelling the future** (assuming you can accurately predict future events)

   ____ **Mind-reading** (assuming you know what others are thinking)

   ____ **Catastrophizing** (thinking that things are much worse than they really are)

   (b) What **evidence** appears to **support** the hurtful thought? (What reasons do I have to believe it?):

   _____

   What **evidence does not** appear to **support** the hurtful thought?

   _____

   (c) Choose a helpful thought: what's a more positive and constructive way of looking at the situation?

   _____

   _____

   Re-rate the intensity of the emotion you are feeling (0–10):

HANDOUT 1.48

Check-Out Feedback Form

Session topic: Identifying and Challenging Hurtful Thoughts

Your date of birth: _____

Today's date: _____

Facility: _____

What about today's session was most useful to you? Which activities and materials were the most helpful?

_____

_____

_____

What specific suggestions do you have for how to make the group better?

_____

_____

_____

How comfortable were you about today's topic? (Please circle a number.)

1	2	3	4	5
Extremely uncomfortable	Fairly uncomfortable	Somewhat comfortable	Fairly comfortable	Very comfortable

What were you thinking and feeling during today's group?

_____

_____

_____

_____

How are you feeling now?

_____

_____

_____

_____

HANDOUT 1.49

Five Steps to Getting Support

1. **"What do I want?"**

    (a) **Look inside yourself**: "What am I thinking and feeling that I could use support in dealing with?" Do I want:
      - Someone to just listen and try to understand?
      - A hug?
      - Companionship?
      - To feel needed?
      - Encouragement that I can handle a difficult situation?
      - Reassurance that someone is there for me if I need them?
      - Feedback or advice?

    (b) **Look outside yourself**: "What's happening in my life that I need support in dealing with?" Do I want:
      - Advice?
      - Help with something?
      - Things/materials/money?

2. **"Whom should I ask?"** Think about your relationships with the people you know. Who has been, or could be, a good source of support for what you want?

    - Which of my relationships has been a *good source of this type of support in the past*? Could I go to a parent? A guardian? A sibling? A close friend?
    - Do I have *other relationships that I could use to create the type of support that I want*?

    For example, even though I have never done this before, do I have an aunt or uncle, or a family friend, who I think would be a good listener if I asked? What about a favorite teacher?

    - Could I *develop a new relationship* to meet my needs? For example, if I want companionship, do I know someone my age who I could invite to do something fun?

3. **Find the right time to ask.**

    - "Do you have the time to talk right now?"
    - "When would you have the time to talk?"

4. **Ask with an "I" message.**

    - Tell them how I'm feeling.
    - Tell them about my situation and how it led me to feel the way I do.
    - Tell them what I want them to do.

    Example: "I'm feeling sad right now because of something I heard at school this afternoon. Can we talk about it?" "I just want you to listen for now, without telling me what to do about it."

5. **Express sincere appreciation.**

    - Graciously thank them and let them know what their support means to you.
    - Be specific, if you can, about HOW they have helped you and the difference that it has made.

    This feedback will encourage them and help them know how to help you in the future.

HANDOUT 1.50

Practice Exercise: "I" Message for Sharing

Name: _____

Date: _____

1. I'm feeling:

    _____

    _____

    _____

2. When ... (describe what happened outside and inside you):

    Outside me: (Who? What? Where? When?)

    _____

    _____

    _____

    Inside me: (Hurtful thoughts? Helpful thoughts?)

    _____

    _____

    _____

3. I want you to:

    _____

    _____

    _____

4. Potential problems:

    _____

    _____

    _____

HANDOUT 1.51

Things That *I* Can Do: My Personal Coping Toolkit

Challenge hurtful thoughts with helpful thoughts

- Use the Three-Step Model I have learned.

Seek support from others

- Use the five steps to getting support that I learned.

Relax

- Breathe deeply and slowly.
- Listen to relaxing music.

Take a time-out

- Walk away and calm down – do something else for a while.

Write in my journal

- Write about the situation, my thoughts and feelings.

Exercise regularly

- Walk, hike, jog, play soccer, tennis, swim, bike, lift weights, go to the gym.

Distract myself through positive activities

- Get my mind off things by going to a positive film, working on hobbies, socializing with friends, reading a book, listening to music, writing poems or stories, etc.

Keep a consistent daily routine

- Get up at the same time and prepare for sleep at the same time. If I have trouble sleeping, this practice can be especially helpful. (I may also find it helpful to use my bed *only* for sleeping.)

Reward myself

- Treat myself to something positive when I do something well. Praise myself, buy myself something healthy, or engage in a favorite (healthy) activity.

Spiritual

- Read an uplifting book.
- Pray or meditate.
- Listen to inspiring music.
- Participate in religious services or other uplifting group activities.
- Memorize uplifting quotes and use them as "helpful thoughts."

HANDOUT 1.52

Group Goals Worksheet

Check only the items that are still a goal for you to work on. Please also add any new goals you have since you filled out your first worksheet.

By the end of this intervention:				
I want to feel *LESS*: *(please circle all that apply)*				
Nervous	Scared	Angry	Upset	Sad
I want to feel *MORE*: *(please circle all that apply)*				
Happy	Calm	Excited	Relaxed	
I want to change the way I do things and think about things: *(please check all that apply)*				
☐	Calm myself down when I feel upset.			
☐	Think about things that happened without feeling upset.			
☐	Talk about things that happened without feeling upset.			
☐	Stop avoiding things that made me nervous.			
☐	Do more of the things that I used to do.			
☐	Think more about things before I do them.			
☐	Make better decisions.			
☐	Have fewer problems with my family.			
☐	Have fewer problems with my friends.			
I also want to change:				

HANDOUT 1.53

Check-Out Feedback Form

Session topic: recruiting support, and gathering feedback on Module 1

Your date of birth: _____

Today's date: _____

Facility: _____

What about today's session was most useful to you? Which activities and materials were the most helpful?

_____

_____

_____

What specific suggestions do you have for how to make the group better?

_____

_____

_____

How comfortable were you about today's topic? (Please circle a number.)

1	2	3	4	5
Extremely uncomfortable	Fairly uncomfortable	Somewhat comfortable	Fairly comfortable	Very comfortable

What were you thinking and feeling during today's group?

_____

_____

_____

_____

How are you feeling now?

_____

_____

_____

2 Working through Traumatic or Loss Experiences

Session 2.1: Preparing to Share Personal Trauma or Loss Experiences (Sharing our Stories)
Session 2.2: Group Narrative Sharing Sessions
Session 2.3: Review of Group Sharing and Exploration of Beliefs and Expectations
Session 2.4: Guide for Conducting Individual Narrative and Pull-Out Sessions

Introduction

Narrative Work with Adolescents

In Module 2, the clinician guides the adolescent to select and then systematically "revisit" a traumatic experience central to their life. The sessions of the module progress from a more restricted account to an in-depth and highly personal "unpacking" of their experience. In doing so, the adolescent is helped to better appreciate and address the profound impact on their emotional and interpersonal lives, their emerging self-identity, their expectations and aspirations for the future, and their developmental trajectory. This work is challenging and poignant for the youth, the clinician, and other group members.

At the same time, the process of constructing and sharing a trauma narrative in a safe and supportive setting has multiple therapeutic benefits: it provides access, increases tolerance, and lends coherence to memories and emotions that may have been avoided for years; it reduces reactivity to these memories; it provides insight into the formation of current triggers and self-defeating beliefs and expectations; and, through the act of sharing and having others bear witness, it reduces isolation and opens a path to a softening of self-recriminations.

At the beginning of Module 2 it is important to review with the adolescent the skills they have acquired in Module 1. These skills include managing psychological and physiological reactivity, managing strong emotions, and recruiting appropriate social support to help with recurring distress. They have practiced identifying, anticipating, and managing trauma and loss reminders, and understand how these are linked to their past experiences and current reactions. And because the trauma narrative is, in and of itself, a powerful reminder and a source of renewed temporary distress, the Module 1 skills will boost their confidence to meet the challenge of Module 2. The clinician encourages them by explaining how this work will help connect details of their subjective experience with a wider range of reminders and trauma and loss themes in their daily lives. The payoff for the adolescent will be a greater awareness

and control of his or her memories and reactions. Given the inherent adolescent push for independence, this should be a motivator to undertake the narrative work in this module.

Don't underestimate the capacity of adolescents to do the work of this module. They are good at it. The trauma narrative work is interactive. It is assisted remembering, co-constructed, and shared. Clinicians have to be prepared to hear everything, however horrifying or painful. The adolescents must be supported in speaking in the most direct and genuine manner about the traumatic details and their most personal thoughts, feelings, and attributions of motivation and accountability. Techniques in each session are designed to facilitate this type of exploration and communication. Mobilization of the adolescent's sense of courage underlies accomplishing the therapeutic work of this module. Keep in mind that the adolescent may not have felt courageous during the traumatic experience, and that these sessions may restore this important facet of the adolescent's self-concept.

The Complexity of Traumatic Experience

Module 2 draws on a comprehensive model of the complexity of traumatic experiences. Traumatic situations involve a *convergence of external and internal threats and dangers* represented by "What's happening outside of me" and "What's happening inside of me," that culminate in irreversible moments of life threat, violation, or injury to oneself or others. The internal threat can arise from multiple sources. The acceleration and intensity of affective and physiological responses can, themselves, feel threatening and intolerable. A sense of *devastating personal consequence* can set in even while the event is still unfolding. For example, adolescents may experience damage to their psychosexual self-concept and life plans ("No one will want me now") while being sexually assaulted or after receiving a disfiguring injury. Further, an adolescent shooting victim may foresee the destruction of his future plans ("Now I will never go to college") while his life still hangs in the balance during the ambulance ride to the hospital.

A traumatic experience, however brief in duration, is complex and made up of many different moments. Each moment can contain a unique configuration of sensory information, changing appraisal of threat and danger, emotional and physical reactions, and thoughts regarding wishes for prevention or protective interventions. There is no "single" traumatic event – rather there are many moment-to-moment reactions and responses. Among these moments there may be a series of "traumatic moments'" where perceptions of external threat converge with internal perceptions of helplessness and the failure of any protective thoughts or actions. Each of these moments may be linked to different sets of reminders or triggers that continue to elicit problematic responses from the adolescent. A key therapeutic approach involves helping the youth identify active trauma or loss reminders, appreciate how these continue to exert influence, and develop strategies to moderate their impact.

Worst Moments

This model also recognizes the importance of what we refer to as "worst moments." These can be highly idiosyncratic and searing memories that are sequestered into a private part of the self. Clinicians can be surprised when youth nominate their worst moment(s). They may coincide with an external traumatic moment but be focused on an internal threat from their bodies' response that made them feel like a participant in their own assault or endangerment. For example, a teenage girl described her worst moment as drowning on her own swallowed blood after being shot in the face. A worst moment may capture the horrific experience of receiving an unacceptable apology. For example, an adolescent described the most painful moment of her mother's murder was when her father, who had committed the murder and was in a holding cell at the police station, said to her, "I'm sorry." A worst moment can come days after the initial traumatic situation. A youth was the driver of the car when his best friend was shot and killed in a road rage incident. At the funeral, the father of the dead teen refused to shake hands or acknowledge him in any way implying that he was to blame for the death. While identifying traumatic moments and understanding how they are linked to symptoms and current reminders represents an important part of the work in Module 2, a careful search for a worst moment (or moments) can capture what still hurts the most.

Protective Intervention Thoughts

One of the best ways to understand the appraisal and response to the moments of danger, and to appreciate the convergence of external and internal threat, is to explore the protective intervention thoughts as they change over the course of a traumatic situation. Protective intervention thoughts share a common theme of envisioning an action that could have altered the course of events and consequences. For example, an adolescent is helpless to stop his father from shooting his mother and thinks, "I wish I had unloaded his gun when I had the chance last week." Protective intervention thoughts can be wishing for outside parties to intervene, like straining to hear the distant sounds of an ambulance siren. Sometimes even thoughts during a rape can be about social justice, "I need to remember his face so I can get him arrested and put in jail."

Clinical studies of remembering traumatic experiences among children and adolescents indicate that intervention thoughts and fantasies are integral to traumatic memories, and that efforts at recall invariably mobilize these accompanying thoughts or fantasies, whether they were entertained during or immediately after the trauma or as they have evolved over time. As adolescents are assisted in approaching different moments of their traumatic experience, so too will they be confronted by intervention considerations. As they are helped to identify perceived failures of the social contract (at home, at school, in the wider community), there is an opportunity for constructive pro-social considerations that can supersede and diminish the force of thoughts and fantasies that erode their impulse control, which is a specific task of Module 4.

Layering of Threat to Self and Others

There can be a complex layering of threat to self and others in traumatic situations. Adolescents are often with peers or family during traumatic experiences. Their reactions can shift back and forth from a focus on their own safety to concerns about harm to others. When the threat to self during a traumatic event becomes imminent, adolescents may experience an unsettling moment of "losing track of" or "forgetting about" others as they become consumed by threats to their own survival, the "tunnel vision" of extreme terror. Identifying these moments are important because they can serve as a precursor to subsequent estrangements and inform strategies to bridge them with family members and close friends. Estrangements also occur when family members or friends serve as reminders to one another. This aspect of the experience should sound an alert to the clinician to anticipate which portions of the traumatic experience may be responsible for interpersonal distancing or disruptions. For example, one group member who witnessed her best friend being shot by a stray gang bullet identified "seeing her face screaming, 'I'm gonna die'" as a powerful intrusive image. She was deeply saddened and hurt that although she was "there for her and helped her when it happened," her friend now avoided her because "she told me that being with me makes her think about when she almost got killed" (Layne et al., 2001).

Adolescents may be particularly susceptible to interpersonal conflicts that arise at different moments within the experience. Loyalty to friends can be profoundly challenged by attributions about the ways in which they or others behaved, with concerns over actions that increased harm, with failed protection or intervention, or left them feeling abandoned or deserted, even by those who were not there. Similar issues can arise with family members or adult mentors. There is particular adolescent vulnerability to what we refer to as "an existential dilemma," where an adolescent is forced to choose between seeking self-protection versus coming to the aid of others, whether friends or family members. This can be an agonizing dilemma, often made even more intense by cries of distress and pleas for help.

There are often different foci of concern over time. There is a radical shift in attention when physical integrity is violated or injury occurs. Whereas prior to being physically assaulted or injured, youth are focused on appraising and responding to an imminent threat, now attention is on their pain and concerns about how badly they have been hurt, about prospects of rescue, and the need for urgent medical attention. In addition, during physical violation, including sexual assault, and serious injury, self-protective measures may be mobilized, including dissociative responses, to contend with the internal threat and pain.

Clinicians should also bear in mind that a traumatic "event" is not over once the violence ceases and the immediate threat recedes. The adolescent's attention may quickly be drawn to seeking outside help (e.g. police, paramedics, adults), trying to aid injured family members or friends, receiving acute medical care, and the ensuing separation from others including family members or friends who are seriously injured or dead. The modularized design of TGCTA reflects an understanding that many traumatic situations involve both trauma *and* loss, in which adolescents may experience acute grief reactions to witnessing a death even while the threat to themselves continues. This flexible design builds tolerance for "unbearable" moments when, for instance, adolescents cannot go to a dying family member or friend even to comfort them in their last minutes because of the ongoing threat to their own life. In Module 3, which provides an avenue to understand and address initial and ongoing grief, mourning, and bereavement, the adolescent has the opportunity to answer in a personal way this profound feeling of incompleteness.

Developmental Themes

Module 2 takes into account the developmental dimensions that adolescents bring to their experience of traumatic situations. The sessions help youth to revisit their experiences, and gain an enriched appreciation of the influence of these experiences on their life while not allowing them to eclipse their identity and development (e.g. "I am a rape victim"). Their increasing awareness that death includes consideration of their own mortality is countered by a protective assertion of their own invulnerability. Further, whereas adults might describe feeling "resigned" at the moment of the infliction of harm or injury, adolescents often express a sense of protest and rage at "surrendering" to such an unavoidable moment of physical helplessness. Other general developmental themes of adolescence include physical prowess, sexual attractiveness, interpersonal intimacy, cooperation, and competitiveness. Furthermore, emerging group and self-identity have a role in the adolescent's experience of traumatic situations. These adolescent issues all

contribute to the moment-to-moment calculations of adolescents in appraising and responding to danger, in protecting themselves and others, and in seeking to secure safety, rescue, and repair.

The Trauma Narrative Process

There is a precise sequence to the narrative work in the manual so that the work is spread out over multiple "passes." The first pass takes place in the pre-treatment screening interview. At that point, the clinician elicits a brief journalistic account of selected trauma or loss experiences, which maps out the basic event without emotional or personal details. This is necessary in order to be protective of the youth, who may have never shared the experience. These are powerful stories that can be extremely evocative. Safe and productive sharing requires a "holding environment" provided by trusting relationships and a structured approach.

After the adolescent completes Module 1 and has been equipped with information about posttraumatic stress and grief, a personalized "toolbox" of coping strategies to manage reminders and strong emotional and behavioral reactions, and there is sufficient trust and familiarity built into the group and/or clinician relationship, then the adolescent may undertake the narrative work in Module 2. This entails a full retelling of the selected experience with the group or individual clinician acting as witness and support. A detailed guide is provided to help the clinician elicit the narrative in a way that weaves together the many strands of the experience: what was going on inside (emotions, thoughts, and sensory components) with what was going on outside (people, place, actions, etc.). It begins by establishing the context in the adolescent's life in which the event took place, focuses on the moment-to-moment experiences just before, during, and immediately after key events, and then concludes with supportive feedback from group members and the clinician. To personalize and enrich the adolescent's narrative, adolescents are also invited to use any media they like (music, rap, art, mix-tapes, etc.) to help give voice to their experience. During the final portion of the activity the adolescent is helped to reflect on the possible worst moments of the experience and ways in which the experience continues to intrude and impact his or her life.

A third collective narrative pass is accomplished in the final session in Module 2, in which group members are invited to share their experiences of telling and hearing the powerful narratives. Adolescents are helped to speak about ways they were touched or surprised by their own and other's narratives. Common themes and issues as well as shared misattributions or interpretations are discussed along with common characteristics of their personal worst moments. This gives way to a structured discussion of ways in which their personal trauma experiences have shaped them. Leaders help group members explore the impact of worst moments on group members' view of their future, their ability to feel safe and secure, their willingness to become close to others, their ability to feel in control of their lives, and their expectations about laws and society. Steps are provided to link specific experiences with current beliefs and expectations that may be obstacles to developing and living a good life. The final exercises are designed to help group members identify specific changes they would like to make in their lives, their beliefs, and their actions, and they are asked to commit to a first small step they will take in the weeks that follow.

Indicators for Individual Narrative Work or Pull-Out Sessions

There are a several indicators that support having one or more individual narrative sessions with an adolescent. A single pull-out session may be helpful if adolescents have difficulty identifying a primary experience on which to focus their narrative. This may be the case for youth who have experienced multiple or chronic forms of trauma. If a youth's selected experience includes graphic, violent, or disturbing scenes whose retelling may provoke strong reactions in a group, you may opt for pull-out sessions. You can conduct the narrative work in a series of individual sessions or have a single session in which the youth prepares an "impact-focused narrative" that focuses on the youth's thoughts and feelings rather than the details of the actual event.

Adolescents whose traumatic experiences are heavily stigmatized and may strain or exceed the group's capacity to fully contain and accept, such as sexual abuse or assault, may require pull-out sessions. Other examples of appropriate individual treatment, especially in juvenile justice and war-zone settings, are cases in which youths participated in acts involving malicious physical harm to others or had been tortured themselves.

Finally, adolescents who present with a dissociate subtype of posttraumatic stress disorder (PTSD) are likely to require more individual narrative work. The neurobiological signature of dissociation is emotional over-modulation and down-regulation of heart rate and other physiological reactions in approaching their traumatic experiences. New evidence suggests that individual trauma narrative work is especially helpful to these adolescents through a gradually assisted approach.

Options for Conducting the Narrative

The intent of the narrative work is to allow the youth to recount his or her selected trauma or loss experiences with sufficient engagement to begin to develop tolerance for the painful memories and to provide a window on their moment-to-moment experiences. The facilitator's task is to help guide the narration to the separate moments and their constituent sensations, appraisals, and emotions, and to help weave together what was happening "inside" the narrator and "outside" the narrator into an accessible whole. This is a key part of coming to terms with the past, making sense of it within the larger arc of their life, and uncovering guideposts for how they want to live their life going forward.

Alternative Ways to Share a Narrative

This section provides a general way to conduct a narrative whereby the youth shares his or her experiences via a sequentially related story. When this program was implemented in various school and juvenile justice settings, we also made available alternative creative methods of sharing the trauma or loss experience. We have had adolescents write and share original raps, make custom "mixtapes" with sequenced songs and lyrics, and drawn, collaged, and constructed visual presentations, all used to tell their story in a very personal and compelling manner. These are acceptable ways to accomplish the goals of this exercise. The key criteria are whether the approach serves to help the youth organize and make sense of his or her experience, whether it provides the youth with exposure to the experience through intense participation during the sharing, and whether it provides a means to access personal thoughts, feelings, and beliefs related to the experience. Feel free to explore these options with your group, though you would need to provide enough guidance before and during the sharing to ensure the therapeutic goals are met.

Option to Create a Timeline

During the narrative, you may also choose to draw a "timeline" that captures the key moments of the group member's story and provides a summary graphic document. This may be done by the facilitator or the second group leader, if there is one. Guidelines for creating the narrative timeline are provided in Section IV. Although the narrative may be elicited without creating a timeline, it is our experience that this concurrent activity has therapeutic value: it underscores the importance of the experience and provides a concrete product that the youth can refer back to for subsequent processing. It also provides a powerful graphic to help the youth see the experience in perspective as just one part of his or her life.

Indicators of Therapeutic Progress and of Readiness to Transition to the Next Module

The following indicators can be used to gauge ongoing therapeutic progress during Module 2 work and assess readiness to transition on to the next module (Module 3 or 4).

1. Monitoring of PTSD symptoms shows reductions in symptoms, *especially re-experiencing* and *avoidant* symptoms. If a signaling system (e.g. the University of California at Los Angeles (UCLA) Reaction Index "traffic lights") indicates a highest severity level for an intrusive image or memory, an individual session may be required to explore particularly distressing moments that have not yet been addressed.

2. Use the total PTSD symptom score as both a diagnostic indicator and a measure of distress. You should see

measurable symptom reduction before transitioning to the next module.

3. Certain problematic behaviors that may be "driven by" or reflect posttraumatic stress reactions (e.g. reckless or self-destructive behavior) may not demonstrate the same degree of change as, for example, intrusive memories, and will be further addressed in Module 4.

4. Adolescents are able to apply a trauma reminder management skill at least to one new reminder that has emerged during trauma narrative sessions.

References

Layne, C. M., Pynoos, R. S., & Cardenas, J. (2001). *Wounded Adolescence: School-Based Group Psychotherapy for Adolescents Who Sustained or Witnessed Violent Injury*. Washington, DC: American Psychiatric Association.

2.1 Preparing to Share Personal Trauma or Loss Experiences (Sharing our Stories)

Session Objectives

1. Introduce Module 2 and the narrative work.
2. Select an appropriate trauma or loss event on which to focus.
3. Provide an overview of what will happen in the narrative sessions.
4. Identify possible stress reactions to this work and put in place appropriate coping strategies.
5. Assign a home practice activity for the week.

An overall goal for this module is for group members to learn to tolerate recalling and describing stressful or traumatic events in their lives, to organize these experiences into a coherent account, and to better make sense of their experiences in a constructive fashion. To do this, a structured approach is provided to help select, organize and share their stories in a supportive environment. Additionally, group members learn to "bear witness" to each other's stories and provide support.

Pre-Session Preparation

Before the session, review the group members' personal timelines elicited during the pre-session interview to become familiar with the range of trauma or loss experiences reported by each youth. Note any experiences that may be challenging to address in the group setting. Also, have on hand the group members' workbooks with their Trauma Goals Worksheet and Personal Goal Worksheet (Handouts 1.02 and 1.03) and Handout 2.02, Selecting My Event.

Group leaders may choose to have individual meetings with group members to help them select an experience or develop a productive way to share experiences that may have violent, disturbing, or stigmatized aspects. Some group members who have experienced repeated or chronic forms of trauma may have difficulty identifying a single representative experience; others may wish to recount very recent trauma or loss experiences that evoke very strong reactions; while others may have endured severe or stigmatized experiences such as sexual assault or the suicide of a family member.

The purpose of the individual meeting is to make sure the youth selects an appropriate experience and is able to share the experience in a manner that will be productive and safe for all concerned. Many victims of sexual crimes have experienced other traumas that they can share with the group while working on the sexual trauma history in individual sessions. For violent or graphic experiences that a group member is reluctant to share with the group, she or he may be guided on how to provide a narrative that focuses on internal thoughts and feelings rather than specific details of the actual event. This is referred to as an *impact-focused narrative* and offers the benefit of a shared narrative that avoids extreme stress during the session.

Section number	Session overview
I	Check-in and Feeling Thermometer
II	Review practice assignment
III	Introduction to narrative work
IV	Selecting a specific event for the narrative work
V	Prepare for the group narrative sessions
VI	Practice assignment
VII	Check-out

Supplies

Every session	This session
• Group member workbooks	Summary of youth group goals worksheets from Session 1.1
• Flipchart	
• Large paper or easel pad	
• Colored markers or crayons	
• Pencils/pens	
• Kleenex	
• Tape	

Handouts in Workbook

Handout 2.01	Feeling Thermometer
Handout 2.02	Selecting My Event Worksheet
Handout 2.03	Telling My Story
Handout 2.04	Things That *I* Can Do: My Personal Coping Toolkit
Handout 2.05	Check-Out Feedback Form

Flipcharts

2.1a Session Highlights

1. Check-in and Feeling Thermometer
2. Review practice assignment
3. Select a specific traumatic event to work on
4. Prepare for the narrative sessions
5. Using the personal coping toolkit to manage reminders
6. Summary and calming exercise
7. Check-out

2.1b Three Steps to Take Charge of Your Thoughts and Feelings

Answer these questions:
1. "What am I feeling?"
2. "Why am I feeling this way?"
   • Look outside
   • Look inside – "What am I thinking?"
3. "How can I feel better?"

Session 2.1: Preparing to Share Personal Trauma or Loss Experiences (Sharing our Stories)

I. Check-In and Feeling Thermometer

- *How are you feeling right now?* (Use Handout 2.01, the Feeling Thermometer.)
- Practice with the group doing five to ten abdominal breaths.
- *Is anything going on that may make it difficult for you to keep your mind on the group today?*
- Briefly review (or have a group member review) Today's Highlights (Flipchart 2.1a).

II. Review Practice Assignment

- Direct group members to think about times during the past week when their Feeling Thermometer went higher or when they numbed out. Have each group member report on one such event and describe his/her reactions (thoughts, feelings, sensations, and actions). Then ask them which coping strategies they used: were they coping strategies that can "mess you up" (MUPS) or did they choose coping skills from Handout 2.04, Things That I Can Do: My Personal Coping Toolkit? Briefly

explore the outcomes and troubleshoot coping skill efforts for the next week.
- Use the Trauma Goals or Personal Goals Worksheets (Handouts 1.02 and 1.03) to provide feedback and encouragement about how the upcoming sessions can help them achieve these goals: for example, to avoid overreacting to small things, to feel less chronically angry, to sleep better, or to learn how to calm themselves.

III. Introduction to Narrative Work

- Provide a brief introduction and overview of the narrative work in this module.
- Explain the rationale for developing and sharing narratives of personal trauma or loss experiences.
- Answer any questions or concerns.

Note: Make sure to read the introduction to this module for a broad understanding of the theory and model on which the work in this module is based.

Broadly cover the following content:

- *This next part of the program involves revisiting your trauma or loss experiences in a structured, safe, and supportive way.*
- *The research is clear that by going over and sharing painful and difficult experiences in this kind of a supportive setting, you can develop greater control of your thoughts and memories and weaken the power of these*

memories to upset you or stress you out. It can also help you to make sense of what happened and, by sharing your story, help you to feel understood and supported.

- *We will do this work in steps: today we will clarify which experience you would like to focus on for these sessions. For some group members we will schedule individual meetings to further assist in this process. Then each of you will have an opportunity to share your experience with the group. At all points, you are in charge of what you talk about and what you share.*
- *It is our experience that this part of the group can be very rewarding and beneficial for group members and will call upon each of you to trust and support each other, and "have each other's backs." Most people say it is the best part of the group, so let's work together to ensure everyone has a good experience and feels respected and comfortable and safe. Any questions?*
- **Note**: This activity can also be done without a worksheet. You can do the primary steps simply as a group discussion.

IV. Selecting a Specific Event for the Narrative Work

Activity: Select a Specific Event for the Narrative Work

- Lead the group in a structured activity to select a specific event on which to focus for this part of the program. This can be either a trauma or a loss experience.
- The newly selected event may or may not be the experience identified in the pre-group interview.
- Determine if a group member would benefit from an optional individual session to select and prepare for the group narrative sharing.

Part 1

Part 1 of the worksheet is to help group members characterize their significant trauma and loss experiences in terms of "level of intensity *at the time*" and "level of intensity *now*" (when they think about it).

Group leaders should circulate around the group as members are filling out Part 1 and consult with them individually to help them select the event that will be most useful to focus on at this time. Keep in mind that they do not have to choose the event that is most extreme or currently provokes the most distress. The group leader should help make the judgment as to which event is currently most workable and may render the most benefit. Consideration should also be given to which events are appropriate for sharing with the group. For example, severe personal experiences such as child sexual abuse should be addressed in individual sessions rather than in this group.

During the pre-group interview, each of you selected one or more trauma or loss experiences that had a large influence on you and that you have continued to think about. Even though many of you have had more than one experience of this kind, we explained that this part of the group works best by focusing on one main experience.

- *Now we want to simply check back in with you to make sure you get a chance to work on an experience that will work well with this program and result in the most benefit for you.*
- *We are going to use a simple worksheet to help us do this.* (Have group members turn to Handout 2.02 on selecting an event or pass out copies of it.)
- *Keep in mind that you can choose to stick with the same event you chose before or you can choose a different one today.*

Part 2

Once group members have selected an event, they should fill out the checklist in Part 2. The selected experience should prompt mostly "Yes" responses on the questions provided.

Group leaders should circulate among group members to check in privately on their selected events and to answer any questions.

Deciding Whether to Have an Individual Pull-Out Session

As mentioned previously, you might choose to invite selected group members to have an optional individual meeting in the following circumstances:

- The group member seems agitated or is having difficulty selecting an experience.
- The group member is considering focusing on an extreme, violent, graphic, or stigmatized experience such as sexual assault or abuse.
- The group member is having difficulty with selecting a single experience because trauma occurred repeatedly over a long period of time.
- The group member does not have sufficiently clear memories of the event.

Or, you may simply wish to provide an opportunity for a more intensive and personalized narrative experience. In any case, you may schedule an individual session prior to or during the group narrative meetings.

Please refer to the guide for individual and pull-out sessions at the end of this module.

V. Prepare for the Group Narrative Sessions

- Briefly discuss what will transpire in the group narrative sessions, including the sequence of events and a description of the roles of the group member sharing the narrative, the group leaders, and the other group members.
- (Optional) Refer youth to Handout 2.03, Telling My Story, to look over as they think about what to include as they write or tell their stories. This lists suggestions for the kinds of content to include but does not need to be followed rigidly.
- Ask one to two group members to volunteer to tell their story in the next session.

Scheduling Group Narrative Sessions

During Module 2, it is expected that all group members will have an opportunity to share their narrative in the group and have time to draw upon the group for new perspectives on how they see themselves, their current concerns, and their future. This will generally be accomplished across two sessions as it is frequently difficult to engage in group discussion immediately after the narrative sharing experience, which can be emotionally taxing.

In terms of planning for a 50–60 minute group, it is recommended that two group members be prepared to share their narrative at each session even though there is usually only time for one sharing in an hour session. The second person is a backup in case the selected group member chooses not to share that day or is absent. Of course, longer sessions (70–90 minutes) are preferred, especially for this module. The longer period would provide time for up to two narratives per week plus additional time for processing and transition.

Provide Descriptions of the Group Narrative Sessions to Group Members

With the understanding that a "no surprises" approach is the best way to proceed in this sensitive portion of the program, provide a detailed description of how these sessions will be conducted. Highlight the roles and responsibilities for the group leaders, the group members, and the youth sharing his or her narrative. Invite group members to ask questions or comment at any point.

OVERVIEW OF THE GROUP SESSIONS

During the narrative sharing part of the program, the sessions will start with the usual check-in and then quickly transition to the narrative sharing activity.

Leader's role: During the narrative sharing, one group member will share his or her narrative. While the narrative is being shared, the group leader will support the youth, check in occasionally to see where he or she is at on the Feeling Thermometer and, sometimes, ask questions about what the youth was thinking or feeling at different moments in the experience.

Co-leader's role: If there is a co-leader, he or she should monitor group members' reactions, especially if anyone appears to be having a very strong reaction to the narrative sharing. As necessary, the co-leader may pull a group member aside to check in. Otherwise, the co-leader is alert to key themes and potential hurtful thoughts or problematic beliefs indicated in the story.

Narrative sharer's role: The group member designated to share a narrative is responsible simply for sharing his or her experiences before, during, and after the selected trauma or loss event. He or she will be guided by the leader to describe what was going on "outside" (events and actions) and "inside" (thoughts, feelings, interpretations, etc.). If the member has had an individual session to prepare a limited or "impact-focused narrative" he or she will be guided in doing just that.

Group member's role: While the narrative is being shared, group members will listen respectfully, without commenting. It is hoped that they will support the group member by listening from their heart and try to understand and feel what the experience was like for the person telling the story. And while group members may offer supportive utterances or words during the sharing, any comments should be reserved till after the narrative is completed, at which point they will be invited.

Group members should be prepped in terms of what kinds of comments are most helpful after a personal narrative is shared. You can encourage them to praise the person sharing for their courage or comment on their own reactions to the story and what they learned in the telling. Very often youth may start telling their own stories and experiences in a way that pulls the group focus onto them and away from the person who just shared. Group leaders should make it clear that the group focus should stay on the youth sharing his or her experiences and that each of them will have their own opportunity to share their experiences during their designated session.

In this preparatory session group leaders should explain that group members may become activated or experience upsurges of their own trauma or loss memories while listening to others' narratives. Explain that this is normal and that this provides an opportunity to think about and explore their own experiences. If they find themselves becoming stressed or anxious, they may use one or more of their personal coping strategies or speak with the group leader after the session.

At the end of this section, the leader should check in with the group, perhaps with the Feeling Thermometer, to see if there were any upticks in stress levels or concerns about this piece of work. If there seems to be the need, you may want to conduct a stress-reduction or grounding activity for the group.

VI. Practice Assignment

Describe the practice assignment for the coming week using Handout 2.04 (Things That *I* Can Do: My Personal Coping Toolkit). Group members should continue to identify situations that evoke a stress response (high on their Feeling Thermometers) and utilize one or more of their coping strategies as listed in Handout 2.04. They should come to the group prepared to share one or more of these experiences.

VII. Check-Out

- *How are you feeling now?* (Use the Feeling Thermometer ratings.)
- *What did you learn about yourself today?*
- *Please fill out the Check-Out Feedback Form (Handout 2.05). The title of today's session was "Preparing to Tell our Stories."*

If any group members are visibly agitated or troubled or report high levels of distress on the Feeling Thermometer, keep them after the group and determine an appropriate way to transition back to their settings.

2.2 Group Narrative Sharing Sessions

Session Objectives

1. Review the practice exercises.
2. Introduce the narrative activity and session structure.
3. Elicit one or more individual trauma narratives.
4. Group leaders take note of key aspects of the narrative including worst moments, hurtful thoughts, and revenge or prevention fantasies.
5. Provide opportunities for vicarious working through for those who listen.
6. Help group members to practice being supportive to each other.
7. Create an atmosphere of support, validation, and sympathetic understanding to allow the group members to be a "container" for the range of thoughts and feelings that will be expressed.

Pre-Session Preparation

Check In with the Candidates Prior to the Session

Prior to the group-meeting day, if possible, a group leader should contact the two group members who were identified in the previous session as candidates to tell their story. The purpose is to see if they need any help in preparing or are experiencing significant distress in anticipation of sharing their narrative. The group leader should make sure to contact group members who have worked on "impact-focused narratives" in order to productively share sensitive, graphic, or violent experiences. Additional support or restructuring of the planned narrative may be necessary.

If a candidate is unable to share his or her narrative for some reason, the alternate candidate should be chosen with the understanding that the first candidate can share his or her story in a later session. At the beginning of the group or just before, a group leader should again check in with the candidates. If there is any question about the readiness of the planned candidates, group leaders may identify alternate group members to share their narrative during the session. Keep in mind the following considerations:

- Although group leaders may know beforehand who appears to be ready, daily events can throw even higher-functioning youth members off balance, so that allowing group members to volunteer to go first on days they feel ready may be advisable.
- Many young people are eager to tell their stories and look forward to the opportunity.
- Youth who will be discharged soon from a facility should be given the opportunity to share their stories before discharge.

Format of Narrative Sessions

This session is optimally staffed by two group leaders: one to facilitate the narrative construction and one to monitor group reactions and take notes of the narrative itself.

The facilitating group leader should sit adjacent with his or her chair angled toward the group member sharing the narrative. He or she should also take notes of key points during the narrative so that both group leaders may contribute to a summary of the narrative.

Section number	Session overview
I	Check-in and Feeling Thermometer
II	Review practice assignment
III	Introduce the narrative activity and review the session structure
IV	Steps for eliciting the narrative
V	(Optional) Create a timeline during the narrative
VI	(Optional) Gentle updating of problematic thoughts and beliefs
VII	Summary and practice assignment
VII	Check-out

Supplies

Every session	This session
• Group member workbooks	For optional timeline activity, large piece of paper, colored markers (black, green, yellow, orange, and red)
• Flipchart	
• Large paper or easel pad	
• Markers	
• Pencils/pens	
• Kleenex	
• Tape	

Handouts in Workbook

Handout 1.06	Instructions for Deep (Abdominal) Breathing
Handout 2.06	Muscle Relaxation Guide
Handout 2.07	Timeline Template
Handout 2.08	Challenging and Replacing Hurtful Thoughts
Handout 1.42	Common Errors in Thinking
Handout 1.30	Sizing Up a Situation
Handout 2.09	Examining the Evidence For and Against
Handout 2.10	Check-Out Feedback Form

Flipcharts

2.2a Session Highlights

1. Check-in
2. Review practice assignment
3. Introduce narrative activity
4. Share the trauma narrative
5. Summary and practice assignment
6. Check-out

2.2b What Type of Support Do I Want?

1. Emotional closeness
2. Social connection
3. Feeling needed
4. Reassurance of self-worth
5. Being there for me when I need you
6. Information (feedback and advice)
7. Physical assistance (acts of service)
8. Material support

Session 2.2 Group Narrative Sharing Sessions

I. Check-In and Feeling Thermometer

- *How are you feeling right now?* (Use the Feeling Thermometer ratings.)
- Practice with the group doing five to ten abdominal breaths.
- *Is anything going on that may make it difficult for you to keep your mind on the group today?*
- Briefly review (or have a group member review) Today's Highlights (Flipchart 2.2a).

II. Review Practice Assignment

- Direct group members to think about times during the past week when their Feeling Thermometer went higher or when they numbed out. Have each group member report on one such event and describe his/her reactions (thoughts, feelings, sensations, and actions).

- Then ask them which coping strategies they used: were they strategies that "mess you up" (MUPS) or did they choose coping skills from their personal coping toolkits (Handout 2.04)?
- Briefly explore the outcomes and troubleshoot coping skills efforts for the next week.

III. Introduce the Narrative Activity and Review the Session Structure

Briefly provide a rationale and overview of the narrative construction process, especially for the first time or two that this is done in the group. After that, group members will not require this review.

As you prepare for this session with the group, select from the following:

- *As you remember, today we start having each group member share his or her story about the traumatic or stressful experiences you have chosen to work on. Keep in mind that this special way of telling your story will help to give you more control over your memories.*

- *It will give you a clearer understanding of what happened and how it has influenced your life.*
- *The way to do this is by telling a detailed story about what happened and what you and other people did.*
- *We also want you to describe what was happening outside of you as well as what was happening inside of you, including your sensations, emotions, and thoughts.*
- **Optional** (if doing a timeline):*While you are sharing your experience, I will write down the key parts on this timeline so that we can go over it later.*
- *For group members, keep in mind that hearing these stories may provoke some strong reactions. Take care of yourselves during the sharing by using your coping skills or asking for help from* (name of the other group leader).
- **My job** *is to check in with you every so often to see how you are doing and to help you stay in the story.*
- **The rest of you** *will have the job of supporting the group member who is telling his/her story by listening respectfully from your hearts. This means that you really try to understand and feel what the experience was like for the person telling the story. If there are supportive things you want to say, such as comments or questions, please keep them in mind until the end of the story, when you'll have an opportunity to share them.*
- *Any questions before we begin?*

Notes on Conducting the Trauma Narrative Exercise

- This trauma narrative exercise is designed to allow narrators to re-work their traumatic experiences and to develop tolerance for their painful memories within a safe and supportive therapeutic setting.
- It organizes the pieces of what happened *outside* of the narrator and *inside* of the narrator into a coherent story.
- Remember that our purpose is not simply to review what happened on a superficial level. Rather, it is to remember with a sense of immediacy the narrator's memories and feelings connected to the event. If the re-working is of sufficient personal relevance (i.e. identifying salient worst moments), depth, and duration, and if it takes place within the "working range of anxiety," narrators will develop a greater capacity to tolerate these memories and feelings, and greater insight into their personal reminders. In many cases, they will also experience a reduction in the intensity of, and an improved ability to manage their posttraumatic stress reactions. It also helps to discriminate more clearly between their prior traumatic experiences and current situations that can serve as reminders. Make sure that enough time (we recommend at least 20 minutes per narrative) remains in the session to do this exercise.
- If the narrative is very brief or the group member is disengaged in the telling, you may use sensory prompts ("What did you see, hear, smell, etc.") or

explorations of feelings and thoughts to heighten the intensity ("What was going through your mind then?" What were you feeling inside?").

- As a general guide you should let the retelling unfold without interruption unless you think the narrator is skipping over important moments or aspects of his or her experience. In recounting a painful experience, narrators frequently skip over or move quickly through the most stressful or difficult parts of their experience. At those times it is important to gently ask the narrator to go back to a certain point in the story and slow down the description.
- Throughout, you should attempt to have the narrator describe what was happening *outside* of him or her and also what was happening *inside* in terms of thoughts and feelings. You may use the guide below to elicit salient or missing pieces of the narrative as it unfolds. Once again, your primary goal is to "get out of the way" of the person sharing the story.
- In sharing his or her experiences the youth may provide a window on personal thoughts, beliefs, and expectations that may be the source of current difficulties. Note these and be especially attentive to self-blame, distortions about whether the event could have been predicted or prevented, and/or whether the group member telling the story feels guilty in any way about what happened or seeks revenge.

IV. Steps for Eliciting the Narrative

Activity: Eliciting the Narrative

The following is a step-by-step guide for helping the youth tell his or her story in a safe and productive way.

1. Begin the narrative
- Get a baseline rating on the Feeling Thermometer ("What's your rating right now?")
- *Why don't you begin by describing the events that led up to what happened? How did it start?*

2. Continue the narrative construction
- Use a combination of "objective" and "subjective" questions to construct a story that weaves together what happened *outside* of the youth with what happened *inside* of them.
- Generally speaking, you can allow the youth to tell his or her story fairly uninterrupted as long as key *outside* and *inside* information is being shared and the youth is engaged in the telling. You may draw upon Figure 2.2a, the guide for narrative prompts, for guidance on how to help move through the narrative. Even if the youth is using an alternative approach to the narrative, e.g. sharing music or a rap, you can use prompts to focus the work.
- If a youth stops at any point, you can repeat back the last sentence he or she said and ask, "What happened next?" or "What did you do next." Or "You said [...] Tell us more about that."

Figure 2.2a: Guide for narrative prompts. (Use these selectively.)

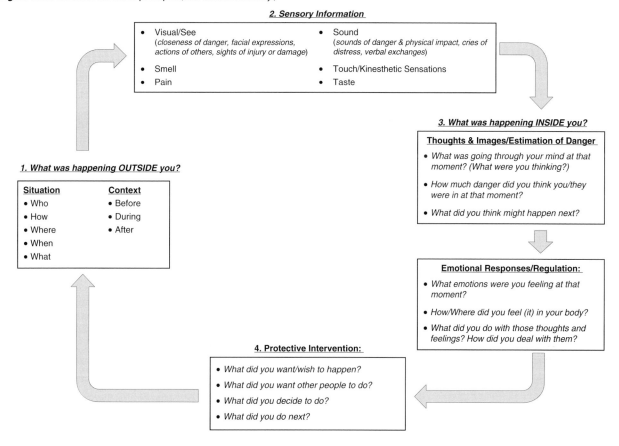

3. **Regularly check on how the narrator is doing.**
   - *How did you feel while this was happening? How are you doing right now?* (Check Feeling Thermometer reading.)
   - This helps to keep the youth within the "working range" of feeling intensity by communicating that they are in control. Look for signs of becoming overwhelmed by intense recollections and emotions – especially when exploring highly distressing material. If the youth reports becoming extremely distressed, you can re-direct his or her focus to less distressing parts of the trauma scene. In addition, you can decrease intensity by guiding the narrator to focus on facts rather than feelings and sensations, and have them "close the book" by recounting how it ended and what happened afterwards. **It can reinforce avoidance to just stop in mid narrative, so it is important to tell the story, even briefly, to the end.**
   - If the group member appears to be disengaged from the retelling (e.g. is not within the working range of anxiety, which is typically between 5 to 8 on a 10-point Feeling Thermometer), you may seek to increase engagement by asking about feelings or by probing for sensory details of the experience: *What did you feel? What did you see (hear, smell, feel in your body)?*
   - You can also slow them down to focus on the more difficult portions of what happened and inquire about moment-to-moment experiences.

4. **Conclude the narrative and check in with the group member.**
   - Get a thermometer reading and explore thoughts and feelings about what happened and about the experience of sharing the story.
   - *How do you feel now as you share these things with us?*
   - This may be appropriate after the narrator has made a revealing disclosure and shows signs of discomfort. Revealing disclosures are frequently accompanied by feelings of guilt, shame, embarrassment, fear that one has said too much, or feeling vulnerable to disapproval or rejection. Sympathize, normalize, and reassure as appropriate.

5. **After working *through* the immediate traumatic experience, bring closure to the narrative by exploring the immediate aftermath.**
   - Direct the focus of the narrator to an exploration of the *immediate aftermath* (e.g. medical treatment received, what the funeral was like, being relieved that you survived, feeling distant from certain friends or family members, etc.), and to begin to reflect on the *ongoing hardships* they currently face (e.g. worrying that you would get arrested or gang members would come after you, having less money because a parent is dead, having to move or change schools, etc.).

6. **(Recommended): If the narrator has described the death of a family member or friend, it can help calm them by asking them to think back to their fondest memories of this person.**
   - Ask the group member to tell you about their fondest of happiest memories about this friend or family member.

"What are your happiest memories about your mom?" "You said you and Jason were best friends. What did you two used to do for fun when you were little?"

7. Close the narrative by providing sincere praise and highlighting strengths.

- Thank the youth and share your sincere praise for the courage shown in sharing these very personal and important experiences. If possible, highlight examples of strength and resilience evidenced in the narrative.

8. Invite group members to share their comments.

- Remind group members about the type of feedback that is most useful, as discussed last session. You can also remind the group of the sharer's personal goals in doing this work and any specific types of feedback that were requested. Facilitate supportive sharing and prevent other group members from speaking too long or pulling the focus too much to themselves through detailed sharing of their own experiences. Each will have a turn to share their story and this moment of group time is primarily for the one sharing the story.

9. As necessary, conduct a calming and transitioning activity. Examples are noted below.

- Deep breathing (see Handout 1.06)
- Progressive muscle relaxation (see Handout 2.06)
- Listening to music

V. (Optional) Create a Timeline during the Narrative

This section provides steps for drawing a timeline concurrently with the narrative. During the narrative, you may choose to draw a "timeline" that captures the key moments of the group member's story and provides a summary graphic document. This may be done by the facilitator or the second group leader, if there is one. The timeline may be useful in that it underscores the importance of the experience and provides a concrete product that the youth can refer back to for subsequent processing, and provides a powerful graphic to help the youth see the experience in perspective as just one part of his or her life.

Optional Activity: Creating a Timeline

1. Prepare the Timeline

You should have available five markers: black, green, yellow, orange, and red. You may choose to draw the timeline either on a single large piece of paper on which you hand-draw the thermometer and timeline as shown on Handout 2.07. For either it can be helpful to color in the quadrants of the thermometer with green, yellow, orange, and red markers in ascending order. The lowest "green zone" indicates experiences that were comfortable, with minimal stress; the "yellow zone" for experiences that were somewhat stressful; "orange zone," very stressful; and "red zone" for experiences that were extremely stressful and uncomfortable. Along the horizontal axis, from left to right, the experiences will be noted in approximate chronological order. The multiple copies of the handout can be laid next to each other so that you can continue the story from left to right, adding more copies as needed and reserving the last page for related experiences during the past month.

2. Begin the Narrative

On the timeline, locate the beginning of the selected trauma or loss event a few inches to the right along the horizontal axis to allow room to the left for the events or context that led up to the trauma or loss experience.

Why don't you begin by describing the events that led up to what happened? How did it start?

Figure 2.2b: Example of a personal timeline

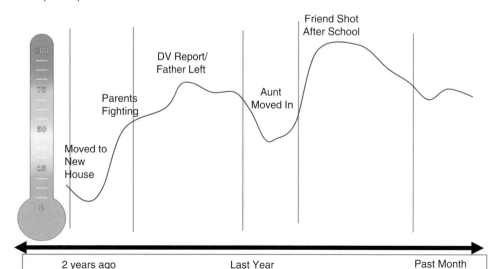

3. Continue the Timeline Construction

As the youth describes his or her moment-to-moment experiences, you will write them into the timeline in vertical clusters moving left to right in chronological order (see Figure 2.2b). Write down a brief phrase capturing what was going on *outside*, and key words that describe what was going on *inside*. Also write down, verbatim, important thoughts, beliefs, or interpretations, especially those that imply distortions regarding self-blame, shame/guilt, or excessive responsibility.

Levels of relative stress for each "moment" or part of the experience will be indicated by circling the written description in either green, yellow, orange, or red ink. This is done *after* the narrative is shared so as not to distract the youth from the telling and reduce the exposure value of the activity.

4. Conclude the Timeline

Comment on the multiple challenges, difficult moments, and examples of strength and resilience evidenced in the experiences shared. Take this opportunity to confirm color-coding for any moments you were not sure how to rank. Cite specific examples in which the youth persevered, succeeded, or demonstrated character. Thank the youth and share your sincere praise for the courage shown by the youth in sharing these very personal and important experiences.

VI. (Optional) Gentle Updating of Problematic Thoughts and Beliefs

This section contains guidelines for briefly working on problematic thoughts and beliefs indicated during the narrative sharing. In the telling of the narrative you may have heard clues to important interpretations and beliefs about *self* ("I am stupid," "I am helpless"), *others* ("You can't trust anyone"), and *the world* ("Bad things always happen to me," "The doctors didn't even try") that may have been shaped by the experience. When heard, they should be written onto the timeline. These are important because they can lead to on-going painful rumination and traumatic expectations and behaviors that may derail normal development ("I shouldn't get close to anyone," "It doesn't matter what I do, I'll be dead before I'm twenty"). Likely suspects for problematic thoughts include the following:

- *Hurtful* and *inaccurate thoughts* regarding shame, guilt, or exaggerated responsibility for what happened (additional examples may be seen on Handout 2.08, Challenging and Replacing Hurtful Thoughts, or on Handout 1.42, Common Errors in Thinking).
- *Prevention fantasies* that include unrealistic statements about the predictability and preventability of what happened along with expressed wishes to have intervened, prevented, or been able to repair the bad outcome.
- *Revenge fantasies* that include the expressed desire to retaliate or seek revenge for a loss, death, or other traumatic event.

If potentially problematic thoughts and beliefs were indicated in the narrative and the group member is not too emotionally extended after the narrative (and there is time) you may choose to begin some of the cognitive processing work.

Activity: Updating of Problematic Thoughts and Beliefs

1. **Identify a hurtful thought**. Provide a few examples of hurtful thoughts that can "mess you up." Ask the group and the narrator if they noticed any of these during the narrative. Mention one or more that the group leaders heard or thought were operative. Check in with the narrator.
2. **Validate the hurtful thought** and why it made sense given the trauma or loss experience.
3. **Discuss the current accuracy and utility of the thought**. Use Handout 1.30, Sizing Up a Situation, to discuss how the thought or belief currently plays out in terms of resulting feelings, behaviors, and consequences. If it is problematic in any way and the youth is motivated to update the thought, continue with the next step.
4. **Explore more accurate and helpful alternatives**. Rather than "challenging" or "confronting" what are often referred to as "cognitive distortions," we suggest you work collaboratively with the youth to see if he or she can see ways in which the thought or belief is no longer accurate or helpful. From that vantage point, the youth becomes more open to explore alternatives. And while you may enlist the tools in Handout 2.09, Examining the Evidence For and Against, seeking out instances in which the negative thought or belief is shown to be inaccurate, and Handout 1.42, exploring possible common errors in thinking, etc., the overall approach should be respectful and not discounting towards previous ways of thinking and behaving.

A similar gentle and respectful approach should be taken with prevention and revenge fantasies. Guidelines are provided in the boxes to first acknowledge why these responses make sense given the youth's experience and then to explore options that might be more realistic and positive.

Guidelines for Interpreting Prevention Fantasies

Prevention (wishing it hadn't happened)

Goal: accept the *reality of the loss* and experience its accompanying pain.

- *These thoughts let us know how much you wish this had never happened.*

Protection (wishing for protective intervention)

Goal: increase tolerance for memories of how *threatening* the trauma was, and how *defenseless, trapped,* and *helpless* the youth felt.

- *These thoughts help us to understand how threatening this experience was for you, and how **vulnerable,*** *helpless, and scared* you felt while it was happening.

Repair (Wishing the Harm or Loss Could Be Undone, Reversed, or Repaired)

Goal: *gently* process the *finality* and *irreversibility* of the injury or loss.

- *It sounds like it is scary to think about what your life will be like without (your loved one) in your life.*
- *It sounds like you're wishing that this were only temporary – it's hard to accept that it's really going to be like this from now on.*

Prevention of Future Trauma

Goal: help them understand how this relates to their needs for safety and security, both now and in the future.

- *These thoughts let us know what you believe it would take to help you feel safe if something like this were to happen again.*
- *These thoughts help us understand what you believe it would take to keep something like this from happening again to you or to people you care about.*

Guidelines for Exploring Revenge Fantasies

Introduce the concepts of retaliatory fantasies and desires for revenge. Call attention to how difficult it must be to be placed in the position of having these angry and violent feelings. Explore their reactions to being forced to experience themselves as vengeful, and how this has changed them in ways they perhaps did not want. How do these fantasies help them feel stronger or safer?

1. Facilitate a deeper exploration and acceptance of the terror, horror, helplessness, and catastrophic loss that one experienced during the worst moments:

   - *By imagining the suffering of the boys who killed your cousin, it seems like you are showing how much losing him has made you suffer.*
   - *Imagining that the man who shot at you is in a terrifying situation and is certain that he's going to die, lets us know just how terrible those moments were like for you.*

2. Explore members' perception of the perpetrators – their ruthlessness, violence, and malevolence – through an exploration of retaliatory fantasies of what is needed to eliminate the threat that the perpetrator poses:

   - *Imagining that the people responsible for this have it done back to them lets us know what you think would have to happen for something like that to never happen again. They would have to actually go through it themselves – to feel as scared and sad and helpless and hurt as much as the people they did it to – before they would truly understand what it feels like and never do it again.*
   - *Imagining the death of the boys who did this lets us know that you believe that nothing short of death would stop them from ever doing something like this again. It*

tells us that it's the only way you would feel safe and that justice has been done.

Summarize as needed:

- *The more terrified, horrified, and helpless people feel during the worst moments of what happened, the stronger their motivation to protect themselves from having to go through that kind of experience ever again. (This is one reason why we avoid trauma reminders – we don't want to go re-experience that horror in our memories!)*
- *Thus, the presence and nature of these thoughts and feelings help us to know more about what your own experience was like–about the terror, horror, helplessness, and pain that you felt in the face of a malevolent, violent, menacing threat.*
- *These thoughts and feelings also tell us about your perception of the people responsible for this – of the violence and ruthlessness that you believe they are capable of, and what you think it would take to stop them from ever doing this again.*

(As appropriate): Lead a discussion about appropriate ways to express/channel retaliatory fantasies and desires for vengeance.

- *It is completely understandable why some of you have these thoughts and desires, at least occasionally. These thoughts and feelings don't mean that you're a bad person, and instead, they tell us a lot about what this experience means to you and what it was like for you to go through.*
- *But feeling this way also doesn't mean that you have to act on your desires. Remember that you, your thoughts, and your feelings are independent. A feeling doesn't prove that the thought that generated it is true, nor does it mean that you have to slavishly act on your feelings.*
- *Let's work together to help you express how honestly you feel about this.* (Facilitate a problem-solving activity that helps them to transform or convert their anger into constructive social action, such as advocacy, supporting others who are recently affected by such experiences, or preventing crime.)

VII. Summary and Practice Assignment

- Summarize and bring closure to the session.
- Normalize group members' reactions to the disclosures made today.
- Gain members' commitments that they will use Handout 1.39, Three Steps to Taking Charge of Your Thoughts and Feelings, and their coping skills to contend with distressing events during the week.
- As necessary, help members to emotionally recover and reconstitute themselves.
- Refer to Flipchart 2.2b and discuss with group members what kinds of support would be helpful for them during the week.

In order to bring closure to the session, the group leaders can comment on the strengths (courage, support, persistence, kindness, etc.) evidenced in the group today. Group member reactions to the narrative can also be normalized with some guidance on what to expect during the upcoming week and what they can do to take care of themselves and each other. For example, it is normal for the narrator to experience an increase in memories, strong feelings, and even trauma-related symptoms such as trouble sleeping. This is temporary, and coping skills can be used to ease the impact of these reactions.

For youth in residential treatment facilities, it is wise to alert the cottage or unit staff so that they can be supportive and assist group members to practice their coping strategies and avoid MUPS.

Meanwhile, the regular practice assignment for the week for all group members should be reviewed. This involves continuing to identify situations that evoke a stress response (high on their Feeling Thermometers) and utilize one or more of their coping strategies. They should come to group prepared to share one or more of these experiences.

VIII. Check-Out

- *How are you feeling now? (Use the Feeling Thermometer ratings.)*
- *What did you learn about yourself today?*
- *Please fill out the Check-Out Feedback Form (Handout 2.10) The title of today's session was "Group Narrative Sharing Exercises."*

If any members are visibly agitated or troubled or report high levels of distress on the Feeling Thermometer, keep them after the group and determine an appropriate way to transition back to their settings.

2.3 Review of Group Sharing and Exploration of Beliefs and Expectations

Session Objectives

1. Provide a summary experience for the narrative-sharing portion of the group.
2. Facilitate a group discussion about what they have learned from each other and the narrative-sharing experience.
3. Establish linkages between personal trauma or loss histories and current beliefs and expectations.
4. Evaluate usefulness and accuracy of beliefs/expectations and demonstrate a process whereby problematic beliefs/expectations may be changed.
5. Provide praise and support for the group's efforts throughout this module.

Pre-Session Preparation

- Review the group leader worksheets that highlight salient information on the narratives shared during this module. Have available summary information for each group member's narrative, including primary events, worst moments, likely reminders, helpful and unhelpful thoughts or beliefs, and prevention and revenge fantasies.
- Prior to the group, write down bullets on a flipchart to aid your discussion and provide an anchor to the discussion.

Supplies

Every session	This session
• Group member workbooks	• Blank flipchart
• Flipchart	
• Large paper or easel pad	
• Markers	
• Pencils/pens	
• Kleenex	
• Tape	

Handouts in Workbook

Handout 2.01	Feeling Thermometer
Handout 1.30	Sizing Up a Situation
Handout 2.11	Check-Out Feedback Form

Section number	Session overview
I	Check-in and Feeling Thermometer
II	Review practice assignment
III	What we learned from sharing our stories
IV	Practice assignment
V	Check-out

Flipcharts

2.3a Session Highlights

1. Check-in and Feeling Thermometer
2. Review practice assignment
3. What we learned from sharing our stories
4. Practice assignment
5. Check-out

2.3b Discussion Questions

[Review the discussion questions below and select those you would like to use and write them on the flipchart.]

2.3c What Type of Support Do I Want?

1. Emotional closeness
2. Social connection
3. Feeling needed
4. Reassurance of self-worth
5. Being there for me when I need you
6. Information (feedback and advice)
7. Physical assistance (help with my chores, etc.)
8. Material support (money, clothes, food, books, etc.)

Session 2.3 Review of Group Sharing and Exploration of Beliefs and Expectations

I. Check-In and Feeling Thermometer

- *How are you feeling right now?* (Use the Feeling Thermometer ratings.)
- Practice with the group doing five to ten abdominal breaths.
- *Is anything going on that may make it difficult for you to keep your mind on the group today?*
- Briefly review (or have a group member review) Today's Highlights (Flipchart 2.3a).

II. Review Practice Assignment

- Briefly check in with group members on their home exercise, troubleshoot difficulties, and refine practice for the upcoming week.
- Direct group members to think about times during the past week when their Feeling Thermometer went higher or when they numbed out. Have each group member report on one such event and describe his/her reactions (thoughts, feelings, sensations, and actions).
- Then ask them which coping strategies they used: were they strategies that "mess you up" (MUPS) or did they choose coping skills from Handout 2.04 (Things That I Can Do: My Personal Coping Toolkit).
- Briefly explore the outcomes and troubleshoot coping skills efforts for the next week.

III. What We Learned from Sharing our Stories

- Note that all members have now shared their narratives. Praise their work.

- Facilitate a discussion that invites all to comment on their experiences of sharing their narrative and hearing others' stories.
- Invite group members to explore how their experiences may have influenced their beliefs and expectations.
- While validating the ways in which their beliefs and expectations make sense in light of their experiences, introduce a process whereby they can update and shift beliefs that they see as unhelpful.

The following activity marks the end of the narrative sharing part of the group. It is an important time to review the experience and use the group process to consolidate learning. The ensuing discussion will also offer an opportunity to reflect on ways that group members' trauma or loss experiences have impacted their beliefs and expectations and whether those views are helpful or unhelpful.

Activity: Learning From Sharing Our Stories

Review the discussion prompts below and feel free to use these or generate some of your own. You can write these on a flipchart or share them verbally. Keep this discussion open and engaging. Take a back seat and let the youth carry the ball. Avoid lecturing. This is their chance to hear from each other and to consolidate the valuable lessons of their unique group experience.

Today marks the end of the part of the group in which we share our personal stories. So this is a good time for us to look back on what we experienced together, what we felt, and what we learned.

To help start out, I have written some basic questions, but we can change things as we go.

Discussion Questions

1. **The experience of telling your story.**
   - *What surprised you the most?*
   - *What did you think the most about afterwards?*
   - *What did you learn about yourself in telling your story?*

- *What did you most appreciate from the group?* (Group leaders can comment on this as well.)

2. **Hearing others' stories**
   - *What touched you the most in hearing others' stories?*
   - (If appropriate) *What wishes do you have for those who are still blaming themselves or feeling guilty about what happened?*
   - (If appropriate) *What wishes do you have for those who still believe they could have (and should have) done something to change what happened?*
   - (If appropriate) *What wishes do you have for those who would like to get revenge for what happened?*
   - *What wishes overall do you have for others who shared their stories?* (Group leaders can comment on this as well.)

3. **How my experience has shaped me.** *Powerful experiences can have a powerful influence on how we see ourselves, others and the world. Most importantly, they can influence our beliefs and our expectations. These are important because to a large extent, they can determine what we hope for, what we try, and what we do.*

   For example, people who believe that nothing they do matters or have the expectation that they won't live long may not work hard or try new things. And people who have the belief that they can't trust others or expect others will always let them down, will probably not build strong or close relationships. Those beliefs and those resulting behaviors can have a devastating impact on your life.

   So let's talk about your beliefs and expectations and maybe how your experiences have helped shape them. I have listed some important areas that you can talk about. Or you can choose ones that are more important to you.

   (Write the following on a flip chart or white board)

   - My view of the future
   - Feeling safe and secure
   - Closeness to others
   - Feeling in control of my life
   - Laws and society

As group members share their beliefs and expectations, help to offer linkages to their trauma or loss experiences ("… that makes sense when I think about what you shared …"). Make sure to acknowledge the ways even extreme or problematic beliefs and expectations make sense in light of their experiences. There will be an opportunity for the group to identify ways that these beliefs may not be helpful and that they can take small steps to change them.

At an appropriate point in the conversation, ask group members to comment on whether they think their beliefs or expectations have been helpful or unhelpful. Unhelpful beliefs or expectations may be considered those that result in the youth feeling badly, not getting what he or she wants, or have opportunities or options foreclosed.

If the group identifies any unhelpful beliefs or expectations, you may use any of the prompts below to work with the group overall or with an individual to explore change opportunities. Use Handout 1.30, Sizing Up a Situation, to help with the discussion below. We have found that youth often help each other with this process of updating their trauma-based beliefs and expectations, and the group leaders can support this while staying pretty quiet.

Identify motivation to change:
How is that belief or expectation not working?
How does it play out in how you feel or act and how others respond?
Is there any part of it you would like to change?

Find an alternative view:
While the belief makes sense based on what you experienced back then, is anything different now? Are you different now?
Is there any proof that it is no longer completely true?
What is the evidence that it is true?
What is the evidence that it is not?
Is there another way to look at it?
How would your life be different in the future if you did not believe this?

Commit to a small first step:
What would it look like if you took a small step towards changing it?
How would you think, feel, act? How might responses from others or consequences change?
Will you try it?

Summarize the key points of the discussion. Close this section by praising their work throughout the narrative module, including the courage and openness they have shown in doing the narrative work, and the support and help they have provided each other. Highlight progress made by individuals and the group overall in becoming a safe place to share stories and to support each other in this important work.

IV. Practice Assignment

- Discuss with group members possible challenging or stressful situations that may arise during the week.
- Explore with group members which of their coping strategies have been most useful and which they would like to use.

Discuss with group members upcoming challenges for the week and selected coping strategies they will use. They should come to the group prepared to share one or more of these experiences.

V. Check-Out

- *How are you feeling now?* (Use the Feeling Thermometer ratings and be especially attentive to distress in group members who have limited experience in doing this kind of work.)
- *What did you learn about yourself today?*

- *Please fill out the Check-Out Feedback Form (Handout 2.11). The title of today's session is "Review of Group Sharing and Exploration of Beliefs and Expectations."*

If any group members are visibly agitated or troubled or report high levels of distress on the Feeling Thermometer, keep them after the group and determine an appropriate way to transition back to their settings.

Guide for Conducting Individual Narrative and Pull-Out Sessions

Session Objectives

This additional session may be used with individual group members in two ways:

1. For those group members who had difficulty selecting a single event because of the chronic or repeated nature of their exposure, or for those whose selected event involves violent or graphic images or stigmatized experiences, Section II provides guidance on selecting an event even in complex circumstances. Section III provides guidance on generating an "impact-focused" narrative to share in the group. This is a narrative that focuses primarily on the youth's moment-to-moment internal experiences, thoughts, and feelings, rather than a depiction of the external event.

2. For clinicians who wish to provide a group member with a more intensive and personalized narrative experience or for clinicians conducting individual therapy, this session may be used to guide narrative work over single or multiple sessions. Section III provides guidance for eliciting a trauma or loss narrative while generating a graphic "timeline," which captures the highs and lows along with salient thoughts and interpretations that accompany the moment-to-moment experience. Guidelines are provided for subsequent individual sessions in which the timeline is used to gently explore and update problematic thoughts, beliefs, and expectations.

Pre-Session Preparation

Review the following documents for the youth:
- Pre-session personal timeline
- University of California at Los Angeles (UCLA) Reaction index
- Youth's most recent version of his or her Trauma Goals Worksheet and/or Personal Goals Worksheet (Handouts 1.02 and 1.03)

Number section	Session overview
I	Check-in and Feeling Thermometer
II	Select an experience and provide guidance on narrative sharing
III	Option to elicit a narrative and co-create a timeline
IV	Review the narrative timeline
V	Additional narrative processing for subsequent sessions
VI	Practice assignment
VII	Check-out

Supplies

Every session	This session
• Group member workbooks	• Large pieces of paper and five colored markers (black, green, yellow, orange, and red)
• Flipchart	
• Large paper or easel pad	
• Colored markers or crayons	
• Pencils/pens	
• Kleenex	
• Tape	

Handouts in Workbook

Handout 2.01	Feeling Thermometer
Handout 2.02	Selecting My Event
Handout 2.04	Things That *I* Can Do: My Personal Coping Toolkit
Handout 2.13	Check-Out Feedback Form

Flipcharts

2.4a Session Highlights

1. Check-in and Feeling Thermometer
2. Select an experience
3. Share my narrative
4. Discuss it
5. Summary and calming exercise
6. Check-out

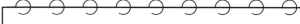

2.4b Three Steps to Take Charge of Your Thoughts and Feelings

Answer these questions:
1. "What am I feeling?"
2. "Why am I feeling this way?"
   • Look outside
   • Look inside – "What am I thinking?"
3. "How can I feel better?"

2.4 Optional Individual Pull-Out Session and Guide for Eliciting an Individual Narrative Timeline

I. Check-In and Feeling Thermometer

First, check in with the youth in the usual way:

- You may choose to use the Feeling Thermometer.
- Discuss purpose of the meeting.
- Elicit any questions or concerns.

There may be a number of reasons why you invited a group member to have an individual session. It may be because of a difficulty in identifying a primary experience on which to focus their group narrative, to help prepare the group member to share an especially sensitive or graphic experience in a manner that will be productive, to address other concerns about the youth or work on coping skills, or to provide an opportunity to do more intensive narrative work than would be possible in the group setting. In any case, be clear about the intent of the meeting and address any questions or concerns.

Depending on your purpose, pick from the sections below for guidance: Section II for simply selecting an experience for the narrative and Section III for eliciting an individual narrative and developing an impact-focused version to share in a group. Sections IV and V provide guidance for reviewing and processing the narrative. For clinicians conducting individual therapy, this work may be extended over multiple sessions.

II. Select an Experience and Provide Guidance on Sharing

The purpose of this exercise is to review and trouble-shoot selection of focal trauma or loss experience. As necessary, follow guidelines for managing and preparing the youth to share with the group violent, stigmatized, or chronic forms of exposure.

Activity: Selecting an Experience

Clarify the reason for current difficulties in either selecting or preparing to share a trauma or loss experience in the group. As a general course of action you may review with the youth their pre-session personal timeline that should indicate the range of trauma or loss experiences identified at that time. Discuss the various experiences in terms of the prompts provided in Part 2 of Handout 2.02, on selecting an event ("I still think about it a lot," "When I think about it I get stressed or have strong feelings," "I remember it well enough to tell the story," "If I could do some healing about this experience it would help me.")

Violent, Graphic, or Stigmatized Forms of Trauma

Some youth may consider focusing on experiences that include graphic, violent, or disturbing scenes whose retelling for the group session may provoke strong reactions. Note that you can choose to accommodate graphic retelling in an individual session if it serves the client's therapeutic goals. If the intent is to prepare the youth to share a narrative in the group setting you can use the individual session to help the youth prepare an "impact-focused narrative." In these accounts, the youth shares his or her thoughts and feelings rather than the details of the actual event. Guidance for how to coach the youth in doing this is provided at the end of the next section. Essentially, you elicit the narrative and draw a representative timeline that captures the key moments with the attendant thoughts and feelings. After the narrative you go through the timeline with the youth and identify the key moments in consecutive order and highlight the subjective aspects, the thoughts and feelings that comprise the "impact" of the experience. The youth is then coached on how to tell his or her story in terms of the subjective impacts of the sequenced events rather than sharing external details of what happened.

For youth whose selected experience includes stigmatized forms of trauma, such as sexual abuse, the group leader should consider whether the group composition and focus is appropriate for this kind of narrative. For example, it may be appropriate for a female youth to share her narrative of sexual abuse in a group comprised primarily of other female teens in which other sexual assaults have been or will be shared. It may also be appropriate to counsel the narrator to use impact statements to navigate difficult passages of the experience and develop an impact-focused narrative as described above.

Ultimately, the decision to green-light a sensitive narrative topic is a clinical one that must be made by the group leader, ideally, in consultation with others. It should be noted, however, that in previous implementations, group leaders have been surprised at the willingness and capacity of groups to work on these important experiences. With regard to the individual session, however, the leader can choose to elicit a full narrative if it is in keeping with therapeutic goals.

Chronic or Repeated Forms of Trauma

Youth who have experienced complex or chronic forms of trauma often have difficulty identifying a single event on which to focus the narrative. Chronic traumatic exposure often leaves vague and remote memories that have many gaps. Your task will be to try and assemble some semblance of an experiential chronology that may draw upon multiple occurrences or a single representative event that evokes the most important responses and feelings. To accomplish this you may use the narrative timeline technique described below in Section III. With this technique, you can chart and discuss the occurrences over time and see if the youth can identify a single representative event or map out the common elements of the repeated trauma. Once you either have a selected occurrence or an overall description of the repeated experience you can then continue with the narrative timeline work as described.

III. Elicit a Narrative with the Option to Co-Create a Timeline

The intent of this activity is to allow the youth to recount his or her selected trauma or loss experiences with sufficient engagement to begin to develop tolerance for the painful memories and to provide a window on their moment-to-moment experiences. The facilitator's task is to help guide the narration to the separate moments and their constituent sensations, appraisals, and emotions and weave together what was happening *inside* the narrator and *outside* the narrator into an accessible whole. This is a key part of coming to terms with the past, making sense of it within the larger arc of their life, and uncovering guide-posts for how they want to live their life going forward.

During the narrative, you may also choose to draw a timeline that captures the key moments of the group member's story and provides a summary graphic document. Guidelines for creating the narrative timeline are provided below. While the narrative may be elicited without creating a timeline, it is our experience that this concurrent activity has therapeutic value: it underscores the importance of the experience, places the trauma or loss event in context to the arc of the youth's life, and renders the experience more accessible for subsequent processing and repeated therapeutic exposure.

General Tips for Eliciting a Trauma or Loss Narrative

At the beginning, and intermittently, check the narrator's Feeling Thermometer level. For the bulk of the session you should try and keep the youth in the "working range," which is above the bottom "green zone" but below the top "red zone." The intent is to make sure the youth is engaged and not just telling the narrative in a rote fashion, while at the same time watching out for signs that the youth is becoming over-involved or activated in the retelling. The danger here is that the narrator may then shut down or distance him or herself from the narrative task, thereby reducing the amount of therapeutic exposure that takes place and undermining the goal of building tolerance to painful memories.

If the narrative is very brief or you want to increase engagement you can slow the narrative down and focus on detailed aspects of the story, especially of intensive parts of the experience; you can ask the narrator to describe what he or she was seeing, hearing, smelling, or tasting (sensory details will increase the intensity of the immediate experience), or simply ask what he or she was "feeling inside at that moment." To reduce the intensity or activation during the narrative you can ask the youth what he or she was thinking or "What went through your mind at that point," or move the story past a highly evocative sequence by asking, "What happened next?".

As a general guide, you should let the retelling unfold without interruption unless you think the youth is skipping over important moments or aspects of his or her experience. In recounting a painful experience, narrators frequently skip over or move quickly through the most stressful or difficult parts of their experience. At those times, it is important to gently ask the youth to go back to a certain point in the story and slow down the description.

Throughout, you should attempt to have the youth describe what was happening *outside* of him or her and also what was happening *inside* in terms of thoughts and feelings. You may use the guide below to elicit salient or missing pieces of the narrative as it unfolds. Once again, your primary goal is to "get out of the way" of the person sharing the story.

Activity: Eliciting a Narrative with a Co-Created Timeline

1. Prepare the timeline

- You should have available five markers: black, green, yellow, orange, and red. You may choose to draw the timeline either on a single large piece of paper on which you hand-draw the thermometer and timeline as shown on Handout 2.07 or by having available three to four copies of that handout. For either it can be helpful to color in the quadrants of the thermometer with green, yellow, orange, and red markers, in ascending order. The lowest "green zone" indicates experiences that were comfortable, with minimal stress; the "yellow zone," experiences that were somewhat stressful; "orange zone," very stressful; and "red zone," experiences that were extremely stressful and uncomfortable. Along the horizontal axis, from left to right, the experiences will be noted in approximate chronological order. The multiple copies of the handout can be laid next to each other so that you can continue the story from left to right, adding more copies as needed and reserving the last page for related experiences during the past month.

- As the youth describes his or her moment-to-moment experiences, you will write them into the timeline in vertical clusters, moving left to right in chronological order (see Figure 2.4a). Write down a brief phrase capturing what was going on *outside*, and key words that describe what was going on *inside*. Write down, verbatim, important thoughts, beliefs, or interpretations, especially those that imply distortions regarding self-blame, shame/guilt, or excessive responsibility.

- You will assign levels of stress for each part of the experience *after* the narrative during a review process described in Section IV. Inquiries into stress rankings for each part of the experience are withheld until after the narrative so as not to take the youth out of the immediate experience of the story and reduce the exposure value of the activity.

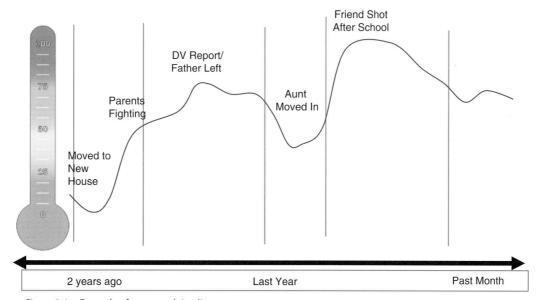

Figure 2.4a: Example of a personal timeline

2. Introduce the narrative activity

- *One of the most powerful tools for working on past trauma or loss experiences is to simply tell your story in a way and in a place that you feel safe and supported.*

- *By choosing to face these difficult memories you will get a clearer understanding of what happened and how it has influenced your life.*

- *It will also put you in a position where you can decide how and when to think about those events and what you will take forward as you build the life you want to have.*

- *The way to do this is to tell your personal story, here in this safe place.*

- *Share what was going on **outside** of you, as well as the thoughts, feelings, and even sensations that were going on **inside** of you.*

- *While you are sharing your experience, I will write down the key parts on this timeline so that we can go over it later.*
- *I will also check in with you from time to time to see where you are at on the Feeling Thermometer.*

3. **Begin the narrative**
   - On the timeline, locate the beginning of the selected trauma or loss event a few inches to the right along the horizontal axis to allow room to the left for the events or context that led up to the trauma or loss experience.
   - Get a baseline rating on the Feeling Thermometer. (*What's your rating right now?*)
   - *Why don't you begin by describing the events that led up to what happened? How did it start?*

4. **Continue the narrative construction**
   - Generally speaking, you can allow the youth to tell his or her story fairly uninterrupted as long as key *outside* and *inside* information is being shared and the youth is engaged in the telling. You may draw upon Figure 2.4a for guidance on basic prompts to help move through the narrative. Keep in mind that you don't want to ask so many questions that you undermine the youth's engagement in the process – unless it is your specific intent to do so for therapeutic reasons.

5. **Regularly check on how the narrator is doing.**
   - *How did you feel while this was happening? How are you doing right now?* (Check Feeling Thermometer reading.)
   - This helps to keep the youth within the "working range of anxiety" by communicating that they are in control. Look for signs of becoming overwhelmed by intense recollections and emotions – especially when exploring highly distressing material. If the youth reports becoming too distressed, you can re-direct his or her focus to less distressing parts of the trauma scene. In addition, you can decrease intensity by guiding the youth to focus on facts rather than feelings and sensations, and have them "close the book" by recounting how it ended and what happened afterwards. **It can reinforce avoidance to just stop in mid narrative, so it is important to tell the story, even briefly, to the end.**
   - If the youth appears to be disengaged from the retelling (e.g. is not within the working range of anxiety, which is typically between 5 to 8 on a 10-point Feeling Thermometer or in the "green zone" or "red zone"), you may seek to increase engagement by asking about feelings or by probing for sensory details of the experience:
   - *What did you feel? What did you see (hear, smell, feel in your body)?*
   - You can also slow the youth down to focus on the more difficult portions of what happened and inquire about moment-to-moment experiences.

6. **Conclude the narrative and check in with the youth.**
   - Get a thermometer reading and explore thoughts and feelings about what happened and about the experience of sharing the story.

- *How do you feel now as you share these things with me?*
- This may be appropriate after the youth has made a revealing disclosure and shows signs of discomfort. Revealing disclosures are frequently accompanied by feelings of guilt, shame, embarrassment, fear that one has said too much, or feeling vulnerable to disapproval or rejection. Sympathize, normalize, and reassure as appropriate.
- *Although I want to encourage you to explore as much of this as you can, I don't want you to talk about things that you think would overwhelm you or be too uncomfortable to talk about with me. Shall we move on?*

7. **After working *through* the immediate traumatic experience, bring closure to the narrative by exploring the immediate aftermath.**
   - Direct the focus of the youth to an exploration of the **immediate aftermath** (e.g. medical treatment received, what the funeral was like, being relieved that you survived, feeling distant from certain friends or family members, etc.), and to begin to reflect on the *ongoing hardships* they currently face (e.g. worrying that you would get arrested or gang members would come after you, having less money because a parent is dead, having to move or change schools, etc).

8. (**Recommended**) **If the youth has described the death of a family member or friend, it can help calm them by asking them to think back to their fondest memories of this person.**
   - Ask the member to tell you about their fondest or happiest memories about this friend or family member. "What are your happiest memories about your mom?" "You said you and Jason were best friends. What did you two used to do for fun when you were little?"

9. **Bring the youth's attention to the timeline where you have left space on the right to talk about stressors, challenges, and also positive experiences *during the past month*.**
   - You may prompt this by asking about events at school, at home, and in his or her social life. As before, when the youth describes an experience, write down key words that capture the experience, thoughts, and feelings. As the exposure aspect of the activity is over, you may ask whether each experience is in the "green," "yellow," "orange," or "red zone". Circle the written descriptions with the appropriate color.

10. **Provide sincere praise for the work done.**
    - You may comment on the courage the youth has shown in sharing and confronting these difficult memories. You may also reflect on the number of challenges and adversities encountered by the youth, and cite specific examples in which the youth has persevered or evidenced strength and resilience.

IV. Review the Narrative Timeline and Coach on "Impact-Focused Narrative"

Activity: Reviewing the Narrative Timeline

The timeline may be used to accomplish key therapeutic goals:

- Follow the directions for assigning stress rankings and identify the worst moment in the narrative content.
- Support perspective-taking by using the timeline to review the full arc of the youth's experience, highlighting strengths and successes when possible.
- As necessary, use the timeline to coach the youth on doing an impact-focused narrative for the group meeting.

Assign Stress Rankings

After the narrative is completed, you should go back over the timeline to assign stress rankings to the sequenced parts of the experience. This is done by reviewing each "moment" written on the timeline and asking the youth whether this was a "green" (non-stressful), "yellow" (somewhat stressful), "orange" (stressful), or "red" (extremely stressful) experience. After being told, circle the written description on the timeline with a green, yellow, orange, or red line.

Identify Worst Moments

These will be the single or multiple moments in which the youth felt most fearful, vulnerable, or helpless.

Summarize the Timeline and Highlight Strengths

Invite the youth to take a look at the entire filled-in and color-coded timeline and ask what his or her impression is and take-away message. What the youth focuses on is significant and can lead to a discussion that advances the youth's ability to develop perspective on this experience. Your goal is to support efforts to place the experience in a meaningful context within the youth's overall life and highlight the youth's strengths, resilience, and courage in dealing with the many challenges presented by this experience.

(If Needed) Create an Impact-Focused Narrative for Group Sharing

For those youth who need coaching on how to present an impact-focused narrative for group sharing, you can use the timeline to scaffold their presentation. You may review the moments described on the timeline and probe for further information on the sensations, thoughts, and feelings that accompanied these experiences. Note these on the timeline. This content along with the moment-to-moment stress rankings and information on worst moments can be used to flesh out an impact-focused narrative. In this way, group members can authentically share their experiences of violent, embarrassing, or stigmatized experiences without going into details about the objective event. After reviewing the contents have

the youth practice going through the narrative focusing on the internal "impacts." The youth may choose to bring into the group the narrative timeline to help share the experience. If this is the youth's wish, you may need to redraw or cross-out information on the timeline that the youth does not want shared. Clinical experience has shown that these narratives are well-received by group members and elicit the same level of empathy and support as objectively detailed retellings.

Completion of Narrative Task

For most circumstances, the session should be brought to a close after the review and, if indicated, the development of an impact-focused narrative. If the clinician is conducting on-going individual therapy or if there will be additional opportunities to work individually on the narrative after the youth has shared his or her story with the group, you may draw upon the exercises outlined in the next section.

As necessary, conduct a calming and transitioning activity. An example is shown below.

Calming Exercise

As necessary, conduct a calming and transitioning activity.

Deep breathing

- Practice doing five to ten abdominal breaths.
- Check again with the Feeling Thermometer to monitor any changes.

Other activities may include:

- Progressive muscle relaxation by tensing and relaxing muscles from head to toe
- Playing cards
- Listening to music.

V. Additional Narrative Processing for Subsequent Sessions

- Two forms of post-narrative processing are described that focus on thoughts, beliefs, and expectations. These may be initiated in subsequent sessions.
- Review and gently address problematic thoughts and beliefs.
- Review and gently address problematic beliefs and (traumatic) expectations.

Activity: Additional Narrative Processing

A. Gentle Review and Updating of *Specific* Thoughts and Beliefs

In the telling of the narrative you may have heard clues to important interpretations and beliefs about *self* ("I am stupid," "I am helpless"), *others* ("You can't trust anyone"), and *the world* ("Bad things always happen to me," "The doctors didn't even try") that may have been shaped by the experience. When heard, they should be written onto the timeline. These are important because they can lead to on-going painful rumination and traumatic expectations and behaviors that may derail normal development ("I shouldn't get close to anyone," "It doesn't matter what I do, I'll be dead before I'm twenty.") Likely suspects for problematic thoughts include the following:

- **Hurtful and inaccurate thoughts** regarding shame, guilt, or exaggerated responsibility for what happened (additional examples may be seen on Handout 1.35, Hurtful Thoughts Checklist, or on Handout 1.42, Common Errors in Thinking).
- **Prevention fantasies** that include unrealistic statements about the predictability and preventability of what happened along with expressed wishes to have intervened, prevented, or been able to repair the bad outcome.
- **Revenge fantasies** that include the expressed desire to retaliate or seek revenge for a loss, death, or traumatic occurrence.

For this part of the work, you can review the timeline focusing on the noted problematic thoughts and beliefs. The key here is to validate why these thoughts and beliefs made sense and may have even been useful at one time. Explore with the youth ways in which they may not be so useful now or even may result in unwanted feelings, behaviors, and consequences. You may use Handout 1.30, Sizing Up a Situation. Rather than "challenging" or "confronting" what are often referred to as "cognitive distortions," it is recommended that you work collaboratively with the youth to see if he or she can see ways in which a certain way of thinking or believing is no longer accurate or helpful. From that vantage point, the youth becomes more open to explore alternatives. And while you may enlist the tools of Examining the Evidence For and Against (Handout 2.09), seeking out exceptions, explore possible common errors in thinking (Handout 1.42), etc., the overall approach should be respectful and not discounting towards previous ways of thinking and behaving.

A similar gentle and respectful approach should be taken with prevention and revenge fantasies. Guides are provided to first acknowledge why these responses make sense, given the youth's experience, and then to explore options that might be more realistic and positive (see the boxes containing guidelines for interpreting intervention fantasies, and guidelines for exploring revenge fantasies in Session 2.2).

B. Gentle Review and Updating of General Beliefs and Expectations

Youth who have experienced a single major trauma or loss may be able to talk about ways that their beliefs and views on such things as feeling safe, in control of their life, trusting others, having trust in laws and society, and feeling optimistic about their future, have changed as a result of their experiences. For many, the legacy of traumatic or loss experiences is to shake the bedrock of their assumptions and move them towards a greater sense of vulnerability and questioning of these "givens." When the outcome is a more clear-eyed understanding of the self and

world that can lead to more realistic expectations and adaptive functioning, then the shift may be considered as a gain. When it results in an exaggerated sense of helplessness or hopelessness with regard to securing a positive future, staying safe, building relationships, or working within society, then this shift in outlook may have far-reaching negative developmental consequences for the youth. In the latter case, the youth may be seen as harboring "traumatic expectations," which come at a cost.

Youth who have had many traumatic or loss experiences in a context of ongoing racial bias and socio-economic disadvantage may have more pervasive trauma-related beliefs or expectations, which may pose a similar threat to development. The difference is that these traumatic expectations may be harder for the youth to identify as problematic because they are so self-evident. For example, it may be assumed that police and people in authority are not there to help and protect, or that it is clear that they cannot keep themselves safe. In determining which of the expectations are realistic and useful and which are out-sized and problematic, we must also factor in some of the grim realities of life in high-risk communities. It may, in fact, be accurate to say that the police are not in all instances looking out for them and that they can keep themselves and their loved ones safe.

The clinician's task is to begin a conversation to explore with the youth his or her beliefs and expectations with regard to the listed topics below (view of future, feeling safe, etc.). Then the clinician validates and contextualizes the youth's beliefs and expectations given his or her trauma and loss history ("This makes sense …"). Then a collaborative process is described in which the clinician and the youth explore the costs and benefits of specific potentially problematic beliefs or expectations, and the youth is helped to decide if he or she wants to make any desired changes. For those "traumatic beliefs/expectations" slated for change, a gentle process is described whereby a personalized "belief problem statement" is crafted and simple steps provided for envisioning and then initiating change.

DISCUSSION OF BELIEFS AND EXPECTATIONS IN KEY AREAS

Begin a conversation with the youth in which you explore his or her beliefs or expectations with regard to the following areas. You may draw upon content shared in the narrative or knowledge about the youth. Write down key phrases on a white board or piece of paper you both can view.

- My view of the future.
- Feeling safe and secure.
- Closeness to others.
- Feeling in control of my life.
- Laws and society.

VALIDATE AND LINK TRAUMATIC BELIEFS/EXPECTATIONS TO TRAUMATIC EXPERIENCES

- Discuss youth's expressed views. Do not challenge them or try and talk them out of even problematic beliefs.
- Put beliefs/expectations in context with what you know about the youth's trauma and loss experiences. You may reference the timeline.

- Normalize and validate ("It makes sense that you would believe you can't trust people when over and over you have reached out to people and they have let you down.")
- Praise positive and hopeful beliefs that have weathered single or multiple difficult experiences and related adversities.

DISCUSS THE COSTS OF MAINTAINING SPECIFIC TRAUMATIC BELIEFS/EXPECTATIONS

- If you have identified one or more traumatic beliefs/expectations that may undermine the youth's current functioning and future prospects, explore with the youth the "costs and benefits" of this view. You may use the grid that highlights short-term and long-term costs and benefits (see Handout 2.12).
- You may also do a cost–benefit analysis of positive and hopeful assumptions and expectations to highlight the concrete value of realistic yet optimistic assumptions.
- You may also help the youth evaluate the accuracy of the belief or expectation by examining the evidence for and against and looking for exceptions, when the belief or expectation was not true.
- For youth who come to the conclusion that one or more assumption comes at too high a cost, help him or her craft a "belief problem statement" that has the following elements:

Creating a Belief Problem Statement

(Believing that …) + (doesn't work for me because …) + (and that makes me feel …)

"Believing that I can't trust anybody + doesn't work for me because it means that I can never get close to people + and that makes me feel sad and alone."

DISCUSS POSSIBLE PATHWAYS TO CHANGE THE TRAUMATIC BELIEF/EXPECTATION

For each belief problem statement, go through the following steps with the youth.

1. Work with the youth to craft a more realistic and helpful version of the belief/expectation. Draw upon the previous discussion that explored "evidence for and against" and "exceptions" to the belief or expectation.
    - (Example: *"There are a lot of people I can't trust but I also am good at identifying a few that I can."*)

2. Help the youth explore what it would be like to have the new more realistic and helpful belief or expectation.

Use Handout 1.30, Sizing Up a Situation, to explore the following:
- **Thoughts**: *How would you think differently? In what situations would there be the most difference?*
- **Feelings**: *How would you feel differently?*
- **Behaviors**: *What would you do differently? What changes would other people notice?*
- **Consequences**: *What new or different consequences might you encounter?*

3. Describe a first small step towards changing the problematic belief or expectation. Describe what that first step would look like and create an "experiment" to see if you can do it during this next week.

C. Review of Current Stressors, Challenges, and Positive Experiences Identified in Timeline

During the latter part of the narrative, the youth was asked to describe stressors, challenges, and positive experiences encountered during the past month. These were color-coded and provide a window on current issues and themes in the youth's life. There are numerous ways to use this information. One is to engage in a discussion in which you help the youth prioritize the current difficulties and see if these can inform or update the goals set for participation in the treatment. You can also look for themes related to the trauma or loss experiences highlighted in the narrative. Current problems in living may include reactivity to trauma and loss reminders that were indicated in the narrative sharing; they may also be related to problematic thoughts, beliefs, and expectations identified in the previous exercises.

VI. Practice Assignment

Describe the practice assignment for the coming week using Handout 2.04, Things That *I* Can Do: My Personal Coping Toolkit. Have the youth anticipate one or more situations or events that may occur during the next week that may be stressful or triggering. Help the youth select one or more of the coping strategies in the youth's personal coping toolkit to use in response or to pre-empt difficulties. Arrange to check in on this at the next meeting.

VII. Check-Out

- *How are you feeling now?* (Use the Feeling Thermometer ratings.)
- *What did you learn about yourself today?*
- *Please fill out the Check-Out Feedback Form (Handout 2.13). The title of today's session was "Individual and Pull-out Sessions."*

MODULE 2 HANDOUTS

HANDOUT 2.01

Feeling Thermometer

What emotion do you feel right now? Name the feeling you are having and rate how strong or weak it is on this thermometer: 10 means extremely strong, 5 means medium, and 1 means you have the feeling just a little bit.

10	EXTREME
9	
8	A LOT
7	
6	
5	MEDIUM
4	
3	
2	A LITTLE
1	
0	NOT AT ALL

What distressing feelings do you have right now? Rate the strength of these feelings from 1 to 10.

HANDOUT 2.02

Selecting My Event

Part 1 — Describe an event:

One sentence description of event	Distress when reminded
Event 1 _____ _____	
Event 2 _____ _____	
Event 3 _____ _____	

Part 2 — Answer questions below for your selected event:

Y / N   I still think about it a lot.

Y / N   When I think about it, I get stressed or have strong feelings.

Y / N   I remember it well enough to tell the story.

Y / N   If I could do some healing about this experience, it would help me.

HANDOUT 2.03

Telling My Story

The Facts

Everything that happened – from the beginning to the end

The Feelings

What did I feel while it was happening?

What do I feel when I remember it?

The Senses

Sight, sound, touch, smell, taste during the experience

How did your body feel?

What were the worst moments?

The Thoughts

What did you tell yourself at the time? What do you tell yourself now?

Do you have thoughts about whose fault it was?

How has this experience changed you?

How has this experience changed how you think?

Others

What advice would you give others who have been through experiences like this about how to survive them so they can move on with their lives?

HANDOUT 2.04

Things That *I* Can Do: My Personal Coping Toolkit

Challenge hurtful thoughts with helpful thoughts. Use the Three-Step Model you have learned.

Seek support from others

- Use the five steps to getting support that you learned.

Relaxation

- Breathe deeply and slowly.
- Listen to relaxing music.

Take a time-out

- Walk away and calm down – do something else for a while.

Write in your journal

- Write about the situation, your thoughts, and your feelings.

Exercise regularly

- Walk, hike, jog, play soccer, basketball, swim, bike, lift weights.

Distraction through positive activities

- Get your mind off things by going to a positive film, watching something funny on YouTube, working on hobbies, socializing with friends, reading a book, listening to music, writing poems or stories, etc.

Keep a consistent daily routine

- Get up at the same time and prepare for sleep at the same time. If you have trouble sleeping, this practice can be especially helpful. (You may also find it helpful to use your bed *only* for sleeping.)

Reward yourself

- Treat yourself to something positive when you do something well. Praise yourself, buy yourself something healthy, or engage in a favorite (healthy) activity.

Spiritual

- Read an uplifting book.
- Pray or meditate.
- Listen to inspiring music.
- Participate in religious services or other pro-social group activities.
- Memorize uplifting quotes and use them as "helpful thoughts."

HANDOUT 2.05

Check-Out Feedback Form

Session topic: Preparing to Share Personal Trauma or Loss Experiences

Your date of birth: _____

Today's date: _____

Facility: _____

Unit/Cottage: _____

What about today's session was most useful to you? Which activities and materials were the most helpful?

_____

_____

_____

What specific suggestions do you have for how to make the group better?

_____

_____

_____

How comfortable were you about today's topic? (Please circle a number.)

1	2	3	4	5
Extremely uncomfortable	Fairly uncomfortable	Somewhat comfortable	Fairly comfortable	Very comfortable

What were you thinking and feeling during today's group?

_____

_____

_____

_____

How are you feeling now?

_____

_____

_____

HANDOUT 2.06

Muscle Relaxation Guide

Get yourself in a comfortable position. (PAUSE)

Now make a tight fist with your right hand.

Feel the tension in your hand.

Open your hand and let the tension fly away.

Let's get rid of the tension in your body.

Now, tighten the muscles in your face. (PAUSE)

Do you feel tension? (PAUSE)

Sigh deeply and let it go.

Now, tighten the muscles in your shoulders. (PAUSE)

Sigh deeply and let it go.

Now, tighten the muscles in your arms. (PAUSE)

Sigh deeply and let it go.

Now, tighten the muscles in both of your hands and fingers. (PAUSE)

Sigh deeply and let it go.

Now, tighten the muscles in your stomach. (PAUSE)

Sigh deeply and let it go.

Now, tighten the muscles in your thighs. (PAUSE)

Sigh deeply and let it go.

Now, tighten the muscles in your feet and toes. (PAUSE)

Sigh deeply and let it go.

If you feel any remaining tension in your body, tighten those muscles. (PAUSE)

Now sigh deeply and let it go.

Reprinted with permission from UCLA Center for Community Health (TALK LA)

Timeline Template

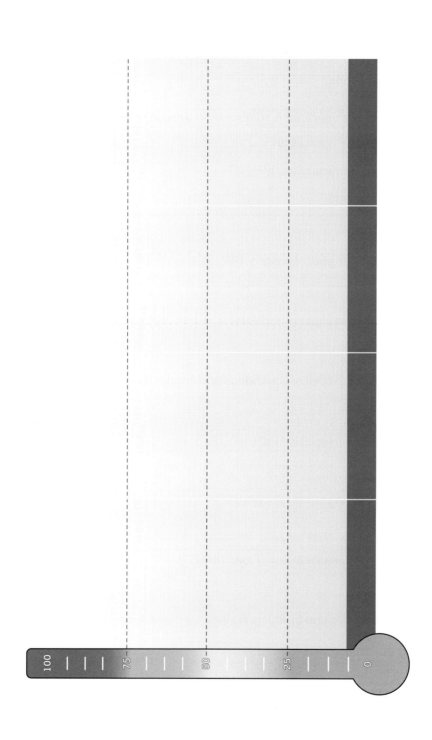

HANDOUT 2.08

Challenging and Replacing Hurtful Thoughts

First: Help the group member clearly state the hurtful thought. You may refer to Handout 1.35, the Hurtful Thoughts Checklist, to help clarify the central thought.

Second: With the group's help, guide the member to consider whether the thought makes sense and whether it is the most helpful way of looking at what happened.

- For this work you can elicit facts that support and do not support the thought. You can refer to Handout 2.09, Examining the Evidence For and Against.
- You can also help the member identify possible errors in thinking and refer to Handouts 1.41 and 1.42 on common thinking errors.
- Finally, even if the thought is accurate you can ask the member if the thought and subsequent feelings and behaviors are "working" or are helpful.

Third: Construct a more accurate or helpful thought. Draw upon the group for suggestions and feedback.

HANDOUT 2.09

Examining the Evidence For and Against

Evidence that supports the belief	Evidence that does not support the belief (possible questions/facts)
What evidence do you have for believing the hurtful thought? List your responses here: _____ _____ _____ _____ _____ _____	• Did your **circumstances permit you** to do what you wanted (and tried) to do? • Could you have known what was about to happen? ("crystal ball" beliefs) • Could you have done anything to stop it? ("Superman" or "Superwoman" beliefs) • You were in a **terrible predicament (Was there any satisfactory choice available?)** • There was **little time** to prepare or to decide what to do • There was **little information available** • You were very **young** and **inexperienced** • You were **terrified, horrified, confused, panicked**, and felt **helpless** • You were **doing the best you could** under the circumstances

HANDOUT 2.10

Check-Out Feedback Form

Session topic: Group Narrative Sharing Sessions

Your date of birth: _____

Today's date: _____

Facility: _____

What about today's session was most useful to you? Which activities and materials were the most helpful?

_____

_____

_____

What specific suggestions do you have for how to make the group better?

_____

_____

_____

How comfortable were you about today's topic? (Please circle a number.)

1	2	3	4	5
Extremely uncomfortable	Fairly uncomfortable	Somewhat comfortable	Fairly comfortable	Very comfortable

What were you thinking and feeling during today's group?

_____

_____

_____

_____

How are you feeling now?

_____

_____

_____

_____

HANDOUT 2.11

Check-Out Feedback Form

Session topic: Review of Group Sharing and Exploration of Beliefs and Expectations

Date of birth: _____

Today's date: _____

Facility: _____

What about today's session was most useful to you? Which activities and materials were the most helpful?

_____

_____

_____

What specific suggestions do you have for how to make the group better?

_____

_____

_____

How comfortable were you about today's topic? (Please circle a number.)

1	2	3	4	5
Extremely uncomfortable	Fairly uncomfortable	Somewhat comfortable	Fairly comfortable	Very comfortable

What were you thinking and feeling during today's group?

_____

_____

_____

_____

How are you feeling now?

_____

_____

_____

HANDOUT 2.12

Consequences of my Choices: "What Would Happen if I Did It?"

	Short-term	Long-term
Positives		
Negatives		

HANDOUT 2.13

Check-Out Feedback Form

Session topic: Individual and Pull-out Sessions

Your date of birth: _____

Today's date: _____

Facility: _____

What about today's session was most useful to you? Which activities and materials were the most helpful?

_____

_____

_____

What specific suggestions do you have for how to make the group better?

_____

_____

_____

How comfortable were you about today's topic? (Please circle a number.)

1	2	3	4	5
Extremely uncomfortable	Fairly uncomfortable	Somewhat comfortable	Fairly comfortable	Very comfortable

What were you thinking and feeling during today's group?

_____

_____

_____

_____

How are you feeling now?

_____

_____

_____

_____

3 Working through Grief Experiences

General Objectives for All Module 3 Grief Sessions

Work together to create a group atmosphere of support, validation, acceptance, and sympathetic understanding that:

- Can tolerate, accept, and bear witness to intense and painful emotions that often accompany loss, including deep sorrow, longing, intense anger, guilt, and despair.
- Allows the group to serve as a safe and supportive "container" for the often intense and poignant thoughts and feelings that will be expressed.
- Helps group members feel comfortable experiencing and sharing their grief-related thoughts, emotions, and efforts to cope with and adjust to the loss.
- Increases group members' motivation and commitment to engage in grief work.
- Validates members' grief reactions by explaining that these reactions reflect how deeply each of them still feels the loss and what this loss personally means to them.
- Normalizes group members' experiences and strengthens group cohesion by pointing out commonalities among group members' grief-related experiences.
- Strengthens group members' re-connection with (living) members of their social networks in the form of supportive exchanges (e.g. giving and receiving emotional support, feedback). These supportive exchanges include:
  - exchanges *among group members themselves*
  - exchanges between group members and their *significant others*, such as family members, close friends, or romantic partners, outside of the group.

Introduction

Module 3 is designed to help bereaved adolescents reduce their distressing grief reactions and cope in adaptive ways with the death of a family member or close friend. An innovative aspect of Module 3 is its *strength-based focus*, reflecting the basic assumption that *grief is not inherently pathological, but is instead a generally beneficial process that facilitates adjustment to the death and the accompanying loss* (Layne et al., 2012). Thus, a unique feature of Module 3 is its dual emphasis on *regulating* and *reducing* maladaptive grief reactions (so that they recede over time) on one hand, while *facilitating, encouraging,* and *cultivating* adaptive grief reactions (so that they promote positive adjustment over time) on the other. This strength-based emphasis makes Module 3's therapeutic activities not only poignant, edifying, and fulfilling for clinicians and youth, but also engaging, energizing, hopeful, and often fun.

Overview of Multidimensional Grief Theory

Multidimensional grief theory proposes that grief reactions consist of responses to *three central challenges* posed by the death of a loved one (Layne et al., in press). Each of these three challenges forms the conceptual basis of a separate dimension of grief. The first conceptual dimension (*Separation Distress*) centers on responding to distress over the permanent, irreversible, physical separation from the deceased. The key challenge of separation distress involves addressing the problem, "How do I find a way to feel meaningfully connected to the person who died, even though he or she is now physically absent from my life?" Normative manifestations of separation distress are characterized by missing the deceased person; sadness and heartache over his or her failure to return; and yearning or longing to be reunited with him/her. More maladaptive manifestations of separation distress in bereaved youth can involve intrusive, unwelcome, unconstructive thoughts or mental images of the deceased (e.g., "I keep on thinking of him or her, even when I don't want to"); persisting suicidal ideation (motivated by a wish to be reunited in an afterlife with the deceased); identifying with unhealthy or dysfunctional elements of the deceased's values, habits, or behaviors as a way of feeling close to him/her; and developmental slowing or regression (motivated by desires to stay connected with the deceased by remaining rooted in the same developmental stage, life circumstances, or now-immature behavior patterns one engaged in while he or she was still alive) (Kaplow et al., 2013; in press).

The second conceptual dimension (*Existential/Identity Distress*) focuses on responding to an existential crisis, or threat to one's personal identity, evoked by the death. The key challenge of this dimension involves addressing the problem of "who am I as a person, and what is the meaning and purpose of my existence, now that my loved one is physically absent from my life?" Normative manifestations of existential/identity distress involve efforts to cope with disruptions to one's sense of self, daily routines, life ambitions, life plans, and future aspirations as a result of the loss; striving to find personal meaning in the loss; and striving to find meaning and fulfillment in one's personal life after an important life figure has died. More maladaptive manifestations of existential/identity distress in bereaved adolescents can involve a perceived loss of personal identity (e.g., "I feel like a big part of me died with him"); feeling deeply ashamed or embarrassed (e.g., "I feel weird or different from other kids now that I don't have a dad anymore"); nihilism (e.g., "I've lost what I cared about most, so nothing else really matters"); or hopelessness, despair, or resignation in anticipation of a grim future without the deceased (e.g., "I'll never find someone like her again. My life is ruined"). Loss-related identity or existential crises may also manifest as risky behaviors, recklessness, or indifference to one's safety (e.g. not buckling one's seat belt, risky drug use), well-being, or social standing (e.g., "I don't care what happens to me"), survivor guilt ("I should be dead, too"), neglect of self-care, or failure to develop positive future aspirations appropriate to one's life circumstances and developmental stage (e.g., "Even if I keep on living, I don't have a future") (Kaplow et al., 2013; in press).

The third conceptual dimension (*Circumstance-Related Distress*) focuses on responding to *how* the person died – that is, the specific *manner* of his or her death. The key challenge of circumstance-related distress involves addressing the question: "How do I think about, feel about, and come to terms with the way in which this person died?" Circumstance-related distress consists of troubling thoughts and emotional pain over *how* the person died. Within the normative/adaptive range, such distress typically recedes over time, and often motivates bereaved youth to engage in constructive social action – whether public or private – that addresses (answers, or speaks to, in a helpful way) *how* the person died. Examples of constructive social action include advocacy (focused on preventing similar deaths from occurring in the future), becoming a counselor (to help youth find alternatives to gang life), becoming a doctor (to keep people from dying prematurely), or becoming an engineer (to make cars safer). More maladaptive expressions of circumstance-related distress can involve persisting feelings of rage, guilt, shame, retaliatory fantasies, and intense desires for (often violent) revenge (Kaplow et al., 2013; in press).

A growing body of research is helping to identify potential causal risk factors for circumstance-related distress. These include deaths that may involve *violence* (e.g. violent murders, gruesome accidents), *volition* (e.g. human agency with malicious intent such as murder; also suicide), or *violation* of the social contract (e.g. deaths arising from human negligence, failure to protect, or professional malpractice) (Rynearson, 1994). The risk for severe circumstance-related distress may increase in youth who are dually exposed to direct life threat themselves and to witnessing traumatic death of a close person, given that these youth must contend with posttraumatic stress reactions, grief reactions, and their interplay (Pynoos, 1992 Layne et al., in press). Nevertheless, evidence indicates that even "anticipated" deaths, such as those due to terminal illness, can also produce circumstance-related distress in youth, especially youth who have been exposed to potentially traumatic scenes (e.g., witnessing progressive physical deterioration of a loved one, disfiguring medical procedures, intense suffering; Kaplow et al., 2014a).

Multidimensional grief theory helps clinicians to understand that, even if bereaved youth are not notably distressed by the circumstances of the death, they may still experience separation distress and/or existential/identity distress. Put simply, circumstance-related distress relates to *how* the person died, whereas separation distress and existential/identity distress relate to the fact *that* the person died, regardless of the circumstances. This distinction not only underscores the advantages of a multidimensional framework for understanding grief, but is key to identifying different subgroups of youth who are at risk for experiencing different forms of maladaptive grief (Layne et al., 2012, in press).

Overview of Module 3 Sessions

Module 3 session activities are designed to reduce the specific maladaptive grief reactions outlined above, while also promoting adaptive grief reactions. *Session 3.1* focuses on psychoeducation about grief and provides an overview of different types of grief reactions (separation distress, existential/identity distress, circumstance-related distress) addressed by multidimensional grief theory. Discussion-based activities emphasize that there are a wide range of grief responses and courses of bereavement, and that there is no one way or single "best" way to grieve in healthy ways. The discussion also notes the roles played by developmental and cultural factors that shape and influence the experience of loss and expression of grief (Kaplow & Layne, 2014). Bereaved adolescents are often distressed by inappropriate expectations held by themselves or others about their course of adjustment to bereavement. For example, many adolescents believe that something may be wrong with them because of unrealistic expectations about how long their grief reactions persist. Describing the wide range of potential grief responses helps youth to appreciate and understand their own reactions, as well as those of fellow group members, family, and friends (Kaplow et al., 2014b). The discussion can also be guided to clarify how *differences in levels* or *types of exposure* to the death (i.e. direct life threat or injury, witnessing the death of a loved one, attempting to revive the person) can influence the ways in which family members react to their experiences. These may include differing levels of posttraumatic stress and grief reactions that create powerful dissonances in the ways in which members experience, exhibit, and cope with their reactions – especially circumstance-related distress (Kaplow et al., 2013; Howell et al., 2015). Helping youth become aware of how traumatic circumstances can make bereavement more difficult can help them to identify, label, understand, and process their own grief reactions, including managing their circumstance-related distress and having compassion for themselves and each other (Kaplow et al., in press).

Session 3.2 focuses on the connections between *loss reminders* and bereavement-related *thoughts, feelings*, and *consequences*. This session helps to validate the various types of grief reactions that many adolescents experience and offers words they can use to label their own deeply-held (and often unspoken or misunderstood) internal responses. In addition, identifying personal loss reminders and understanding how they evoke their grief reactions helps adolescents to feel more "in control" as they become better able to predict when and how their grief may arise (Kaplow et al., in press). The clinician also uses an illustration-based exercise to teach youth how to challenge "unhelpful" grief-related thoughts, while leveraging the safe distance these illustrations create between the imagined scenario and the bereaved youth's own experiences. This self-distancing "third-person" approach creates opportunities for insight and self-reflection by using fictitious characters and hypothetical scenarios, thereby helping to protect youth from feeling overwhelmed by their personal emotions (Kross & Ayduk, 2011; Wardecker et al., 2013). Session 3.2 activities can be tailored to the types of grief reactions that are most prominent among group members by having the therapist select illustrations that depict the specific grief reactions and bereavement-related experiences that group members have endorsed (e.g. avoiding situations that remind him/her of the person who died, being afraid of getting close to others, feeling like they have lost what matters most; Kaplow et al., in press).

Session 3.3 focuses on helping adolescents to identify intense negative emotions that can contribute to their maladaptive grief reactions, including guilt, shame, anger, or regret. Youth use the coping skills they learned in Session 3.2 to challenge their "unhelpful" thoughts and beliefs related to self-blame or preoccupations with revenge. This may also include identifying and processing difficult last interactions with the person who died (which can arise when the person died by suicide or overdose) and addressing regrets. As appropriate, the clinician can therapeutically reframe adolescents' efforts to maintain behaviors and attitudes that used to evoke negative interactions with the person while they were alive, but which the youth has now outgrown, as a reunion fantasy. This fantasy helps to preserve the feeling of "having them back again" (e.g. "Sometimes we wish our dads would come back and show their love by protecting and guiding us, like telling us to stop dating losers, stop getting high, or stop skipping school") (Kaplow et al., 2013; in press). This can introduce the idea of maladaptive *separation distress* and set the stage for identifying more constructive ways to feel close to the person who died.

Session 3.4 is designed to help adolescents deal with their ambivalent feelings about the deceased. Many youth – especially those with extensive trauma histories – report having had a "difficult" relationship with the deceased person. Session 3.4 activities help youth to make sense of potentially *ambivalent* feelings about the deceased person, to reflect on the deceased person's desirable and undesirable traits or behaviors, and to learn to selectively choose *positive* aspects of the deceased that they would like to carry with them over time and incorporate into their own identity. This session is also designed to help adolescents use those positive traits/behaviors of the deceased to not only honor their memory, but to improve the adolescents' own lives in practical ways by encouraging the adolescent to try to become a better person. This exercise can help to alleviate both *existential/identity distress* (by incorporating positive attributes of the person into the youth's identity and personal life) and *separation distress* (by feeling positively connected to the "better" parts of the deceased) (Kaplow et al., in press).

Session 3.5 is designed to help adolescents renegotiate their relationship with the deceased from one of physical presence to one of memory (and for some, spiritual presence). Many youth need assistance in finding healthy ways of connecting to the deceased. Session 3.5 helps adolescents form connections in developmentally and culturally sensitive ways through memories of the person, precious items they now hold close, mourning rituals, and, where appropriate, prayer. This session focuses on helping adolescents to find ways of maintaining a healthy connection with the deceased that works for them and can alleviate separation distress.

Session 3.6 is designed to normalize and validate bereaved adolescents' difficult interpersonal interactions that have arisen as a result of the death. Adolescents practice their support-seeking skills to help (a) decide which types of disclosures are most appropriate in which settings and with whom, and (b) recruit specific types of support depending on the specific bereavement-related challenge they are facing. The death of a loved one can be especially challenging for adolescents, given that this developmental period centers on issues of emerging personal identity and constructing a more elaborate conceptual framework of "my past, present, and future" by which to plan their lives. Bereaved adolescents may thus feel self-conscious, different, or "abnormal," or may have altered beliefs about what they may be able to accomplish in their future (Kaplow et al., 2012; in press). Bereaved adolescents may also feel the incentive to inhibit their developmental progression based on the distressing assumption that, by moving forward with their lives, they are actively letting go of and abandoning the deceased person (so that they *really are* dead and gone). Developmental achievements or transitions, such as graduations, can serve as loss reminders and may signify that the adolescent is "moving on" in life and leaving the deceased person behind permanently. This may increase adolescents' fears that they will forget important things about their loved ones, such as the sound of their voice, their smile, the way they smelled, or the warmth of their embrace. Session 3.6 is tailored to address adolescents' developmentally linked need to "fit in," but balances this with a focus on harnessing adaptive grief reactions (e.g. carrying on a positive legacy) to prepare for future challenges and accomplish future goals while still maintaining a positive connection to the deceased (Kaplow et al., in press). These activities are intended to address both *existential/identity distress* (by problem-solving how to move forward with life in adaptive ways) and *separation distress* (by problem-solving how to bring and update a positive connection to the deceased while moving forward).

Concluding Thoughts

Consistent with the proposition of multidimensional grief theory that grief is a generally beneficial and ongoing process of adjustment and adaptation (Kaplow et al., 2013; Layne et al., in press), the goal of Module 3 is not to eliminate all grief reactions. Indeed, grief reactions may continue long into the future. Instead, a realistic goal is to furnish adolescents with more effective tools to cope in comforting and constructive ways with loss-related challenges. Recommended intervention objectives include:

1. Reduced maladaptive grief scores (on the PCBD Checklist, etc.).
2. Reduced grief-related impairments (e.g. withdrawal from friends, restrictions in developmental tasks and opportunities) in developmentally salient life domains.
3. Improved ability to manage loss reminders, including reduced negative reactivity to reminders, reduced behavioral and cognitive avoidance, and improved coping skills.
4. Improved ability to access positive and comforting memories of the deceased (especially if the relationship was supportive while they were alive).
5. Reduced encroachment and interference by distress over the circumstances of the death (if the manner of death was violent, tragic, or otherwise deeply disturbing) upon adaptive grief reactions.
6. Meaningful improvements in adaptive grief responses including adopting a more optimistic outlook on their own sense of self, life purpose, interpersonal relationships, daily activities, and future aspirations.

References

Howell, K. H., Kaplow, J. B., Layne, C. M., et al. (2015). Predicting adolescent posttraumatic stress in the aftermath of war: Differential effects of coping strategies across trauma reminder, loss reminder, and family conflict domains. *Anxiety, Stress, & Coping*, 28, 88–104.

Kaplow, J. B., Layne, C. M., Pynoos, R. S., Cohen, J., & Lieberman, A. (2012). DSM-V diagnostic criteria for bereavement-related disorders in children and adolescents: Developmental considerations. *Psychiatry*, 75, 242–265.

Kaplow, J. B., Layne, C. M., Saltzman, W. R., Cozza, S. J., & Pynoos, R. S. (2013). Using multidimensional grief theory to explore effects of deployment, reintegration, and death on military youth and families. *Clinical Child and Family Psychology Review*, 16, 322–340.

Kaplow, J. B. & Layne, C. M. (2014). Sudden loss and psychiatric disorders across the life course: Toward a developmental lifespan theory of bereavement-related risk and resilience. *American Journal of Psychiatry*, 171, 807–810.

Kaplow, J. B., Howell, K. H., & Layne, C. M. (2014a). Do circumstances of the death matter? Identifying socioenvironmental risks for grief-related psychopathology in bereaved youth. *Journal of Traumatic Stress*, 27, 42–49.

Kaplow, J. B., Layne, C. M., & Pynoos, R. S. (2014a). Persistent Complex Bereavement Disorder as a call to action: Using a proposed DSM-5 diagnosis to advance the field of childhood grief. *Traumatic Stress Points* (available online: http://sherwood-istss.informz.net/sherwood-istss/archives/archive_3773102.html)

Kaplow, J. B., Layne, C. M., & Pynoos, R. S. (2014b). Parental grief facilitation: How parents can help their bereaved children during the holidays. *Traumatic Stress Points* (http://sherwood-istss.informz.net/admin31/content/template.asp?sid=40989&brandid=4463&uid=1019024255&mi=4449102&mfqid=17980717&ptid=0&ps=40989).

Kaplow, J. B., Layne, C. M., Pynoos, R. S., & Saltzman, W. (in press). *Multidimensional Grief Therapy: A Flexible Approach to Assessing and Supporting Bereaved Youth*. Cambridge: Cambridge University Press.

Kross, E., & Ayduk, O. (2011). Making meaning out of negative experiences by self-distancing. *Current Directions in Psychological Science*, 20, 187–191.

Layne, C. M., Kaplow, J. B., & Pynoos, R. S. (2012). Using developmentally-informed theory and evidence-based assessment to guide intervention with bereaved youth and families. In C. M. Layne (Chair), *Integrating Developmentally-Informed Theory, Evidence-Based Assessment, and Evidence-Based Treatment of Childhood Maladaptive Grief*. Symposium presented at the International Society for Traumatic Stress Studies, Los Angeles, CA, November 2012.

Layne, C. M., Kaplow, J. B., Oosterhoff, B. Hill, R., & Pynoos, R. S. (in press). The interplay between posttraumatic stress and grief reactions in traumatically bereaved adolescents: When trauma, bereavement, and adolescence converge. *Adolescent Psychiatry*.

Pynoos, R. S. (1992). Grief and trauma in children and adolescents. *Bereavement Care* 11, 2–10.

Rynearson, E. (1994). Psychotherapy of bereavement after homicide. *Journal of Psychotherapy Practice and Research*, 3, 341–347.

Wardecker, B. M., Kaplow, J. B., Edelstein, R. S., Kross, E., & Layne, C. M. (2013). Linguistic correlates of adaptive functioning in parentally bereaved children. In J. B. Kaplow (Chair), *Correlates and Predictors of "Good Grief" in Bereaved Children and Adolescents: Implications for Intervention*. Symposium presented at the Annual Meeting of the International Society for Traumatic Stress Studies, Philadelphia, PA, November 2013.

3.1 Learning about Grief

Session Objectives

1. Normalize and validate grief as a normal, expectable, and generally helpful reaction to loss.
2. Describe and explore grief reactions in terms that are relevant to group members' losses and experiences.
3. Expand group members' vocabularies for labeling, understanding, and expressing grief reactions.
4. Explain how the course of grief reactions often fluctuates over time.
5. Explain *why* we grieve – what is the purpose of grieving and mourning over our losses? What helpful function does it tend to serve?
6. Identify and review group members' own personal goals for coping with painful grief reactions.

Section number	Session overview
I	Check-in
II	Review practice assignment
III	Transition to a focus on loss
IV	Grief psychoeducation: what is grief?
V	Grief psychoeducation: grief reactions
VI	Summary and practice assignment
VII	Check-out

Supplies

Every session	This session
• Group member workbooks	
• Flipchart	
• Large paper or easel pad	
• Markers	
• Pencils/pens	
• Kleenex	
• Tape	
• Post-it notes and pencils	

Handouts in Workbook

Handout 3.01	Feeling Thermometer
Handout 3.02	Rating My Grief Reactions
Handout 3.03	Learning about Different Grief Reactions
Handout 3.04	Grief Goals Worksheet
Handout 3.05	Check-Out Feedback Form

Flipcharts

> **3.1a Today's Highlights**
>
> 1. Check-in
> 2. Review practice assignment
> 3. Turn to a focus on loss
> 4. What is grief?
> 5. Grief reactions
> 6. How does grief change over time?
> 7. What are your own personal goals for coping with grief?
> 8. Summary and practice assignment
> 9. Transitional activity and check-out

> **3.1b What Is Grief?**
>
> Grief is a normal reaction to the loss of someone or something we care about.
> - Many different types of losses can cause grief reactions
> - Grieving is healthy, normal, and helpful
> - Grief reactions usually change over time
> - Grieving can be both public and private
> - Grief can last a long time, even forever
> - Healthy grieving does not mean forgetting or no longer caring about the people or things we love

Session 3.1: Learning About Grief

I. Check-In and Feeling Thermometer

- Check in via Handout 3.01, the Feeling Thermometer.
- *What happened or what did you do since we last met that you feel good about?*
- *Is anything going on that may make it difficult for you to keep your mind on the group today?*
- Briefly review (or have a group member review) Today's Highlights (Flipchart 3.1a).

II. Review Practice Assignment

- Ask group members if they practiced the deep breathing this week. If they did, how did it go?
- Practice with the group doing five to ten abdominal breaths.
- Check in again with the Feeling Thermometer to monitor any changes.

III. Transition to a Focus on Loss

Hint: Keep this exercise relatively light and brief – your goal is to transition from trauma-focused work (the primary focus of Modules 1 and 2) to the loss-focused work of grief processing.

For the past several months, we have been focusing on stressful, scary, or traumatic experiences and how these experiences have influenced your lives.

*We're now going to shift our focus away from these traumatic or scary experiences to ways in which the deaths of people you cared about, and the circumstances surrounding their death (or the **way** they died) may continue to influence your lives.*

*We're shifting away from the theme of **trauma** to the themes of **loss** and **grief**.*

Activity: Sharing the Loss

*We would like to ask each of you to **briefly** tell us about the death that you would like to focus on in this group. It can be the same one you described before in our trauma-focused work, or it can be some other death that you feel would be most helpful to focus on now.*

*Please describe the death you have chosen to focus on, including **whom** you lost, **what** happened (how they died), and **when** it happened. Please also share **one situation or part of your life that has become more difficult**, because the person is no longer physically present in your life. This may be a difficult situation that their loss has created (like money problems after losing a parent), or something that you still really miss, like talking or having fun with him or her.*

Tips: Help group members keep their sharing brief and then **sympathize, normalize,** and **validate**. Ask clarifying questions as needed. Be mindful that **this may be the first time that these youths have discussed the death publicly.**

After all group members have briefly described their experience(s), check in with the group and, as necessary, help group members relax or recover using some of the skills they have already learned (e.g. sharing encouraging words of support, deep breathing, relaxation, distraction, or journaling).

Thank you all for sharing your experiences. We can all see how much experiencing the death of someone you care about can affect you in so many different ways. We are confident that the work we will be doing in the coming weeks will help you gain a better understanding of your reactions to these losses and how to deal with your grief in ways that can be helpful to you and bring feelings of comfort.

IV. Discuss Grief Psychoeducation: What Is Grief?

(Cover the general points below in your own words.)

Almost everyone will have someone close to them die at some point in their lives. For many people your age though, the loss of someone they love is one of the hardest and most painful experiences they have ever had. Even years after it happened, there are still times when it feels as if their family member or friend died just yesterday, and they miss them with all their heart.

*It's helpful to think about both **public** and **private** parts of dealing with losses.*

*Let's start by talking about two different words that people use to describe these situations – **grief** and **mourning**.*

*The word **grief** refers to the **private** part of reacting to a loss. Grief reactions are our own thoughts, feelings, dreams, and even physical feelings that we have inside our own bodies, like feeling our hearts ache, feeling a sinking feeling in our stomachs, or feeling empty inside. It can also include warm, comforting feelings like remembering fun times together or how much you like to do things that would make him or her proud. So grief can feel painful at times, and comforting at others, but it is a personal, private experience that we feel deeply inside.*

*The word **mourning** often refers to the **public** part of reacting to a loss (the part that other people can see and participate in). Mourning often involves **rituals** that help us to remember, honor, share memories about, and feel close to the person who died. Examples of public mourning rituals include attending wakes, funerals and memorial services, candlelight ceremonies, writing an obituary, creating memorials or shrines, wearing clothes in public that memorialize the person (like a T-shirt with their name or picture on it, or wearing all black), getting tattoos of them where others can see them, and posting about them on Facebook.*

*Mourning can also have **private** parts as well, such as **private mourning rituals** we create to help us remember and feel closer to them. This may include lighting a candle in private, going to church or a quiet place to pray for them, holding a personal moment of silence for them, planting a flower for them, keeping a memento, putting their picture next to our bed, or putting a T-shirt on our bedroom wall.*

*Both the personal and public parts of grief and mourning can help you deal with your loss. You can use our time together as a safe place, so that **as you begin to feel more comfortable**, you may want to share things that so far have only been part of your **personal** grief and not part of what you show others. This can help you to get the support you need and help you make sense of the feelings you're having, because grief can involve many different feelings. It's important to remember that there is no "right" or "wrong" way to grieve, and everyone's grief reactions are unique in some ways. How you grieve tells us a lot about what this person and your relationship with them meant to you and continues to mean to you.*

Activity: Answer True–False Grief Statements

For this activity, select specific questions below based on which topics are most relevant to your group members and on how much time is available. The following are some hints to remember when leading this activity:

- This activity should move along quickly, without in-depth explanations. The lengthy italicized passages after each question are to help you prepare beforehand, so you can explain these concepts in your own words based on the specific needs of your members. Do not read every phrase out loud. The intent is to simply introduce and normalize common grief reactions.
- You also don't need to read every statement. Pick the ones that you think are most relevant to the group, or add items that are not included here.
- To decrease a sense of competition among individual group members, consider dividing group members into pairs who will work together to answer each true/false question.
- After each statement is read and responded to, reinforce correct answers. When group members select an incorrect answer, normalize it (e.g. "a lot of people think that, but in fact … "). After reading each fact, call on a group member who chose the correct answer and ask him/her to share his/her thoughts on why it's true or false. Then, fill in the remaining facts as appropriate.

Although grief can involve some very strong emotions – maybe among the strongest we've ever felt – some people don't talk about grief openly. This can make it difficult for teenagers to learn what there is to learn about grief, and especially to find out whether what they're feeling is normal. So let's try an activity that helps us to think about how people grieve. I'm going to read some statements about grief and then ask you to answer whether you think it is true or false.

1. Most types of grief reactions can be *normal* and *healthy*.

ANSWER: TRUE

(Only as needed) *Most types of grief reactions are normal and understandable. Those strong feelings of grief are signs that we are still missing the person we have lost. These feelings can be healthy and beneficial in the long run, because they help us to adapt and adjust to the loss. Although some grief reactions **can** be painful and upsetting, they can also be comforting, reassuring, and they can even bring us relief over time, such as when we have a good cry or enjoy a sweet memory of a loved one. In our work together, we are not going to try to make your grief reactions go away. Instead, we'll try to increase the types of grief reactions that can be helpful and comforting to you, and decrease those that are less helpful to you.*

2. After someone close dies, teenagers get over their painful feelings after about 6–12 months.

ANSWER: FALSE

(Only as needed) *People grieve in individual ways. There is no "normal" time limit when grief is supposed to be over. Many grieving kids talk about their very strong feelings of sadness and loss decreasing more and more over time, so that painful memo-*

ries are replaced by more positive memories as time passes. This process can take weeks, months, or years and there is no "right" or "wrong" time limit. People can often experience an "uptick" in their grief reactions on certain occasions when they are reminded of the person, such as the anniversary of their death, their birthday, or during holidays when you would have been together with them.

3. It is best not to talk about the person who died – that way, it will be easier to move on with your life.

ANSWER: FALSE

(Only as needed) *Actually, talking about the loss and sharing our feelings is one of the best ways to work through painful feelings of grief. People who have the hardest time moving on with their lives often are working hard to avoid thinking or talking about their loss. Pushing these feelings down or out of your mind takes mental energy that can be draining and can close off important parts of yourself and your life. Working to keep strong feelings hidden, and distancing yourself from others, can make it harder to grieve in helpful ways, and can leave you feeling more lonely, misunderstood, sad, or angry. It also prevents you from benefitting from the public part of mourning, which is a powerful tool for giving and receiving support after a loss.*

4. Grief reactions always stay the same over time.

ANSWER: FALSE

(Only as needed) *Grief reactions can change from day to day, year to year, or even moment to moment. Some teens may not have very strong grief reactions right after the death, but may start to have them as time passes. For others, their grief reactions may be strongest right after the death, but then become less intense over time. Grief is different for everyone and may go up and down over time, often in response to* **loss reminders***. When loss reminders are there – such as hearing the deceased person's name, being someplace they used to be, doing something they used to do, their birthday, or during holidays or graduations – grief reactions can be very intense, especially soon after a loss. When loss reminders aren't around, grief reactions often* **decrease** *and may not feel as intense.*

5. Healthy grieving means that we forget or stop thinking about our loved one who died.

ANSWER: FALSE

(Only as needed) *Healthy and helpful grieving will never mean that you must try to replace, forget, or cut your emotional ties to the person who died. Instead, our goal is to* **change our relationship** *with them – to shift them from the physical world to a different world, which can be in our memories, minds, and hearts, or more of a spiritual world where they are watching over us in a comforting way – so that we have room in our lives for new relationships and activities. We each know that the person who has died is irreplaceable, and that's why losing them hurts so much. We will always keep a special place for them in our memories and hearts. We can honor their memory by remembering them and especially by carrying on part of what we admire the most about them. But while we grieve, we will also work on making space in our lives for new, enriching activities and new relationships with*

living people. These new relationships will never take the place of our loved one, and they don't need to, but they can help us move forward and live the kind of lives that our deceased loved one would want for us.

6. Everyone in the same family or group of close friends grieves in the same way, and "finishes" grieving at about the same time.

ANSWER: FALSE

(Only as needed) *Different people in the same family or group of close friends can have very different reactions to the same death, including when and how strongly they experience grief reactions. This may be due to different things. For example, they may have had a* **different type of relationship** *with the person who died – some may have been closer to the person than others, while others had a more difficult relationship. People may also have* **different levels of exposure to the death***. For example, some teens may have seen the actual death firsthand, or witnessed events that led up to it. Some teens may even have been with the person when it happened, and perhaps were injured themselves or felt their lives were in danger. They may be struggling with* **both posttraumatic stress reactions** *(to what they witnessed and went through at the time of death), and* **grief reactions** *(to the loss). All of these things can affect how they react to the person's death.*

People also have very different **personalities** *and* **styles of coping** *that can strongly affect how they grieve. Some people may "wear their hearts on their sleeve" and may be very open and expressive about how they feel about the death, whereas other people may be grieving a lot on the inside but are not that comfortable showing their feelings to others. Differences in how people react to a death can be a source of confusion, stress, misunderstanding, miscommunication, and even anger within a family or group of friends that can strain relationships at a time when they could really use one another's support. Family members and close friends often need to talk to each other more after a loss so they can understand each other's grief reactions and know how to support each other when someone is having a hard time.*

7. After someone we love or feel close to dies, we can never be truly happy again.

ANSWER: FALSE

(Only as needed, depending on assessment profiles) *People can feel this way right after someone dies. They often feel lots of strong emotions, like deep sadness, anger, or confusion. They may feel lost and alone. But although it may feel like you and your life are now very different because of what you have lost, you can still live a happy, fulfilling life. It may be different, but it can still be a good and meaningful life that is well worth living. Many teens find that there are important lessons that the person and their death can teach them – lessons that help them know how to better live their lives. Learning and applying these lessons often helps teens to find meaning and happiness again, by knowing that this is something that the person would want for them. It is also a comforting way to help keep the person's memory and influence alive.*

8. If we do not have a strong reaction to a death, it means we did not care about the person who died.

ANSWER: FALSE

(Only as needed) *How people initially react to a death depends on many things. Sometimes people who cared deeply for someone who died may not show strong reactions. This can be related to their personality, their life history, or just the fact that it's painful to think about the deceased person. Sometimes it takes a while for the reality of the death and the loss (what it means to live without the person's physical presence) to really sink in. Sometimes, especially if it was a difficult death and they were there when it happened, they may still feel numb and not be able to feel grief-related emotions. Sometimes, grief reactions can be delayed and appear only later in response to certain reminders or changes in their lives, such as when they get a bit older and start to make important life choices, like getting serious with someone, choosing a profession, or getting married. All these things take time, and we should give ourselves and others time and space to grieve.*

9. Sometimes we may feel relieved when a person dies.

ANSWER: TRUE

(Only as needed) *People sometimes feel relieved or even happy about a death. For example, the person may have been very sick, such as from cancer, and it was a relief when they finally passed away. They may have thoughts like, "I'm glad it finally happened because now I can move on with my life" or "I'm glad he/she doesn't have to suffer anymore." These thoughts are completely normal and, although they may be hard to talk about, many, many people have these thoughts and feelings after a death.*

In some cases people have had a very difficult relationship with the person who died and felt deeply hurt by them, so they felt a sense of relief or even happiness at their passing. In other cases, people can have very mixed feelings about the person who died, like a "love–hate" relationship, so they feel torn about the loss. They sometimes feel sad and miss the person, and other times they feel very angry at the person and tell themselves they're glad that the person is gone. These feelings sometimes leave teenagers feeling confused, or even guilty or ashamed, and they may try to hide or suppress their feelings.

V. Grief Psychoeducation: Grief Reactions

Activity: Identifying Different Grief Reactions

1. Have markers and either a board or paper to write on.
2. Open with the idea that people have very different reactions to a death over time. Introduce each of the three main grief categories listed below (write their names on the paper or the board) and briefly describe some typical thoughts that might be part of each category.
3. Give group members Handout 3.03, Learning about Different Grief Reactions, and ask them to put a check mark next to the reactions that they have had. Encourage the group members

to talk about their own reactions and to identify which ones have bothered them the most.
4. Ask whether each group member has any other grief reactions that you haven't talked about, and how he/she might categorize those reactions.
5. Call attention to the fact that, within each category, you will be giving examples of grief reactions that are often hard to deal with because they are painful and upsetting, and reactions that are more comforting. You can talk about both kinds of reactions and how often they feel each type.

The Three Categories of Grief Reactions

CATEGORY 1: MISSING THEM (SEPARATION DISTRESS)

- Missing the person.
- Wishing we were together again.
- Feeling lonely.
- Wanting to go look for them.
- Wanting to cry for them.
- Feeling angry that we aren't together.
- Avoiding any reminder that they are gone.
- Feeling afraid to get close to other people, because I could lose them too.
- Feeling bad that we didn't get to say goodbye the way we wanted to.
- Feeling bad (regret or guilty) that we didn't treat the person better while they were alive.

(Normalize as appropriate) Possible additional comments for describing separation distress:

- *Cry.*
- *Search for the deceased or be "on the lookout" for them to show up, such as imagining that it's them whenever they hear the front door open, or seeing their face in a crowd.*
- *Grief reactions that can be comforting when you're really missing them:*
- *Thinking I can see or hear or feel them nearby in a comforting way.*
- *Feeling like the person is watching over me and looking out for me.*
- *Wanting to do positive things that he/she used to do that I liked or admired.*

CATEGORY 2: FEELING LOST WITHOUT THEM (EXISTENTIAL DISTRESS)

- Feeling like part of myself died with them.
- Feeling lost without them.
- Not knowing what to do without them.
- Losing hope that I can still have a good life.
- Losing my desire to work hard to have a good life.
- Feeling like nothing matters anymore.
- Not caring what happens to me anymore.

(Normalize as appropriate) Possible additional comments for describing existential distress:

Grieving teenagers also may change how they act around other people. They may experience:

- *A decrease in their interest and motivation to form relationships (because they see no rewarding future).*
- *They may feel bored or indifferent towards life, or feel like nothing is worth working for.*
- *They may get easily irritated, angry, and critical of others.*
- *They may withdraw from others, even though they feel lonely and bored.*

Grief reactions that can be comforting when you're feeling lost without them:

- *Feeling like I want to help other teens who are going through difficult times.*
- *Wanting to live the kind of life that he or she would have wanted for me.*

CATEGORY 3: EMOTIONAL PAIN OVER THE WAY THEY DIED (CIRCUMSTANCE-RELATED DISTRESS)

- Feeling angry about the way they died.
- Feeling guilty that I didn't do more.
- Being so upset over how they died that it's hard to remember the good times.
- Wanting revenge on whoever I think is responsible.

(Normalize as appropriate) Possible additional comments for describing these reactions:

- *Many people describe feeling **angry** about their loss. Sometimes they also feel guilty or ashamed over what happened, especially when the person died in a **violent or tragic way.** We'll focus on these difficult feelings during our next sessions.*
- *People who experience loss through violent death can sometimes have upsetting pictures come into their minds about how the person died. These thoughts can be so upsetting that it makes it hard to enjoy pleasant memories about them. Thoughts of how the person died can be so unpleasant that people start to avoid even thinking or talking about the special person who died. This avoidance interferes with grieving.*

Grief reactions that can be comforting when I'm upset about the way they died:

- *Wanting to do things to prevent other people from dying the same tragic way.*

Other Types of Grief Reactions

Some grieving teens also have what they call "weird", "abnormal", or even "paranormal" experiences, such as when:

- *You sense the presence of the person nearby.*
- *You seem to "see" or "hear" them, such as catching a glimpse of their face in a crowd or hearing their voice just for a moment.*
- *Believing that certain animals or situations are "signs" from the deceased person.*

These experiences can be interpreted in different ways depending on our different belief systems. For example, when this happens, it may be telling us how much we wish that the loss didn't happen and that our loved ones would come back to us. Or some people believe that the spirit of the deceased person can visit us from time to time to let us know that he/she is still around to comfort or protect us. The point isn't to decide what is "real" and what is "in our heads" – it's really more about what feels most helpful and comforting at this point in time. A grief reaction we had during childhood may have been comforting back then, but is less so now, and vice versa. Our beliefs may have changed, or we may learn new things as we grow. The ways in which we grieve, and what feels comforting to us, can change over time, and this is normal and OK.

Optional Activity: Riding the Waves of Grief (How Grief Changes over Time)

Follow the steps below:

1. Draw this wave/timeline on a board or large piece of paper attached to a wall so everyone can see:

Riding the Waves of Grief

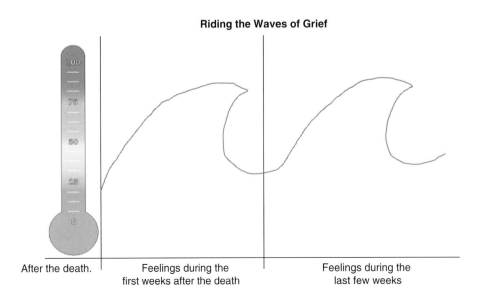

After the death. | Feelings during the first weeks after the death | Feelings during the last few weeks

2. Introduce the exercise. You can use language like the following: *We can think of grief-related feelings like **waves** in the ocean. Waves come and go. They can be strong (sometimes even as strong as a tsunami), medium, or weak. One day you can be swept up by a wave of anger, and then after a while it begins to weaken, and you are next picked up by a wave of guilt, or sadness* (use the predominant emotions/grief reactions that you just reviewed together, making sure to include anger, guilt, and sadness). Note the distress rating scale on the left side of the chart and explain that the higher the wave, the stronger the emotion.

3. Give each group member a pencil and two post-it notes and provide the following directions: *On the first post-it note, please write down **at least two grief reactions** you had **within the first few weeks** after the person died. On the second post-it note, write down at least two grief reactions you've had much more recently, during the **last few weeks**. These can be the more upsetting grief reactions we discussed, or more comforting reactions, or both. There are no right or wrong answers.*

4. Have each group member come up to the wave chart and place their first post-it with the feelings during the first few weeks on a wave at the height that describes how intense the feelings were (lower on the wave = less intense, higher on the wave = more intense). Have them place their second post-it note in the second area that describes the feeling intensity during the past few weeks.

Comment on the range of different reactions and how reactions may change or stay the same over time. Invite group members to describe their experience regarding how their own reactions may have changed or stayed the same since the death.

VI. Summary and Practice Assignment

Summarize the session: *Today we talked about grief and loss. What were some of the main things you learned?*

Have the group respond first and then show Flipchart 3.1b and review the points listed.

- *Grief is normal.*
- *Grief is generally healthy because it helps us adjust to a loss.*
- *Grief is expressed in lots of different ways.*
- *Grief can last a long time.*
- *Grief reactions can go up and down over time, and even from minute to minute.*

Have group members complete Handout 3.04, the Grief Goals Worksheet. Explain that you will be revisiting these goals at the end of Module 3 to see how much progress they have made in terms of achieving these goals.

Then give the following practice assignment:

- Introduce the grief thermometers (Handout 3.02, Rating My Grief Reactions) and ask them to fill out the thermometers at some point during the week.

- Inform group members that they will be using these thermometers in each of the following sessions focusing on grief in order to track the strength and type of grief reactions that they experience over time.
- **Bring a photo of the deceased next week**: For many groups it has been a positive practice to have group members bring a photo of their deceased to put on a memory board that is displayed during each group. Use your judgment to decide if this is what you would like to do for your group.

Note: For groups in residential training centers or juvenile justice facilities, this may not be practical.

VII. Check-Out

- *How are you feeling now?* (Use Handout 3.01, the Feeling Thermometer.)
- *What did you learn about yourself today?*
- *Please fill out* Handout 3.05, *the Check-Out Feedback Form. The title of today's session is "Learning about Grief."*

If any group members are visibly agitated or troubled or report high levels of distress on the Feeling Thermometer, keep them after the group and determine an appropriate way to transition back to their settings.

Implementing Module 3, Session 3.1 with Individual Clients

PREPARATION: Make printed copies/handouts of Handout 3.01, the Feeling Thermometer, Handout 3.02, Rating My Grief Reactions, Handout 3.03, Learning about Different Grief Reactions, and Handout 3.04, the Grief Goals Worksheet.

I. **Check-in via Handout 3.01, the Feeling Thermometer**. Have the client complete Handout 3.01. After sharing his/her current feeling(s), ask the client to share anything that happened since the last session that may have influenced his/her feelings (in either a positive way or a negative way).

II. **Review practice assignment and previous sessions**. Deliver the exercise as written but omit references to the group.

III. **Transition to a focus on loss.** This content can be delivered conversationally, with the client sharing information about his/her loss and any secondary adversities (or things that have become harder for your client since the death) that he/she has encountered. As appropriate, call attention to themes involving loss that have already emerged in treatment, such as losses that were discussed in the Module 2 narrative-building exercise, or in Module 1 coping skills exercises focusing on loss reminders.

IV. **Grief psychoeducation: what is grief?** This content can be delivered conversationally. You can ask your client to share any personal examples of both "private" (e.g. feelings, prayers) and "public" (attending memorial services, visiting grave site with family members) parts of grieving that he/she has experienced. For the "true/false" activity, it can be helpful to enlist a parent or caregiver in the session. You can create a "true/false" card (with true on the front, false on the back) that can be given to each person. Ask them each to indicate whether the grief-related statement you (the clinician) read aloud is true or false by turning the card onto the appropriate side. You can make this into a game by asking them to reveal their responses at the same time or make it more conversational by having the client discuss his/her response first and then asking the caregiver to explain his/her own response. This is a good opportunity to begin to facilitate more open communication between the caregiver and the client about grief reactions in general. If a caregiver is not available, then you can simply have the client respond to the questions himself/herself and engage in a discussion about each statement.

V. **Grief psychoeducation: grief reactions**. Present Handout 3.03, Learning about Different Grief Reactions, and describe each of the three different categories. You can then ask your client to put a checkmark next to the reactions that he/she has felt the most in the last few weeks. Use this as an opportunity to obtain more information about those reactions that your client is experiencing more regularly. This activity nicely segues into the "riding the waves of grief" activity. Provide your client with a sheet of paper and a marker. Ask him/her to choose two grief reactions that bothered him/her the most during the first few weeks following the death and draw what those waves looked like (higher waves indicate stronger feelings). Then, ask your client to identify the two grief reactions that have bothered him/her the most during the last few weeks (which were already identified in the last activity) and draw what those waves look like. Discuss the ways in which these reactions may (or may not) have changed over time.

VI. **Summary and practice assignment**. Summarize the session and complete Handout 3.04, the Grief Goals Worksheet, with your client. You can also introduce Handout 3.02, Rating My Grief Reactions, to be completed for the next session. Also ask the client to bring a photo of his/her deceased loved one to the next session.

VII. **Check-out**. Deliver this step as written.

3.2

Understanding Connections between Loss Reminders, Grief Reactions, and Consequences

Session Objectives

1. Describe loss reminders as understandable, predictable, and manageable.
2. Link loss (or trauma) *reminders* to bereavement-related *feelings*, hurtful *thoughts* (inaccurate or unhelpful), and related *behaviors* and their consequences. Learn how helpful thoughts can lead to more positive feelings, behaviors, and consequences.

Section number	Session overview
I	Check-in
II	Review practice assignment
III	Grief psychoeducation: review loss reminders
IV	Activity: linking bereavement-related situations, grief reactions, and consequences. "Helping a friend" exercise
V	Summary and practice assignment
VI	Check-out

Supplies

Every session	This session
• Group member workbooks	
• Flipchart	
• Large paper or easel pad	
• Markers	
• Pencils/pens	
• Kleenex	
• Tape	
• Post-it notes and pencils	

Handouts in Workbook

Handout 3.01	Feeling Thermometer
Handout 3.02	Rating My Grief Reactions
Handouts 3.06–3.13	Illustrations
Handout 3.14	Loss Reminders and Grief Reactions Practice Exercise, Parts 1 and 2
Handout 3.15	Check-Out Feedback Form

Flipcharts

3.2a Today's Highlights

- Check-in
- Review practice assignment
- How do we grieve?
- Review loss reminders
- Linking loss reminders with grief reactions and consequences
- Summary and practice assignment
- Hurtful thoughts
- Check-out

3.2b Loss Reminder Examples

Missing reminders:
- An empty seat at the table
- His or her favorite food or song
- Activities that you used to do with them
- Big events or holidays such as graduations, birthdays, and Christmas

Changes or hard times:
- Moving to a new house or town
- Difficulty adjusting to a new school
- Not as much money as before
- More work

3.2c Sizing Up a Situation

Draw this diagram with the word "You" in place of the drawing of the young man.

Sizing Up a Situation

Session 3.2: Understanding Connections between Bereavement-Related Thoughts, Feelings, and Consequences

I. Check-In and Rating My Grief Reactions

- Introduce the idea that feelings related to grief tend to come and go, and that this is completely normal.
- Show Handout 3.02, Rating My Grief Reactions, and explain that some grief reactions can be more or less helpful than others. You may have these feelings "not at all" (0), "very much" (10), or somewhere in between, on any particular day. In this module we will be working on both *encouraging* or *increasing* helpful grief reactions, and *decreasing* less helpful grief reactions, over time.
- Invite each group member to use the sheet as a guide for sharing his/her current grief reactions during a "check in" exercise:
  - *What happened or what did you do since we last met that you feel good about?*
  - *Is anything going on that may make it difficult for you to keep your mind focused on our group today?*
  - Briefly review (or have a group member review) Today's Highlights (Flipchart 3.2a).

(Optional) **Recommended** (but may not be possible in juvenile justice/residential treatment settings): Display board with photos of deceased brought last week. Ask if any additional pictures were brought. Encourage those who

have not yet brought a photo to do so. Leave the board in prominent sight for the duration of the group.

II. Review Practice Assignment

Start by asking group members if they practiced the deep breathing this week. If they did, how did it go?

- Practice with the group doing five to ten abdominal breaths.
- Check in with the Feeling Thermometer, to monitor any changes.

Present Flipchart 3.2b. Review the practice assignment from last week and troubleshoot difficulties.

Refer group members to Handout 3.02, Rating My Grief Reactions, and ask them to report on what their ratings were on the day that they chose during that week. Did anything (either in their environment, such as reminders, or their own internal experience, such as times when they feel bored or lonely) prompt them to feel that way?

III. Grief Psychoeducation: Review Loss Reminders

Review Loss Reminders

*So far we have talked a lot about **trauma reminders** and how they can bring up different feelings, including posttraumatic stress reactions. Trauma reminders can be very different from **loss reminders**.*

*When it comes to our loved ones who have died, **trauma reminders** make us think about the **circumstances*** surrounding the death (**how** the person died). In contrast, **loss reminders** make us think about the fact that the person who died is **no longer physically here** with us (**that they died**). Trauma reminders typically arise when there are parts of the death that we find disturbing or hard to accept. On the other hand, loss reminders can arise even when a person dies a peaceful death. Loss reminders simply tell us that we really miss not having them physically present in our lives.

(**Note**: Though the following information was presented in Module 1, you may want to review it here.)

A loss reminder is something that reminds us of the physical absence of someone important to us and what it means to be without them. Loss reminders can lead to feelings of sadness and wishing to be with the person that we love.

Loss reminders generally fall within two categories (present Flipchart 3.2b).

Missing reminders:
- Situations or things that remind us of the person, like an empty seat at the table, a favorite chair, his or her favorite food or song, fun places you used to visit, or fun things you used to do together.
- People they used to be with, such as their family, friends, or people they used to work with.
- Activities that you used to do with them.
- Big events or holidays such as graduations, birthdays, or Thanksgiving.

Changes or hard times since the death:
- Moving to a new house or town.
- Difficulty adjusting to a new school.
- Not as much money as before.
- More work or responsibilities at home.
- Changes in routines.
- Just feeling like things aren't the same as they used to be.

IV. Linking Loss Reminders, Grief Reactions, and Consequences

Activity: Personal Loss Reminders

Ask group members to share some of their current loss reminders.

What are some of the things that remind you of your person who died? What are situations that make you think about your person?

If group members have difficulty identifying personal reminders, mention examples from the list below. Write their reminders on a page of the flipchart. After you list a number of reminders, invite group members to discuss their reactions to being reminded: How do they tend to feel, think, and cope or behave after being reminded?

Examples of Loss Reminders

- Hearing their name
- Their belongings
- Pictures or videos of them

- Places they used to be (their place of work, the chair where they used to sit)
- Things they used to do (their chores)
- Their favorite things (their favorite song, dish, flavor of gum, or favorite saying)
- Family time (like breakfast, dinnertime, or Sunday afternoons)
- People connected to them (family, friends, or workmates)
- Smells connected to them (the scent of their perfume, smelling a dish they used to prepare)
- People who look like them
- Family gatherings, social events (parties, holidays, birthdays, graduations, marriages)
- Difficult times when I wish I had their support
- Seeing other people spend time with their loved ones
- Being around other people who are also grieving
- Hardships created by their loss (like not having enough money, having to move to a new house, starting a new school, strained relationships among family members caused by the loss, having new caregivers, being treated differently by other kids, being teased in mean ways)
- Seeing other people show strong emotions, such as sadness, anger, or fear
- Your own feelings (like times when you are feeling sad, lonely, scared, angry, alone, or bored)

Sizing Up a Stressful Situation (Display Flipchart 3.2c)

Work with one or two group members who described having strong or problematic reactions to a reminder. Use Flipchart 3.2c, the Sizing Up a Situation graphic, to demonstrate the connections between: being triggered by a loss reminder and experiencing grief-related thoughts and feelings; and how these thoughts and feelings may, in turn, be linked to behaviors and their consequences.

Using a group member's reminder example, walk him/her through the graphic, helping him/her to describe: (1) a specific situation that contains a loss reminder, (2) the thoughts and feelings that the reminder evoked, and (3) the behavioral response. If the behavioral response is problematic (e.g. becoming irritable or angry, withdrawing, or acting out in a negative manner), then (4) ask about potential negative consequences for the problem behaviors.

Go through the chart with at least two group members so that they get a clear sense of the linkages between strengths situations (e.g. loss reminders), thoughts, feelings, behaviors, and their consequences.

Activity: "Helping Out a Good Friend" Exercise

This exercise helps group members identify and work on *loss reminders* and other stressful situations that pull up strong grief-related thoughts, feelings, and behaviors that create problems. Handouts 3.06–3.13 show sketches of various grief scenarios that may be used to discuss how to cope with each stressful or risky situation. Guidelines for how to structure the discussion for the illustrations are provided in the boxes accompanying this section. Be sure to prepare for this session in advance by reading the guidelines for the selected illustrations.

1. Select two or three handout sketches for this exercise, depending on the time available and the needs of your group based on their particular grief profiles (i.e. separation distress, existential distress, or circumstance-related distress).

2. Show one of the sketches to the group and ask them to imagine that the teenager in the sketch is a close friend who is having a really hard time after someone they cared about has died, and he/she is turning to you for help. You really care about this friend, so your job is to give him or her your very best advice and support.

3. Show Flipchart 3.2c and explain that we will use the Sizing Up a Situation graphic to figure out what is going on in the situation, what the stressful situation is. It may involve a loss reminder, trauma reminder, or temptation to do something dangerous. Then, we'll problem-solve how to think, feel, and behave in a more helpful way.

4. Use Handout 1.35 and go over *hurtful thoughts*. You may summarize the following points: *There are two basic types of hurtful thoughts:*

   (a) **Inaccurate thoughts**, *which don't accurately reflect the known facts about what happened, like taking complete responsibility for a bad choice that someone else made, and*

   (b) **Unhelpful thoughts**, *which are technically true, based on the facts, but they take away our power by filling us with negative feelings like helplessness, hopelessness, guilt, bitterness, and despair.*

The goal is to help your friend identify the hurtful thought, figure out why it's hurtful, and come up with helpful thoughts instead. The key to winning the war with hurtful thoughts is understanding that for every hurtful thought, there is at least one helpful thought that you can use to counter it.

5. Practice with the first selected sketch. Use the chart and ask the group the following questions:

   - *What is the stressful or risky situation?*
   - *What is the main hurtful thought the person is having (see thought bubble in sketch)?*
   - *What unpleasant feelings did the thoughts bring up?*
   - *What problem behaviors might he/she engage in if he/she is thinking that way?*
   - *What are some likely negative consequences?*

Depending on time and the capacity of the group, you may choose to review Handout 1.35, the Hurtful Thoughts Checklist, from Module 1. Whether you use this list or not, explore with the group possible hurtful thoughts (in addition to the one depicted) that might be involved in the sketch scenario, and then invite the group to generate believable and accurate helpful thoughts. Use prompts such as: "Can you help him/her think differently about the situation? Are there more helpful ways of looking at what happened?" (See below for guidelines to discuss each of your selected sketches).

Guidelines for Handout 3.06: Avoiding Loss Reminders (*Separation Distress*)

Description: *This teen's father died of a sudden heart attack three weeks ago. He and his dad used to do lots of fun things together, including going to basketball games. In fact, that was this teen's favorite activity to do with his dad. Now, going to any sports events, but particularly basketball games, serves as a strong loss reminder.*

Facilitating questions (group leaders should allow group members to generate their own responses and offer answers only when necessary):

What is the **situation**? Mother handing her teenage boy two season tickets to a basketball game, saying, "Your dad would want you to enjoy these tickets. Why don't we go to the game together?"

What is his **hurtful thought**? "I can't ever go back there anymore. It won't ever be the same without him."

How might he be **feeling** *if he is thinking this way?* (Sadness, emptiness, feeling lost, always feeling bored, feeling like a big part of him died, feeling like life has lost its excitement, feeling like nothing matters anymore, feeling hopeless, despair.)

What **behaviors** *might he be tempted to engage in if he is thinking and feeling this way?* (Acting like he doesn't care anymore, giving up activities that he used to enjoy, avoiding relationships that may remind him that his dad is gone, missing out on fun opportunities.)

What might be some **negative** *or* **harmful consequences** *of thinking, feeling, and behaving this way?* (Becoming isolated, feeling lonely, leading a boring and unfulfilling life, feeling suicidal, engaging in more risk-taking behaviors.)

What believable **helpful thoughts** *could you suggest as replacements?*

- "It won't always hurt so bad. Waves of grief come and go, and I can get through them."
- "I know Dad would want me to have fun and do the things we used to enjoy doing together. He'd want me to spend some time with mom, because he loved us both."
- "Even though my life will be very different, it can still be a good life. I don't have to throw it all away or give up trying just because I'm feeling discouraged right now."
- "It may feel really sad to do activities without him now, but maybe there are other people who I could enjoy spending time with and do fun things with."
- "Instead of giving up hope that I can have a good life, I might want to become a doctor or nutritionist or physical trainer who works on preventing heart disease, so that other families don't have to go through the pain my family is going through."

(As appropriate):

Could **you** *believe these thoughts if you were in his situation?*

How could choosing to **think about the situation** *in these ways change how he* **feels** *and* **behaves**?

What kinds of **consequences** is he likely to face if he chooses to have these different kinds of thoughts, feelings, and behaviors about this situation? (Better, the same, or worse?)

Guidelines for Handout 3.07: Reunification Fantasies (*Separation Distress and Existential Distress*)

Description: *This teenager's closest friend died of a drug overdose and she misses her every single day. They used to do everything together, including driving together, so driving alone is a loss reminder. To her, being alone and feeling lonely are painful loss reminders that keep reminding her that her friend is no longer there.*

Facilitating questions (group leaders should allow group members to generate their own responses and offer answers only when necessary):

What is the **situation?** Scene: Teenage girl in a car without her seat belt on, windows rolled down, wind in her hair, tears running down her cheeks, mournful expression on her face.

What is her **hurtful thought?** "If I crash, the bad news is I die, but the good news is I get to see my friend again."

How might she be **feeling** if she is thinking this way? (Sadness, emptiness, missing her friend, longing to be reunited with her friend, feeling lost, feeling like a piece of her died, no longer caring what happens to her.)

What **behaviors** might she be tempted to engage in if she is thinking and feeling this way? (What she is doing – driving recklessly without a seatbelt, picking the wrong romantic partners who mistreat her, unprotected sex, neglecting her health, acting like she doesn't care about anything anymore, cutting off other important relationships, using drugs to escape her pain and to maybe feel closer to her friend who died from an overdose.)

What might be some **harmful consequences** of thinking, feeling, and behaving this way? (Crashing her car and hurting herself or other innocent people, attempting suicide, dropping out of school, becoming socially isolated and lonely, getting an expensive traffic ticket, losing her insurance so she can't drive, getting arrested, getting a sexually transmitted disease, getting pregnant, becoming addicted to drugs.)

What might be more **helpful thoughts** that she could believe instead as replacements? Ideas for *substitute thoughts* include:

- "My friend wouldn't want me to die. She would want me to make the most of my life."
- "I can do things with my life that would make her proud to call me her friend."
- "I can use this experience to help other teens – maybe I can prevent other kids from ending their lives."
- "I still have other people in my life who care about me."
- "I'll never be able to replace her, and I would never want to. But I can form other relationships that will bring me

and others some happiness and make the world a better place."
- "Bringing other special people and activities that I cherish into my life doesn't mean that I'm replacing her. I'll always keep a special place for her in my heart. But my heart can grow bigger!"

(As appropriate):

Could you believe these helpful thoughts if you were in her situation?

How could thinking about the situation in these ways change how she feels and behaves?

What kinds of consequences are likely to follow if she chooses to have these different kinds of thoughts, feelings, and behaviors about this situation? (Better, the same, or worse?)

Guidelines for Handout 3.08: Fear of Getting Close (*Separation Distress*)

Description: *This teenage girl lost one of her closest friends when she was killed in a drunk driving accident several months ago. Ever since, she has been avoiding the other girls who made up their same circle of friends who are strong loss reminders for her. Being in their company reminds her that her close friend who died is not there with them anymore.*

Facilitating questions (group leaders should allow group members to generate their own responses and offer answers only when necessary):

What is the **situation**? Teenage girl walking away from a small group of friends who are saying, "Hey, why don't you hang with us anymore?"

What is her **hurtful thought**? "It's better not to get too close to people. I don't want to feel the pain of losing someone else ever again."

What **negative feelings** might this hurtful thought bring up? (Sadness, loneliness, fear, anxiety.)

What **behaviors** might she be tempted to engage in if she is thinking and feeling this way? (Pull away from friends and other relationships, isolate herself, hurt herself or cut herself to try to distract herself from negative feelings, etc.)

What are some likely **negative consequences** of these behaviors? (Being lonely all the time, missing out on fun opportunities, doing poorly in school, injuring herself, having suicidal thoughts or behaviors.)

Can you help her **think differently** about the situation in a more constructive way? Are there more helpful ways of looking at what happened? Ideas for *substitute thoughts* include:

- "I'll bet they miss her, too, and we can support each other through this."
- "Being close to other people can help me to deal with my grief – pulling away from them will just make it harder in the long run. We can remember and share positive memories about our friend together."

- "If I can open up to my friends about how I'm feeling, it will be easier for them to open up to me about difficult feelings they may be having. Helping each other creates good friendships."
- "It's unlikely that I'll have to lose my other friends. What happened to my close friend was a terrible accident, but the chances of that happening again are highly unlikely."
- "My friend would never want me to become isolated. She always wanted the best for me, including having good friends."
- "It's better to have loved and lost than to never love at all. Even though I lost my friend way too soon, our friendship was worth the pain I'm feeling now."
- "I can take one of her most positive qualities, like her friendly personality, and try to be more like her in that way. That way I can keep feeling close to her by enjoying her gift to me."

(As appropriate):

*Could **you** believe these thoughts if you were in her situation?*

*How could **thinking about the situation** in these more positive ways change how she is **feeling** and **behaving**?*

*What kinds of **consequences** is she likely to face if she chooses to have these different kinds of thoughts, feelings, and behaviors about this situation? (Are they an improvement over what is most likely to happen if she doesn't make these choices?)*

Guidelines for Handout 3.09: Giving Up on Future Plans (*Existential Distress*)

Description: *This teenage girl's father was killed as an innocent bystander in a drive-by shooting several months ago. He was very supportive of her staying in school and had high hopes that she would graduate from high school and go to college. She just found out she was accepted to a local university that is willing to give her a scholarship. But since her dad died, it's hard to feel excited about it. In fact, the college acceptance letter is a strong loss reminder because she doesn't have her dad here to celebrate her acceptance with her. She knows that he won't be around to cheer her on during her studies, and he won't be there when she graduates.*

Facilitating questions (group leaders should allow group members to generate their own responses and offer answers only when necessary):

*What is the **situation**?* Teenage girl reading a college acceptance letter and throwing it in the trash.

*What is her **hurtful thought**? "*I don't care about my future anymore if he's not going to be a part of it. He'll never see me graduate anyway, so what's the point?"

*How might she be **feeling** if she is thinking this way?* (Sadness, emptiness, feeling lost, feeling like a big part of her died, feeling like life has lost its meaning, feeling like nothing matters anymore, feeling hopeless and in despair, feeling like her life is over, feeling like it's not worth trying anymore.)

*What **behaviors** might she be tempted to engage in if she is thinking and feeling this way?* (What she is doing now – throwing away an acceptance letter with a scholarship! Not trying to really make something of her life, giving up on her hopes for a good future, passing up valuable opportunities to succeed, acting like she doesn't care about anything anymore, not trying anymore, dropping out of school, hanging out with the wrong crowd, getting a boring, low-paying job with no real opportunities for moving up (or advancement).)

*What might be some **harmful consequences** of thinking, feeling, and behaving this way?* (Not making something out of her life, underachievement, feeling unsatisfied and unfulfilled, being bored, regretting having passed up big opportunities, losing a chance to make a positive difference in the world, dropping out of school, cutting off relationships with good friends who can help her keep her life on track, feeling suicidal because nothing seems worth it anymore)

*What believable **helpful thoughts** could you suggest as replacements?*

- "I know Dad would want me to do good things with my life – he would have been thrilled that I got accepted, and so proud of me if I decided to go to college."
- "Even though my life will be very different, it can still be a good life. I don't have to throw it all away just because I'm feeling discouraged right now. There is a big difference between having a life that's different, and having a life that's not worth living."
- "If I take advantage of this opportunity and actually go to college, maybe I could do something important with my life, like help other kids who have suffered the way I have."
- "My spiritual beliefs tell me that Dad is watching over me and will see me succeed if I try."

(As appropriate):

*Could **you** believe these thoughts if you were in her situation?*

*How could choosing to **think about the situation** in these ways change how she **feels** and **behaves**?*

*What kinds of **consequences** is she likely to face if she chooses to have these different kinds of thoughts, feelings, and behaviors about this situation? (Better, the same, or worse?)*

Guidelines for Handout 3.10: "Why Not … Nothing Matters Anymore" (*Existential Distress*)

Description: *This teen's father died of cancer three weeks ago and he has felt like a different kid ever since. Sometimes he can't believe that the world still keeps turning and that everyone is acting the way they normally would, even though his dad is gone. He feels like the world, for him, has stopped, and that there is no good reason to hope or keep trying any more.*

Facilitating questions (group leaders should allow group members to generate their own responses and offer answers only when necessary):

*What is the **situation**?* Scene: A diverse group of teenage boys standing next to a fence overlooking a repair shop with motorbikes leaning up against the wall. One says to the bereaved teen: "Why not do it? Nothing matters."

*What is his **hurtful thought**?* "Why not do it? Nothing matters anymore."

*How might he be **feeling** if he is thinking this way?* (Sadness, emptiness, feeling lost, feeling like a big part of him died, feeling like life has lost its meaning, feeling like nothing matters anymore, feeling hopeless and in despair, feeling like his life is already pretty much over and not worth investing in and preparing for.)

*What **behaviors** might he be tempted to engage in if he is thinking and feeling this way?* (Just what he is considering doing right now! Letting other kids talk him into doing stupid things that aren't worth it like skipping school and using drugs/alcohol, giving up on his hopes for a good future, acting like he doesn't care about anything anymore, not trying anymore, hanging out with the wrong crowd.)

*What might be some **harmful consequences** of thinking, feeling, and behaving this way?* (Getting in serious trouble with the law, doing more risky things that get him into trouble and hurt people, becoming addicted to drugs/alcohol, feeling suicidal because nothing seems worth it anymore, dropping out of school, cutting off relationships with good friends who can help him keep his life on track.)

*What believable **helpful thoughts** could you suggest that he could replace these with?* Ideas for *substitute thoughts* include:

- "It won't always hurt so bad. Waves of grief come and go, and I can get through them."
- "I know Dad would want me to do good things with my life – not waste it doing stupid things."
- "Even though my life will be very different, it can still be a good life. I don't have to throw it all away just because I'm feeling so lost right now."
- "My dad didn't raise a quitter, and I'm not going to quit trying to become the man he wanted me to be. This (making bad decisions that can get me into trouble) is not that."
- "I want to become a doctor or someone who works on a cure for diseases like the one that killed my dad, so others don't have to go through the same pain my family is going through."

(As appropriate):

*Could **you** believe these thoughts if you were in his situation?*

*How could choosing to **think about things differently** change how he **feels** and **behaves**?*

*What kinds of **consequences** is he likely to face if he chooses to have these different kinds of thoughts, feelings, and behaviors about this situation? (Better, the same, or worse?)*

Guidelines for Handout 3.11: "I Will Never Love Again ..." (*Existential Distress*)

Description: *This girl's boyfriend was killed in a car accident four months ago. He was her first real love. She was hoping and planning to marry him after they graduated from high school. Her boyfriend's photo serves as a loss reminder.*

Facilitating questions (group leaders should allow group members to generate their own responses and offer answers only when necessary):

*What is the **situation**?* Scene: Teenage girl holding a picture of her deceased boyfriend, tears running down her face, mournful expression.

*What is her **hurtful thought**?* "I'll never love anyone the way I loved you. I will never love again."

*What might she be **feeling**?* (Sadness, emptiness, hopelessness, feeling like a big part of her died, feeling like life has no meaning, despair, feeling like the light went out of her life.)

*What **behaviors** might she want to engage in if she is thinking and feeling this way?* (Give up on life, not try, not hope or plan for the future, withdraw from friends and family, turn down social invitations or dating opportunities, spend all her time at her boyfriend's grave or in places he used to be while thinking about the good old days or "what might have been," using drugs or alcohol or sex to distract herself or numb away her pain.)

*What might be some **serious consequences** of her thinking, feeling, and behaving this way?* (Cutting off other relationships, loneliness, dropping out of school, giving up on life, thinking about suicide, getting hooked on alcohol or drugs, engaging in risky sexual behaviors to escape her pain, etc.)

*What are some believable **helpful thoughts** that you could suggest to her?* Ideas include:

- "It won't always hurt so bad. Waves of grief come and go, and I can get through them."
- "I can tell how much I loved him by how much I still miss him. I need to give myself time to figure out what the "new normal" is, because things will never be quite the same."
- "Even though my life will be very different, it can still be a good life. I don't have to throw it all away just because I'm feeling really sad and hopeless right now. I won't always feel this way."
- "I know he would want me to do good things with my life – not waste it. If *he* can't be around to love me, then he would want me to find someone who can. He wouldn't want me to waste my time in cheap relationships."
- "No one will ever replace him, but I may still be able to find love again, and he would want that for me."
- She might also have spiritual beliefs that bring her comfort, such as believing she will see her boyfriend in an afterlife, but it can wait until after she has led a good life.

(As appropriate) *Could **you** believe one or more of these thoughts if you were in her situation?*

*How could **thinking about the situation** in these ways change how she **feels** and **behaves**?*

*What kinds of **consequences** are likely to follow if she chooses to have these different kinds of thoughts, feelings, and behaviors about this situation? Do you think that choosing to think differently can really make a difference for the better for her?*

Guidelines for Handout 3.12: Shame over Circumstances of the Death (*Circumstance-Related Distress*)

Description: *This teenage girl recently started attending a new high school and is just beginning to make some new friends. Her new friends know that her dad died several months ago, but what they don't know is **how** he died (by suicide). She feels very self-conscious and a little ashamed, and she worries about what her new friends might do if they found out about the way he died. She thinks that it's best to just play it safe and make only superficial friendships, even though it will make her life very lonely and boring.*

Facilitating questions (group leaders should allow group members to generate their own responses and offer answers only when necessary):

*What is the **situation**?* Scene: Teenage girls sitting at a table in the high-school cafeteria, gesturing to the bereaved girl to come sit with them.

*What is her **hurtful thought**?* "They'll never want to hang out with me once they know the truth about how my dad died."

*What **negative feelings** might this hurtful thought be bringing up?* (Shame, embarrassment, anxiety, etc.)

*What **behaviors** might she be tempted to engage in if she is thinking and feeling this way?* (Pull away from friends and other new relationships, isolate herself, hurt herself, or cut herself to try to distract herself from negative feelings, etc.)

*What are some likely **negative consequences** of these behaviors?* (Dropping out of school, injuring herself, having suicidal thoughts or behaviors.)

*Can you help her **think differently** about the situation in a more constructive way? Are there more helpful ways of looking at what happened?* (Ideas for *substitute thoughts* include):

- "If they're true friends, it won't put them off to know how my dad died."
- "All families have difficult problems to deal with – I'm sure these girls have had upsetting things happen to them, too."
- "Just because my dad had some mental health problems doesn't mean that I do, too."
- "If I choose to talk one day about my dad's suicide and help people understand what caused it, I may be able to

prevent other people from taking their own lives the way my dad did."
- "My dad would have wanted me to have friends who cared about me and supported me, no matter what has happened in my family."
- "If I choose to open up to new friends about what happened to my dad, it will be easier for them to open up to me about bad things that may have happened to them. That openness and trust is what helps to create lasting friendships."

(As appropriate):

*Could **you** believe these new thoughts about what happened if you were in her situation? Do they accurately reflect the **facts** that are known about what happened? Are they believable to **you**?*

*How could **thinking about the situation** in these more positive ways change how she is feeling?*

*How could these more positive thoughts and feelings help her **behave** in more positive ways?*

*What kinds of **consequences** are likely to follow if she chooses to have more positive thoughts, feelings, and behaviors about this situation? (Are they better, the same, or worse than the negative consequences?)*

Guidelines for Handout 3.13: "Can't Stop Thinking about the Way He Died" (*Circumstance-Related Distress*)

Description: *This girl's brother was killed in a drive-by shooting a year ago. Although she **wants** to enjoy positive memories of him, any reminder of him (like **seeing his picture** or **hearing his name**) keeps bringing up upsetting feelings. They remind her he is no longer physically present in her life (a loss reminder). They also remind her of the terrible night he was killed (a trauma reminder) when everyone was screaming and crying. She wishes her family would put away their pictures of her brother and not talk about him. She believes that if she doesn't think about him, she won't get overwhelmed with the pain she still feels about his death.*

Facilitating questions (group leaders should allow group members to generate their own responses and offer answers only when necessary):

*What is the **situation**?* A girl sits on a couch next to a photo of her brother on an end table, a troubled expression on her face.

*What is her **hurtful thought**?* "Every time I see his picture, I can't help thinking about the night he got killed. It gets me so mad that it's hard to remember the good times."

*What **negative feelings** might this hurtful thought be bringing up?* (Anger, frustration, rage, fear, sadness, wanting to get revenge, regret.)

*What **behaviors** might she be tempted to engage in if she is thinking and feeling this way?* (Trying not to think about her brother at all, staying away from anything that reminds her of her brother – including his friends and family, thinking of getting revenge by hurting other people, not being able to concentrate in school, drinking or taking drugs to try to make the pain go away.)

*What might be some **harmful consequences** of these thoughts and feelings and behaviors?* (Getting put in detention or suspended for fighting at school, dropping out of school because of low grades, getting in trouble with the law for hurting other people, having a hard time making and keeping good friends or going on dates, becoming an angry loner, getting herself hurt or killed.)

*What might be a more **helpful thought** that you could suggest she could replace these with?* (Ideas include):

- "Maybe I just have to accept that I'm going to feel mad and sad for quite a long time. But that doesn't mean I'll feel this way forever."
- "My brother would want me to remember him as the great person he was and not by the tragic way he died."
- "Letting bad memories of his death go and letting good memories in does not mean that I think the way that he died is 'acceptable.' I can *always* believe it is wrong, and I can *always* want justice to be served, but I don't have to let these things keep me from moving on with my life."
- "If I get myself hurt or killed, then my family will lose two children, not one. I can do my best to live for my brother as well as for myself, to try to make up for the good his life would have brought."
- "By not allowing myself to remember my brother the way he would want me to, it's like I'm letting the people who shot him and treated him like dirt win."
- "I can work in therapy on coming to terms with what happened to my brother, so that I don't get overwhelmed by it every time I get reminded and I can start to enjoy good memories of him."

(As appropriate):

*Could **you** believe these thoughts if you were in her situation?*

*How could **thinking about the situation** in these more positive ways change how she is **feeling** and **behaving**?*

*How could these more positive thoughts and feelings help her **behave** in more positive ways?*

*What kinds of **consequences** is she likely to face if she chooses to have these different kinds of thoughts, feelings, and behaviors about this situation? (Are they an improvement over what is most likely to happen if she doesn't make these choices?)*

Process the "Helping Out a Good Friend" Exercise

Point out the following:
- How effectively and compassionately they used their skills to help a friend in need.
- They are learning to be a good friend to *others* and to *themselves* by choosing to *think* about difficult *situations*

in more positive and empowering ways. They will *feel* better and *behave* in ways that lead to more positive *consequences*.
- These skills can prevent them from getting so upset by loss reminders, trauma reminders, or other stressful situations that they "lose it," act out, make poor choices, put themselves in danger, and create trouble for themselves and other people.

V. Summary and Practice Assignment

Summarize the session:

- *Today we learned about grief work. What was the main thing you learned today?*
- *If you can support a friend by giving him or her good advice about how to handle a stressful or dangerous situation differently, then you can do the same thing to yourself. You can be a good friend to yourself, just like you are to other people.*
- *Learning to care **about** yourself, and care **for** yourself, is an important step in growing up and becoming **your own man or woman**.*
- *So when you feel like saying, "Hey, I can take care of myself," remember that it doesn't just mean being independent. It also means that you know how to be a good friend to yourself, to care for yourself and stay out of trouble when you run into stressful or risky situations, just like we practiced doing today.*

Then give the following practice assignments:

- *Practice identifying stressful situations that contain loss reminders, as well as negative thoughts, feelings, and problem behaviors, and being your own "best friends" by thinking of more hopeful and helpful beliefs.*
- *You can also think of types of social support from other friends that might help you deal with a stressful situation involving a loss reminder.*
- For groups that are willing to do written homework, you may have them fill out Handout 3.14, Loss Reminders and Grief Reactions, Parts 1 and 2.
- *Continue breathing practice.*

VI. Check-Out

- *How are you feeling now?* (Use Handout 3.01, the Feeling Thermometer.)
- *What did you learn about yourself today?*
- *Please fill out Handout 3.15, the Check-Out Feedback Form. The title of today's session was "Understanding Connections between Loss Reminders, Grief Reactions, and Consequences".*

If any group members are visibly agitated or troubled or report high levels of distress on the Feeling Thermometer, keep them after the group and determine an appropriate way to transition back to their settings.

Implementing Module 3, Session 3.2 with Individual Clients

Preparation: Make printed copies of Handout 3.02, Rating My Grief Reactions, Flipchart 3.2c, Sizing Up a Situation, and Handout 3.14, Loss Reminders and Grief Reactions Exercise, Parts 1 and 2. Also select three to four illustrations from Handouts 3.06 to 3.13 that appear to be most relevant to your particular client (e.g. which domains of grief is he/she struggling with the most?).

I. **Check-in via Handout 3.02, Rating My Grief Reactions.** Have your client complete Handout 3.02 by writing a number (on a scale from 1 to 10) next to each grief thermometer. After sharing his/her current grief reactions, ask the client to share anything that happened since the last session that may have influenced his/her grief reactions (in either a positive way or a negative way). Briefly review today's highlights.

II. **Review practice assignments and previous sessions.** Deliver the exercise as written but omit references to the group. Have your client share any photos of his/her deceased loved one in the session. This is a good opportunity to allow your client to share more information about the person who died. What was he/she like? What are your client's fondest memories of the person? What made him/her choose that particular picture(s)?

III. **Grief psychoeducation: review loss reminders.** This content can be delivered conversationally, while presenting information contained in the "Examples of Loss Reminders" section.

IV. **Linking loss reminders, grief reactions, and consequences.** This content can be delivered as written. You can ask your client to share any personal examples of loss reminders, while recording them on a sheet of paper. You can have your client identify those loss reminders that bother him/her the most right now. It may also be helpful to identify potential loss reminders that are comforting or helpful to your client (e.g. a cherished necklace, a favorite photo, Dad's shirt that still smells like him, etc.). Next, use the Sizing Up a Situation graphic (Flipchart 3.2c) to help your client draw links between a loss reminder, thoughts, feelings, and behaviors. Next, conduct the "helping a friend" exercise as written, eliminating references to the group. Even if the specific illustration does not depict an exact situation that your client has dealt with, it is often just as helpful to use illustrations that exemplify specific grief domains that he/she may be grappling with. In fact, a slightly different context/situation can allow for more self-distancing and facilitate greater insight. Note that this session can be divided up into two sessions, especially if your client may benefit from reviewing multiple types of grief reactions as depicted in the illustrations. For example, if he/she is experiencing intense separation distress as well as circumstance-related distress, you may want to have an additional session to process up to five or six different illustrations.

V. **Summary and practice assignments.** Summarize the session and provide information about Handout 3.14, Loss Reminders and Grief Reactions Exercise, Parts 1 and 2, to be completed for the next session.

VI. **Check-out.** Deliver this step as written.

3.3 Dealing with Distress over the Circumstances of Tragic Deaths

Session Objectives

In completing this session, group members will be able to:

1. Identify intense negative emotions that can contribute to maladaptive grieving, including guilt, shame, anger, and regret.
2. Use emotional coping tools to challenge maladaptive beliefs that involve self-blame.
3. Rely on fellow group members to help them challenge maladaptive beliefs about how much can be predicted or prevented.

Section number	Section overview
I	Check-in
II	Review practice assignment
III	Dealing with strong emotions related to how the person died
IV	Identify and change your hurtful thoughts
V	Summary and practice assignment
VI	Check-out

Supplies

Every session	This session
• Group member workbooks	
• Flipchart	
• Large paper or easel pad	
• Markers	
• Pencils/pens	
• Kleenex	
• Tape	
• Photo board (optional)	

Handouts in Workbook

Handout 3.01	Feeling Thermometer
Handout 3.02	Rating My Grief Reactions
Handouts 3.16, 3.17, 3.19, 3.20	Illustrations
Handout 3.18	Feeling Angry About a Death
Handout 3.21	Wishes and Regrets
Handout 3.22	Check-Out Feedback Form

Flipcharts

3.3a Today's Highlights

1. Check-in
2. Review practice assignment
3. Things I wish I could change: guilt and anger
4. Identify changes in my life since the death

3.3b Sizing Up a Situation

Draw this diagram with the word "You" in place of the drawing of the young man

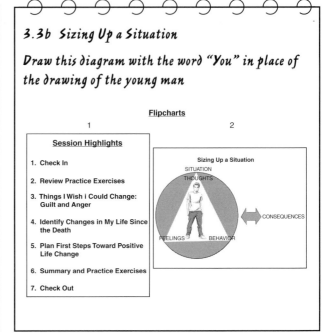

3.3c Hurtful Thoughts

Two types:
1. Inaccurate thoughts
2. Unhelpful thoughts

How they affect you:
- Keep you feeling down
- Rob you of hope
- Get you angry and out of control
- Make you blind to positive choices
- Fool you into thinking they must be true
- Rob your power with helplessness, hopelessness, guilt, bitterness, despair
- Make you into an angry loner
- Make you make bad choices that bring bad consequences

3.3d Facts about Angry Feelings

- Everyone who loses someone close feels angry at times.
- It's OK to feel angry.
- Being angry doesn't mean you need to hurt yourself or others. How you respond is your choice.
- "Hard" feelings of anger, irritability, and frustration often cover "softer" feelings of sadness, pain, and longing.
- If you give up being angry about the death, it doesn't mean you have forgotten him or her.
- Some anger does not go away, but it does not have to run your life.

Session 3.3: Dealing with Strong Emotions after a Death

I. Check-In and Rating My Grief Reactions

- Check-in via Handout 3.02, Rating My Grief Reactions.
- Introduce the idea that grief-related feelings tend to come and go, and this is completely normal.
- Show the handout and explain that some grief reactions can be more or less helpful than others. You may have these feelings "not at all" (0) or "very much" (10) or somewhere in between on any particular day. In this module, we will be working on both *increasing helpful grief reactions* and *decreasing less helpful grief reactions* over time.
- Invite each group member to use the sheet as a guide for sharing his/her current grief reactions.
- *What happened or what did you do since we last met that you feel good about?*
- *Is anything going on that may make it difficult for you to keep your mind in our group today?*

- Briefly review (or have a group member review) Today's Highlights, Flipchart 3.3a.
- (Optional) Display board with photos of deceased brought last week.

Ask if any additional pictures were brought. Encourage those who have not yet brought a photo to do so. Leave the board in prominent sight for the duration of the group.

II. Review Practice Assignment

Start by asking group members if they practiced the deep breathing this week. If they did, how did it go?

- Practice with the group doing five to ten abdominal breaths.
- Check in with the Feeling Thermometer, to monitor any changes.

Then, either conduct the review of the practice assignment with the entire group or, as a fun change, break the group into pairs and have group members interview each other about any loss reminders that they faced over the last week, and to trace how they may have led to hurtful (inaccurate or unhelpful) *thoughts*, and negative *feelings, behaviors*, and *consequences*.

Hand out copies of Handout 3.14, Loss Reminders and Grief Reactions Practice Exercise, Part 1, from last week to help guide their interviews with each other. The questions are also listed below. Group members who filled out the sheet can review these with one another.

- What was the *situation* where the loss reminder happened?
- What *hurtful thoughts* went through your mind when you were faced with this situation?
- What *unpleasant feelings* did it bring up for you?
- What *problematic behavior(s)* did you show after these thoughts and feelings about the loss reminder?
- What were the *consequences* of those actions or behaviors?
- What *believable and helpful thought* could you use in the future if you're ever faced with a similar situation? What can you choose to do in future situations like this?
- In contrast, look for and praise instances in which group members coped effectively with a loss reminder or other difficult situation. Did they use their coping skills? If so, what positive beliefs did they use to challenge the maladaptive belief? Did it change the outcome compared to what normally happens?

III. Dealing with Strong Emotions Related to How the Person Died

*In our last sessions, we've been developing skills to deal with our most difficult thoughts and feelings connected to the death(s) of people we care about. These feelings include guilt, regret, and anger. We've learned that these difficult thoughts and feelings can be set off by **trauma reminders** (which*

*remind us of how they died) or **loss reminders** (which remind us that they are physically absent from our lives).*

These painful feelings can be strongly connected to how the person died, especially if the person died in a tragic or violent way. Painful feelings can also come up if we feel ashamed about what happened or if we somehow feel responsible for not having done more to keep it from happening.

Guilt-Related Hurtful Thoughts

Display Flipchart 3.3c. *People's guilty thoughts often fall into two main categories: **inaccurate thoughts**, which don't match up with the facts and usually exaggerate things so they seem worse than they really were or are; and **unhelpful thoughts**, which may be accurate, but keep us feeling down and depressed and discouraged. Remember that for every hurtful thought, there is at least one helpful, hopeful thought that is at least as believable.*

Activity: "Helping a Good Friend" Exercise – Part 1

Continue with the "helping a good friend" exercise, this time focusing on scenarios in which the youth feels guilty for not having done more to prevent the death of a friend, or feels angry about the circumstances of the death. Select as many illustrations as appear relevant given group members' grief profiles (especially circumstance-related distress) and as you have time for. (If time is short, only use one of them.)

To begin, let's practice using two of the sketches from the same "helping a good friend" role play exercise that we practiced during our last session. These sketches focus on tragic deaths of people they cared about that have left your friends feeling really guilty.

Guidelines for Handout 3.16: Feeling Guilty about a Friend's Murder (*Circumstance-Related Distress*)

Description: *This boy was supposed to go out with his friends a couple of nights before, but his mother needed him to take care of his brother and sister while she picked up an extra night shift at work. His friends ended up getting into serious trouble. They decided to rob a jewelry store and his best friend got shot and killed. This boy is now faced with **a trauma reminder** – a newspaper article that describes how his friend died.*

Facilitating questions (group leaders should allow group members to generate their own responses and offer answers only when necessary):

*What is the **situation**?* Scene: Teenage boy looking at a newspaper article that says "Teen shot to death after suspected armed robbery"

*What is his **hurtful thought**?* "If only I'd hung out with him that night, this wouldn't have happened."

*What **negative feelings** might this hurtful thought be bringing up?* (Guilt, regret, shame, etc.)

What **behaviors** might he be tempted to engage in if he is thinking and feeling this way? (Try to get revenge on the person who shot him; get angry and act out; hurt himself; take drugs or alcohol to numb the pain, get in a car and speed recklessly down the highway.)

What are some likely **negative consequences** of these behaviors? (Getting into trouble with the law, hurting himself, hurting someone else, hurting his family and his friends, overdosing, wrecking the family car.)

Can you help him **think differently** about the situation in a more constructive way? Are there more helpful ways of looking at what happened? Ideas for *substitute thoughts* include:

- "There is no way I could have known they would do this and that this would happen."
- "I'm not so sure I could have stopped them, even if I had been there."
- "Who knows? If I'd been there, they might have talked me into going along with it, and then where would I be now?"
- "I don't have to make excuses to anyone for choosing to take care of my family. In a way I'm lucky I was not involved; maybe my life was spared for a reason."
- "I may feel *regret* about what happened (wishing it had never happened; wishing I had known what was about to happen so I could've done more to stop it), but I don't have to feel *responsible* for it (because I didn't *cause* it to happen). Regret and guilt are two very different things."
- "He wouldn't want me to feel guilty."
- "I'm going to try and prevent something like this from happening to other kids – maybe by volunteering as a Big Brother or mentoring kids in my neighborhood."

(As appropriate):

Could **you** believe these new replacement thoughts about what happened if you were in his situation? Do they accurately reflect the **facts** that are known about what happened? Are they believable to **you**?

How could **thinking about the situation** in these more positive ways change how he is **feeling**?

How could these more positive thoughts and feelings help him **behave** in more positive ways?

What kinds of **consequences** are likely to follow if he chooses to have more positive thoughts, feelings, and behaviors about this situation?

Guidelines for Handout 3.17: Feeling Guilty about a Friend's Suicide (*Circumstance-Related Distress*)

Description: *This teenager is grieving the loss of his friend, who recently committed suicide.*

Facilitating questions (group leaders should allow group members to generate their own responses and offer answers only when necessary):

What is the **situation**? Scene: He's holding one of the notes she left behind, which says "too much pain."

What **hurtful thought** is going through his mind? "It's all my fault. If I would have paid more attention to what was going on with her, this never would have happened."

What **negative feelings** might this hurtful thought be bringing up? (Guilt, regret, remorse, shame, depression, etc.)

What **behaviors** might he be tempted to engage in if he is thinking and feeling this way? (Get angry and act out, zone out like a zombie, hurt himself, take drugs or alcohol to try to numb out.)

What are some likely **negative consequences** of these behaviors? (Hurting himself, hurting someone else, hurting his family and friends, getting into trouble with the law, failing at school.)

Can you help him **think differently** about the situation in a more constructive way? Are there more helpful ways of looking at what happened? Ideas for *substitute thoughts* include:

- "No one knew this was going to happen, including me. You really can't predict the future, no matter how much you want to."
- "I may feel very bad about what happened, but there have been many times when I was kind to her and showed that I cared about her."
- "I may feel *regret* about what happened (wishing it had never happened; wishing I had known what was about to happen so I could've done more to stop it), but I don't have to feel *responsible* and *guilty* for it. Regret and guilt are two very different things."
- "Instead of torturing myself with guilt, which she wouldn't want and doesn't do anyone any good, I'll do my best to do something kind for someone she cared about, like her friends or family."
- "I want to do something to help stop tragedies like this, like volunteering with at-risk kids."

(As appropriate):

Could **you** believe these new replacement thoughts about what happened if you were in his situation? Are they believable to **you**?

How could **thinking about the situation** in these more positive ways change how he is **feeling**?

What kinds of **consequences** are likely to follow if he chooses to have more positive thoughts, feelings, and behaviors about this situation? (Are they better, the same, or worse than the negative consequences?)

Activity: Discussion of Angry Feelings

One of the most common emotional reactions to loss – especially a traumatic death – is anger. People who have suffered these types of losses often report feeling anger, and even rage, at those responsible for the death, at God (for letting this happen), and sometimes at the person who died.

Distribute Handout 3.18, Feeling Angry About a Death, which shows different types of anger with rating scales by each type.

Ask group members to fill out the worksheet indicating the degree to which they experience these different types of anger.

Facilitate a discussion about group members' angry feelings. Read each type from the worksheet and ask for a show of hands of those who rated the item "very angry." If few people are acknowledging these levels of anger, you may ask for those who endorsed "somewhat angry." Note that "anger at yourself" is a special type of anger that may be related to feelings of guilt, which we talked about earlier in this session.

Different Types of Anger about a Death

1. About the way they died:
   - It's not right
   - He/she deserved better

2. At the people responsible:
   - They should have done more
   - They should be punished

3. At the world:
   - I need him/her
   - It's not fair
   - He/she was too young
   - We didn't deserve this
   - All my hopes, plans, and wishes involving him/her must be altered or abandoned

4. At God:
   - For letting it happen
   - For not protecting us

5. At the people around me:
   - For the way people treat me since the death
   - Because others go unharmed while we struggle and suffer

6. At the person who died:
   - For leaving us when we really need you
   - For the hardships your death has created for us
   - For unkind things you did while you were alive
   - For not keeping your promise that you'll always be there for me, that we'll have a future together

7. At yourself (guilt):
   - For not being there to help
   - For not preventing the death/injury
   - For things you have said or done (or not said and done)

You can use the following process questions:
- *Do you relate to the angry feelings I have described?*
- *What sort of angry feelings do you experience?*
- *What part of the loss do you feel most angry about?*
- *When do you feel angry? Are there certain times when you feel more angry, like when you're facing a trauma or loss reminder?*
- *What do you do when you feel this way? (Whom do you turn to? How do you cope?)*
- *What helps you to feel better when you feel this way?*

Activity: "Helping a Good Friend" Exercise – Part 2

Continue with the helping a good friend exercise, this time focusing on scenarios in which the youth feels angry about the circumstances of the death. You may select one or all of the illustrations presented here. (If time is short, only use one of them.)

Now, let's practice using sketches from the same helping a friend role-play exercise that focus on deaths of people they cared about, that have left their friends feeling really angry.

Guidelines for Handout 3.19: Anger at People Responsible for the Death (*Circumstance-Related Distress*)

Description: *This teen just lost his brother in a gang-related drive-by shooting. He feels so driven to find out who was responsible that it has taken over his life and is about the only thing he thinks about. He tells himself that he can't grieve for his brother until he gets revenge. For him, anyone who looks like a gang member serves as a trauma reminder (reminding him of how his brother was killed) or a loss reminder (reminding him that his brother is gone) and can get him so angry that he can't think straight.*

Facilitating questions (group leaders should allow group members to generate their own responses and offer answers only when necessary):

*What is the **situation**?* Scene: A teenage boy sees a gang of kids hanging around an outdoor basketball court.

*What is his **hurtful thought**?* "I'll bet they're the ones who killed Jessie. They're going to pay for what they did."

*What **negative feelings** might this hurtful thought be bringing up?* (Anger, rage, guilt.)

*What **behaviors** might he be tempted to engage in if he is thinking and feeling this way?* (Get revenge on the people responsible by hurting/killing them, hurt himself, take drugs to try to relieve his pain and anger.)

*What might be some **harmful consequences** of these thoughts and feelings and behaviors?* (Go to jail or get killed so his family loses two sons, hurting or killing the wrong people, provoking another attack that may hurt or kill more people he loves and keep the cycle of violence going, having a murder on his hands that he will regret for the rest of his life, etc.)

*What might be a more **helpful thought** that you could suggest he could replace these with?* Ideas include:

- "They may not be the ones who did it at all! I could hurt or kill innocent people."
- "Just because I feel angry at them doesn't mean they are guilty." (Emotional reasoning.)
- "My brother wouldn't want me to become a killer and end up in jail."

- "If I kill someone, it will just keep the cycle of violence going and won't bring him back."
- "If I did something like that it would break my mother's/father's/grandparents' heart."
- "I have my whole life ahead of me – I know my brother would want me to make the most of it."
- "My family already lost one son. I don't want to put them at risk for losing another (me) or at risk for losing their own lives in retaliation for things I've done (like taking the law into my own hands)."
- "My brother's murder is being investigated by forensic experts. I need to let them do their job."

(As appropriate):

Could **you** *believe these thoughts if you were in his situation?*

How could **thinking about the situation** *in these more positive ways change how he is* **feeling** *and* **behaving***?*

What kinds of **consequences** *is he likely to face if he chooses to have these different kinds of thoughts, feelings, and behaviors about this situation? (Are they an improvement over what is most likely to happen if he doesn't make these choices?)*

Guidelines for Handout 3.20: Anger and Blame for Not Preventing Brother's Death (*Circumstance-Related Distress*)

Description: *This boy just lost his older brother in a tragic car accident. The doctor has just informed the family that he died. The boy is shocked and confused, but mostly enraged at the doctor. He believes that the doctor could have done more to save his brother, and probably just gave up on him too soon. He can't imagine trusting another doctor ever again. Now, doctors in white coats or the sound of an ambulance serve as trauma reminders.*
Facilitating questions (group leaders should allow group members to generate their own responses and offer answers only when necessary):

What is the **situation***?* Scene: A boy is in the Emergency Room with his family when the doctor tells them that his brother has died.

What is his **hurtful thought***?* "I know they could have done more to save him. If they had just tried harder he would still be alive. I'll never trust these people again."

What **negative feelings** *might this hurtful thought be bringing up?* (Anger, rage, guilt.)

What **behaviors** *might he be tempted to engage in if he is thinking and feeling this way?* (Get revenge on the doctors responsible by hurting them, hurt himself, become suicidal, take drugs to try to relieve his pain and anger, never see another doctor again.)

What might be some **harmful consequences** *of these thoughts and feelings and behaviors?* (Go to jail or get killed so his family loses two sons, hurting the wrong people, physical pain and

stress from carrying that much anger/rage, health problems from not seeing a doctor again).

What might be a more **helpful thought** *that you could suggest he could replace these with?* Ideas include:

- "Maybe the doctors probably *did* do everything they could. They didn't want my brother to die, either. There was only so much they could do."
- "Just because I feel angry at them doesn't mean they are guilty." (Emotional reasoning.)
- "My brother wouldn't want me to get revenge and end up in jail."
- "If I hurt or kill someone, it won't bring him back."
- "If I did something like that it would break my mother's/father's/grandparents' heart."
- "I have my whole life ahead of me – I know my brother would want me to make the most of it."
- "My family already lost one son. I don't want to put them at risk for losing another (me) by not taking care of my health or by doing something stupid that could get me in jail."
- "I want to become an ER doctor so I can try and save kids like my brother."

(As appropriate):

Could **you** *believe these thoughts if you were in his situation?*

How could **thinking about the situation** *in these more positive ways change how he is* **feeling** *and* **behaving***?*

What kinds of **consequences** *is he likely to face if he chooses to have these different kinds of thoughts, feelings, and behaviors about this situation? (Are they an improvement over what is most likely to happen if he doesn't make these choices?)*

Optional Activity: Facts about Angry Feelings Review

Before we move on, let's talk about some facts about angry feelings.

Display Flipchart 3.3d (text shown below). Review these points in an interactive manner.

Facts about Angry Feelings

1. Everyone who loses someone close feels angry at times.
2. It's OK to feel angry.
3. Being angry doesn't mean you need to hurt yourself or others. *How you respond is your choice.*

   It is your decision how to respond to your feelings. This means that you do not have to push your anger on to others, punish yourself even though you are feeling guilty, have suicidal thoughts, or take unnecessary risks.

4. "Hard" feelings of anger, irritability, and frustration often cover "softer" feelings of sadness, pain, and longing.
   Angry feelings are often based on feelings of loss, helplessness, and sadness. It is sometimes easier to feel angry rather than to feel these other emotions. But feeling these other

emotions – feeling sad, lonely, lost, or confused – is what grieving is all about, especially in its early stages.

5. If you give up being angry about the death, it doesn't mean you have forgotten him or her.

   Some people feel that they must hold on to their anger or else it will mean that they are disloyal and will somehow forget about the people who have died. We want you to consider a different possibility: holding onto the anger helps to keep your painful feelings alive, and may make it more difficult to have good memories of this person you cared about as they would want to be remembered. By letting their anger diminish, many young people find that they begin to have more good memories.

6. Some anger does not go away, but it does not have to run your life.

Explore and problem-solve ways in which teens can cope constructively with anger. Elicit ideas from the group.

Ideas include:

- Talk about your feelings with others
- Replace hurtful thoughts with helpful thoughts
- Carry out a constructive activity (this may be related to the mode of death, such as participating in a drunk-driving awareness campaign, etc.)
- Exercise to "get it out of your system"
- Refer to the personal coping toolkit from Module I, Session 1.8, for other strategies to cope with anger.

IV. Identify and Change Your Hurtful Thoughts

Activity: Challenging Hurtful Guilt-Related Thoughts

Hint: Some issues, especially those involving ambivalent feelings such as physical abuse or neglect, may require individual attention and/or referral to a specialist. Obtain expert consultation as appropriate.

- Hand out Handout 3.21, Wishes and Regrets, and have group members fill it out. Normalize the fact that when someone dies, people usually carry forward some regrets about what they did or didn't do either before or after the person's death. This worksheet helps to flesh out some of these thoughts.
- Provide each group member with several strips of paper. Ask them to write at least two of their own hurtful thoughts from the handout, *one hurtful thought per strip.*
- Ask everyone to *fold their strips of paper and place them into a bowl* in the middle of the room.
- Generate additional hurtful thoughts as needed, based on your own experience and clinical judgment about what thoughts will resonate with group members, and also add them to the bowl.
- Once everyone has placed their strips of paper in the hat, say:

*You are all becoming experts in challenging many of the hurtful grief-related thoughts we've been talking about. Let's try a **different version** of the **helping a friend** exercise and practice being good friends by **helping one another out** with difficult thoughts and feelings about our **own family members** or **friends** who have died.*

- Invite each group member to draw one hurtful thought out of the hat and read it. If they run into their own hurtful thought, they can put it back and draw another one, or just pretend that it isn't theirs.
- Using Flipcharts 3.3b and 3.3c, facilitate group discussion regarding the hurtful thought (is it inaccurate? unhelpful?), what feelings the thought might call up in the (anonymous) person, how these thoughts and feelings might affect his/her behavior, and possible negative consequences.
- Help them generate one or more helpful thoughts, and discuss how adopting this belief may help to improve the person's feelings or mood, behavior, and the consequences.
- Give every group member a chance to read at least one hurtful thought. Praise group members' efforts and comment on how their skills are developing. Encourage them to keep practicing and using these skills with themselves and others around them.

V. Summary and Practice Assignment

Summarize the session:

- *Today we explored our emotional reactions to grief, and focused on guilt, regret, and anger.*
- *We discussed how, depending on the way the person died and our beliefs about what we should or shouldn't have done, we may have painful thoughts and feelings that continue to bother us.*
- *We learned about ways to recognize these kinds of thoughts and how to challenge and replace them with more accurate and helpful thoughts.*

Then give the following practice assignment:

- *In addition to continuing with the breathing practice, you should keep track of times during the week that you notice painful thoughts or feelings about your person who died. Use the techniques practiced in group to be a "good friend" to yourself and develop a more accurate and helpful thought or way of thinking about the situation.*
- *Next week, come prepared to talk about one time that you had painful thoughts or feelings and what you did to help yourself feel better.*

VI. Check-Out

- *How are you feeling now?* (Use Handout 3.01, the Feeling Thermometer rating.)
- *What did you learn about yourself today?*

- *Please fill out Handout 3.22, the Check-Out Feedback Form.*

If any group members report high levels of stress on the Feeling Thermometer, take time to process with them before returning them to their classrooms or residences.

Implementing Module 3, Session 3.3 with Individual Clients

I. **Check-in via Handout 3.02, Rating My Grief Reactions.** Have your client complete Handout 3.02 by writing a number (on a scale from 1 to 10) next to each grief thermometer. After sharing his/her current grief reactions, ask your client to share anything that happened since the last session that may have influenced his/her grief reactions (in either a positive way or a negative way). Briefly review today's session highlights.

II. **Review practice assignments and previous sessions.** Deliver the exercise as written but omit references to the group. Have your client share his/her homework assignment, Handout 3.14, Loss Reminders and Grief Reactions Practice Exercise, Parts 1 and 2, if completed. If not completed, you can do the worksheet together in the session.

III. **Dealing with strong emotions related to how the person died.** This content can be delivered conversationally, while presenting the information in the Hurtful Thoughts Checklist (Handout 1.35 from Module 1).

Next, conduct the "helping a friend" exercise using Handouts 3.16 and 3.17.

Next, discuss any angry feelings your client may have while using Handout 3.18, Feeling Angry About a Death.

Again, conduct the "helping a friend" exercise using Handouts 3.19 and 3.20.

You can also review the facts about angry feelings activity in a conversational way. Have the client discuss healthy ways in which he/she deals with anger.

IV. **Identify and change your hurtful thoughts.** Have your client complete Handout 3.21, Wishes and Regrets, as written. Instead of conducting the exercise with strips of paper, have your client choose one or two of his/her wishes or regrets and help him/her to generate more helpful thoughts while using the Sizing Up The Situation graphic (Flipchart 3.3b).

V. **Summary and practice assignment:** Summarize the session and provide information about the practice assignment.

VI. **Check-out:** Deliver this step as written.

3.4 Identifying Positive and Negative Traits

Session Objectives

1. Identify and discuss *desirable* traits, characteristics, or behaviors of the person who died that each group member loved or admired about him/her.
2. Identify and discuss *less* desirable or negative traits, characteristics, or behaviors of the person who died that can bring up ambivalent feelings when group members remember and reminisce about the deceased.
3. Normalize and validate ambivalent feelings that group members may have towards the deceased.
4. Help group members to choose selectively which *positive* aspects of the deceased they would like to hold on to and carry with them over time as a means of maintaining a positive connection with the deceased.
5. Help adolescents to use the positive traits/behaviors of the deceased to honor their memory and to improve their own lives in some way.

Section number	Session overview
I	Check-in
II	Review practice assignment
III	Identifying both positive and negative traits
IV	Summary and practice assignment
V	Check-out

Supplies

Every session	This session
• Group member workbooks	Tape
• Flipchart	Activity option 1: waterproof markers, popsicle sticks, small stones, bowl, water in a container
• Large paper or easel pad	Activity option 2: purple and yellow construction paper pre-cut into 3-inch strips
• Markers	
• Pencils/pens	
• Kleenex	

Handouts in Workbook

Handout 3.01	Feeling Thermometer
Handout 3.02	Rating My Grief Reactions
Handout 3.23	Connecting in a Positive Way
Handout 3.24	Check-Out Feedback Form

Flipcharts

3.4 Today's Highlights

1. Check-in
2. Review practice assignment
3. Discussion of positive and negative traits
4. Elevation exercise
5. How we can stay connected to the person who died through identifying with their positive traits
6. Summary and practice assignment
7. Check-out

I. Check-In

- Check-in via Handout 3.02, Rating My Grief Reactions.
- Introduce the idea that feelings related to grief tend to come and go, and that this is completely normal.
- Show the handout and explain that some grief reactions can be more or less helpful than others. They may have these feelings "not at all" (0) or "very much" (10) or somewhere in between on any particular day. In this module, they will be working on both *increasing helpful grief reactions*, and *decreasing less helpful grief reactions*, over time.
- Invite each group member to use the sheet as a guide for sharing his/her current grief reactions.
- *What happened or what did you do since we last met that you feel good about?*
- *Is anything going on that may make it difficult for you to keep your mind in our group today?*
- Briefly review (or have a group member review) Today's Highlights, Flipchart 3.4.

II. Review Practice Assignment

First, ask group members whether they practiced the deep breathing this week. If they did, how did it go?

- Practice with the group doing five to ten abdominal breaths.
- Check in with the Feeling Thermometer, to monitor any changes.

Then review the practice assignment from last week and troubleshoot difficulties.

- *This week, did you notice any painful thoughts or feelings about the person who died, such as when you encountered a loss reminder?*
- *Were you able to develop a more accurate and helpful thought or way of thinking about the situation?*
- *What did you do to help yourself feel better? Did it work for you?*

III. Identifying Both Positive and Negative Traits

*When someone dies, it's often easier to think and talk about things we **loved** or **admired** about him/her. But oftentimes, teens have mixed feelings about the person who died, including both memories of things they **admired** about the person, as well as memories of things that were **not so positive** about the person, such as negative personality characteristics or behaviors.*

*Now we know that no one is perfect, including our loved ones, but the fact that they're imperfect doesn't make it any easier for us to grieve over their loss. In fact, holding bitter or deeply mixed feelings (feeling torn) over your relationship with a lost loved one can actually make grieving for them more difficult. Learning how to deal with **all** of our feelings for them – both the positive and the less positive – is our main focus for today.*

*Just as it is normal to have some **angry** feelings toward the deceased person (as we talked about last time), it is also normal to remember some of their negative traits as well. In fact, these may be things that you **still** feel somewhat angry about. It can be helpful to keep in mind that everyone has some admirable as well as not-so-admirable traits, and that it's normal to have both positive **and** negative feelings about the deceased person at the same time.*

*But also remember that it is up to us to choose **which** traits to focus on – we don't have to forget about their negative traits, but we can **choose to focus on, learn from,** and **cherish** their positive traits. Learning to focus on a person's positive traits is a valuable and important skill. It will help you draw strength from other people, despite their flaws, and forgive other people when they make mistakes. So as you think of the life of your loved one(s), you can ask yourself, "Which of their good traits or habits do I want to remember and bring with me into my future? And which not-so-good or negative traits and habits can I outgrow and leave behind?"*

Young people can often still feel connected to the deceased person by carrying forward certain qualities of that person or behaving in the same ways that he/she did when he/she was alive. This can be useful and helpful if those qualities or behaviors are healthy and beneficial; but at the same time, we can create all sorts of problems for ourselves if we choose to carry on their negative qualities.

*In other words, sometimes it can help us to feel more connected to the person who died, or feel like we're honoring their memory, when we behave the same way or do the same things they did. We can **choose** to focus on and carry their **positive** qualities with us, while still being aware of their less admirable qualities and accepting them as imperfect people.*

With this in mind, our activity today will help us to think about and choose which of the person's positive qualities we value the most and would like to keep with us over time, almost like one of their gifts to us.

Note: There are two options for this activity: The first is preferred though it requires more materials (pens, popsicle sticks, stones, bowl, and water), whereas the second option is somewhat simpler and requires only purple and yellow construction paper and pens. Review both and decide which one is better for your setting.

Activity Option 1: "Sticks and Stones" (Promoting the Positive, Normalizing the Negative)

Pass out waterproof pens (e.g. Sharpies), two popsicle sticks (representing good attributes), and two stones (representing undesirable attributes) to each group member. Place a large clear plastic bowl in the center of the table along with a pitcher of water.

First, invite group members to write up to two positive traits, habits, or behaviors that they admire about the person who died on the popsicle sticks, one trait per stick, and to write up to two negative traits, habits, or behaviors that they do **not** admire or that created problems for the person on the stones, one per stone.

- Acknowledge that talking about not-so-positive parts of a deceased person's life can sometimes make people uncomfortable, because it may feel disloyal to their memory, but no one is perfect, and it's ok to remember those parts, too. It's important to remember our loved ones realistically, imperfections and all, if we are going to relate to them as real people as we grieve.
- Look out for inappropriately detailed descriptions of undesirable traits or actions and direct the focus back on the activity – leaving these things behind.
- If group members cannot identify positive attributes that the person exhibited during his/her life, invite them to select attributes that they personally *wish* that person had exhibited in life.
- Encourage group members to notice how each object (popsicle stick versus stone) feels. Note that the positive qualities are lighter, and *easier to carry* with them. The more negative qualities are heavier, and can *weigh them down*.

Second, invite each group member to share the things they *admire* about their loved one, that they want to *keep* with them and incorporate into their own behavior as they move forward with their lives.

- Invite that group member to also describe (in general terms) the person's traits, habits, or behavior that may have created problems for them in the past that they would like to *leave behind*.
- As each group member describes the positive and negative qualities of the person who died, the group member should place the popsicle sticks and the stones in a large, clear plastic bowl in the middle of the table.
- Reflect, normalize, and validate as necessary. Praise the selection of truly adaptive "positive" attributes, and if they are not truly adaptive (e.g. "He was a crazy dirty fighter and no one messed with him"), then encourage group members to fine-tune or replace them with more adaptive traits using their practice exercise lists.

Third, after all group members have put their objects into the bowl, say:

*Thank you for sharing. The most important part of this exercise is to understand how our work together in this group can help us to bring those positive traits to the surface, so we can connect with them more easily, while letting those more negative traits become smaller and less powerful. We have the power to **choose** to keep their positive traits in the foreground, and their less positive aspects in the background. But how can we do this?*

Group leader pours pitcher of water into the bowl. The popsicle sticks should rise to the top while the stones stay at the bottom of the bowl. The group leader can then make waves in the water and ask group members to comment on what they observe:

Notice what happens to the popsicle sticks (or the positive qualities) and the stones (negative qualities) when we make waves in the water. The positive qualities stay afloat and ride the waves, kind of like the waves of grief that we've talked about. So when you find that you're experiencing a wave of grief, if you're able to hold on to those positive traits and behaviors of the person who died, it will be easier for you to stay afloat even when waves of sadness or anger or loneliness wash over you. But what happens if you grab on to those negative traits or behaviors? They'll pull you down and you'll start sinking.

Also, notice how the popsicle sticks cluster together, almost forming a raft. So when we "stick together" as a group, the positive qualities of all of our deceased loved ones can become even stronger and help to carry all of us through the tough times. We can not only learn from each other – we can learn from each other's loved ones as well (if on display, point to the pictures group members have brought in). They still have things to teach us, if we learn to listen.

Group Discussion

Now, let's focus again on the positive qualities or behaviors that our loved one has left us, but this time think of these qualities as a gift or "legacy" that the person would want us to carry forward.

How can this positive quality help you make positive changes in your life?

How can you use this positive quality to help other people in some way? (This can be something as simple as making use of the deceased person's friendly smile and kindness by smiling at other people or giving someone a hug when they're having a tough time.)

Remember that making positive changes requires courage and commitment. How can their gift to you really help you now? What will it take for you to use this gift in your everyday life? Monitor reactions: *How is everyone doing?*

Process: Help group members to calm themselves as needed using the skills they have learned (deep breathing, relaxation, distraction, or journaling).

Summarize and lead into the next section.

Thank you for sharing your experiences. By understanding the things we share in common (both positive and negative) with the person who died, we can choose to keep healthy qualities that make our lives better, and begin to let go of unhealthy qualities that will create problems for us.

Activity Option 2: "Yellow and Purple Paper" – Choosing What to Keep and Cherish, and What to Let Go

1. Pass out pens, three strips of yellow construction paper (representing good attributes), and three strips of purple construction paper (representing undesirable attributes) to each group member.

   *In this exercise, we will symbolically **keep** the parts of the person that we cherish (which we will write on the yellow strips), and **let go and leave behind** our unhealthy connections to the person by discarding what we have written on the strips of purple paper.*

2. Invite the group members to write up to three positive traits, habits, or behaviors that they admire about the person who died on the yellow strips of paper, one trait per strip, and to write up to three negative traits, habits, or behaviors that they do not admire or that created problems for the person on the purple strips, one per strip.
   *We invite each of you to write down on these three **yellow** strips of paper three positive qualities (traits, characteristics, or behaviors, like having a good sense of humor) of the person who died that you really liked and still admire. On these three **purple** strips of paper, we'd like you to write down up to three qualities of the person that you don't admire (these may be things that bothered or upset you, or bad habits that caused problems for them or people around them). Feel free to write down whatever comes to mind.*
   Then, think about both the positive and negative traits and behaviors that you have chosen to focus on. Do you yourself

*share any of the same qualities (traits, habits, or behaviors) that you **admire** in your loved one? On the other hand, are there any **negative** or **unhealthy** qualities (traits, habits, or behaviors) that you also share with them that could be creating **problems** for you either now or in the future?*

3. Emphasize that talking about not-so-positive parts of a deceased person's life can sometimes make people uncomfortable, because it may feel disloyal to their memory. For example, you can tell them,
   *We want to be respectful of the fact that it may feel uncomfortable or disloyal to speak about the not-so-positive aspects of your special person, and we encourage you to write and speak only in **general** terms about the not-so-good trait or behavior. This is not a speech about the person, and it's not a confession of their faults and crimes. No one is perfect, and we need to remember them as real people – flaws as well as strengths, if we are going to remember and reminisce about them as real people. This is about a **choice** you are making about which parts of their lives you want to remember and keep, and which parts you want to leave behind. You can just share a few general words if you wish.*
   Look out for inappropriately detailed descriptions of undesirable traits or actions and direct the focus back on the activity – leaving these things behind. If group members cannot identify (1) positive attributes that the person actually exhibited during his/her life, then invite them to either (2) select attributes that they personally *wish* that he or she had exhibited in life, or (3) select positive attributes that the deceased person hoped that they (the group member) would acquire, or (4) positive attributes they already possess that the deceased person admired or praised them for having while they were alive.

4. Invite each group member, in turn, to select a yellow strip and to share with the other group members the thing they admire about their loved one, that they want to keep with them as they move forward with their lives. They can *keep these strips as mementos with their other precious things.* During the same turn, invite that group member to also describe (in general terms) one part of the person's traits, habits, or behavior that could really create problems for them or others if they "kept" it, and to *leave this behind by placing the purple strip in the container* (located in the middle of the circle). Go around the circle as many times as the time (and group members' written slips) allows, with each group member describing and "keeping" one positive attribute on a yellow slip, and "leaving behind" one negative attribute on a purple slip in the container, in a single turn.

5. Reflect, normalize, and validate as necessary, inviting the group's help to evaluate the positive attributes that each group member chooses to cherish and keep. Praise the selection of truly adaptive "positive" attributes, and if they are not truly adaptive (e.g. "He was a crazy dirty fighter who no one messed with"), then encourage group members to fine-tune or replace (from their practice exercise lists) them with more adaptive traits that will serve them well as they mature. Encourage group member-to-group member interaction (questions, feedback, encouragement, praise) where appropriate.

6. After all group members have completed the activity say: *Thank you for sharing. It can feel uncomfortable, even scary, to let go of negative qualities that we share in common with the person who died. It might feel a bit like we are losing them. But we can choose to replace these with positive qualities that we share in common with them. In our practice assignment and group session next week, we will be focusing on the positive traits or habits you have chosen to keep and cherish. We'll be problem-solving how to use these positive qualities to help you feel connected to your loved one, make good choices, and move forward with your life.*

7. Monitor and process reactions: *How is everyone doing?* Help group members to calm themselves as needed using the skills they have learned (deep breathing, relaxation, distraction, or journaling).

8. Summarize and lead into the next section.

Thank you for sharing your experiences. By understanding the things we share in common (both positive and negative) with the person who died, we can choose to keep healthy qualities that make our lives better, and begin to let go of unhealthy qualities that will create problems for us.

Processing for Both Activity Options

Point out the following:

- How they were able to identify both positive and negative qualities of the person who died.
- How it can be helpful to acknowledge and accept those negative qualities, but not make them the focus.
- How choosing to focus on positive qualities of the person who died can help them to: (1) feel more connected to the deceased person, (2) honor the deceased person, (3) make their own lives better, and (4) help the people they care about.

IV. Summary and Practice Assignment

Summarize the session:

- *Today we talked about both positive and negative traits, characteristics or behaviors of your deceased family member or friend.*
- *We also talked about ways in which we may take on similar behaviors or traits because we believe that this will help to honor the person's memory or help us feel close to him or her.*
- *It's important to be able to identify both the positive and the negative qualities of the person who died and make good choices about which qualities to remember, cherish, and bring into your lives, and which to let go.*
- *Sometimes young people who've lost a special person feel reluctant to move forward with their lives. They worry that doing so will show they didn't really need their loved one because they can get along without them. Sometimes teenagers worry that if they move forward they'll forget precious things about their loved one (like the sound of their voice or the good times they shared). Today's exercise helped us learn that we don't have to leave our loved ones behind. We can bring the best parts of them with us as we* move forward with our lives. *This can help us feel close to them. It also gives more meaning to our lives by inspiring us to be better people for having known them.*

Then give the following practice assignment:

*We just completed an activity that helped to symbolically let some of the negative traits or habits of the deceased person go, so they recede into the background as we move forward with our lives. While that's an important first step for improving your lives, it may leave you feeling kind of **empty** inside – like something is missing, or like you don't quite know what to do with yourselves. This practice assignment is designed to help deal with this empty or confused feeling.*

Formal Version of Assignment (Using Handout 3.23)

- *For next week, we invite you to complete Handout 3.23, Connecting in a Positive Way: Pick one of the **positive** traits, characteristics, or habits that you believe you have in common (or want to have in common) with the person who died and that helps you to feel connected to him or her, that you think will help you as you move forward with your life. It can be something you wrote on the popsicle stick or another trait or behavior.*
- *During this next week, pay close attention to ways in which you can bring out that trait or behavior in yourself either while you are with your friends, when you're in class or group, or when you're by yourself. Make a mental note about whether you feel closer to the person who died, like enjoying a positive memory of things you did together or feeling like they are still an important part of your life.*
- *Please support one another in this. Share your trait or behavior you will be working on, and encourage one another to keep trying during the coming week.*

Informal Version of Assignment

Have group members pick one or two positive traits of their person who died and think about how they would like to emulate or copy these traits during the week. Next week they will report on how they acted on these traits and describe their experiences.

Optional Assignment

(Use this assignment if you plan to implement the sharing mementos activity in the next session.)

Next session, *we will be learning about other ways in which you can feel connected to the person who died while you move on with your lives. One of these is to keep **mementos**, or physical objects that help us to remember positive things about the person who died. These can be pictures of them, things that they created like letters they wrote, or things that belonged to them.*

Please bring a memento of your special person to our next session that you can share with the group, along with a positive memory that the memento can help you to remember about them. If you don't have a memento, then you can draw a picture or write a poem or a story – something you can share that helps you to remember something positive about them.

V. Check-Out

- *How are you feeling now?* (Use Handout 3.01, the Feeling Thermometer).
- *What did you learn about yourself today?*
- *Please fill out* Handout 3.24, *the Check-Out Feedback Form. The title of today's session was "Promoting the Positive, Normalizing the Negative."*

If any group members are visibly agitated or troubled or report high levels of distress on the Feeling Thermometer, keep them after the group and determine an appropriate way to transition back to their settings.

Implementing Module 3, Session 3.4 with Individual Clients

Preparation: Make printed copies of Handout 3.02, Rating My Grief Reactions, and Handout 3.23, Connecting in a Positive Way. You will also need a waterproof marker, two popsicle sticks, two white stones (large enough to write on), and a clear, plastic bowl.

I. **Check-in via** Handout 3.02, **Rating My Grief Reactions.** Have the client complete Handout 3.02 by writing a number (on a scale from 1 to 10) next to each grief thermometer. After sharing his/her current grief reactions, ask the client to share anything that happened since the last session that may have influenced his/her grief reactions (in either a positive way or a negative way). Briefly review today's session highlights.

II. **Review practice assignment and previous sessions.** Deliver the exercise as written but omit references to the group. Have the client share his/her homework assignment if completed. If not completed, you can do it together in the session.

III. **Identifying both positive and negative traits.** This content can be delivered conversationally as written, eliminating references to the group. Next, conduct the "sticks and stones" exercise (recommended) or the "yellow and purple paper" exercise, depending on availability of materials. The sticks and stones exercise can be very powerful even in an individual, one-on-one setting. In fact, clients may be more open to discussing negative traits or behaviors of the person who died in this setting, especially if those behaviors involved abuse, neglect, or interpersonal problems. Both of these activities can be conducted as written, with minimal wording changes. You can invite your client to generate as many positive attributes and as many negative attributes as you have time to cover (be aware that processing negative attributes often takes more time than positive attributes).

IV. **Summary and practice assignment.** Summarize the session and provide information about Handout 3.23, Connecting in a Positive Way, to be completed for the next session. Also remind your client to bring a memento (that helps him/her feel more connected to the person who died) to the next session.

V. **Check-out.** Deliver this step as written.

3.5 Reminiscing Together (Connecting to the Deceased in a Healthy Way)

Note: This session may be more difficult to do in residential or juvenile justice settings because group members may have no access to mementos of the deceased. If this is the case, you can invite group members to draw a picture that calls to mind a positive memory of their deceased loved one.

Session Objectives

1. Expand group members' vocabularies for labeling, understanding, and expressing grief reactions.
2. Practice skills for giving and receiving grief-related social support.
3. (Group leaders) facilitate group members' re-negotiation of their relationships with the deceased from one of physical presence to one of memory or, for those who hold strong spiritual beliefs, one of spiritual presence.
4. The overarching goal of this session is to help group members understand that they can still find ways of connecting in a healthy way to the deceased person through their memories of the person, precious items that they hold close to their heart, mourning rituals, or even through prayer.

Session Overview

Section number	Session overview
I	Check-in
II	Review practice assignment
III	Why stay connected after a loss?
IV	Sharing our mementos and memories
V	Summary and practice assignment
VI	Check-out

Supplies

Every session	This session
• Group member workbooks	• Have art materials available for group members who did not bring a memento; their drawing will function as a memento
• Flipchart	• If possible, provide refreshments
• Large paper or easel pad	
• Markers	
• Pencils/pens	
• Kleenex	
• Tape	
• Photo board (where possible)	

Handouts in Workbook

Handout 3.01	Feeling Thermometer
Handout 3.02	Rating My Grief Reactions
Handout 3.25	Things I Admire About the Person That I Want to Keep
Handout 3.26	Check-Out Feedback Form

Flipcharts

3.5a Session Highlights

- Check-in
- Review practice assignment
- Why stay connected after a loss?
- Sharing our mementos and memories
- Summary and practice assignment
- Check-out

3.5b How We Try to Stay Connected After a Loss

1. Physical connection:
   - Visiting their grave
2. Symbolic connection:
   - Remembering them
   - Reminiscing about them
   - Dreaming about them
   - Grief rituals
   - Keeping mementos
   - Following their good example
3. Spiritual connection:
   - Prayer or meditation
   - Asking for their guidance
   - Unusual experiences

Session 3.5: Reminiscing Together

I. Check-In and Rating My Grief Reactions

- Check-in via Handout 3.02, Rating My Grief Reactions.
- Introduce the idea that feelings related to grief tend to come and go, and that this is completely normal.
- Show the handout and explain that some grief reactions can be more or less helpful than others. You may have these feelings "not at all" (0), "very much" (10), or somewhere in between on any particular day.
- In this module, we will be working on both *increasing* helpful grief reactions and *decreasing* less helpful grief reactions over time.
- Invite each group member to use the sheet as a guide for sharing his/her current grief reactions.
- *What happened, or what did you do, since we last met that you feel good about?*
- *Is anything going on that may make it difficult for you to keep your mind in our group today?*
- Briefly review (or have a group member review) Today's Highlights, Flipchart 3.5a.

II. Review Practice Assignment

Start by asking group members if they practiced the deep breathing this week. If they did, how did it go?

- Practice with the group doing five to ten abdominal breaths.

- Check in with the Feeling Thermometer, to monitor any changes.

Depending on whether you assigned the "formal" or "informal" version of the practice assignment, select one or more group members to report on their experiences doing the assigned activity.

III. Why Stay Connected after a Loss?

Tip: Do not spend too much time on this discussion, as the main activity for this session is the sharing of mementos that follows. Your primary objective in this preliminary discussion is to acknowledge and normalize group members' *desires to maintain a sense of connection with their loved ones*, regardless of whether the connection is adaptive (e.g. reassuring or comforting) or maladaptive (e.g. creepy, risky, taking on dysfunctional attributes of the deceased).

*During the past several weeks we have spent a lot of time talking about **common grief reactions**. (Invite group members to share common grief reactions.) Examples include:*

- *Thoughts and feelings we have about the person*
- *Participating in mourning rituals (whether public or private) to help remember and pay our respects to the person who died*

*Keep in mind that grief reactions can include **spiritual experiences** that can sometimes feel comforting or, in some cases, strange, weird, or even a little creepy. These experiences include seeing or hearing the deceased person, sensing their* presence, or having life-like dreams about them. Although these experiences may seem unusual to you, many people (young and old) have these experiences but choose not to talk about them because they are afraid others will think they are "crazy" or "weird." (Invite any group member who feels comfortable to share experiences they have had such as those described above).

So what is all of this about? Why do we all think about, talk about, dream about, and sometimes sense the presence of, someone we know is physically dead?

We do this because, after having lost a very special person, we naturally try to find ways to stay connected to them. All of these different grief reactions that we've talked about share a common purpose: **To keep us feeling close and connected to the person who died.** *Let's focus on a few main ways in which grief reactions often help us feel connected to a special person who died.*

Display Flipchart 3.5b and go over it while using some of the phrasing below (as appropriate). Lead an interactive discussion in which you briefly describe different ways of staying connected with the deceased person, then invite them to share their experiences of things they do to feel connected to their loved ones in ways that feel helpful and comforting.

The **first way** *is to imagine or fantasize about* **being with them again in a physical sense** *– that is, sometimes teens* **imagine** *the person is still alive and that they are* **physically reunited.** *This is especially common when people are still having trouble accepting that the person is truly dead.*

For example, does anyone remember feeling the **urge to search** *for your special person – to go to places they used to go, or the last place you saw them, to see if they were still there, even if you "knew in your mind" for a fact that they had died?*

(Process and normalize as appropriate, based on group members' grief profiles.) *This urge to search is quite common, especially soon after a loss. Sometimes, it is not until we have searched – often multiple times – for the person in places they used to be that we come to accept that they are physically absent and will not physically return. Although these episodes of searching for and not finding them can make us feel even stronger waves of sadness, they can also teach us to accept and adjust to their death.*

The **second way** *in which people often try to stay connected to a special person who* **died** *usually happens after they begin to accept that the person is never coming back in their physical body. They do this by learning to connect with their special person in* **symbolic ways** *– that is, by finding ways to feel close to them not by being physically reunited, but in their* **minds and hearts** *and in* **the way they live.**

Some of these symbolic connections (like using **mementos,** *grief rituals, talking to them in our minds or out loud when we are alone) may feel very personal and private.*

Finally, people may also maintain a **spiritual connection** *with the deceased. Individuals from different cultures or religious/spiritual backgrounds may have very different ways of*

maintaining spiritual connections with people who have died. These can include saying prayers, lighting candles for them in church, feeling grateful that they were and are an important part of our lives, or planting a tree for them.

Invite group members to share different ways in which they (or group members of their religious or cultural background) spiritually connect with loved ones who have died, and how these connections can feel comforting because they help them to feel closer to the person.

IV. Reminiscing with Mementos

This activity is designed to help youth reminisce about their loved ones and provide support to each other. Keep in mind the following helpful hints:

- Take your time with this exercise – (it requires at least 20, preferably 30 minutes). Help group members express their grief in a genuine voice and support each other with compassion and understanding.
- You may not have to make many comments. This activity's power grows as each group member shares his or her memento in an atmosphere of respectful, quiet listening. Group members do not need to speak aloud in order to support one another during this poignant exercise.
- Introduce the activity and allow time as necessary for those who have not brought an object to draw (by hand) a memorable experience or object that they can then use as a memento.
- Once the sharing begins, simply sit quietly and let individual members share as they are ready. After speaking, they should place their memento on a central table or area.

Activity: Reminiscing with Mementos

Have group members sit in a circle, and place a small table or stand in the middle of the group on which group members may place their mementos when they are done speaking.

We've been learning about ways to feel connected to a loved one even when we can no longer be physically together and reunited with them. Mementos are powerful tools for remembering positive things about them that we admire and want to cherish or help us to maintain positive memories involving the deceased person. This week you each brought or created a personal memento of the person who died. Each of you will have an opportunity to share your memento with the group and describe what it means to you, such as a special memory or a positive quality that you admire about the person.

If there are group members who need to draw their memento, state something like:

If you did not or could not bring a memento, we have some materials here to draw a picture of a memento you'd like to talk about. This can be a special experience you had with your person, or an object that reminds you of something positive about that person. (Distribute drawing materials.)

If needed, take several minutes to let group members draw their mementos. In the meantime, re-assure group members that this is an informal exercise and they don't need to prepare a speech.

Invite group members to share their mementos by answering the following questions:

1. Why did you choose this memento (or drawing)?
2. What positive memories about the person does this memento help you to remember?
3. How do you feel as you remember (reminisce about) your special person who died?

(Process as appropriate) I noticed that several of the stories we shared about our mementos had some things in common. Did anyone notice some things in common? What did you see or hear? What have we learned today about ways in which we can feel connected to our loved ones in a positive way – something that feels uplifting or reassuring?

Keep in mind that connecting to our loved one in a positive way does not mean that we won't sometimes feel sad or miss their physical presence, or feel like crying over the fact that they are no longer physically here. Actually, sometimes having a "good cry" can bring a sense of relief that feels good. But as we find ways to connect with our loved ones in a symbolic or spiritual way, we can still feel connected to them and know they are still an important part of our lives, and this can feel comforting and good. This is part of healthy grieving.

(Conclude: as appropriate)

- Invite members to comment on how it felt to share (reminisce with) their mementos.
- Share your impressions and reactions to the exercise, calling attention to and expressing admiration for the courage and trust that members have shown.

V. Summary and Practice Assignments

Summarize today's session, focusing not only on what occurred but also on your own reactions to the poignant stories that were shared today.

- Comment that healing from a loss does not mean forgetting your special person, but it does require learning to relate to them in a different way (in a symbolic or spiritual way) – one that does not require them to be physically here.
- Encourage group members to find other opportunities and ways to reminisce and connect to their deceased loved ones in a healthy way.

For the practice assignment, we invite you to fill out Handout 3.25, Things I Admire About the Person That I Want to Keep.

As you work on this, try to list as many of their positive qualities as you can, but pay special attention to things you

want to cherish – that is, to keep with you moving forward and use in your life to better handle the problems and challenges you will face in your future. As you work, remember to be honest, and don't "sugar coat" things to make them sound better than they really were like in life. It is important to be realistic in how we remember and think about our loved ones, because we want them to be believable and useful to us.

VI. Check-Out

- *How are you feeling now?* (Use Handout 3.01, the Feeling Thermometer.)
- *What did you learn about yourself today?*
- *Please fill out Handout 3.26, the Check-Out Feedback Form. The title of today's session was "Reminiscing Together".*

If any group members are visibly agitated or troubled or report high levels of distress on the Feeling Thermometer, keep them after the group and determine an appropriate way to transition back to their settings.

Implementing Session 3.5 with Individual Clients

Preparation: You will need a clear Mason jar or a shoebox with markers and other decorative materials.

I. **Check-in via** Handout 3.02, **Rating My Grief Reactions.** Have the client complete Handout 3.02 by writing a number (on a scale from 1 to 10) next to each grief thermometer. After sharing his/her current grief reactions, ask the client to share anything that happened since the last session that may have influenced his/her grief reactions (in either a positive way or a negative way). Briefly review today's session highlights.

II. **Review practice assignment and previous sessions**. Have client share his/her homework assignment if completed. If not completed, you can do the worksheet together in the session.

III. **Why stay connected after a loss**? This content can be delivered conversationally as written. Have your client provide examples of ways in which he/she stays connected to the person who died using Flipchart 3.5b, on how we try to stay connected after a loss, as a guide.

IV. **Reminiscing with mementos**. Although much of this exercise can be conducted as written, we have found that it can be more meaningful in a one-on-one setting to have the client bring at least three or four mementos to the session that can be easily contained within a shoe box or Mason jar. These can include pictures, tickets to an event, a cherished item, jewelry, etc. Have your client describe each memento and what it means to them. You can then have them decorate their "memory box" or "memory jar" and share it with their caregiver/parent at the end of the session if they're comfortable. This may require preparing the caregiver/parent ahead of time by explaining the activity and providing guidance with regard to ways in which the caregiver can express support and validation toward the client during the activity.

V. **Summary and practice assignment**. Summarize the session and provide information about Handout 3.25, Things I Admire About the Person That I Want to Keep, to be completed for the next session.

VI. **Check-out**. Deliver this step as written.

3.6

Planning for Difficult Days (Relapse Prevention)

Session Objectives

1. Normalize and validate group members' problems in dealing with difficult days and difficult interpersonal interactions.
2. Point out that some interactions they have with others relating to the loss may not feel supportive. For example, people may ask for details that group members do not want to share. People may be genuinely interested in helping, but need guidance about what types of support are needed and when. (Link this concept with the Five Steps to Getting Support skill that group members learned in Module 1.)
3. Practice effective support-seeking skills to help group members (a) decide which types of disclosures are most appropriate in which settings and with whom, and (b) obtain specific types of support depending on the specific challenge they are facing.

Session overview

Section number	Session overview
I	Check-in
II	Review breathing exercises
III	Review practice assignment
IV	Life changes and secondary adversities
V	Planning for difficult days
VI	Summary and practice assignment
VII	Check-out

Supplies

Every session	This session
• Group member workbooks	• This activity requires either a large chalk or drawing board or a large piece of butcher paper taped to the wall so that group members can write on it
• Flipchart	
• Large paper or easel pad	
• Markers	
• Pencils/pens	
• Kleenex	
• Tape	
• Photo board (where possible)	

Handouts in Workbook

Handout 3.01	Feeling Thermometer
Handout 3.02	Rating My Grief Reactions
Handout 3.27	Changes in My Life Since the Death
Handout 3.28	Making Positive Life Changes to Further Adjust to the Loss
Handout 3.29	My Relationships Before and After the Death
Handout 3.30	Ideas for Getting through Special Days
Handouts 3.31–3.33	Illustrations
Handout 3.34	Check-Out Feedback Form

Flipcharts

3.6a Today's Highlights

1. Check-in
2. Review practice assignment
3. Life changes and secondary adversities
4. Planning for difficult days
5. Summary and practice assignment
6. Check-out

3.6b Problematic Daily Occurrences

- Whom to tell about the death?
- How to speak about the death?
- How to get the support you want
- Dealing with rumors
- Dealing with expectations that you should be "over it"

3.6c Five Steps to Getting Support

1. What do I want?
2. Whom should I ask?
3. Find the right time.
4. Request with an "I" message:
   - Tell them what I am feeling.
   - Tell them what happened (outside and inside).
   - Tell them what I want them to do.
5. Express sincere appreciation.

3.6d Sizing Up a Situation

Draw this diagram with the word "You" in place of the drawing of the young man

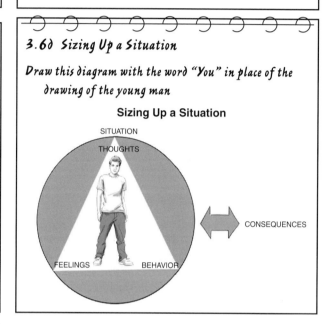

Sizing Up a Situation

Session 3.6: Planning For Difficult Days (Relapse Prevention)

I. Check-In and Rating My Grief Reactions

- Check-in via Handout 3.02, Rating My Grief Reactions.
- Introduce the idea that feelings related to grief tend to come and go, and that this is completely normal.
- Show the handout and explain that some grief reactions can be more or less helpful than others. You may have these feelings "not at all" (0) or "very much" (10) on any particular day. In this module, we will be working on both increasing helpful grief reactions and decreasing less helpful grief reactions over time.
- Invite each group member to use the sheet as a guide for sharing his/her current grief reactions.
- *What happened, or what did you do, since we last met that you feel good about?*
- *Is anything going on that may make it difficult for you to keep your mind on the group today?*
- Briefly review (or have a group member review) Today's Highlights, Flipchart 3.6a.

II. Review Practice Assignment

Start by asking group members if they practiced the deep breathing this week. If they did, how did it go?

- Practice with the group doing five to ten abdominal breaths.
- Check in with the Feeling Thermometer to monitor any changes.

Then, review Handout 3.25, Things I Admire About the Person That I Want to Keep. If group members have not completed this handout, they may answer the questions with your prompts. Have group members brainstorm about the ways in which these positive traits or behaviors can help them, especially in situations that are now more difficult as a result of the death.

III. Identify Life Changes and Secondary Adversities

Activity: Identifying Life Changes

The objectives of this activity are to:

- Identify changes in their relationships, circumstances,

and activities since the death.

- Discuss changes that have been difficult for them.
- (Optional) Draw "emotional proximity maps" to describe relationships before and after the death.
- Provide an opportunity for group members to talk about changes in their relationships and to acknowledge losses and gains.

Allow group members to express their thoughts and feelings regarding the adversities and challenges they now face as a result of their losses. Normalize and validate as appropriate.

*Deaths are not only difficult to deal with themselves, but can also create many **changes** in our lives. Learning to adjust to these changes is an important part of grieving a loss. Healthy grieving involves **making changes**, both inside of ourselves and outside of ourselves, to adjust to the physical absence of the person from our lives. We've talked about ways in which your loved one died that you wish you could change, but can't. Now, let's talk about changes in your personal relationships and day-to-day activities, and changes that you **can** make in your own personal behavior that will help you adjust to all these changes.*

Group Completes Worksheet (Optional)

*Although many of the changes we just discussed **are** out of our direct control, there are some aspects of these life situations that we **can** control and begin to change. This next exercise will help you to think about things that you would like to change in your lives, and to figure out **how** to take your first steps toward making those changes.*

Use your discretion in inviting group members to fill out either Handout 3.27, Changes in My Life Since the Death, Handout 3.28, Making Positive Life Changes to Further Adjust to the Loss, or Handout 3.29, My Relationships Before and After the Death, depending on group members' needs.

Facilitate a discussion regarding the changes that group members have experienced in their relationships and daily lives:

- Which changes have been easiest to make, and which are still the hardest to deal with?
- Which loss-induced changes do they need to adjust to the most in their relationships? What first steps should they take?
- For youth in residential facilities, what was it like before they entered the facility and what might they expect when they return home?

IV. Planning for Difficult Days (Relapse Prevention)

Explain that difficult days involving trauma and/or loss reminders can often be anticipated. The following exercises can be used to assist members in identifying their own (often idiosyncratic) difficult days.

A. Group Activity: Anticipating Difficult Days

Draw six equally placed vertical lines across the board /paper, creating six columns that represent the next six months. Write the name of the current month at the top of the far left column and continue writing the names of consecutive months at the top of each successive column to the right. Provide each group member with a different colored marker or piece of chalk, so that each group member is represented by a unique color.

Invite all group members to go up to the board/paper at the same time and write, under the appropriate month, special dates that may serve as trauma or loss reminders during the next six months. These days should include specific times or settings in which they may expect to be reminded either of the traumatic event that resulted in their special person's death or of his/her continuing absence. These difficult days may include birthdays, anniversaries, holidays, seasons of the year, or special events such as graduations, reunions, religious events like bar mitzvah's and catechisms, athletic events, or musical/theatrical performances involving the group member.

Help each group member identify one or two days that he/she expects will be the most difficult to handle, and to think of why. Invite group members to describe their difficult days and aspects of those days that they expect will be most difficult to deal with.

B. Group Discussion: Dealing with Difficult Days

Now that we have each identified one or two difficult days and aspects of those days that will be most difficult to handle, let's work on developing a plan that will help us to cope with these days as best as we can.

During this discussion/exercise, invite group members to review their *personal coping plans* to identify which coping strategies may be most effective for that day and place. (These plans were created in Module 1, Session 1.5, on coping skills.)

For holidays and special occasions, direct the discussion to aspects of the upcoming event that may be most painful or difficult to negotiate. Prompts for engaging group members in this task include:

- "The holiday I am most worried about is …"
- "What I fear the most is …"
- "I will miss (deceased person, "my brother," etc.) the most when we …"
- "I start getting upset when …"
- "It's hardest for me when …"

Review Handout 3.30, Ideas for Getting through Special Days.

Prompts:

*One of the important tasks for grieving is to remember the past while moving into the future. One way you can do this is to **set aside a special time** during which you and others remember your special person. Perhaps you can each share a special memory of a time you shared with your special person, or have a moment of* *silence, or pray together. Then, you can create some new rituals that are all your own, so you can create new pleasant memories.*

Lead a problem-solving discussion using such statements as:

- "One way I would like to honor the memory of (deceased person) during (the holiday or event) is …"
- "I'm going to try something new by …"
- "One thing I've done in the past that has really helped is to …"
- "One thing I've done in the past that didn't help (and that I'd like to avoid doing again) was to …"
- "I'd like the group's help in figuring out a better way to …"

C. Group Discussion: Dealing with Daily Occurrences

Hint: This discussion is designed to provide an opportunity for group members to share daily interactions at school or with friends and family members that can be difficult because of their loss. Convey the message that you don't really know which particular incidents are difficult for them on a daily basis – that you have some ideas based on your conversations with other teens, but that you hope to learn from them. Given the opportunity, group members will often start a passionate discussion in which they share "horror stories" of bad moments with teachers, peers, neighbors, and family members.

*In addition to special days, **certain everyday conversations and situations** can be another source of stress for people who have lost a special person. Kids tell us that it's hard to know **whom to tell and whom not to tell** about the death, and exactly what to tell them, or how to tell them. Sometimes other people who know about what happened can treat you differently, like avoiding you, or acting nervous about mentioning the word "death" or the name of your special person who died. Some kids who have had a parent die say they feel uncomfortable when they are in awkward situations where their parent is supposed to be involved, like getting permission slips signed, or back-to-school nights, or setting up teacher–parent meetings.*

So let's spend some time talking about whether this happens to you. You tell me: what kind of everyday situations feel awkward or uncomfortable to you, or are difficult to deal with?

Lead the discussion, taking notes of everyday situations that feel awkward or stressful, pointing out common themes and identifying problem situations that you can address in the next activity. Common themes may include the following:

- Not knowing whom to tell or how to talk about the death.
- How to help friends and teachers provide the kind of support that you need at the time.
- How to deal with situations that usually involve your deceased family member (conferences, permission slips, etc.).
- Dealing with rumors about the death.

- Dealing with other's expectations that you should be over the death by now.

D. Group Discussion: Speaking Authentically About Your Loss and Asking for What You Want

Hint: There are no easy answers to these problems. Your role as group leader is not to have all of the answers, but rather to act as a sympathetic listener who is ready to hear about the pain and isolation that these circumstances may cause. Use "leading" questions as appropriate to encourage group members to generate their own ideas. Help them shape their ideas into a form that is supportive and useful.

Summarize the discussion, focusing on the range of common situations that the group members find uncomfortable and difficult. Use the list you gathered in the previous activity.

Present Flipchart 3.6b. After each topic, invite a "group think tank" about how to deal with this issue. As needed, mention some of the ideas in italics below. You can also choose to use specific cartoon cards that exemplify specific difficult situations, as well as Flipchart 3.6d. You can use Flipchart 3.6c to remind group members of the five steps to getting support.

Problem Situation: Not knowing Whom to Tell About the Death

Give serious thought to the question of whom to tell about the death. The decision is easier for close friends and family members, less clear for teachers and acquaintances. The key factor is whether telling will make things easier for you in the long run. For instance, even though you would prefer not to tell a school counselor or certain teachers, it may be in your best interest to do so rather than having it brought up in a group or classroom with everyone around. It can also help to tell teachers if you foresee yourself asking for an extension on assignment or test deadlines, or to tell a guidance or health counselor at school if you think it would help to have them advocate for your needs, like talking to teachers for you.

Problem Situation: Not Knowing How to Speak About the Death

You might want different people to have different amounts of information about what happened. Keep in mind that you want them to know enough so that they can support you without exposing them to too many upsetting details. For this reason, it may be a good idea to have in mind a brief "news release" that you can use to let people know about what happened without getting into details that aren't helpful for you to get into in that setting. If someone gets curious and presses you for details that you don't wish to discuss, you can say, "I'd rather not go into details, but I can tell you that it was one of the worst days of my life."

Optional activities: have each group member develop their own "news release." Alternatively, you can use Handout 3.31 to generate a "helping a good friend" exercise focusing on the topic of intrusive questioning by peers.

Guidelines for Handout 3.31: Insensitive Expressions of Support (*Secondary Adversity*)

Description: *This teenage boy is a member of his high-school basketball team. Two weeks ago his older brother died by suicide, and today is his first day back to practice. The boy's parents gave his coach permission to tell his teammates that he was missing practice because his brother had died and that he needed time with his family. After his return, his teammates surround him sympathetically and are curious about what happened. One teammate lays a sympathetic hand on his shoulder and says, "Sorry about your brother. What happened?"*

Facilitating questions (group leaders should allow group members to generate their own responses and offer answers only when necessary):

*What is the **situation**?* Scene: Teenage boy's first day back at practice following the death of his brother. His teammates are curious and ask him an uncomfortable question about the death.

(Discuss): *His teammates are like a lot of teenagers. They are both sympathetic and curious. They're not trying to be mean or hurtful, but that question makes him feel really uncomfortable and puts him on the spot. He doesn't want to talk about how his brother died. He wants to drop the subject and get back into playing basketball so he can feel normal and get his mind off things, just for a little while.*

*How might he **react** to his teammate's question?*

*How might **you** feel if you were in his situation?* (Ideas may include):

- "I feel ashamed that I come from a family where things like this (brother's suicide) happen."
- "It's none of their business."
- "If I tell them, they'll never treat me the same again."
- "They don't really care about me or what I'm going through. They just want all the dirty details."

*What **negative feelings** might these thoughts bring up?* (Anger, shame, embarrassment, anxiety, feeling self-conscious and awkward in front of his teammates, etc.)

*What **behaviors** might he be tempted to engage in if he is thinking and feeling this way?* (Get angry and lash out at his teammates, storm out of the room, drop out of the team, get into a fight with someone, take drugs or alcohol to "chill out" or escape, take it out on his family members when he gets home, withdraw from his friends and family.)

*What are some likely **negative consequences** of these behaviors?* (Getting suspended from school for fighting, getting kicked off the team, undermining team morale, getting himself or someone else hurt in a fight, overdosing or getting drunk and doing something stupid or reckless that creates more problems.)

*Can you help him **think differently** about the situation or behave in a more constructive way? Are there more helpful ways of looking at and responding to what happened?* (Ideas for *substitute thoughts* include):

- Being honest and saying, "I don't want to go into the details, but it was the worst thing we've ever been through."
- Enlisting coach's support by letting him know what happened to his brother and also letting him know what he's comfortable sharing and what he would like to keep to himself.
- "They mean well and they're probably just curious. Some of them may have even known my brother. Maybe they really could support me if I let them and showed them how."
- "It's up to me to decide how much I want to share. I get to define the boundaries of what I'm comfortable talking about and not talking about."

(As appropriate):

*Could **you** believe these new replacement thoughts about what happened if you were in his situation? Do they accurately reflect the **facts** that are known about what happened? Are they believable to **you**?*

*How could **thinking about the situation** in these more positive ways change how he is **feeling**?*

*How could these more positive thoughts and feelings help him **behave** in more positive ways?*

*What kinds of **consequences** are likely to follow if he chooses to have more positive thoughts, feelings, and behaviors about this situation?*

Problem Situation: How to Help Friends and Teachers Provide the Kind of Support that Feels Good to You

*Remember in our exercise on learning to get support that **different types of stressful situations may require different types of support**. You may be confused over an important choice and not know what to do. Here, **information and advice** can be most helpful. In other cases, if you are bored or feeling lonely, **being with friends** can really pick up your spirits. Sometimes, a hug and maybe a shoulder to cry on are exactly what you need.*

- Lead a discussion in which group members explore the specific types of responses and supportive exchanges that have been most helpful, versus least helpful.
- Point out that when friends or family offer support that we don't want, we may respond with irritation and frustration, or we may simply ignore them. This can confuse them or hurt their feelings and put additional strains on our relationships.
- We can sometimes make things easier if we let our friends and family know what type of support they could offer that would be useful to us. A good way to do this is to use the Five Steps to Getting Support, which we learned in Module 1, Session 1.8, and have practiced since then in some of our sessions. This will also help your friends feel more comfortable, because they often mean well but simply don't know what to say or do to be helpful. Sometimes the smart thing to do is not burn bridges by storming off or shutting down emotionally, but instead, "coach" people about what type of support would feel most helpful.

Optional activity: use Handout 3.32 to generate a "helping a good friend" exercise focusing on inappropriate expressions of support from a teacher.

Guidelines for Handout 3.32: Well-Meaning Teacher (*Secondary Adversity*)

Description: *Last fall, this boy lost his mom to cancer. It is now the spring of the same school year. He missed quite a few days of school while his mom was sick and after her death, and even after he came back, his grades continued to suffer. He looked sad all the time and had a hard time paying attention and remembering things, or feeling motivated to do homework or study for tests. Several months have passed, and he is doing a bit better at school, but he still feels sad and misses his mom all the time. He often feels like crying inside, although most of the time he doesn't show it. Today, he gets back a test and sees that he has earned an "A+". His teacher says, "It's good to see you are doing better."*

Facilitating questions (group leaders should allow group members to generate their own responses and offer answers only when necessary):

What is the **situation**? Scene: Teenage boy sitting at his desk with his teacher handing back his test and saying, "It's good to see you are doing better."

How might he **react** *to his teacher's comment? How might you feel if you were in his situation?* (Ideas may include):

- "Just because I'm *doing* better doesn't mean I'm *feeling* any better."
- "I know he means well, but he really doesn't have a clue about how I'm feeling."
- "I don't *want* to do better in school. I'm never going to get over this."
- "If I let myself do better in school, then it would mean that I don't miss her as much. And that would be disloyal."

What **negative feelings** *might these thoughts bring up?* (Anger, feeling misunderstood, resentment that the teacher is assuming too much, guilt over disloyalty to mother's memory, feeling self-conscious in front of his classmates, etc.)

What **behaviors** *might he be tempted to engage in if he is thinking and feeling this way?* (Getting angry and lash out at the teacher, doing worse on his next test to prove that he's not "over it," getting into a fight with a classmate, taking drugs or alcohol to "chill out.")

What are some likely **negative consequences** *of these behaviors?* (Getting suspended from school, failing the class, getting himself or someone else hurt in a fight, overdosing or getting drunk and doing something stupid.)

Can you help him **think differently** *about the situation or behave in a more constructive way? Are there more helpful ways of looking at and responding to what happened?* Ideas for *substitute thoughts* include:

- "I could talk with a counselor at school and tell him/her about what happened. I could let the counselor offer advice

to teachers who want to help but don't know what to say."
- "The teacher means well, so maybe I can cut him some slack. Maybe all he's talking about are my grades – he may not be assuming that he knows how I'm feeling inside."
- "My mom would be happy that my grades are improving, so I can look at this as a good thing – even though I still really miss her."
- "Even when my teacher does not understand me, there are other people who do, and I can turn to them for support."

(As appropriate):

Could **you** *believe these new replacement thoughts about what happened if you were in his situation? Do they accurately reflect the* **facts** *that are known about what happened? Are they believable to* **you**?

How could **thinking about the situation** *in these more positive ways change how he is* **feeling**?

How could these more positive thoughts and feelings help him **behave** *in more positive ways?*

What kinds of **consequences** *are likely to follow if he chooses to have more positive thoughts, feelings, and behaviors about this situation?*

Problem Situation: How to Deal with Situations That Usually Involve your Deceased Family Member (Conferences, Permission Slips, etc.)

You can avoid some of these situations by letting key people know (like teachers or coaches) about the death beforehand. If this is not possible, then consider speaking with people privately. For example, if a teacher asks that both parents sign a permission slip, speak privately with him or her after class.

Problem Situation: Dealing with Rumors about the Death

Consider taking the first step and being the first one to talk with key adults and people you want to know. Once they hear the news from you, the need for gossip may go down. Remember also that rumors are very common, especially among teenagers, but they generally go away more quickly if you don't react to them in a defensive or angry way.

Optional activity: use Handout 3.33 to generate a "helping a good friend" exercise focusing on feeling ostracized after an accident.

Guidelines for Handout 3.33: Feeling Ostracized after Fatal Accident in Which Friend Was Killed (*Secondary Adversity*)

Description: *Several weeks ago, this boy was out driving on a Friday night with his girlfriend and his best friend. They were heading off to a party when they hit a patch of ice in the road and spun out of control and flipped over. His girlfriend was seriously injured* *and his best friend, who was not wearing a seatbelt, was ejected and died at the scene. The boy himself was also hurt pretty badly. All three of them attend the same school. He has been out of school for two weeks to recover and attend his friend's funeral. The accident and the death of his friend were covered in the local news and are public knowledge. Today is his first day back to school, and he's about to enter his homeroom class.*

Facilitating questions (group leaders should allow group members to generate their own responses and offer answers only when necessary):

What is the **situation**? Scene: Teenage boy returning to class after getting into an accident in which his friend was killed and his girlfriend was seriously injured. Today is his first day back after missing two weeks of class. He knows that his classmates probably all know what happened.

What is his **hurtful thought**? "They're all looking at me weird. I know it's because I was the one who was driving."

(Discuss): *How might he be feeling after thinking this hurtful thought? How might you feel if you were in his situation?* (Ideas may include):

- He might be worried that they will blame him for what happened. They may never want to be his friend again or may even try to punish him for what happened, such as by spreading rumors at school or posting mean things about him on social media.
- He could be feeling ashamed and guilty about what happened.
- He may have lots of regrets, like not insisting that his friend wear a seatbelt, getting distracted by the loud music on the radio, not recognizing how slippery the road was, going too fast around a curve given the road conditions, etc.
- He could be feeling very awkward and self-conscious, and not have any idea about what to say about what happened.
- He might be afraid that no one will ever trust him or feel safe with him again, so he may not have people to hang out with.
- He could be feeling misunderstood, like no one else was there to know what it was like and how scary it was to go through.

What **behaviors** *might he be tempted to engage in if he is thinking and feeling this way?* (Skip school or drop out of school, get into a fight with a classmate, use drugs or alcohol to distract himself from how bad he feels about what happened, start driving recklessly to prove that he actually *is* a good driver and is in control in dangerous places, do other reckless things that put his and other people's safety at risk, and even start to think about taking his life.)

What are some likely **negative consequences** *of these behaviors?* (Not getting an education, getting suspended from school, getting himself or someone else hurt in a fight, overdosing or becoming addicted to drugs or alcohol, getting into another accident, actually ending his own life.)

Can you help him **think differently** *about the situation or behave in a more constructive way? Are there more helpful ways of looking at and responding to what happened?* (Ideas for *substitute thoughts* include):

- "This is a difficult situation for everyone – not only for me, but also my teacher and my classmates. No one here doubts how bad I feel about what happened. Just because people may be "looking at me funny" doesn't mean they are rejecting me. They just may be feeling bad for me and not know what to say."
- "Heavy things like this take time to deal with. It's gonna feel awkward at first, but it won't always feel this way. Things will get better with time."
- "My life may never be quite the same as before, but that doesn't mean that it won't be a good life – one that's still worth living."
- "My friend would have wanted me to my live life to the fullest. If he were here, he'd tell me how short and precious life really is and to make the most of it – not throw it away."
- "I want to do things that my friend would have been happy about or proud of. Even though his life was short, I want to make sure he leaves his mark in the world by doing good things in his memory."

(As appropriate):

Could **you** *believe these new replacement thoughts about what happened if you were in his situation? Do they accurately reflect the* **facts** *that are known about what happened? Are they believable to* **you**?

How could **thinking about the situation** *in these more positive ways change how he is* **feeling**?

How could these more positive thoughts and feelings help him **behave** *in more positive ways?*

What kinds of **consequences** *are likely to follow if he chooses to have more positive thoughts, feelings, and behaviors about this situation?*

Problem Situation: Dealing with Stigmatized Deaths

There are many publicized circumstances in which a family member or friend dies because of a murder, drug overdose, suicide, gang violence, or other "stigmatized" causes of death. Survivors are often left feeling ambivalent, angry, or ashamed while still feeling a profound sense of loss. People who grieve for someone who died in a difficult way not only have to deal with their grief over the loss, but also with other feelings over how the person died that can make grieving more difficult. People around them often don't know what to say and can often come across as unsupportive. Comments from others such as: "She should have seen this coming and left him," "She was an addict – what did you expect?" "People kept telling him to stop dealing drugs, and he just would not listen," are all too common on these occasions. Because these deaths often get reported in the news, the grieving person may feel for a few days that there is no place to get away from loss and trauma reminders and from curious questions. You can say things like:

- "I'd rather not go into details, but I can tell you that it was one of the worst days of my life."
- A simple statement such as, "She meant a lot to me, and I'll always miss her/him" may help stop the questioning. If they don't, it may be best to say, "This is too hard for me to talk about right now." Remember that it is your choice about how much you want to discuss with a given person at a given time and place. If it doesn't feel helpful, you don't need to go into details.

Problem Situation: Dealing with Other's Expectations That You Should Be Over the Death By Now

Dealing with other people's expectations can be difficult, especially if they don't understand very much about grief. People can feel pressured by comments like "It's been a month now; you better start concentrating on your grades." Sometimes the pressure is more subtle, like when all mention of the person who died stops and people only talk about you getting on with your life.

*It's during times like this that knowledge about the normal process of grief can be helpful, both for you and for those around you. Think about handing some of our materials to family, teachers, or friends who may benefit from reading them. Remember that grief is a very individual process. There is no set time for it to be resolved. When the death occurred under difficult circumstances, or when your last meeting with them was difficult (such as having an argument), grieving can be harder. **In truth, you will grieve in some way or another for as long as you feel the absence of your special person in your life. This is not a bad thing. It shows how important your relationship with that person was to your life, and what they meant to you. You can live with grief. Grief tells you that you have lived and loved.***

V. Summary and Practice Assignment

- Summarize and bring closure to the session.
- Motivate group members to initiate desired changes in their support network, circumstances, and activities.

We call this our "relapse prevention" session because it is designed to give you a "heads up" for difficulties that may be waiting for you. The road to healing is often bumpy. There may be times, maybe even tomorrow, when you will feel strong waves of sadness, anxiety, or really miss your special person. You may even feel like the world around you is distant and uncaring. That is when you can think back to your experience, training, and practice in our group, so that you can begin to put things in perspective and, hopefully, try one of your personal coping strategies. This group cannot magically take away the pain you have experienced or the pain you may continue to experience, but we can help you to manage your grief better so you can find ways to remember and keep a place for your loved one as you move forward with your life.

VI. Check-Out

- *How are you feeling now?* (Use the Feeling Thermometer.)
- *What did you learn about yourself today?*
- *Please fill out Handout 3.34, the Check-Out Feedback Form. The title of today's session was "Planning for Difficult Days."*

If any members are visibly agitated or troubled or report high levels of distress, keep them after the group and determine an appropriate way to transition back to their settings.

Implementing Module 3, Session 3.6 with Individual Clients

I. **Check-in via** Handout 3.02 **Rating My Grief Reactions.** Have the client complete Handout 3.02 by writing a number (on a scale from 1 to 10) next to each grief thermometer. After sharing his/her current grief reactions, ask the client to share anything that happened since the last session that may have influenced his/her grief reactions (in either a positive way or a negative way). Briefly review today's session highlights.

II. **Review practice assignment and previous sessions**. Have the client share his/her homework assignment if completed. If not completed, you can do the worksheet together in the session.

III. **Identify life changes and secondary adversities**. This content can be delivered conversationally as written. Use your discretion in inviting your client to fill out either Handout 3.27, on changes in life since the death, or Handout 3.29, on relationships before and after the death, depending on his/her needs.

IV. **Planning for difficult days (relapse prevention)**. The "anticipating difficult days" exercise can be conducted as written. However, instead of writing on a large sheet of paper, you can use a personal calendar or write the months on a sheet of paper. It is often helpful to share this calendar with the client's parent or caregiver so they can be aware of potential upcoming trauma or loss reminder dates. Similarly, the "dealing with difficult days" exercise can be conducted as written. You can review Handout 3.30, Ideas for Getting through Special Days. Finally, you can conduct the "dealing with daily occurrences" and "speaking authentically about your loss and asking for what you want" exercises as written, making use of the illustrations in the handouts as needed.

V. **Summary and practice assignment**. Summarize the session as written.

VI. **Check-out**. Deliver this step as written.

MODULE 3 HANDOUTS

HANDOUT 3.01

Feeling Thermometer

Sometimes we feel a feeling *just a little bit*, and other times we feel a feeling so strongly that we feel like we might *burst* with that feeling! You can rate or measure your feelings, just like a thermometer measures temperature. The number tells how intense the feeling is.

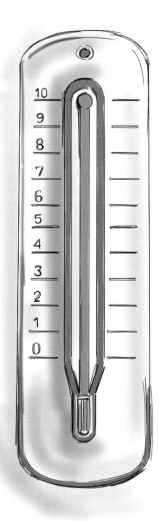

What distressful feelings are you having right now? How would you rate each of these feelings (on a scale of 0 to 10)?

HANDOUT 3.02

Rating My Grief Reactions

Directions: Write one number (from 1 to 10) in the line next to each thermometer to show how strongly you are feeling each grief reaction.

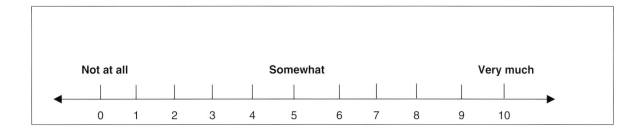

 Missing the person a lot

_____

 Feeling lost without them

_____

 Feeling so upset about the way that they died, that it's hard to remember the good times

_____

 Feeling afraid of forgetting important things about them

_____

 Wanting to avoid things that remind me they are no longer here physically (loss reminders)

_____

 Feeling like they're watching over me in a comforting way

_____

 Wanting to live the kind of life they would want me to have

_____

 Wanting to make the world safer so other people don't die in tragic ways

_____

 Wanting to avoid things that remind me of the way they died (trauma reminders)

_____

 Feeling like they are still an important part of my life

_____

HANDOUT 3.03

Learning about Different Grief Reactions, page 1

1. **Emotional pain over being separated from them (Separation distress)**

Reactions that this group can help you with:

___ Missing the person

___ Feeling sad that we are no longer physically together

___ Wishing we could be together again

___ Feeling lonely for their company

___ Feeling my heart ache inside for them

___ Wanting to sigh a lot

___ Wanting to go search for them in places where they used to be

___ Wanting to cry for them

___ Feeling angry or frustrated that we aren't together

___ Thinking of where they are now; wondering whether I'll ever see them again

___ Thinking I can see them (like their face in a crowd) or feeling their presence nearby

___ Avoiding loss reminders (things that remind me they are gone)

___ Feeling afraid to get close to other people, because I might lose them too

Positive reactions that can develop over time:

___ Feeling like they are watching over me and looking out for me

___ Wanting to do positive things he or she used to do that I admired

___ Feeling grateful for the time we had together

2. **Feeling lost without them (Existential/identity distress)**

Reactions that this group can help you with:

___ Feeling like part of myself died with them and is gone

___ Feeling lost and directionless without them

___ Not knowing what to do with myself without them

___ Losing hope that I can still have a good life without having them here

___ Not caring what happens to me anymore since they died

Learning about Different Grief Reactions, page 2

____ Feeling bored, like nothing matters any more since they died

____ Losing my desire to work to have a good life

Positive reactions that can develop over time:

____ Wanting to live the kind of life that he or she would have wanted for me

____ Wanting to spend my life helping other people who are going through very hard times

3. **Pain over the *way* they died (Circumstance-related distress)**

Reactions that this group can help you with:

____ Feeling angry about the way they died (thinking their death was violent, tragic, preventable, unnecessary, or senseless)

____ Feeling guilty or angry at myself that I didn't do more to keep them from dying

____ Feeling ashamed over how I acted at the time of their death

____ Feeling angry at other people for not doing more to keep them from dying

____ Being so upset over how they died that it's hard to remember the good times

____ Wanting revenge on whoever is responsible

____ Feeling angry at them for contributing to their own death (not taking better care of themselves, using drugs or alcohol, taking their own life)

Positive reactions that can develop over time:

____ Wanting to do positive things that keep other people from dying the way my loved one did

____ Wanting to help others in need

____ Deciding to be more safe and careful with my life

HANDOUT 3.04

Grief Goals

By the end of this group, I want to feel *less*: *(check all that apply)*				
☐ Angry	☐ Sad	☐ Alone	☐ Scared	☐ Nervous
☐ Confused	☐ Guilty	☐ Different from other kids		☐ Other _____

By the end of this group, I want to feel *more*: *(check all that apply)*				
☐ Calm	☐ Happy	☐ Hopeful	☐ Confident	☐ Close to others
☐ Understood	☐ Powerful	☐ Cared For	☐ Other_____	

I want to change the way I do things, the way I think about things, or the way I feel about things in the following way(s): *(check all that apply)*

☐	Be able to calm myself down when I really start to miss the person who died
☐	Be able to calm myself down when I get upset thinking about **the way** that the person died
☐	Be able to understand my thoughts and feelings about the person who died a little better
☐	Feel more connected to the person who died, even though they are no longer here physically
☐	Know what to do when my grief starts to feel overwhelming or out of control
☐	Be able to think or talk about the person who died without getting upset
☐	Stop staying away from things that remind me that the person has died and is no longer here
☐	Stop staying away from things that remind me of **the way** the person died (what caused them to die)
☐	Have an easier time dealing with strong or confusing feelings about the person's death
☐	Feel like I can live the kind of life that the person would have wanted for me
☐	Have an easier time talking to family members about the death
☐	Have an easier time talking to friends about the death
☐	Have a better idea of what to do or say when other kids find out about the death
☐	Feel like I can still have a good future even though this death has happened

HANDOUT 3.05

Check-Out Feedback Form

Session topic: Learning about Grief

Your date of birth: _____

Today's date: _____

Facility: _____

Unit/cottage: _____

What about today's session was most useful to you? Which activities and materials were the most helpful?

_____

_____

_____

What specific suggestions do you have for how to make the group better?

_____

_____

_____

How comfortable were you about today's topic? (Please circle a number.)

1	2	3	4	5
Extremely uncomfortable	Fairly uncomfortable	Somewhat comfortable	Fairly comfortable	Very comfortable

What were you thinking and feeling during today's group?

_____

_____

_____

_____

How are you feeling now?

_____

_____

_____

_____

HANDOUT 3.06

Avoiding Loss Reminders

HANDOUT 3.07

Reunification Fantasies

HANDOUT 3.08

Social Withdrawal and Fear of Getting Close

HANDOUT 3.09

Giving Up on Future Plans

HANDOUT 3.10

"Why Not . . . Nothing Matters Anymore"

HANDOUT 3.11

"I Will Never Love Again . . ."

HANDOUT 3.12

Shame over Circumstances of the Death

HANDOUT 3.13

"Can't Stop Thinking about the Way He Died"

HANDOUT 3.14

Practice Exercise: Part 1 – Loss Reminders and Grief Reactions

Purpose: To help you identify your own personal loss reminders and the grief reactions they bring up.

Directions: Using the figure below to guide you, choose a situation that happened this week when you had a *loss reminder*. Loss reminders come in different forms, like the person's picture or name or belongings; places they used to be, things they used to do while they were alive, their favorite food, their family or friends, and hardships created by their loss (like money problems, or feeling lonely). Then, answer five questions about it.

Sizing Up a Situation

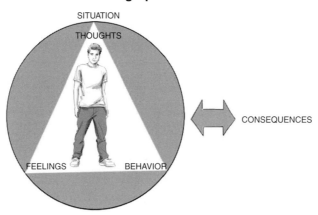

First, describe the *situation* where the loss reminder happened (what happened that reminded you?)

_____

_____

_____

Second, what *thoughts* or mental pictures went through your head (what did you tell yourself)?

_____

_____

_____

Third, what grief reactions did the reminder bring up for you? (Name as many *feelings* as you can.)

_____

_____

_____

Fourth, how did you *behave* when these grief reactions (thoughts and feelings) came up?

_____

_____

_____

Fifth, what were the *consequences* of your behaviors? Were these consequences good or bad?

_____

_____

_____

Practice Exercise: Part 2 – Loss Reminders and Grief Reactions

Next, think about different ways in which your hurtful thoughts about the loss reminder may be either *inaccurate* or *unhelpful*. Put a checkmark next to every type of thought or mental picture that went through your mind when you ran into your *loss reminder*.

___**Filtering and throwing out** (focusing only on the negative, and throwing out the positive or telling yourself that positive things are not real or that they don't matter, like "I was lucky to have a dad like mine, but now that he's dead, that doesn't matter.")

___**Should and musts** (setting really strict rules about how things "should" be, and being really hard on yourself if you don't follow them, like "I should be over this by now!")

___**All-or-none thinking** (seeing things in black and white, things are totally good, or totally bad, like, "If I still get upset when I am reminded of her, then it means I'm not getting any better.")

___***Then* is *now* thinking** (acting like what is happening now is exactly what happened in my past, like, "If I start to feel sad and scared about losing my friend, then it means I'm about to lose someone else I care about.")

___**If it *feels* true, then it *is* true** (taking feelings as proof that a hurtful thought is really true, like, "If I feel hopeless after losing my mother, then it means there really is no hope", "If I feel very angry at the emergency workers because they did not save my grandfather's life, then it must mean they did something wrong and should be punished.")

___**Self put-downs** (putting negative labels like "loser" on yourself and tearing yourself down, like, "If I let myself feel happy or have loving feelings again, then it means I am disrespecting the memory of my boyfriend who died.")

___**Self-blame** (blaming yourself when you had only a small part in what happened, like "It's all my fault I should have known this was coming," "If only I would have done more, this would never have happened.")

___**Permanent thoughts** (using words like *always* and *never*: "Life will *always* be this way," "I will *never* be happy again," "I will *never* get over this," "Things will *always* be this hard.")

___**Playing fortune-teller** (believing you can predict the future and acting as if it will definitely happen, "I already *know* I'll go back to jail, so why even try to stay straight?")

___**Mind-reading** (believing you know what others are thinking, like, "I just *know* you blame me for what happened.")

___**Catastrophizing** (blowing a problem into a huge catastrophe by thinking that things are worse than they really are, like, "If I start to feel nervous about making a new close friend or boyfriend, then I will *always* have this problem, and I will end up always being sad and alone.")

HANDOUT 3.15

Check-Out Feedback Form

Session topic: Understanding Connections between Loss Reminders, Grief Reactions, and Consequences

Your date of birth: _____

Today's date: _____

Facility: _____

Unit/cottage: _____

What about today's session was most useful to you? Which activities and materials were the most helpful?

_____

_____

_____

What specific suggestions do you have for how to make the group better?

_____

_____

_____

How comfortable were you about today's topic? (Please circle a number.)

1	2	3	4	5
Extremely uncomfortable	Fairly uncomfortable	Somewhat comfortable	Fairly comfortable	Very comfortable

What were you thinking and feeling during today's group?

_____

_____

_____

_____

How are you feeling now?

_____

_____

_____

_____

HANDOUT 3.16

Feeling Guilty about a Friend's Murder

HANDOUT 3.17

Feeling Guilty about a Friend's Suicide

HANDOUT 3.18

Feeling Angry About a Death

> **Please indicate how angry you feel about each issue by writing a number on the line beside each thermometer:**
>
> 1 = Not angry   5 = Somewhat angry   10 = Very angry

 At the Person Who Died

_____

 **At the People Responsible**

_____

 **At the World**

_____

 At the People Around Me

_____

 At Yourself

_____

 About the Way They Died

_____

 **At God**

_____

HANDOUT 3.19

Anger at People Responsible

HANDOUT 3.20

Anger and Blame for Not Preventing Brother's Death

HANDOUT 3.21

Wishes and Regrets

(Adapted from M. K. Perschy)

Directions: Reflect on your relationship with your loved one as you fill in the following:

If only I had …

_____

If only I hadn't …

_____

It was my fault when …

_____

I'm so sorry that …

_____

It still hurts to think about the time when he/she …

_____

I still cannot forgive him/her for …

_____

I still get angry when I think about …

_____

I can't forgive myself for …

_____

If we had one more day together, I would …

_____

HANDOUT 3.22

Check-Out Feedback Form

Session topic: Dealing with Strong Emotions after a Death

Your date of birth: _____

Today's date: _____

Facility: _____

Unit/cottage: _____

What about today's session was most useful to you? Which activities and materials were the most helpful?

_____

_____

_____

What specific suggestions do you have for how to make the group better?

_____

_____

_____

How comfortable were you about today's topic? (Please circle a number.)

1	2	3	4	5
Extremely uncomfortable	Fairly uncomfortable	Somewhat comfortable	Fairly comfortable	Very comfortable

What were you thinking and feeling during today's group?

_____

_____

_____

_____

How are you feeling now?

_____

_____

_____

HANDOUT 3.23

Connecting in a Positive Way

Directions: Find ways to feel close to your loved one who died by modeling (or copying) parts of their personality, habits, or behaviors that you like or admire the most.

First: pick a specific positive trait, characteristic, or behavior that you admired about them and write it down in the space below. (This can be from the activity we did in the session.)

Second: during the coming week, try to display that positive trait, habit, or behavior at some point each day. On the chart below, please circle "yes" for each day that you display that quality, and circle "no" for each day that you do not.

	Sunday	**Monday**	**Tuesday**	**Wednesday**	**Thursday**	**Friday**	**Saturday**
Were you able to show that positive trait or behavior today? (Circle Yes or No)	Yes	Yes	Yes	Yes	Yes	Yes	Yes
	No	No	No	No	No	No	No

Third: describe how well the trait or behavior worked for you. Describe a specific situation and what you did. What were you thinking? What were you feeling? What were the consequences?

_____

_____

_____

_____

_____

_____

_____

_____

_____

_____

_____

HANDOUT 3.24

Check-Out Feedback Form

Session topic: Promoting the Positive, Normalizing the Negative

Your date of birth: _____

Today's date: _____

Facility: _____

Unit/cottage: _____

What about today's session was most useful to you? Which activities and materials were the most helpful?

_____

_____

_____

What specific suggestions do you have for how to make the group better?

_____

_____

_____

How comfortable were you about today's topic? (Please circle a number.)

1	2	3	4	5
Extremely uncomfortable	Fairly uncomfortable	Somewhat comfortable	Fairly comfortable	Very comfortable

What were you thinking and feeling during today's group?

_____

_____

_____

_____

How are you feeling now?

_____

_____

_____

_____

HANDOUT 3.25

Things I Admire About the Person That I Want to Keep

Directions: Think about the things you value the most about the special person who died, such as their personality or good things they did. What were they good at? It might be being funny, being loving, being a hard worker, being honest, caring about other people, or always being there for you.

List as many of their positive qualities as you can, especially qualities you believe can be of help to you in the future, like help to make you a better person, to make better life choices, or being good at handling different situations.

- _____

- _____

- _____

- _____

- _____

- _____

- _____

- _____

HANDOUT 3.26

Check-Out Feedback Form

Session topic: Reminiscing Together (Connecting to the Deceased in a Healthy Way)

Your date of birth: _____

Today's date: _____

Facility: _____

Unit/cottage: _____

What about today's session was most useful to you? Which activities and materials were the most helpful?

_____

_____

_____

What specific suggestions do you have for how to make the group better?

_____

_____

_____

How comfortable were you about today's topic? (Please circle a number.)

1	2	3	4	5
Extremely uncomfortable	Fairly uncomfortable	Somewhat comfortable	Fairly comfortable	Very comfortable

What were you thinking and feeling during today's group?

_____

_____

_____

_____

How are you feeling now?

_____

_____

_____

HANDOUT 3.27

Changes in My Life Since the Death

Directions: Below are different areas of your life that may have changed since the death of the person you cared about. For each area, write down any ways in which things in your life have changed.

- Living situation and finances

- Meals

- School and homework

- Chores and responsibilities

- Day-to-day interactions with my family and friends

- Holidays and other special days

- Favorite activities and hobbies

- (Other)

HANDOUT 3.28

Making Positive Life Changes to Further Adjust to the Loss

My desired relationships map:

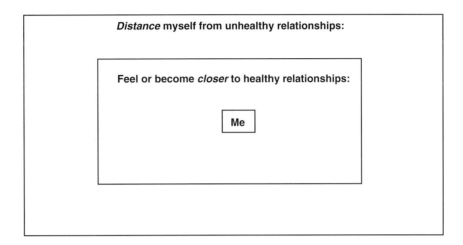

Parts of my life I want or need to change to more fully adjust to the loss:

	Overall change I want/need	First steps I need to take
• Living situation and finances		
• Meals		
• School and homework		
• Holidays		
• Daily interactions with people		
• Favorite activities and hobbies		
• Chores and responsibilities		
Other (describe)		

HANDOUT 3.29

My Relationships Before and After the Death

- Depending on how close or distant you felt to specific people Before the Death, write their names in Chart 1 (below) either closer or further away from you (Me).

- Depending on how close or distant you feel to specific people at the present time (Now), write their names in Chart 2 either closer or further away from you (Me).

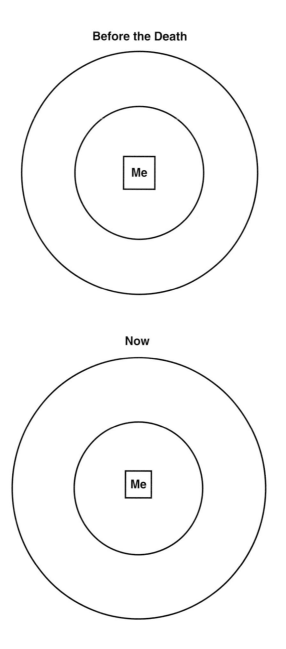

HANDOUT 3.30

Ideas for Getting through Special Days

Holidays and special family occasions such as birthdays, anniversaries, graduations, and reunions can be very stressful for people who have lost someone close.

Maintain good health routines. On holidays or special occasions, normal sleeping, eating, and exercise routines can be thrown off. Keep healthy routines as much as possible – before, during, and after these events. That means getting enough sleep, avoiding too many sweets, and getting enough exercise.

Plan time with someone whom you can talk about your feelings. Seek out a friend or family member who is comfortable talking about these issues. This may also be an important time for you to write in a journal – to note and further explore your feelings and other reactions to the loss.

Plan fun activities. If your family is unable to engage in fun activities at this time, make sure you spend some time with people who can do fun things ahead of time. Try to structure your days so that you aren't sitting around for long periods of time.

Beware of using alcohol or drugs. Alcohol or drugs can make sadness or depression worse and contribute to impulsive, or even dangerous, behaviors. You may experience a strong desire to "forget about" painful feelings and circumstances by drowning your feelings with drugs or alcohol. This is a form of avoidance and can make things much worse for you, in both the short and long term.

Use the coping strategies discussed in the group. During this group, you have identified coping strategies that you have used on your own, and practiced others that may also help you. Look at your list often, and pick one or more that may help you the most with the problem you currently face.

Other ways to take care of myself. List other ways that you can support yourself during special days. You should take your needs seriously and treat yourself as well as a good and caring friend would.

_____

_____

_____

_____

HANDOUT 3.31

Insensitive Expressions of Support/Intrusive Questioning by Friends

HANDOUT 3.32

Well-Meaning Teacher

HANDOUT 3.33

Feeling Ostracized/Alienated after Fatal Accident in Which Friend Was Killed

HANDOUT 3.34

Check-Out Feedback Form

Session topic: Planning For Difficult Days (Relapse Prevention)

Your date of birth: _____

Today's date: _____

Facility: _____

Unit/cottage: _____

What about today's session was most useful to you? Which activities and materials were the most helpful?

_____

_____

_____

What specific suggestions do you have for how to make the group better?

_____

_____

_____

How comfortable were you about today's topic? (Please circle a number.)

1	2	3	4	5
Extremely uncomfortable	Fairly uncomfortable	Somewhat comfortable	Fairly comfortable	Very comfortable

What were you thinking and feeling during today's group?

_____

_____

_____

_____

How are you feeling now?

_____

_____

_____

_____

Preparing for the Future

Introduction

This final module is forward-looking in outlook, optimistic in tone, and rewarding to implement. Its aim is to promote and harness adolescent strivings for independence while helping adolescents maintain and build upon their recently developed therapeutic gains. These gains include reductions in distress symptoms, improved emotional regulation skills, a greater awareness of personal trauma and loss reminders, and greater self-confidence in handling personal reminders. These therapeutic gains also include a more compassionate understanding of oneself and fellow survivors, a greater ability to recruit and furnish social support, and the ability to recognize, challenge, and replace traumatic expectations with more adaptive core beliefs. The sessions of Module 4 recruit these enhanced adolescent resources to help adolescents improve their current situations where possible, invest in the social contract, and prepare adaptively for their future.

Adolescence is characterized by substantial cortical reorganization. Enhanced pre-cortical function not only prepares adolescents to "take danger into their own hands," but also furnishes them with executive functioning skills that they can (with appropriate adult supervision and facilitation) utilize to plan and direct their lives. Adolescents are primed not only to *plan*, but also to *take action*. Prior therapeutic work with Modules 1, 2, and 3 has deepened adolescents' insight into how trauma and loss-related experiences may have derailed, delayed, restricted, or accelerated their personal development. Module 4 sessions build upon these insights, guiding adolescents to initiate "action plans" to take charge of their own developmental trajectories. Accordingly, Module 4 sessions focus on practical, incremental steps forward that adolescents can take prior to the end of treatment.

In this spirit, we offer two constructive caveats. A first caveat is to avoid approaching Module 4 lightly, as if the "real" therapeutic work is done and these are optional "feel-good" sessions. To the contrary, much of the therapeutic work in prior modules was dedicated to preparing adolescents to engage in Module 4 work by freeing youths from the heavy burden and frequent distractions of managing reminders, distress reactions, and pessimistic beliefs.

A second, related caveat is to not underestimate the potential life-long preventive impact of Module 4 on adolescents' developmental trajectories, many of which have been put in extreme jeopardy. A *trauma-informed* assessment, case formulation, and treatment plan begins with conceptualizing traumatic events during childhood and adolescents as *causal risk factors* for developing posttraumatic stress reactions and related mental health problems, including functional impairment and risky behavior (Layne et al., 2017). However, a *developmentally informed* assessment, case formulation, and treatment plan begins with conceptualizing childhood traumatic events and losses as potential *developmental insults* that carry significant risks for developmental disruptions in developmental tasks and developmental opportunities that can, in turn, cascade forward across developmental transitions into subsequent developmental stages and tasks (Layne et al., 2014a). The risk for developmental disruption – including *developmental derailment*, or major alterations in the life trajectory such as school dropout or incarceration – may increase if trauma-related distress and functional impairment interfere with key developmental tasks in developmentally salient domains (e.g. school, family, peer, romantic relationships), that cascade forward, creating their own risks as they take on a life of their own (Layne et al., 2014b). Although comparatively brief, Module 4 sessions may have the most lasting impact on youth's lives by helping them to reflect on, invest in, and make course corrections in their personal development as they prepare for the transition to young adulthood and the responsibilities of full citizenship.

Supporting an Integrated Sense of Personal Identity

Trauma and loss can create a powerful sense of historical discontinuity, leading to disruptions in the emerging sense of self that can developmentally "freeze" the adolescent into their "traumatized" adolescent personality. The opening sessions of Module 4 are designed to bridge this sense of discontinuity by promoting the resumption of interrupted activities and encouraging developmental progression by initiating new age-appropriate activities. Therapeutic exercises invite adolescents to recognize and reflect on ways in which *traumatic expectations* may still be impeding their developmental progression. Adolescents learn to take concrete "course correction" steps forward in developmentally important life domains to challenge and reformulate traumatic expectations into more adaptive core beliefs, and to make constructive plans for their future.

Transitioning from a Focus on the Past to the Present and Future

Pivoting away from a more *retrospective* exploration in prior modules of traumatic experiences and losses and their continuing impacts, Module 4 *prospectively* focuses on the present and future. It takes a hopeful yet pragmatic approach to developing future goals and aspirations, taking concrete developmental steps forward, and dealing with current and anticipated life adversities. Adolescents are often weighed down by an array of secondary adversities in their lives that were either caused or worsened by traumatic experiences and losses. The group provides a supportive setting in which adolescents put their coping skills to practical use in problem-solving day-to-day life adversities and developmental challenges. The aim of these exercises is to promote adaptive developmental progression by helping adolescents to undertake age-appropriate developmental tasks, pass developmental milestones, and negotiate developmental transitions. The group also harnesses the power of *social referencing* by offering a relevant peer group (one another) that adolescents can use to compare themselves and correct traumatic expectations that may still be impeding their developmental progression. These highly pessimistic expectations often focus on themselves, others, social agencies, and the future, and typically involve themes of danger, prevention, protection, trust, and control over one's life and future.

Module 4 sessions also take a practical approach to addressing problematic behaviors by inviting youth to evaluate the risks, benefits, and consequences of various scenarios that may play out in adolescents' current and future lives. Adolescents often surprise clinicians with their "brain-storming" capabilities, including their capacity to detect ongoing dangers. This work builds on new advances in neuroscience regarding the different neurobiological signatures of danger and safety. In particular, achieving safety by preventing an anticipated harm not only leads to reduced fear, but also activates the brain's reward center in ways similar to the effects associated with substance use. Accordingly, Module 4 sessions focus on helping adolescents detect danger and seek safety in responsible ways including discriminating between *developmentally appropriate adolescent thrill seeking and experimentation* on one hand, and *risky behavior* (which is objectively dangerous) on the other (Steinberg, 2014). Adolescents are helped to recognize ways in which their ability to make responsible choices about danger, protection, and safety can be compromised by their reactivity to trauma and loss reminders, pessimistic beliefs and biased appraisals, and undermined by alcohol and substance use.

Transitioning from a Focus on Self to a Focus on Others

A major developmental achievement of adolescence is the maturation of the capacity for self-care and altruistic behavior. Module 4 is designed to therapeutically harness and cultivate this potential. As adolescents become less mired down by their own trauma and loss-related distress in the preceding modules, they often express an impressive degree of altruism. Indeed, many adolescents have already taken on precocious parental-like functions within their own families due to losses or impaired family members. Thus, a primary aim of Module 4 is to help adolescents acknowledge and balance their altruistic desire to help and protect others (including severely stressed and distressed parents, siblings, and peers) while also taking into account realistic limitations on what they *can* do and what it is *appropriate to do on behalf of others*. This work validates adolescents' pro-social desires while also helping to protect them from unrealistic expectations and excessive burdens. Building on pioneering work with bereaved families (Sandler et al., 2010), a key exercise in Module 4 focuses on discriminating between "problems that are *my* job to fix versus problems that are *other* peoples' job to fix." The key aim of this exercise is to free up resources and create a larger personal space in which to concentrate on self-care and build a healthy future.

Identifying Developmental Disruptions and Developmental Derailment

Prior modules of TGCTA have emphasized the role that development plays in trauma and loss, including developmental capacities, tasks, milestones, transitions, opportunities, and developmentally linked risks. The "pivot" in perspective to the present and future in Module 4 calls for both careful reflection regarding the diverse ways in which trauma and loss can affect ongoing developmental processes, and for effective strategies to remedy developmental disruptions if they are detected. To the extent that trauma- and loss-induced disruptions occur within developmentally salient domains, they can impede the achievement of developmental tasks, cascade forward across developmental transitions in *risk factor caravans*, and increase the risk for serious developmental derailment (Layne et al., 2014b; Pynoos et al., 1999). The impacts of trauma and bereavement on development can vary in complex ways, producing both premature developmental *accelerations* and developmental *decelerations* (Steinberg, 2014). Thus, it is helpful to be vigilant to the different ways in which trauma and bereavement may impede adaptive developmental progression. We propose six potential types of *developmental disruption*, which – if sufficiently severe and prolonged – can accumulate in number, accrue in their effects, and "cascade forward" into more serious *developmental derailment* (i.e. a fundamental change for the worse in the life course, such as school drop-out or incarceration). Developmental disruptions are varyingly addressed in different modules and components throughout TGCTA. Theorized disruptions include:

1. **Interruption of ongoing age-appropriate developmental tasks**. Trauma or bereavement may induce youths to socially disengage or discontinue previously enjoyable pro-social activities. Manifestations may include dropping out of school clubs or sports teams, avoiding friends one had before the death, or reluctance to initiate new friendships. Other manifestations include refusal to participate in or avoidance of age-appropriate activities, such as maintaining age-appropriate bodily appearance and dress. For example, feeling anxious and withdrawn at school may decrease the likelihood that youths will exhibit positive peer relationships, successful school performance, and engage in pro-social extracurricular activities. Additionally, constrictions in emotions and behavior can adversely affect attachment relationships by making youths appear "difficult to read," withdrawn, or reclusive by caregivers, families, and friends (Saltzman et al., 2006).

2. **Precociously accelerate development**. Traumatized or bereaved youths can engage in developmentally precocious and even "adult" roles, such as reaching sexual maturity early, becoming sexually active early, getting pregnant early, and leaving home early (Pynoos et al., 1995). Developmental accelerations may also depend on the specific type of trauma. For example, a large-scale study found that half of women who reported sexual abuse in childhood experienced *early* menarche (before age 11), whereas half of women who reported physical abuse in childhood experienced *late* menarche (after the age of 15) (Boynton-Jarrett et al., 2013). The potential consequences of premature accelerations (accelerations that, by definition, the youth is not sufficiently prepared to handle) are sobering: Compared to their peers, girls who reach puberty early are at higher risk for depression, obesity, smoking, substance abuse, eating disorders, higher blood pressure, and cardiovascular problems across the life course (Steinberg, 2014).

3. **Developmental slowdowns and regression**. Trauma and bereavement may also slow the rate at which competencies are acquired, and in more severe cases, induce developmental regressions characterized by the loss of previously acquired competencies. Examples include immature behavior in emotional regulation, in interpersonal relationships, or in speech; excessive dependency on adult figures; separation anxiety; a resurgence of previously conquered or mastered fears; decreased school performance; and preference for social interactions with less mature peers (Schoen et al., 2004).

4. **Delayed initiation of age-appropriate developmental tasks once one comes of age**. Trauma and bereavement may also interfere with youths' capacity and motivation to initiate age-appropriate activities as youth "grow" into them. For example, as they grow older, youth may refrain from dating, leaving home, preparing for trade school or college, or finding employment (Saltzman et al., 2006), or avoid forming ambitious life aspirations or growth-inducing developmental opportunities. One theorized mechanism for such delays is *traumatic bracing*, characterized by restrictions in life ambitions and daily activities brought about by the perceived imperative to "survive from day to day" at the expense of thinking about, planning for, and investing in the future. A second theorized mechanism centers on traumatic expectations involving such themes as the dangerousness of the world, the impotence of the social contract, and one's own powerlessness to anticipate and handle danger (Layne et al., 2001, in press).

5. **Risky behavior**. Trauma and bereavement early in life also increase the likelihood for many types of risky behaviors in adolescence (Layne et al., 2014a). A variety of theorized causal mechanisms have been proposed, which are not mutually exclusive. These proposed mechanisms include: (a) *Traumatic expectations* (pessimistic "lessons learned" from traumatic experiences, such as the beliefs that the world is a hostile place, that no place is safe, that relationships are exploitative, and that others have malicious intent), which can prime adolescents to act aggressively when they feel threatened. (b) *Intervention thoughts* (what adolescents *wish* they or others could have done while the trauma was unfolding), which if not appropriately modulated can prime adolescents to engage in reenactment behavior when they encounter trauma reminders, including death- or danger-defying behavior and aggressive behavior. (c) *Disrupted moral development* and *impaired conscience functioning* – such as not knowing you have a conscience, or lacking the willpower to act on your conscience even when you know right from wrong (Goenjian et al., 1999). (d) *Maladaptive coping* in the form of drug or alcohol abuse, compulsive behaviors, or self-harm, that serve the common function of temporarily soothing, alleviating, or distracting youth from their pain.

Further, (e) bereaved adolescents may experience intense *separation distress* characterized by intense pining, yearning, and longing to be physically reunited with the deceased. If sufficiently intense and prolonged, *maladaptive* separation distress reactions (as assessed using such measures as the PCBD Checklist) are theorized to increase the risk for suicidal ideation (reflecting a desperate need to be reunited with the deceased at all costs, even if in the afterlife) (Layne et al., 2012). Separation distress may also lead to taking on the deceased person's unhealthy or risk-taking behaviors as a means of feeling more connected to the deceased, particularly if the relationship prior to the death involved such behaviors (e.g. risky health behaviors such as smoking, drinking, or drug use; aggressive or criminal behavior) or suicidal fantasies or behaviors that involve recapitulating the manner of death (Kaplow et al., 2013). (f) Bereaved adolescents may also experience intense *existential/identity distress*, characterized by the sense that part of you has died, that prospects for a successful life and future were lost with their death, and a nihilistic outlook (nothing matters anymore) on the world and one's future (Kaplow et al., 2013). Maladaptive existential/identity distress reactions, if sufficiently intense and prolonged, can increase the likelihood for risk-taking (delinquency, truancy, promiscuity, drug use, driving recklessly, criminal behavior), as well as failure to take reasonable precautions (e.g, not wearing a seatbelt) or to engage in appropriate self-care. Last, (g) traumatically bereaved adolescents – especially if the death involved perceived negligence or malicious intent that violated the social contract – may also experience *circumstance-related distress* characterized by retaliatory fantasies and desires for revenge. These reactions, if intense and prolonged, can increase the risk that the youth will act on their fantasies, either directly or by recruiting proxies to act on their behalf (e.g. recruiting a boyfriend to carry out one's fantasy; Layne et al., 2012, in press).

6. **Increased susceptibility to illness.** Trauma, bereavement, and their stressful aftermath may also decrease perceived self-efficacy, sense of mastery, and locus of control; trust in adults; and contribute to youths' *allostatic load* – defined as the "wear and tear" physiological and psychological burden imposed by repeatedly adapting to challenges imposed by stress. Increases in allostatic load are linked to a broad range of serious health outcomes (McEwen, 2006). In a cascading-forward effect, physical illness or significant mental distress may in turn lead to impaired role functioning, increased vulnerability to life stressors, and inability to exploit growth-inducing developmental opportunities or successfully negotiate developmental transitions (Layne et al., 2014b).

In summary, it is important to *listen with a developmentally-attuned ear* in order to both identify the location (life domain) of potential developmental disruptions, as well as to formulate appropriate *intervention objectives* that correspond to their nature. For example, cases of precocious developmental accelerations (taking on developmental tasks prematurely, such as running away from home, trying to enter the workforce without a diploma, precocious sexual activity) may call for "developmental slow-downs" to give youth time to catch up on their preparedness. In contrast, interrupted or delayed developmental disruptions may call for "developmental resumptions" or "speed-ups" by encouraging regular, incremental steps towards resuming or taking on the developmental task with the group's support.

Dealing with Termination Issues

Termination issues may surface throughout this module and may be profitably addressed as they emerge. For example, members may show signs of concern regarding whether they are ready to continue without the weekly support from the group. Some group members may show signs of regression or a loss of treatment gains, which often appears as a return to the same level of functioning they exhibited when the group began. These behaviors may be gently interpreted:

These setbacks sometimes show how we are feeling about the group coming to a close. They may show that we don't feel sure about whether we are really ready to go on without the group being physically there for us every week.

During these last sessions, group members may also begin to start new friendships, either with other group members or with others outside the group. These investments may represent group members' anticipation of the loss in social support that will accompany the formal cessation of the group's meetings. This may also be gently interpreted:

Sometimes when a group is ending, we want to start new friendships because we want to have relationships that will continue to last. This helps us to feel better when we think about how we'll miss being with the group.

Be prepared also for some anger that you are willing to let the group end. This can also be gently interpreted:

It sounds like being in the group has been an important part of your life and that you'll miss it.

The last sessions also include attention to the process of group termination. Although concerns over termination are fairly common, adolescents with histories of bereavement and other losses may have special concerns and vulnerabilities. In particular, termination may function as a potent *loss reminder* to youths who never had a chance to say goodbye, or desperately wished that they didn't have to say goodbye to a dying loved one. Such adolescents can benefit from help in discriminating between past *traumatic separations* in which they had little or no chance to say goodbye, versus *non-traumatic* separations like the one the group is now undergoing. This type of separation is different because it is more predictable, voluntary, and an appropriate reflection of the growth and progress that the adolescents have shown. These final sessions are designed to provide repeated opportunities to engage in leave-taking rituals, to say a "good" goodbye, and (if appropriate) to arrange for future "booster" sessions when members can be reunited and share notes about their ongoing lives, accomplishments, and progress. In our experience, many group leaders become closely attached to their group members and also have a hard time saying goodbye. Thus, please give special attention to self-care at this time, and remember that arranging for regular ongoing "check-ins" and booster sessions can also help you feel better, too.

Session activities focus on making this a "non-traumatic" ending. Group discussion helps the adolescents learn and experience that, in many relationships, "saying goodbye" is natural, benign, voluntary, and often reversible. They also learn that by creating personal room in their lives for relationships *without* traumatic endings, adolescents are more free to create healthy intimate relationships. At the same time, termination also opens up doors to an investment in the wider social contract that is essential to an adaptive transition to young adulthood. Given their personal growth, improved skills, and greater sense of personal control, youth can redirect some of the time and energy they invested in the group to benefit others around them. Pro-social discussions invite group members to consider not only how to improve their personal life circumstances and future, but to discuss how they would like to make life better for their generation as they approach adulthood, marriage, and family, and plan activities to improve their school and community.

Traumatized, traumatically bereaved, and bereaved adolescents can each benefit from these pro-social activities. By investing in activities involving the common theme of preventing future trauma and traumatic deaths (e.g. anti-drunk driving campaigns, public advocacy about drugs or suicide), adolescents with histories of trauma and traumatic bereavement can find gratification by modulating and acting on their action plans and fantasies about how such tragedies (e.g. the specific circumstances of the death) could have been prevented. Further, bereaved adolescents can grieve in constructive ways by engaging in pro-social activities that honor and carry on the memory of the deceased. These activities can serve the dual functions of feeling closer to the person who died (a positive response to *separation distress*), while also helping to reconsolidate a sense of personal identity and sense of life purpose of a caring, committed, and compassionate person (a positive response to *existential/identity distress*) (Kaplow et al., 2013; Layne et al., 2012).

Special Considerations: Remorse and Ongoing Risk

As in other modules, situations may arise that call for special considerations. In particular, adolescents may be suffering from understandable *remorse over something they did do* (acts of commission) such as falling asleep that resulted in a fatal car accident, intentionally harming someone, or engaging in provocative behavior that resulted in violent injury to others (e.g. a road-rage incident). They may also be experiencing understandable *remorse over something they did not do* (acts of omission), such as not acting on a friend's or sibling's comment about harming themselves or others before the terrible event. Remorse over acts of commission or omission that result in serious harm or death can remain an extremely painful yet private source of self-condemnation (and may indeed contribute to *worst moments*), especially in adolescence when fears of being judged, rejected, and socially alienated can be so powerful. Such feelings of remorse can increase the risk that youth will "punish" themselves by constantly feeling guilty, engaging in poor self-care or risky behavior, letting future aspirations fade, or believing they shouldn't lead a happy and productive life. These intensely private feelings of remorse and accompanying "if others only knew" fears of rejection should be distinguished from *attributions of excessive responsibility* (e.g. the hurtful thought that "It's all my fault"). Whereas the latter are addressed primarily in the narrative work of Module 2 using such cognitive restructuring procedures as examining

alternative explanations for the outcome (e.g., "That's one way to look at it; what's another explanation for what happened?"), legitimate feelings of remorse can be addressed in Module 4 by inviting youths to consider how to make up for past misjudgments by how they live their lives moving forward.

Addressing issues of guilt can require adolescents to consider what *concrete actions* they can undertake among the people and places around them that could serve as a meaningful response to honest misjudgements in their past. For example, an adolescent who fell asleep at the wheel responded by engaging in public advocacy and educating other youth about the dangers of driving when you're really tired. To move forward, adolescents struggling with guilt often need to do something more than talk through their guilt and thus need guidance in selecting appropriate pro-social goals and activities. Accordingly, the sessions of Module 4 provide multiple opportunities for adolescents to problem-solve ways to respond to their remorse in constructive rather than destructive ways. In so doing, youth can make it part of a wider personal effort to move forward in life and invest more fully in their personal life aspirations, interpersonal relationships, and society at large.

In addition, many adolescents live in *dangerous communities that carry significant risks for violence exposure*. It is important to consider the dangers of youth's day-to-day lives under such circumstances when evaluating treatment outcomes. In particular, stakeholders (including providers, caregivers, school personnel, etc.) should not expect certain symptoms, such as hypervigilance, to disappear, given their adaptive value for the adolescents' current circumstances. Instead, the goal is to reduce hypervigilance to a level that is appropriate for youths' current living circumstances and does not significantly interfere with functioning. As adolescents have told us: "There's no way I'm not going to be on the lookout for danger. That's what it's like on the streets." Thus, discussions of risky behavior versus benefits in Module 4 should focus on helping youth develop realistic strategies for maximizing protection and safety in such ecologies while still taking realistic advantage of developmental opportunities as they arise. Making such plans for the future is especially important when working with youths in juvenile justice settings who, upon their release, will be returning to dangerous communities where they may be tempted to resume risky behaviors and relationships. Youth from high-risk communities can also be therapeutically engaged to take concrete steps in making their schools and communities safer, as well as in making plans to live and work in a safer environment.

Module 4 Suggested Indicators of Therapeutic Progress

Indictors of adolescent therapeutic progress and readiness to terminate include:

1. Taking at least one step – however modest – towards reengaging in a personally relevant developmental

task or goal (one that has been interrupted due to developmental delay, acceleration, derailment, or lost developmental opportunity).

2. Using constructive problem-solving strategies to cope adaptively with at least one current adversity.

3. Taking the initiative to "stop" at least one problematic behavior and "start" at least one constructive behavior. This may involve a direct "swap" of a good behavior in place of the bad behavior (e.g. regular exercise in place of an addictive behavior) or, alternatively, these changes may take place more independently in separate life domains.

4. Engaging in a pro-social action toward someone outside the group. Examples include listening with empathy when practicing a "furnishing support to others" practice exercise, pro-social action at home or school (e.g. modeling coping skills for siblings or classmates), or public advocacy (e.g. speaking at Parents' Night at school).

5. Developing personal plans to successfully negotiate an upcoming developmental transition (e.g. making plans to graduate high school or go to technical school or college, join the military, get a job, etc.).

References

Boynton-Jarrett, R., Wright, R. J., Putnam, F., et al. (2013). Child abuse and age at menarche, *Journal of Adolescent Health*, 52, 241–247.

Goenjian, A., Stilwell, B. M., Steinberg, A. M., et al. (1999). Moral development and psychopathological interference in conscience functioning among adolescents after trauma. *Journal of the American Academy of Child and Adolescent Psychiatry* 38, 376–384.

Greeson, J. K. P., Briggs, E. C., Layne, C. M., et al. (2014). Traumatic childhood experiences in the 21st century: Broadening and building on the ACE Studies with data from the National Child Traumatic Stress Network. *Journal of Interpersonal Violence*, 29, 536–556.

Kaplow, J. B., Layne, C. M., Saltzman, W. R., Cozza, S. J., & Pynoos, R. S. (2013). Using multidimensional grief theory to explore effects of deployment, reintegration, and death on military youth and families. *Clinical Child and Family Psychology Review*, 16, 322–340.

Layne, C. M., Pynoos, R. S., & Cardenas, J. (2001). Wounded adolescence: School-based group psychotherapy for adolescents who have sustained or witnessed violent interpersonal injury. In M. Shafii & S. Shafii (eds.), *School Violence: Contributing Factors, Management, and Prevention*. Washington, DC: American Psychiatric Press, pp. 163–186.

Layne, C. M., Kaplow, J. B., & Pynoos, R. S. (2012). Using developmentally-informed theory and evidence-based assessment to guide intervention with bereaved youth and families. In C. M. Layne (Chair), *Integrating Developmentally-Informed Theory, Evidence-Based Assessment,* *and Evidence-Based Treatment of Childhood Maladaptive Grief*. Symposium presented at the International Society for Traumatic Stress Studies, Los Angeles, CA, November 2012.

Layne, C. M., Greeson, J. K. P., Kim, S., et al. (2014a). Links between trauma exposure and adolescent high-risk health behaviors: Findings from the NCTSN Core Data Set. *Psychological Trauma: Theory, Research, Practice, and Policy*, 6, S40–S49.

Layne, C. M., Briggs-King, E., & Courtois, C. (2014b). Introduction to the Special Section: Unpacking risk factor caravans across development: Findings from the NCTSN core data set. *Psychological Trauma Theory Research Practice and Policy*, 6, S1–S8.

Layne, C. M., Kaplow, J. B., & Youngstrom, E. A. (2017). Applying evidence-based assessment to childhood trauma and bereavement: Concepts, principles, and practices. In M. A. Landholt, M. Cloitre, & U. Schnyder (eds), *Evidence Based Treatments for Trauma-Related Disorders in Children and Adolescents*. Cham: Springer International Publishing AG, pp. 67–96.

Layne, C. M., Kaplow, J. B., Oosterhoff, B., Hill, R., & Pynoos, R. S. (in press). The interplay between posttraumatic stress and grief reactions in traumatically bereaved adolescents: When trauma, bereavement, and adolescence converge. *Adolescent Psychiatry*.

McEwen, B. S. (2006). Protective and damaging effects of stress mediators: Central role of the brain. Protective and damaging effects of stress mediators: central role of the brain. *Dialogues Clin Neurosci*, 8, 367–381.

Pynoos, R., Steinberg, A., & Wraith, R. (1995). A developmental psychopathology model of childhood traumatic stress. In D. Cicchetti & D. J. Cohen (eds.), *Manual of Developmental Psychopathology*, Volume 2. New York: John Wiley, pp. 72–95.

Pynoos, R. S., Steinberg, A. S., & Piacentini, J. C. (1999). A developmental psychopathology model of childhood traumatic stress and intersection with anxiety disorders. *Biological Psychiatry*, 46, 1542–1554.

Saltzman, W. R., Layne, C. M., Steinberg, A. M., & Pynoos, R. S. (2006). Trauma/grief-focused group psychotherapy with adolescents. In L. Schein, H. Spitz, G. Burlingame, & P. Muskin, (eds.), *Group Approaches for the Psychological Effects of Terrorist Disasters*. New York: Haworth, pp. 669–729.

Sandler I., Ayers T. S., Tein J. Y., et al. (2010). Six-year follow-up of a preventive intervention for parentally bereaved youths: A randomized controlled trial. *Archives of Pediatrics and Adolescent Medicine*, 164, 907–914.

Schoen, A. A., Burgoyne, M., & Schoen, S. F. (2004). Are the developmental needs of children in America being adequately addressed during the grief process? *Journal of Instructional Psychology*, 31, 143–149.

Steinberg, L. (2014). *Age of Opportunity: Lessons from the New Science of Adolescence*. New York: Houghton Mifflin Harcourt.

4.1 Next Steps – Promoting Developmental Progression

Session Objectives

1. Help group members to adopt a future-oriented outlook.
2. Encourage group members to form optimistic yet realistic future aspirations.
3. Help group members harness their therapeutic gains to build a better future.
4. Help group members plan to take a positive step forward in their developmental progression.

Section number	Session overview
I	Check-in
II	Review practice assignment
III	"What we have learned" discussion
IV	My next five years exercise
V	First steps: choosing a *start* goal and a *stop* goal
VI	Summary and practice assignment
VII	Check-out

Supplies

Every session	This session
• Group member workbooks	
• Flipchart	
• Large paper or easel pad	
• Colored markers or crayons	
• Pencils/pens	
• Kleenex	
• Tape	

Handouts in Workbook

Handout 4.01	Feeling Thermometer
Handout 4.02	My Next Five Years Worksheet
Handout 4.03	Personal Development *Stop* Goals Worksheet
Handout 4.04	Personal Development *Start* Goals Worksheet
Handout 4.05	Check-Out Feedback Form

Flipcharts

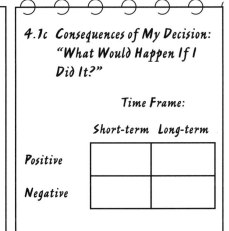

4.1a Today's Highlights

1. Check-in: One good thing that happened and Feeling Thermometer
2. Review practice assignment
3. "What we have learned" discussion
4. My first five years exercise
5. Choosing a stop goal and a start goal
6. Summary and practice assignment
7. Check-out with Feeling Thermometer and feedback form

4.1b Three Ways in Which Trauma and Loss Can Affect My Development

1. Interruptions: healthy things I've stopped doing
2. Delays: healthy things I've kept putting off after I got old enough
3. Skips: growing up too fast, so that I skipped over healthy things I still need to do

4.1c Consequences of My Decision: "What Would Happen If I Did It?"

Time Frame:

	Short-term	Long-term
Positive		
Negative		

Session 4.1: Next Steps – Promoting Developmental Progression

I. Check-In and Feeling Thermometer

- *How are you feeling right now?* (Use Handout 4.01, the Feeling Thermometer.)
- *What happened, or what did you do since we last met, that you feel good about?*
- *Is anything going on that may make it difficult for you to keep your mind on the group today?*
- Briefly review (or have a group member review) Today's Highlights, Flipchart 4.1a.

II. Review Practice Assignment

Start by asking group members if they practiced the deep breathing this week. If they did, how did it go?

- Practice with the group doing five to ten deep breaths.
- Check again with Feeling Thermometer to monitor any changes.

Then, review group members' most recent practice assignment (such as "Using an 'I' Message" and "Five Steps to Getting Support." Review coping skills (Module 1, Session 1.8) as needed.

III. "What We Have Learned" Discussion

Help group members discuss what they have gained from the group (knowledge, skills, confidence, etc.) and what they are now willing and able to do that they may not have been before.

Now that we are beginning the final set of sessions for our group, it's time to start to think about what you want to happen after the group. Specifically, how you would like to use the skills and knowledge gained here to build the life you want?

First, let's talk a bit about what you have learned in the group, what you can do now that you couldn't before, and even how you might feel differently than at the beginning of the group.

Lead a discussion about specific gains from being in the group and how these might be used to build a different and better life for themselves after the group. Make it an open-ended discussion on how they feel they are different as a result of the group. Highlight knowledge, skills, new abilities, and experiences that they may use to build a good life for themselves. Possible discussion topics can include feeling less stressed, less reactive to trauma reminders or even to minor stressors, being better able to stay calm and to concentrate, being better able to find supportive people, being more confident, and being more trusting of others.

As group members identify new knowledge, skills, or areas of confidence that they have gained, explore how they might employ these to build the life they want for themselves. Sample prompts are shown below.

- **General**: *How can you each build on what you've accomplished so far? What strengths have you developed that you can put to good use now that you can imagine actually having a future?*
- **Future orientation**: *Now that you are thinking about your future, can you see yourself having a good life? Getting more education? A good job? Having a family some day?*
- **Concentration**: *Now that you can concentrate better, what can you do? Can you get a high-school degree or a general educational diploma and then attend college, community college, or a trade school?*
- **Emotional modulation**: *Now that you are less reactive to situations, where can you go now that you could not easily when we started in this group, such as a crowded setting at work or school?*
- **Relationships**: *Now that you've learned how to support and rely on one another, can you see yourself being in a caring relationship?*

IV. "My Next Five Years" Exercise

Extend the previous discussion into the concrete task of filling out this worksheet that provides a template of activities and goals desired for the next five years. An important context is addressing missed developmental opportunities due to traumatic events or losses.

Activity: My Next Five Years

Direct group members to Handout 4.02, My Next Five Years, in their workbooks and introduce the activity. You can use your own words or some version of the language below.

Now that you have started to identify some of your new strengths and skills and what you would like to do, let's put it together into a plan that you can use after the group. This worksheet is entitled "My Next Five Years" because you can use it to list some of the specific things you would like to do or have in your life for this next important period of time. It is divided into different areas:

"Things I missed out on that I want to do" *and* ***"Things I avoided or wasn't able to do before"*** *refers to the many things you did not do when other kids were doing them because your trauma or loss experiences interrupted your life. Some youth describe never having had the chance to be a kid and have fun because they had to grow up so fast. Others describe avoiding or delaying opportunities because they became too stressed, withdrawn, or hopeless. In any case, write down some things that you would like to have another chance at now that you have found new strengths and confidence.*

The other items are fairly self-explanatory. They involve things you might want to do that are fun, can help you build your future, grow as a person, feel better, and that can help your family or community.

The next five years are very important years. Make them your own. Put in the things that will make you stronger, happier, and more completely yourself. Take a chance – write down your wishes and dreams. Naming them and committing to them is a big part of making them come true. Let's spend some time now to do that and then share those parts that you would like to with the group.

Allow sufficient time for all group members to go through the handout. Circulate to help those that seem stuck.

At the conclusion, invite group members to share their plans. Model praise and support in your responses so that group members will do the same.

V. First Steps: Choosing a *Stop* Goal and a *Start* Goal

- If there is time in this session, do this exercise. Otherwise, you can do it at the beginning of the next session.
- This activity helps group members define specific simple concrete goals that will place them on the path of implementing their plans for the next five years.

- Conduct the exercise in an interactive fashion having group members share their choices for each of the parts. Use the group to help brainstorm choices.

Activity: *Stop* Goals and *Start* Goals

Refer youth to Handouts 4.03 and 4.04, on personal development goals: *stop* goals and *start* goals. Introduce this activity as a first step towards implementing their desired goals for their five-year plan. The idea is to pick a single "stop goal" and single "start goal" as two things they can start on immediately. They should take out both personal development goals handouts and begin by selecting a stop goal and a start goal (Part I on both handouts). This step is done together because sometimes the two goals may be related. For example, when a stop goal is a problematic way of coping with stress (e.g. drinking or using drugs), the start goal should help accomplish the same goal without the downsides (e.g. exercising, playing a sport, talking with a friend, listening to music, etc.).

Part I: Identify a *Stop* Goal and a *Start* Goal

Have group members each select a stop and start goal. Lead off by defining each (see language below) and then brainstorm with the group their choices.

A ***stop goal*** *is something negative or unproductive that you will stop doing – something that is dangerous, risky, or self-defeating because it prevents you from doing what you want to do in life. It could be as simple as stopping the habit of staying up too late, over- or under-eating, or being lazy. It may also involve swearing off drugs or alcohol, avoiding cutting your arms, avoiding fighting, no longer hanging out with a bad crowd, or saying no to casual sex.*

A ***start goal*** *is a positive change you want to make in your behavior to help you make a developmental step forward – this can be something that is fun, constructive, or uplifting. Pick something that is important and worthwhile to you and celebrates the fact that you are alive, and that will motivate you to work towards a good future worth living. This positive activity can be spending more time with people, making a new friend, renewing an old friendship, working harder at school, finishing high school, getting a job, volunteering, or anything else that deals with getting your life back on track and heading in a direction that you want to go. It may also mean taking up a sport or other activity.*

If your ***stop behavior*** *is a negative habit you developed to reduce tension and help you feel better when you are dealing with trauma reminders, you may want your* ***start behavior*** *to be a replacement that will accomplish the same task. For example, you could choose a skill from your coping strategy toolkit from Module 1, such as deep breathing or talking with a friend, as a start behavior to take the place of smoking weed, losing your temper, or cutting yourself.*

Parts II–V for the *Stop* Goal

Complete Parts II–V for the stop goal, as follows.

Part II stop goal: Help group members think about the different steps that will be involved in achieving their stop goal. Fill these into the worksheet.

Part III stop goal: Guide the group in identifying possible barriers to accomplishing this goal. This is based on Handout 1.39, Three Steps to Taking Charge of Your Thoughts and Feelings.

Parts IV and V stop goal: *Now, let's work together as a group to help you think through solutions to overcome the barriers. Remember you can use things you have already learned here like:*

- *Coping strategies – like abdominal breathing, exercise, self-talk and seeking support that you learned earlier in this group.*
- *How to take charge of your emotions.*
- *How to challenge and change unhelpful thoughts.*
- *How to cope with trauma and loss reminders.*
- *How to identify the type of support you need and ask for it from the right people.*
- *How to carry forward or harness the strengths, positive characteristics, or healthy behaviors of a deceased loved one to help you live the kind of life you want to live.*

Help the group come up with several solutions (fill in Part IV) and then show Flipchart 4.1c (consequences of my decision). Discuss Part V and engage group members in evaluating the costs versus benefits of various proposed solutions. What are the positive and negative consequences of each option in the short term and the long term? Which option may work best, and why? Prompts include:

- *Can you realistically do it? Do you have the resources to carry it out, such as enough know-how, time, money, materials, and helping hands?*
- *What would happen if you did it? Would good things happen that would solve the problem or help me manage it better? Would it make you and other people around you happier or better off? Or, would doing this create more problems for you or others?*
- *Last, choose the best option, based on your evaluation.*

Parts II–V for the *Start* Goal

Now complete Parts II–V for the start goal using the steps above.

VI. Summary and Practice Assignment

Summarize and bring closure to the session. Motivate group members to use these skills.

In today's session, we focused on moving forward in your development in a positive way. Keep these goal sheets and use them for your practice assignment this coming week, which is to begin working on your goals. Focus on one "stop" goal, and one "start" goal. Please be prepared to talk about your progress during our check-in next session.

As needed, problem-solve how they can support one another during the week as they work on their goals.

VII. Check-Out

- *How are you feeling now?* (Use the Feeling Thermometer ratings.)
- *What did you learn about yourself today?*
- *Please fill out the Check-Out Feedback Form* (Handout 4.05). *The title of today's session was "Next Steps."*

If any group members are visibly agitated or troubled or report high levels of distress on the Feeling Thermometer, keep them after the group and determine an appropriate way to transition them back to their settings.

Implementing Module 4, Session 4.1 with Individual Clients

Preparation: Have available the youth workbook.

I. **Check-in using** Handout 4.01, **the Feeling** Thermometer. After sharing his/her current feeling(s), ask the client to share anything that happened since the last session that may have influenced his/her feelings (in either a positive way or a negative way).

II. **Review practice assignment and previous sessions**. Deliver the exercise as written but omit references to the group.

III. **"What we have learned" discussion**. Use the same guidelines provided for the group for the individual session.

IV. **My next five years exercise**. As indicated in the group guide, use the handout and walk through the categories. This can be done more as a conversation rather than as a written assignment.

V. **First steps: choosing a *stop* goal and a *start* goal**. Use the handouts provided in the workbook and coach the youth as needed in filling these out.

VI. **Summary and practice assignment**. Deliver this step as written.

VII. **Check-out**. Deliver this step as written.

4.2 Coping with Difficult Days

Session Objectives

1. Strengthen group members' ability to cope with current life adversities.
2. Further challenge traumatic expectations and loss expectations (beyond the work done in Module 2) that may be impeding adaptive developmental progression.
3. Predict future trauma reminders and loss reminders, and problem-solve for coping with them in more adaptive ways.

Section number	Session overview
I	Check-in
II	Review practice assignment
III	Coping with current life challenges
IV	Summary and practice assignment
V	Check-out

Supplies

Every session	This session
• Group member workbooks	
• Flipchart	
• Large paper or easel pad	
• Colored markers or crayons	
• Pencils/pens	
• Kleenex	
• Tape	

Handouts in Workbook

Handout 4.01	Feeling Thermometer
Handout 1.30	Sizing Up a Situation
Handout 2.12	Consequences of My Choices
Handouts 4.06–4.12	Illustrations
Handout 4.13	Wishing I Could Help When It's Not My Job to Fix
Handout 4.14	Check-Out Feedback Form

Flipcharts

4.2a Today's Highlights

1. Check-in: one good thing that happened, and Feeling Thermometer
2. Review practice assignment (one stop goal, one start goal)
3. Helping a good friend to cope with:
   - Hardships
   - Negative expectations
   - Future reminders
4. Summary
5. Check-out with Feeling Thermometer and feedback form

4.2b Sizing Up a Situation

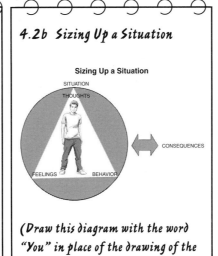

Sizing Up a Situation

SITUATION

THOUGHTS

FEELINGS   BEHAVIOR

CONSEQUENCES

(Draw this diagram with the word "You" in place of the drawing of the young man)

4.2c Consequences of My Decision: "What Would Happen If I Did It?"

Time Frame:

	Short-term	Long-term
Positive		
Negative		

Session 4.2: Coping with Difficult Days

I. Check-In and Feeling Thermometer

- *How are you feeling right now?* (Use Handout 4.01, the Feeling Thermometer.)
- *What happened, or what did you do since we last met, that you feel good about?*
- *Is anything going on that may make it difficult for you to keep your mind on the group today?*
- Briefly review (or have a group member review) Today's Highlights (Flipchart 4.2a).

II. Review Practice Assignment

Start by asking group members if they practiced the abdominal breathing this week. If they did, how did it go?

- Practice doing five to ten abdominal breaths to remind themselves how it feels in their body. Remind them that, by gaining more control over their thoughts, emotions, and bodies, they will be better prepared to prepare for their future.
- Check again with Feeling Thermometer to monitor any changes.

Then, check whether group members worked on their "stop" and "start" goals during the week:
- What were they able to achieve thus far?
- Did they encounter any barriers? If so, problem-solve strategies to cope with barriers.

- As you review the Stop and Start Goal Worksheets, refer as needed to Flipchart 4.2b (Handout 1.30 on Sizing Up a Situation) to point out how situations, thoughts, feelings, behaviors, and consequences are interconnected.
- Use Flipchart 4.3c (Handout 2.12, Consequences of My Choices) as needed to help group members evaluate the desirable and undesirable consequences of various ways of thinking, feeling, and behaving, and to select the best option depending on its consequences.
- Build group members' self-confidence and hope by labeling and praising their coping skills in the problem-solving exercises, and by emphasizing their progress to date. Point out that they can draw on these same strengths as they face their own challenging situations.

IV. Coping with Current Life Challenges

Activity: "Helping Out a Good Friend"

The goal of this exercise is to help group members focus on present and ongoing problems by (1) identifying common adolescent developmental challenges, including daily adversities, traumatic expectations, and distressing reminders, and (2) problem-solving how to cope with them in more constructive and mature ways.

This session includes nine illustrations (Handouts 4.06–4.12). These handouts are designed to help youth problem-solve how to cope with various situations. The illustrations are divided into three sections: (1) *Coping with Current Adversities*, (2) *Challenging Traumatic Expectations*, and (3) *Anticipating Future Reminders*.

Each box below contains guidelines for a specific illustration. Begin with Handout 4.06 as a positively themed example. Then, tailor the exercise by selecting specific illustrations that are most relevant to the youth (e.g. between two and four of the illustrations), or alternatively, create your own scenarios that reflect the youths' particular challenges and life circumstances.

Introduce the Exercise

Last week, you identified a specific **area** *in your lives where you need to move forward in your development. You made a* **goal** *to take a positive step forward and problem-solved how to cope with* **barriers** *that could get in the way. (Acknowledge and praise their progress thus far.)*

Today, we'll use these same problem-solving skills to focus on other challenges you face, both **now** *and in the* **future***.*

(Refer to Flipchart 4.2a, Activity 3 bullet points.) Let's talk about these challenges – things like:

- *Hardships in your lives that you're facing* **now***,*
- *Negative things you've come to* **expect** *about the world and other people,*
- ***Upsetting reminders*** *of your traumas and losses that you may encounter in the future.*

Today's session is about having hope, confidence, and determination as you pursue your life goals – hope and confidence in your new-found strengths, hope in yourselves, and hope in your future. Today's session is designed to help you hold onto your hope even when you face challenges and setbacks.

We're going to role-play this by helping young people (shown in some sketches I'll share) who are facing difficult situations that could hold them back from achieving their life goals. We'll be drawing on all of the skills we've developed so far – any positive coping skill you've learned in this group and in your life is fair game – you can practice using it here.

Let's begin with kids who are facing **hardships** *in their lives. (Show Flipchart 4.2b, Sizing Up a Situation). To help us, we'll use the same skill we've used before to help us understand how the* **situation** *we're in – and the negative or positive ways we choose to* **think** *about our situation – affect our feelings and behavior, and can lead to different consequences – positive or negative. Remember that we* **do** *get to choose our behaviors, but we* **don't** *get to choose the consequences that naturally follow. So the best way for us to gain control of our lives is through the decisions we make about which situations we put ourselves in (Are they safe? Supportive, Discouraging? Risky?), and in how we* **think** *about those situations. We know that it's not always possible to stay away from dangerous situations, but there are almost always things we can do to make ourselves more safe. We'll talk about this in our next session.*

Let's start our "helping out a good friend" exercise by practicing with a positive example. (Turn to Handout 4.06 in workbook: "I Can See My Future More Clearly Now, So I Can Make Better Plans for How to Live My Life.") Use Flipchart 4.2b as a guide for this and all other sketches in this session.

Make sure to read the guidelines for the selected illustrations before your group or session so you are prepared.

Guidelines for Handout 4.06: "I Can See My Future More Clearly Now, So I Can Make Better Plans for How to Live My Life"

Description*: This teenage girl has been through some really bad experiences, but she's worked hard in the group and now she can sleep better and feels more calm and in control. She is now able to think about her future more clearly, with more hope than she had before.*

Facilitating questions (group leaders should allow group members to generate their own responses and offer answers only when necessary):

What is the **situation***?* She's looking over her calendar.

What **thoughts** *might be going through her head?* "I can see my future more clearly now, so I can make better plans for how to live my life." (She's making plans for the upcoming year, looking forward to fun things she wants to do and good things she wants to accomplish.)

How could she be **feeling** *if she is thinking this way?* (Hopeful, excited, optimistic, happy, enthusiastic, maybe a bit anxious, hoping things turn out well.)

What **behaviors** *is she likely to engage in if she is thinking and feeling this way?* (Working at her goals, keep on trying and not giving up.)

What might be some **positive consequences** *of thinking, feeling, and behaving this way?* (Getting more out of life, having more opportunities like going to school, getting a job, earning a good living, feeling happier, feeling more accomplished, feeling more confident.)

Discuss*: What gains have you personally made here that can help you take more control over your lives and prepare for the future? How can you use these strengths to improve your life?*

Guidelines for Handout 4.07: Secondary Adversities Following a Natural Disaster, War or Inner-City Violence (*Coping with Adversities*)

Description*: These teenagers are trying to move on with their lives after having survived/growing up with (natural disaster/war/ inner city violence). There is devastation all around them. There are no jobs, no nice places to go and spend time, no fun things to do. They are feeling bored and discouraged.*

Facilitating questions (group leaders should allow group members to generate their own responses and offer answers only when necessary):

*What is the **situation**?* Scene: Teenagers are hanging around a run-down playground with run-down or destroyed buildings all around them.

*What could be their **hurtful thought**?* "There's nothing to do here. Everything is run down or destroyed."

*How could they be **feeling** if they are thinking this way?* (Feeling bored, discouraged, pessimistic, hopeless, stressed, feeling angry and cheated.)

*What **problem behaviors** could they get into if they are thinking and feeling this way?* (Hang around and not do anything, get into fights, drink or use drugs, get into trouble with the law.)

*What **undesirable consequences** could result from thinking, feeling, and behaving this way?* (Wasting lots of time, getting addicted to drugs/alcohol, getting in trouble with the law, getting hooked by stuff online.)

*What **helpful thoughts** could they use to replace their hurtful thoughts?* (There are things they can do, even with few or no resources, to make their neighborhood a better place. They can volunteer to improve a park in their neighborhood, serve as a tutor for younger kids or special needs kids, or help other people in need.)

(As appropriate):

*Could **you** believe these helpful thoughts if you were in this situation?*

*How could **thinking about the situation** in these ways change how they **feel** and **behave**?* (Getting actively involved in something positive is a powerful protective factor against depression, discouragement, boredom, and getting into trouble with the law.)

*What **positive consequences** are likely to follow if they choose to have more positive thoughts, feelings, and behaviors? How will this situation turn out (better, the same, or worse)?* (It will also help make their school or community a better place for themselves and others.)

Discuss: *Teenagers will be the next generation to inherit the world. How can you make it better for yourselves? How can your organize yourselves and help, even if you don't have much money or other resources besides your time and energy?*

Guidelines for Handout 4.08: Getting Pressured to Do Something I Don't Want to Do (*Coping with Adversities*)

Description: *This girl lost her (clinician choose: father/grandfather/brother) several years ago. They were very close, and losing him was very hard on her. She started dating this past year. A boy she has been dating and likes is now asking her for sex. He's saying "So, what do you think?" and holding out a box of condoms. She doesn't want to, but is worried that turning him down will really disappoint him or make him mad at her, and that he might stop dating her.*

Facilitating questions (group leaders should allow group members to generate their own responses and offer answers only when necessary):

*What is the **situation**?* Scene: Boy and girl are sitting together on a couch (parents are nowhere to be seen) and he's propositioning her to have sex. She's looking uncomfortable.

*What is her **hurtful thought**?* "If I say no, then he'll leave me, and I can't handle another loss."

*How could she be **feeling** if she is thinking this way?* (Sad, worried that he might leave her if she asserts herself and says no, feeling surprised and stressed out.)

*What **problem behaviors** could she get herself into if she's thinking and feeling this way?* (She could decide to do something that she doesn't want to do or doesn't feel ready for.)

*What **undesirable consequences** could result from thinking, feeling, and behaving this way?* (Potential answers include):

- Getting too involved with someone she's not in love with, getting too serious when she doesn't want it or before she's ready, getting a reputation (that will attract more propositions from more boys), losing her self-respect for not standing up for herself, losing her parents' trust if they find out, leading him to expect that they'll keep doing this after every date …
- Getting VD, getting pregnant if the condom doesn't work.

*What **helpful thoughts** could she use to replace her hurtful thoughts?*

- I don't have to do this. I can stand up for myself. I have a lot more to offer than my body.
- Even if he leaves me, I can date other boys. Boys are replaceable, but (dads/brothers/grandfathers) are not. There's a big difference between boyfriends and family members.
- If he leaves me over this, then he didn't care for me for the right reasons.

(As appropriate):

*Could **you** believe these helpful thoughts if you were in her situation?*

*How could **thinking about the situation** in these ways change how she **feels** and **behaves**?* (Thinking this way can make her feel less anxious and pressured, and can give her courage to assert herself.)

*What **positive consequences** are likely to follow if she chooses to have more positive thoughts, feelings, and behaviors? How will this situation turn out (better, the same, or worse)?*

- Discriminating between a "permanent" loss (death of a family member) and a "temporary" loss (sexually frustrated boy not asking her out again) will help to protect her from making a choice that she regrets. Temporary losses are replaceable.
- Understanding why she's afraid of losing other men in her life can help prevent her from making poor decisions in the future.

Discuss: *Losses can make people vulnerable to being pressured into doing things they don't want to do if they become so fearful of (being abandoned/suffering another loss) that they'll do almost anything – even things they really don't want to do – to prevent it. This makes it easier for them to be manipulated by other people who don't have their best interests in mind, who can get them to do what they want by threatening to leave.*

Discuss (for sexually abused youths): *Let's say she was sexually abused when she was younger. She's worried that having sex will be a trauma reminder for her that brings up bad memories from her past.* **What** *can she say about her past experience that will help the partner she chooses to be intimate with be understanding and supportive?* **When** *could she tell him?*

Guidelines for Handout 4.09: Traumatic Bracing (*Coping with Traumatic Expectations*)

Description: *This young man was recently caught in gang cross-fire while playing basketball at the park. Bullets were whizzing all around him, and he saw someone get shot. Now, he always feels unsafe and is always on alert, braced for another terrible thing to happen. It gets him so worked up and distracted that it's hard for him to relax, focus on school, feel hopeful, or think about the future.*

Facilitating questions (group leaders should allow group members to generate their own responses and offer answers only when necessary):

What is the **situation***?* Scene: Boy is walking home from school, sees other kids having fun.

What is his **hurtful thought***?* "I wish I could have fun like them, but I'm always waiting for the next bad thing to happen." (Options: Telling himself he can never let down his guard, telling himself that no one understands, getting down on himself by thinking something's really wrong with him, thinking he'll probably be dead soon so working hard at school or making plans for the future are pointless.)

How could he be **feeling** *if he is thinking this way?* (Sad, lonely, feeling alone and different from other kids, feeling angry and cheated, feeling tense and stressed.)

What **problem behaviors** *could he get into if he's thinking and feeling this way?* (Isolating himself, acting moody and angry, taking drugs, abuse alcohol, spending lots of time online, lashing out at other people, starting to carry a weapon to school.)

What **undesirable consequences** *could result from thinking, feeling, and behaving this way?* (Getting addicted to drugs/alcohol, getting kicked out of school and in trouble with the law for carrying a weapon, feeling lonely and misunderstood, wasting lots of time and getting hooked by stuff online, developing health problems from always feeling stressed and tensed up.)

What **helpful thoughts** *could he use to replace his hurtful thoughts?*

- Reminding himself of the difference between dangerous and safer situations.
- Making good decisions about keeping safe, staying away from danger as best he can.

(As appropriate):

Could **you** *believe these helpful thoughts if you were in his situation?*

How could **thinking about the situation** *in these ways change how he* **feels** *and* **behaves***?* (By telling himself that he is safe and not currently in danger, he can start to relax and focus on school, his development (making friends, uplifting activities), and his future.)

What **positive consequences** *are likely to follow if he chooses to have more positive thoughts, feelings, and behaviors? How will this situation turn out (better, the same, or worse)?* (Being able to tell the difference between dangerous and safer situations will help him be able to focus on the present (like schooling) and his future, and not do risky things (like bringing a weapon to school) that could get him expelled and derail his development.)

Optional discussion: *How can you help keep yourself safe without carrying a weapon to school, etc.?*

Guidelines for Handout 4.10: Sharing the Same Sad Fate as the Deceased (*Coping with Traumatic Expectations*)

Description: *This boy lost his dad* (insert cause: to a heart attack, to violence, to suicide) *several years ago. His dad was very young to die – in his early forties. Now, he believes that he's going to share the same fate as his dad and also die young. He treats it as a certainty – as if it's* **guaranteed** *to happen. He thinks: What's there to look forward to? Why even* **try** *to have a good life? It's not going to last. Why study and hope and prepare for the future? I'm not going to live long enough for it to pay off.*

Facilitating questions (group leaders should allow group members to generate their own responses and offer answers only when necessary):

What is the **situation***?* Scene: Boy is looking at a picture of his father, who died young.

What is his **hurtful thought***?* "I just know I'm going to end up dying early, just like he did." (Expecting that he's going to die young just like dad, so trying to have a good life like getting an education, dating, planning for the future are a waste of time; he's jinxed/doomed with bad luck.)

How could he be **feeling** *if he is thinking this way?* (Sad, lonely, depressed, feeling angry and cheated, apathetic (not caring what happens), stressed.)

What **behaviors** *might he be tempted to engage in if he is thinking and feeling this way?* (Isolating himself, acting moody and angry, taking drugs, abusing alcohol, resignation/giving up, tempting

275

fate with risky behavior like driving too fast, having unsafe sex, stealing, or getting into trouble with the law ("Cause I'm going to die anyway").)

*What **undesirable consequences** could result from thinking, feeling, and behaving this way?* (Getting addicted to drugs or alcohol, kicked out of school or held back a year for failing grades, feeling lonely, getting himself hurt or killed or in jail for risky behaviour.) If he convinces himself he's going to die young and then does risky things "because it's gonna happen anyway", he could create a self-fulfilling prophesy and make it happen.

*What **helpful thoughts** could he use to replace his hurtful thoughts?* (Ideas include):

- Remember that he and his dad are two different people. Although there's always going to be some risk, there are lots of things he can do to stay safe and healthy, including things his dad may not have done. Medical advances are happening all the time, so it's possible now to treat many injuries and illnesses that were fatal a generation ago.
- Thinking about what his dad would want for him.
- Focus on making good decisions about seeking safety, making good choices, staying away from danger as best as he can. He doesn't need to tempt fate in order to take control over his life.

(As appropriate):

*Could **you** believe these helpful thoughts if you were in his situation?*

*How could **thinking about the situation** in these ways change how he **feels** and **behaves**?*

- By seeing himself as separate from his dad, he is free to live his own life (his dad's poor health habits can be some of the things he chooses to leave behind, even as he grieves for him).
- He can feel more hopeful and motivated about his future and try to really make something of his life.
- Advances in medicine are preventing many diseases that claimed lots of lives in the past.

*What **positive consequences** are likely to follow if he chooses to have more positive thoughts, feelings, and behaviors? (Better, the same, or worse consequences?)* (He is more likely to live a full life, like getting a good education, keeping safe and in good health, having a real shot at happiness, making good friends, dating, etc.)

Optional discussion: *How would you want to live your life if you knew it wasn't ruled by fate (giving you no control over it)? How would you want to take initiative and make the most out of your life?*

Optional discussion (for bereaved youth): *How can he stay positively connected to his dad without having to share the same fate (die early)? Can you feel close to someone without having to take on their bad habits and share the way they died? Can he keep the good things and leave the way he died behind?* (Reference the Module 3 exercises that focus on this.)

Guidelines for Handout 4.11: Reluctance to Form New Relationships for Fear of Suffering Further Losses (*Coping with Traumatic Expectations*)

Description: *This girl lost her boyfriend (shown in the picture on her nightstand) six months ago in a* (clinician's choice: car accident/accidental overdose/suicide/drive-by). *He was her first true love, and she told herself* (refer to the Module III sketch of her) *that she'd never find true love again. She is now getting asked* (choose: to the prom/on a date) *for the first time since her boyfriend's funeral. She has very mixed feelings. She's been feeling lonely and doesn't want to miss out on prom/her chance at happiness. But she's also afraid that if she starts to care about someone new, she could lose them, too. She's also worried about being disloyal to her boyfriend's memory because they promised they'd always be together. She still misses him and thinks about the good times.*

Facilitating questions (group leaders should allow group members to generate their own responses and offer answers only when necessary):

*What is the **situation**?* Scene: Girl is on the phone getting invited to (prom/on a date).

*What is her **hurtful thought**? It'd be nice to let myself get close to someone again, but I'd just lose them, too* (expecting that she will suffer another devastating loss).

*How might he be **feeling** if she is thinking this way?* (Stressed, torn, anxious, confused, guilty over perhaps being disloyal to her boyfriend's memory.)

*What **behaviors** might she be tempted to engage in if she is thinking and feeling this way?* (Shut down, not take risks, withdraw, avoid making a decision by putting him off.)

*What **undesirable consequences** might come from thinking, feeling, and behaving this way?* (She could lose out on an opportunity to have fun and socialize, make new friends, and move on with her life, learn that she can love again.)

*What **helpful thoughts** could she believe instead to replace the hurtful thoughts?* (Love always involves risk, but it's worth it; it's not disloyal to find happiness after a loss; I can find ways to preserve the memory of my first love while moving forward with my life; I know this is what he would want for me.)

(As appropriate):

*Could **you** believe these helpful thoughts if you were in his situation?*

*How could **thinking about the situation** in these ways change how she **feels** and **behaves**?* (It could allow her to accept the date, start socializing and dating again, help her move forward with developing into the person she wants to be.)

*What **positive consequences** are likely to follow if she chooses to have these different kinds of thoughts, feelings, and behaviors* about this situation? (Better, the same, or worse?) (She is more likely to live a full life and have a good shot at happiness, making good friends, dating, etc. Dating involves risk, so you sometimes get disappointed and even get your heart broken.)

Optional discussion: *What do you think of her choice to keep her deceased boyfriend's photo by her bed? Does she need that to grieve in a helpful way? Will doing that help her move on with her life?*

Handout 4.12: Anticipating Future Reminders – Sending Out Announcements (*Coping with Future Reminders*)

Description: *This young woman is sending out announcements for her (graduation/wedding). She's looking sad.*

Facilitating questions (group leaders should allow group members to generate their own responses and offer answers only when necessary):

*What is the **situation**?* Scene: She's sitting at a table, addressing announcements and sending them out to her family and friends.

*What is her **hurtful thought**?* "This is supposed to be a happy occasion, but how can it be without Dad there?"

*How might she be **feeling** if she is thinking this way?* (Strong grief reactions like missing dad, yearning to have him back, sadness.)

*What **behaviors** might she be tempted to engage in if she is thinking and feeling this way?* (Not going through with her celebration, being sad and miserable.)

*What **undesirable consequences** might come from thinking, feeling, and behaving this way?* (She could miss out on having an enjoyable gathering where she spends time with her friends and family and celebrates her accomplishment.)

*What **helpful thoughts** could she believe instead to replace the hurtful thoughts?* (Dad will be there in spirit; Dad would want me to celebrate; we can find ways to remember and celebrate Dad as part of the gathering; if I get sad I can turn to my friends and family for support.)

(As appropriate):

*Could **you** believe these helpful thoughts if you were in her situation?*

*How could **thinking about the situation** in these ways change how she **feels** and **behaves**?* (It could help her celebrate and enjoy an important moment in her life – one that her dad would be very proud of.)

*What **positive consequences** are likely to follow if she chooses to have these different kinds of thoughts, feelings, and behaviors about this situation? (Better, the same, or worse?)*

- It would create an opportunity for her and her family to remember and reminisce about her dad. It would make him happy to be remembered.

- It will help her to live a full life by celebrating her accomplishments.

Optional discussion: *How can you set aside time during celebrations to remember loved ones who have died? What can you do if you get strong grief pangs during a celebration and feel like crying?*

IV. Summary and Practice Assignment

Summarize and bring closure to the session. Motivate group members to use these skills.

Refer to Handout 4.13, Wishing I Could Help When It's Not My Job to Fix.

*Next week, we will be learning to deal with situations where someone we care about is facing a problem, and we really wish we could step in and solve it for them. We will be learning to tell the difference between when a problem is our job to fix, and when it is not our job to fix. We'll also learn ways to support the person whose problem it **is** to solve that we **do** care about them without actually taking on their problem and making it our own.*

For your practice assignment this week, we'd like you to think of a situation that is going on right now or in the recent past, where someone you care about is facing a difficult problem and you really wish you could step in and solve it for them, or at least help them deal with it. Please describe the situation in some detail in this sheet, so we know what type of problem they are facing, and can problem-solve with you about the type of support that you or others may be able to give them.

V. Check-Out

- *How are you feeling now?* (Use the Feeling Thermometer ratings.)
- *What did you learn about yourself today?*
- *Please fill out the Check-Out Feedback Form (Handout 4.14). The title of today's session was "Coping with Difficult Days."*

If any group members are visibly agitated or troubled or report high levels of distress on the Feeling Thermometer, keep them after the group and use appropriate coping tools to help them stabilize, regulate their emotions, and transition back to their settings.

Implementing Module 4, Session 4.2 with Individual Clients

Preparation: Have available the youth workbook.

I. **Check-in using Handout 4.01, the Feeling Thermometer.** After sharing his/her current feeling(s), ask client to share anything that happened since the last session that may have influenced his/her feelings (in either a positive way or a negative way).

II. **Review practice assignment and previous sessions**. Deliver the exercise as written but omit references to the group.

III. **Coping with current life challenges**. The very same approach described in the manual can be done with individual clients. You will have a greater ability to truly custom select the illustrations that are most relevant to your client's life. Follow the directions as given.

IV. **Summary and practice assignment**. Deliver this step as written

V. **Check-out**. Deliver this step as written.

4.3

What *Is* and What *Is Not* Your Job

Session Objectives

1. Discuss how some problems *are* my job to fix, and other problems *are not* my job to fix.
2. Challenge hurtful (unhelpful) thoughts (taking too much responsibility for fixing other peoples' problems) with helpful thoughts (about how to help in a responsible way that does not exceed my personal resources).
3. Problem-solve how to responsibly help others when it's *not* my job to fix.
4. Discuss how to help myself through appropriate *self-care*, including distinguishing between "healthy" versus "unhealthy" risks.

Section number	Session overview
I	Check-in
II	Review practice assignment
III	A new unhelpful thought: "I have to fix other peoples' problems"
IV	How can you tell when a problem is not your job to fix?
V	How can I help, even when it's not my job to fix?
VI	Taking good care of yourself (helping the helper)
VII	Summary and practice assignment
VIII	Check-out

Supplies

Every session	This session
• Group member work-books flipchart	
• Large paper or easel pad	
• Colored markers or crayons	
• Pencils/pens	
• Kleenex	
• Tape	

Handouts in Workbook

Handout 4.01	Feeling Thermometer
Handout 4.13	Wishing I Could Help When It's Not My Job to Fix
Handouts 4.15–4.18 and 4.21	Illustrations
Handout 4.19	How to Tell If a Problem Is My Job to Handle
Handout 4.20	How Can I Help When the Problem Is Not My Job to Fix?
Handout 4.22	Three, Two, One Questions
Handout 4.23	Check-Out Feedback Form

Flipcharts

4.3a Today's Highlights

1. Check-in
2. Review practice assignment
3. New unhelpful thought: "It's my job to fix other peoples' problems"
4. How to tell when it's not my job to fix
5. How to help when it's not my job to fix
6. Taking good care of myself
7. Summary
8. Check-out with Feeling Thermometer and feedback form

4.3b Sizing Up a Situation

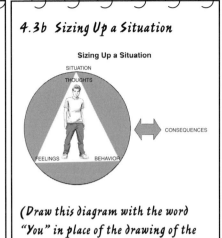

Sizing Up a Situation

SITUATION
THOUGHTS
FEELINGS   BEHAVIOR
CONSEQUENCES

(Draw this diagram with the word "You" in place of the drawing of the young man)

4.3c Consequences of My Decision: "What Would Happen If I Did It?"

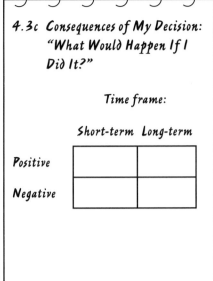

Time frame:

	Short-term	Long-term
Positive		
Negative		

Session 4.3: What *Is* and What *Is Not* your Job

I. Check-In and Feeling Thermometer

- *How are you feeling right now?* (Use Handout 4.01, the Feeling Thermometer.)
- *What happened, or what did you do since we last met, that you feel good about?*
- *Is anything going on that may make it difficult for you to keep your mind on the group today?*
- Briefly review (or have a group member review) Today's Highlights, Flipchart 4.3a.

II. Review Practice Assignment

Start by asking group members if they practiced the abdominal breathing this week. If they did, how did it go?

- Practice doing five to ten abdominal breaths to remind themselves how it feels in their body.
- Check again with Feeling Thermometer to monitor any changes. Then, check whether group members completed their worksheet for today (assigned in Session 4.2), Handout 4.13, Wishing I Could Help When It's Not My Job to Fix. If group members haven't finished, take a few minutes to do so now.
- Review members' progress in taking a developmental step forward during the past week (refer to their personal development goals worksheet, assigned in Module 1, Session 1.1).

- Identify progress towards their goal, barriers encountered, and whether their planned strategies for dealing with barriers have been effective.
- If the barriers continue or new barriers have arisen, problem-solve other strategies using Flipchart 4.3c, on the consequences of their decision) as needed to evaluate them.

III. New Unhelpful Thought: "It's My Job to Fix Other People's Problems"

Activity: Fixing other people's problems

Session 4.3 draws from five illustrations on Handouts 4.15–4.18 for helping youth problem-solve how to cope with situations in which they want to help others who are facing serious problems. The aim of Session 4.3 is to help youth develop realistic expectations about helping others and create appropriate psychological (and sometimes physical) boundaries that can help protect them from getting enmeshed in, and overwhelmed by, other peoples' problems.

Each box below contains guidelines for using a specific illustration.

- Start with Handout 4.15, then tailor treatment by selecting specific illustrations based on their relevance for your clients.
- Use Flipchart 4.3b, Sizing Up a Situation, to emphasize the interconnections between situations, thoughts, feelings, behaviors, and consequences.

- Use Flipchart 4.3c on the consequences of choices to help group members evaluate the desirable and undesirable consequences of various ways of thinking, feeling, and behaving, and to select the best option depending on its likely consequences.
- Each box concludes with at least one optional *discussion* about each topic. Choose these, depending on your clients' specific needs and the time available.
- Build group members' self-confidence in their abilities to help themselves and others by labeling and praising their altruistic motives, compassion for others, creativity, interpersonal skills, and coping skills. Point out how they can draw on these same strengths in their own lives.

Today we are going to work on the unhelpful thought "It's my job to fix other peoples' problems" and its negative consequences. The skills we'll learn today will not only help you still care about others, but increase your ability to support them while protecting yourself from getting overloaded and overwhelmed.

Teenagers can often get stuck thinking it's their job to fix other peoples' problems. They do it because they really care about other people and want to help. They care about their parents' problems, their brothers' and sisters' problems, their relatives' problems, their friends' problems … there's often a long list of people they really care about and want to be happy. That says a lot about their character and what kind and caring people they are. And some teenagers really **have** *been taking care of serious adult responsibilities for a long time and they've gotten used to it. Maybe they feel if they don't do it, nobody else will. The problem is that taking on heavy responsibilities for fixing other people's problems can get teenagers to overdo it and overextend themselves so they become exhausted, discouraged, and miserable. Does this sound familiar?*

Sometimes teens convince themselves to take on other people's problems by thinking (heroic or guilty) thoughts like:

- *"It's all up to me."*
- *"No one can do it but me."*
- *"I just can't stand to see someone I care about in distress."*
- *"I've just got to fix their problem or something terrible will happen."*
- *"If I don't fix their problem, it means I don't love them enough."*
- *"If I don't fix their problem, it means I'm not a good son, daughter, or friend."*

Let's explore how this can work with some more "helping out a good friend" sketches. (Pick one or more of Handouts 4.15– 4.18 that you think are most relevant to your client or group. (Use Flipchart 4.3b to guide discussion for the selected sketches).

Guidelines for Handout 4.15: Boy Considers Dropping Out of School So He Can Help Mom Earn Money

Description: *Here's a story about a teenage boy who wants to help his stressed-out mother by doing something drastic.*

Facilitating questions (group leaders should allow group members to generate their own responses and offer answers only when necessary):

What is the **situation***?* Scene: Teenage boy sitting on the couch, doing his homework. He's looking over at his mom who's stressing over a pile of unpaid bills with a worried look on his face. He knows money is really tight right now.

What is his **hurtful thought***?* "I gotta help her. I better drop out of school so I can make some real money."

How could he be **feeling** *if he is thinking this way?* (Feeling discouraged, pessimistic, hopeless, stressed, worried, concerned, feeling angry and cheated.)

What **problem behaviors** *could he get into if he is thinking and feeling this way?* (Dropping out of school, so he doesn't get a diploma. But without a diploma he probably can't get a good job and make much money, so he might get into selling drugs or other things on the street.)

What **undesirable consequences** *could result from thinking, feeling, and behaving this way?* (Ideas include):

- Selling drugs is dangerous and can get you killed.
- It can also get you into trouble with the law and get you a criminal record, landed in jail, etc.
- You might start with selling drugs, but that might get you into more serious crimes later that could get you into even more serious trouble.
- You set yourself up for not achieving longer-term career goals because you don't have a diploma, so you could be the one facing a pile of unpaid bills a few years from now.

Let's consider what other choices he has that can lead to better consequences.

What **helpful** *thoughts could he use to replace his hurtful thoughts?*

- "My being in school and staying out of trouble might be one of the best things going on in my mom's life right now. It gives her hope."
- "Imagine how much more she'd be worrying if she found out I'm out on the street selling drugs. That would really add to her worries."
- "Things may be tight, but we'll get by. It won't always be this way."
- "I can help out in lots of ways that don't require dropping out of school."

(As appropriate):

Could **you** *believe these helpful thoughts if you were in his situation?*

How could **thinking about the situation** *in these ways change how he* **feels** *and* **behaves***?*

- It could help him stay in school and graduate, so he's in a better position to help, especially over the long term.
- It can also motivate him to think about other ways he can help out.

*What **positive consequences** are likely to follow if he chooses to have more positive thoughts, feelings, and behaviors? How could this situation turn out? (Better, the same, or worse?)*

- Staying in school and graduating is one of the most important things he can do to keep himself (and his family) out of poverty for the rest of his life.
- It will create opportunities for him that he won't have if he doesn't graduate and get the skills he needs.
- It will put him on a very different life course than if he dropped out of school.

Optional discussion: *Do you ever feel like this? Have you ever thought you had to make a big sacrifice (like dropping out) to help someone? What might his mom say if he told her he was dropping out? What if there are other ways to help that don't require making such a huge and risky sacrifice?*

Guidelines for Handout 4.16: Girl Looks with Worry at her Grieving Father and Brother

Description: *Here's a story about a grieving family who lost their mother to cancer last year. The teenage daughter is really worried about her father and younger brother.*

Facilitating questions (group leaders should allow group members to generate their own responses and offer answers only when necessary):

*What is the **situation**?* Scene: Teenage girl is sitting at the dinner table, looking with concern at her father and her younger brother, who both look sad and depressed.

*What is her **thought**?* "They've never been the same since mom died. I've got to help them."

*How could she be **feeling** if she is thinking this way?*

- Feeling stressed, worried, discouraged, even desperate – like she's just *got* to make her dad and brother feel better.
- She may even feel guilty that she's not as devastated as they are. (Does this mean she didn't love her mother as much as they did?)
- She may feel pressure to be the "mother" of the house now and ensure that everyone is doing well (much like her mother used to do).

*What **problem behaviors** could she get into if she is thinking and feeling this way?*

- She may tell herself she shouldn't feel happy because the people she loves are sad.
- She may feel like she has to drop everything she's doing, maybe even school, or all her after-school activities that her mom encouraged her to do.

*What **undesirable consequences** could result from thinking, feeling, and behaving this way?* (She could sacrifice important parts of her adolescence – giving up her hopes to graduate and participate in uplifting activities – to try to make her family happy,

and still not succeed because she can't control what they think and feel.)

*Let's consider what other choices she has that can lead to better consequences. What **helpful thoughts** could she use to replace her hurtful thoughts?*

- "Being in school and doing well is one of the best things going on in my family's life right now."
- "We each grieve in our own way, and the fact that I'm doing OK emotionally and doing well in school doesn't mean I love my mom any less."
- "Doing the things she encouraged me to do helps me to feel closer to her – like I am carrying on with her wishes and honoring her memory."

(As appropriate):

*Could **you** believe these helpful thoughts if you were in her situation?*

*How could **thinking about the situation** in these ways change how she **feels** and **behaves**?*

- It could help her stay in school and graduate.
- It can also help to protect her from becoming discouraged and depressed (because what good would three depressed people be to each other?).
- It can also motivate her to think about other ways she *can* help out at home.

*What **positive consequences** are likely to follow if she chooses to have more positive thoughts, feelings, and behaviors? How could this situation turn out? (Better, the same, or worse?)*

- Staying in school, graduating, and keeping involved in positive activities can help to protect her from sinking into sadness and despair following the death of her mother.
- It can also help her to be better able to support her family members, who are having a tough time right now.

Optional discussion: *Do you ever feel like this girl? Are there people you know (you don't need to say who) that you've been really worried about and wanted to help? (We'll be discussing ways to help others that also help to protect **us** from getting overburdened and exhausted in the next section.)*

Guidelines for Handout 4.17: Boy Vows That "He's Just Got to" Get his Mom to Stop Drinking

Description: *Here's a story about a young man who is living at home with his mom who has a serious problem: she's addicted to alcohol.*

Facilitating questions (group leaders should allow group members to generate their own responses and offer answers only when necessary):

*What is the **situation**?* Scene: Teenage boy is walking through the living room, where his mother is sleeping on the couch.

A bottle of alcohol is in the foreground. He looks sad and discouraged.

*What is his **thought**?* "I've just *got* to get her to sober up."

*How could he be **feeling** if he is thinking this way?* (Feeling sad, stressed, anxious, worried, discouraged, angry, and even desperate – like he's *just got* to get her to stop drinking.)

*What **problem behaviors** could he get into if he is thinking and feeling this way?* (He may not only have to take care of himself (like do the cooking, cleaning, and laundry) and his siblings – he may also feel compelled to intervene in her life (hiding bottles so she can't find them, covering for her absences at work when she's on a binge, etc.).)

*What **undesirable consequences** could result from thinking, feeling, and behaving this way?* (His efforts, although he has the best of intentions, are not likely to succeed – at least on their own. His mother needs professional help and the support of adults (her family, friends, church, community, Alcoholics Anonymous, etc.).)

Guidelines for Handout 4.18: "Even if Life at Home Gets Crazy, I Still Have my Own Personal Space"

What other choices does he have? There are a number of things he can do, including getting adults involved. For now, let's focus on what he can do by himself to cope when his mother goes on a binge.

*What **helpful** thoughts could he use to replace his hurtful thoughts?*

- "Even if life at home gets crazy, I still have my own personal space."
- "I can't be responsible for my mother's behavior – she is an adult who makes her own decisions."

Can you think of any other helpful thoughts he can have?

(As appropriate):

*Could **you** believe these helpful thoughts if you were in his situation?*

*How could **thinking about the situation** in these ways change how he **feels** and **behaves**?* (It can bring some relief and help to protect him from getting too discouraged and depressed as he realizes that he can't control his mother's drinking.)

*What **positive consequences** are likely to follow if he chooses to have more positive thoughts, feelings, and behaviors? How could this situation turn out? (Better, the same, or worse?)* (Having a safe place to go when things are getting crazy around you can help to protect you from sinking into a depression, feeling hopeless, or getting really frustrated and angry.)

Optional discussion: *Do you ever feel like this teenager? Are there people you know (you don't need to say who) who have serious problems, and you've been really worried about them and want to help? (We'll discuss ways to help that can protect us from getting overburdened in the* next section.*)*

IV. How Can You Tell When a Problem Is Not your Job to Fix?

- Refer to Handout 4.13, Wishing I Could Help When It's Not My Job to Fix, which group members completed for today's session.
- Note that some problems can be *fixed* (i.e. solved), whereas others need to be *handled* since some problems don't go away – they have to be managed.
- Help group members understand the difference between inappropriate *enabling* of others (by taking the responsibility for solving their problem off from their shoulders and putting it onto your own), versus appropriately *supporting* the person whose job it is to address the problem (by strengthening their ability to handle the problem).

Activity: How Can You Tell When a Problem Is Not your Job to Fix?

*We just explored how teenagers can get into situations where they want to help someone they care about, but may have **unrealistic expectations** about what they can and should do and then get frustrated when they can't do it. The secret is to care for others by first clarifying **whose job it is** to fix the problem and then developing **realistic** plans for what to do. Keeping this in mind, let's think about the people in your lives you want to help and the problems you wish you could help with.*

Have group members refer to Handout 4.13. Invite them to share the person's problem (they don't have to say who if they don't want) they wish they could fix. Listen sympathetically and respectfully praise their kindness and compassion.

Next, refer to Handout 4.19, on how to tell if a problem is your job to handle. Clarify the difference between situations where it *is*, versus *is not*, your job to fix the problem:

*How can you tell when a problem **is** your job to fix and when it is **not** your job to fix? Ask yourself,*

- *"Is this problem happening to **me**, or **between me and someone else**?" If the problem is **happening to you, or between you and someone else**, then **it's your job to fix**. For example, if you get in trouble with your mother for not cleaning your room, the problem is **between you and her**, and it's your job to work with her to fix it.*
- *"On the other hand, is this problem **happening to someone else, or between other people**?" If this is true, then it's not your direct responsibility to handle or fix the problem – it's **their** responsibility. For example, if your uncle just lost his job and is feeling stressed, is it your job to find him a new job? (No – the problem doesn't involve you directly.)*
- *Describe a situation where you're tempted to step in and try to fix things, but you think it may not be your job to fix. (It can be the same one you described on your practice sheet, or it can be a different one.)*

Invite group members to share their accounts while the others listen empathically.

Next, invite group members to use Handout 4.19 to evaluate the situations they described. Is it their job to handle, or isn't it?

Note: If some youth have been forced by their living circumstances to take care of addicted older family members, tend younger siblings (who would otherwise be neglected) etc., then:

- Acknowledge the compassion shown in their sacrifice on one hand, while also helping them evaluate the costs and benefits – acknowledge the healthy teenage developmental tasks and activities they may be giving up (sports, etc.) in order to do so.
- Offer to work with these youth individually (or make an appropriate referral) to help them lighten or remove these responsibilities, get their loved ones the help they need, and pursue lost or upcoming developmental opportunities they may have passed over.

*Learning to ask yourself "Is this my job to fix?" is a valuable skill because it helps to protect you from getting overinvolved in problems that aren't a teenager's job to fix. If a problem **is your job**, then you should do your best to handle it in a responsible way. If it **isn't**, you can still show support for the person by helping to strengthen them without taking their problem off their shoulders and placing it on yours. Remember there's a big difference between **supporting** someone (so they can better handle their problem) and **trying to fix their problem yourself**, even when you mean well.*

Optional Activity: Problems that *Are* Versus *Are Not* My Job to Fix

Use the following activity if you need examples of each type of problem, or if members have difficulty telling the difference between problems that *are* versus *are not* their job to fix. Consider starting with some of the examples below, and then elicit examples from their own lives. Have group members describe a situation they are not sure whether it is their job to fix and then rely on the group to help them sort things out.

Tips: Read problems from both lists in random order. Continue until they understand, creating your own examples as appropriate (the examples below are derived from high-school students). When group members *correctly* classify the problem, praise them and ask them to explain their reasoning – why does it make sense to them that this is not their job? Main ideas to get across include:

- It's not possible to take over another person's life and live it for them.
- There's a difference between *wanting* someone to feel better and *making them* feel better.
- You can't always make things go the way you want – some things you just have to live with. Learn to pick your battles carefully – be realistic and pick the ones you can win.

When group members *incorrectly* classify a problem that is *not* your job to fix, gently challenge them:

- *How does this problem directly involve you? Why is it your responsibility?*

- *Think of a hurtful thought about **making** their problem your job to fix (e.g. "I've got to get mom and dad to stop fighting or I'm not a good son"; "I've got to make my friend feel better or I'm no good as a friend"). What consequences could come from believing that thought?*

*Let's practice telling the difference between problems that **are** your responsibility to handle or fix, and problems that **aren't**. I'll read a list of problems. Your job is to decide whether the problem would be your job if it happened to you. Think about whether the "problem arrow" is pointing at you (it's **your** job) or whether it's pointing at someone else (it's **their** job).*

Not your Job to Fix

- Your mom argued with your grandma and now they don't talk to each other.
- Your brothers got into a fight over the TV, and now they can't watch it for two days.
- Your parent has a serious drug problem.
- Your sister is depressed and moody.
- Your best friend lost her father in an accident and she misses him all the time.
- Your family doesn't have enough money and your parents worry a lot about bills.
- Your grandma gets sick.
- Your best friend failed a test at school.
- Your neighbors' dog ran away from home.
- Your sister got grounded for staying out too late.
- Your mom's hours got cut back at work.
- Your friend's bike got stolen.
- A grandmother is in poor health, is short of money, and cares for several grandchildren.
- A friend is dealing drugs and you're worried he's going to get killed.
- Two uncles are feuding with each other and both own guns.
- A family member is in poor health but can't seem to give up cigarettes or cocaine.
- A mother is being battered by her husband or boyfriend. (Should a teen handle this alone?)
- A parent has a drinking or drug problem.
- A friend is depressed and you're worried about him/her.
- Your parent/caregiver doesn't have enough money to pay a hospital bill.

Is Your Job to Fix

- You get into a fight with your sister.
- You have a fight with your best friend and you haven't spoken to her in two days.
- You get disciplined for not doing your chores.
- You get picked up by police for skipping school.
- You argue with your mom about your friends.
- You argue with your dad/caregiver about how much time you spend on the phone.
- You get a low grade on your math test.
- Your parent says you can't go out with your friends until you finish your chores.
- You argue with your sister over the phone.

- You want a cell phone but your parent says you'll have to pay for it yourself.
- Your friends at school treat you differently since your mom died.
- Your teacher announces the next test will be on the anniversary of your dad's death.
- You feel down and do poorly in school.
- You like someone and want to call them up.
- A trauma reminder has made you feel irritable and on edge.
- You've run into a loss reminder and are feeling sad and lonely.

V. How Can I Help When It's Not My Problem to Fix?

- Distribute or pull out Handout 4.20, How Can I Help When the Problem Is Not My Job to Fix? (This will build on their homework exercise in which they used Handout 4.13. This exercise also builds on the social support recruitment skill learned in Module 1, except that they are now practicing how to furnish social support to others rather than how to ask for it.)
- Brainstorm helpful thoughts to help you feel better when you see a problem that's not a teenager's job to fix.
- Help group members develop appropriate boundaries (create a healthy distance) between themselves and others.

Activity: How Can I Help When It's Not My Problem to Fix?

*Now that we've learned how to tell whether or not a problem is your job to handle, let's talk about what you can **still do** to help even when the problem is not your job to fix. Using this skill, you'll be able to show the person that you care about them without having to try to fix their problem for them. **Here's the key: When you see a problem that's not your job to fix, support the person whose job it is to handle the problem rather than trying to take it on yourself.***

Go over Handout 4.20. Invite group members to share advice about what each can do to help with situations that are not a teenager's job to fix. Point out that they can still *support* the person whose job it is to fix by telling someone with a substance abuse problem about a local Alcoholics Anonymous meeting, or remind a battered mother that she can seek help from law enforcement or a local shelter. There are many different things they can potentially do, even if they don't have money or other things to share (remember that *material support*, such as money, clothes, food, and equipment, is only one of eight different types of support they can give).

Note: Some youth have family members and friends who are facing serious and potentially life-threatening problems (domestic violence, alcohol addiction, sexual or physical abuse). These circumstances may call for individual pull-out sessions and more intensive intervention/advocacy on the youth's behalf. The aim of such efforts is to recruit the support of responsible adults and agencies (e.g. law enforcement, suicide hotline, Alcoholics Anonymous, extended family members) rather than

leaving the adolescent to try to handle the problem by him or herself.

VI. Taking Good Care of Myself (Helping the Helper)

- Good self-care is a second valuable skill that can also help protect adolescents from becoming exhausted, burned out, and overwhelmed by trying to help others.
- For bereaved youth: employing positive qualities of a deceased loved one (that bereaved youth wish to keep and carry forward) in the service of others can help them in at least four ways. It can help them make that quality their own (inviting personal growth), feel close to the person who died (alleviating separation distress), find a sense of meaning and personal fulfillment, and carry on the person's positive legacy (alleviating existential/identity distress).

Activity: Taking Good Care of Myself (Helping the Helper)

We've learned two valuable skills for helping people who are facing problems.

- *The first skill is knowing how to tell the difference between problems that are **our** job to handle, and problems that are **other people's** job to handle.*
- *The second skill is knowing how to support and care for people whose job it is to handle a problem in a responsible way, without making **their** problem **our** problem.*

*We'll finish today's session by focusing on a third valuable skill: **learning how to support and take care of ourselves in a responsible way**. Supporting other people can be hard work, even if you're not making their problem your problem. Let's finish up with a couple more "helping a good friend" exercises to give us some ideas about how to help ourselves while we help others.*

Re-show Handout 4.17 (boy with alcoholic mother).

Remember this young man whose mother has a drinking problem? Sometimes teenagers have perfectly good reasons to doubt whether their caregiver can handle a serious problem (give examples as appropriate; e.g. drug addiction, mental health problems). When this happens, it's important to problem-solve how to get adults involved who can help, like doctors and nurses or your case manager. But even when things are hard (like for this teen), there are helpful thoughts you can think. What helpful thoughts can he think to help him deal with this situation? (Re-show Handout 4.18. Some examples include):

- *(Reassure yourself): Although this isn't fun, I can handle this. I've got a place to go (my room, a friend's house, Boys and Girls Club, the library) when things get bad.*
- *(Challenge all-or-none thinking/catastrophic thinking): This isn't good, but it's not the end of the world, either. Things are still going well for me in school, with my friends, etc.*
- *(Self-esteem): I care about them and their problem; I just know better than to try to fix everything for them. Taking*

care of myself (going to school, doing my homework, going to bed on time, getting up on time, eating healthy) doesn't mean I'm being selfish.

- (Optimism): They've handled tough problems before, and they can handle this, too. I need to have some confidence in them.
- (Realistic and practical): This is not a problem that I can fix, nor something they can fix alone. They need professional help, and I can talk to adults who can help them get the help they need.
- (**Optional discussion**): Problem-solve ways in which they can take care of themselves, especially during difficult times. Do you have a safe place to go? Do you have a responsible adult you can go to for help? How do you charge your batteries when you get run down?

Refer to Handout 4.21 (girl graduates while family celebrates).

Guidelines for Handout 4.21: "Celebrating My Graduation with My Family"

Another way to take care of yourself, especially when you lose someone you love, is to **keep doing good things that they encouraged you to do and that would make them proud**. This girl's mother valued education and always helped her and her brother to study before she got sick and died. **Working hard at school helped this girl to grieve for her mother in constructive ways**, and by graduating she's set a positive example for her brother and made her mother proud. Remember that **your doing well in something may be one of the best things going on in your family**, so take your success seriously and celebrate it when it happens, and let them celebrate it with you. Celebrating the good things that are happening can help you maintain a sense of bal-

ance and offset things that aren't going so well in other parts of your life.

(**Optional discussion**: especially for youth who completed Module 3: Young people who've lost a loved one and have **qualities about that person that they cherish and want to keep** (like giving good advice, or a sense of humor) find that **it feels good to use those qualities to help others**. This helps them practice that positive quality and make it their own, while feeling close to their loved one as they do good for others. Are there things you cherish and admire about your loved one that you could use to help others in a responsible way? If so, what qualities could you use, and how could you use these to help the people you care about (including people **they** cared about)?

Optional Exercise: Discriminating between Thrill-Seeking versus Risky Behavior

Another way to take care of yourself is to **tell the difference between healthy risks and unhealthy risks**. Healthy risks (like a bit of **thrill-seeking**) can make you feel nervous or excited, but they also help strengthen you (so you're not so frightened in scary situations that you can't think of what to do). For example, teenagers sometimes engage in a bit of **thrill-seeking** as they learn to handle intense emotions, like seeing a scary movie. On the other hand, **risky behavior** involves doing truly dangerous and destructive things that can get you or other people hurt or killed. A bit of thrill-seeking is normal, if it is done safely and responsibly. But risky behavior is always a bad idea and something to stay away from.

(For this exercise, use a large piece or paper or board to make your lists of healthy risks and unhealthy risks. Start with just a few examples that you can draw from the lists below and then have the group come up with their own ideas. Write all of these down.)

Healthy risks	Unhealthy risks
• Riding all the scary rides at a theme park	• Street/drag racing
• Doing a cannonball off the high dive board	• Carrying a gun or knife to school
• Going to a concert	• Getting into a fist fight
• Giving a speech in front of a big crowd	• Walking through a dark alley or unlit park
• Asking someone out who you really like	• Driving with someone who's drunk
• Going to a job interview for the first time	• Driving way over the speed limit
	• Having unprotected sex
• Seeing a scary movie with some friends	• Trying to recreate dangerous things you see on TV (where they say "don't try this at home!")
• Trying to get clean and sober if you've been using (it takes courage!)	• Experimenting with drugs
	• Selling drugs
• Deciding to go back to school if you dropped out	• Seeing whether you can shoplift and not get caught
• Having the courage to say no when you are pressured to have sex or take drugs	• Seeing how far you can go with a girl, even though she says "no!"
• Taking a martial arts class	• Driving without a seat belt
• Standing up to a bully	

Healthy risks	Unhealthy risks
• Trying out for a new sport	• Doing "daredevil" moves on your bike without proper equipment or training
• Taking an acting class	
• Learning how to dance	• Skipping school
• Going to summer camp/school trip away from home	• Skipping a court date
• Avoiding bad influences after you are released from a group home/juvenile justice setting	• Getting into a road rage incident
	• Violating rules of your probation
	• Being disrespectful to the judge

VII. Summary and Practice Assignment

Summarize and bring closure to the session. Introduce the practice assignment, to help group members prepare for the final session.

Activity: Three, Two, One Questions

Next week's session is special, because it's our last session. We'll be taking some time to review all the progress we've made, and share with each other our hopes and plans for our future lives.

To prepare for the activities next session, write some brief answers to the questions on Handout 4.22, Three, Two, One Questions. Let's review them quickly now.

Review the worksheet. Spend a little time reviewing the final question. You may draw upon the following comments:

*One of the best ways to heal, become strong, and move forward is to **make your life a positive answer to the bad things that have happened in your life**. For example:*

- *Kids who were abused by their father or had no father in the picture may decide now to be a good father when the right time comes.*
- *Kids who believe that the ambulance workers or doctors didn't do all they could to help a loved one may choose to go into medicine, so they can be sure that people will get the best help available.*
- *Kids who feel like laws didn't protect them, or didn't do right by their loved ones, may go into government, law enforcement, or the legal system (be a lawmaker, police officer, lawyer, or judge).*
- *(Where appropriate): Some kids feel sincere **guilt** about things they've done, and this may be appropriate if they've truly hurt people in the past. But rather than self-destructing through drugs, risky behavior, or bad relationships, how can they make up for it in a positive way? (**Optional**: lead discussion about compensatory justice, where you make up for your wrongs by serving others.)*
- *(Where appropriate): Some kids have desires to get **revenge** on people who have hurt them or people they love. What positive thing can you do that doesn't involve hurting more people and probably going to jail? Remember that **success is the best revenge of all** (having a good*

*life **despite** the selfish, thoughtless, and hurtful things that people have done to you – don't let them win!).*
- *We look forward to hearing about your life plans next time.*

VIII. Check-Out

- *How are you feeling now?* (Use the Feeling Thermometer ratings.)
- *What did you learn about yourself today?*
- *Please fill out the Check-Out Feedback Form. The title of today's session was "Learning to Help Myself and Others."*

If any group members are visibly agitated or troubled or report high levels of distress on the Feeling Thermometer, keep them after the group and determine an appropriate way to transition them back to their settings.

Implementing Module 4, Session 4.3 with Individual Clients

Preparation: Have available the youth workbook.

I. **Check-in Using** Handout 4.01, **the Feeling Thermometer.** After sharing his/her current feeling(s), ask the client to share anything that happened since the last session that may have influenced his/her feelings (in either a positive way or a negative way).

II. **Review practice assignment and previous sessions**. Deliver the exercise as written, but omit references to the group.

III. **New unhelpful thought: "It's my job to fix other people's problems."** The very same approach described in the manual can be used with individual clients. You will have a greater ability to truly custom select the illustrations that are most relevant to your client's life. Follow the directions as given.

IV. **How can you tell when a problem is not your job to fix**? The individual session will give you a greater ability to make this exercise interactive and collaborative. After giving examples customized to your client, you can brainstorm with him or her regarding actual situations in which the client is unclear whether it is or not his or her problem to address. Take the time to make sure your client is able to discriminate between these scenarios.

V. **How can I help when it's not my problem**? Follow the guidelines provided while omitting references to the group.

VI. **Taking good care of myself**. Deliver this step as written, custom-selecting illustrations to reflect your client's specific needs. Make the exercise engaging and interactive.

VII. **Summary and practice assignment**. Deliver this step as written.

VIII. **Check-out**. Deliver this step as written.

4.4 Graduation and Launching into the Future

Session Objectives

1. Review and reinforce treatment gains.
2. Help group members plan for – and look forward to – life after the group. Give special attention to relapse prevention and to steering youths into adaptive developmental trajectories.
3. Help group members process their reactions to ending treatment by encouraging them to express what participating in the group has meant to them.

Section number	Session overview
I	Check-in
II	Review practice assignment
III	Draw a new personal narrative time-line
IV	What I've learned in the group
V	Ending in a good way
VI	Appreciation activity
VII	Have a celebration!

Supplies

Every session	This session
• Group member workbooks	• Journals
• Flipchart	
• Large paper or easel pad	
• Colored markers or crayons	
• Pens/pencils	
• Kleenex	
• Tape	

Handouts in Workbook

Handout 4.01	Feeling Thermometer
Handout 4.24	My New Narrative Timeline
Handout 1.02	Trauma Goals Worksheet
Handout 1.03	Personal Goals Worksheet

Flipcharts

> ### 4.4 Today's Highlights
>
> 1. Check in
> 2. Review practice assignment (three, two, one questions)
> 3. Draw a new personal timeline
> 4. What I've learned in the group
> 5. Ending in a good way
> 6. Appreciation activity
> 7. Celebrate!

Session 4.4: Graduation and Launching into the Future

I. Check-In and Feeling Thermometer

- *How are you feeling right now?* (Use the Feeling Thermometer ratings.)
- *What happened or what did you do since we last met that you feel good about?*
- *Is anything going on that may make it difficult for you to keep your mind on the group today?*
- Briefly review (or have a group member review) Today's Highlights, Flipchart 4.4.

II. Review Practice Assignment

Start by asking group members if they practiced the abdominal breathing this week. If they did, how did it go?

- Practice doing five to ten abdominal breaths to remind themselves how it feels in their body.
- Check again with Feeling Thermometer to monitor any changes.

Then, review the practice assignment: "Three, Two, One Questions"

- Invite a few group members to share their answers to question 1, then a few more to question 2, and then a few to share their answers to question 3. Each member should share one answer.
- If a group member did not fill out the sheet, he or she can answer on the fly.
- Move along quickly, then summarize and praise responses.
- Describe how this will support the important work to be done in today's session.

III. Draw a New Narrative Timeline

Activity: Draw a new narrative timeline

Hand out copies of Handout 4.24, My New Narrative Timeline, to each group member with drawing pens. Review, as neces-

sary, how to use the timeline. Explain that today they will draw their personal narrative timeline to cover two periods:

- the past month and
- the next five years.

The first part should reflect their actual personal ups and downs over the past four weeks, focusing on those events they would like to share with the group. This is an opportunity for members to share some of their challenges as well as successes in overcoming those challenges, as well as fun and uplifting experiences.

The second part, covering the next five years, should include expected or likely hard times ("orange events" and "red events") as well as positive experiences that they would like to make happen ("green events"). The positive (green) events that they would like to make happen can include any goals or aspirations they have thought about or discussed in the group. It can also include their desire to create a healing and constructive response to the difficult and painful things they have experienced. Accomplishing these restorative goals can empower and uplift group members, help others in need, and make the world a better place. Try to build on last session's discussion (the restorative goal of *choosing to make your life a positive response to bad things that have happened*) by referring to members' restorative goals in this week's practice assignment.

Provide examples of healing and constructive responses to traumatic or loss experiences. You can create your own examples, or draw from the list below.

- *If you didn't have a father around, or your father mistreated you, you can decide to be a **good** father to your children when the right time comes.*
- *If you grew up feeling like you had no choice but to join a gang, you can decide to be a counselor who helps young people like you to find better alternatives.*
- *If you feel like people didn't do their best to **protect** you and your family, then you can aspire to be a lawyer or a judge or a police officer who upholds the law for everyone.*
- *If you wish that more could've been done to **save** your sick loved one, then aspire to be an EMT or a doctor or a nurse who provides the best treatments available, or even a scientist who searches for a cure.*
- *You may feel sincere **guilt or regret** over hurtful or foolish*

things you've done. But rather than punishing yourself through self-destructive behavior, what can you do to help make up for it? How can you put something positive out into the world to make up for any hurtful things you wish you could undo?

- *You may have **desires to take revenge** on people who hurt you. But instead of letting it eat away at you and getting more people hurt, what positive thing can you do?*

Invite group members to share their life plans as well as ideas that spontaneously arise (especially constructive responses to their traumatic experiences and losses). Encourage them to write down any new constructive ideas and plans that arise.

Mapping Out the Key Steps to Accomplishing Your Goal

Explain to group members that they can use the timeline to list some of the major steps that may be necessary to accomplish their goals – not necessarily *all* of the many steps, but the first few important steps needed to give them a good start. Invite them to post these goals in a place where they can see them every day and use them to keep motivated.

As needed, circulate and help group members while they work on their timelines.

Sharing the Timelines

*We'd now like to invite each of you to share your timeline in turn. Our ground rules for sharing are similar to those used during the sharing of personal narratives: **One person shares at a time while everyone else listens respectfully.** You can offer a supportive comment to each person when he or she is finished, if you wish.*

When everyone has presented, summarize the themes, express therapeutic admiration for their plans, and cheerlead for their success.

IV. What I've Learned in the Group

Activity: What I've Learned in the Group

Hand out (or have them look in their workbooks for) the completed goal sheets that they created at the beginning of the group. These can either be Handout 1.02, the Trauma Goals Worksheet, or Handout 1.03, the Personal Goals Worksheet.

We invite you to review your goal sheet, think back on where you were at the beginning of our group, and compare it to where you are now. How were you doing back then at school? At home and with your friends? How were you dealing with your posttraumatic stress or grief reactions? What were your thoughts and hopes for the future? Have these changed during our time together?

- Invite group members to each share one to two ways they have changed as a result of their work in the group.
- Summarize and praise their insights and personal growth.
- Invite group members to reflect on how their trauma or loss experiences have changed them and who they are striving to be now.

- Share your observations, in turn, of the positive changes each group member has made, and your respect and admiration for their courage and hard work.
- As appropriate, briefly share what working with the group has personally meant to you.

V. Ending in a Good Way

Use the following guidelines:

- Focus on personal and collective accomplishments.
- Help group members feel pride and satisfaction for their personal and collective accomplishments.
- Build confidence that members are better equipped with the skills needed to accomplish their (appropriate) personal goals and meet future challenges.
- Process graduation-related thoughts and feelings (sad, nervous, excited, angry, etc.).
- Increase tolerance for healthy separations.
- (If group members have prior losses): Help members distinguish between *traumatic* goodbyes (involuntary, often sudden, and permanent physical separations) versus *good* goodbyes (voluntary and appropriate separations that allow for future physical reunions if you choose). This can be a poignant discussion, so be sure to allow sufficient time for group members to emotionally recover before the session ends.

Activity: Thoughts about Transitioning from Group

Today is the last day of this group. Hopefully this is a "commencement" for you, which means "beginning," not end – a beginning to using the skills you have learned to help you cope with many situations in the future as you move forward with your lives.

Give each member a chance to share his/her feelings about the group coming to an end, and to say goodbye:

We'd like to give each of you some time to talk about how you think and feel about the group ending.

(As appropriate, depending especially on whether group members have histories of traumatic or tragic loss and appear distressed):

*Sometimes, goodbyes like the one we are saying today can remind us of past goodbyes, including times when we didn't get to **say** a proper goodbye or we didn't **want** to say goodbye. Does today's goodbye remind you of other goodbyes in your past? If so,*

- *What is the **same** about today's goodbye compared with other goodbyes in your past? (e.g. Feeling sad that we won't see each other again; I'll miss the group's support.)*
- *What is **different about today's goodbye**? (e.g. We've done our work and are now ready to move forward; we can see each other or get in touch in the future).*

Express confidence in group members' ability to continue on without the regular group meetings. If appropriate, plan for a "booster" reunion session when group members will check in about their lives and progress in pursuing their life goals.

If you have concerns about specific members' ability to function without the group, offer follow-up individual sessions or make referrals for other services as needed.

As appropriate, share your contact information with members, and invite them to share their contact information with each other in case they wish to correspond after the group ends.

VI. Appreciation Activity

Do a final activity that provides an opportunity for group members to express their appreciation for each other. Make this an uplifting final experience. You can decide whether the group leaders should also receive appreciations. Ideas include:

- (Simple version) Do a round in which each person (including the group leader) shares an appreciative word or statement that describes each group member.
- Invite each person to pass around a piece of paper with his or her name at the top, and everyone writes something they admire or appreciate on the paper.
- (Requires preparation): Do the following "pat on the back" activity.

Activity: "Pat on the Back" Exercise

To do this exercise, you need the following:

- Paper (either white or color construction paper)
- Tape
- Scissors
- Pens or a marker for each group member

1. Each group member should have enough cut-out paper hands (a hand traced on paper and then cut out) for each member of the group (and the leader if you like). You can do this before if there will not be time in the group, or you can do this as a group activity (each member tracing his or her hand on paper and cutting out multiple copies).
2. Each group member writes down on a hand cut-out something he or she appreciates or admires about each group member.
3. Group members put tape on the hands and go around taping their hand with a written compliment on the back of each group member. Every member should have a hand cut-out from each other member.
4. Each group member then has his or her "pats on the back" read aloud to the group. This can be read by one person or by the authors of each appreciation.

VII. Have a Graduation Celebration!

- Provide certificates of completion for group members, have a treat, or create some other opportunity to eat and socialize.
- Group leaders or assessors should *complete reassessments of all youth at this point to assess change based upon previous modules of therapy*. This information will also document the need (if any) for

further skills building or processing work. Complete the post-treatment assessments as soon as possible – no more than two weeks after termination. Obtaining quality assessment data, and minimizing missing cases, is of critical importance to evaluating treatment outcomes and quality assurance. If needed, use this final session to assess youth's outcomes, and offer to hold a party next week as your first "booster" session so you can socialize in your new roles as group graduates.

Implementing Module 4, Session 4.4 with Individual Clients

Preparation: Have available the youth workbook.

I. **Check-in using** Handout 4.01, **the Feeling Thermometer**: After sharing his/her current feeling(s), ask the client to share anything that happened since the last session that may have influenced his/her feelings (in either a positive way or a negative way).

II. **Review practice assignment and previous sessions.** Deliver the exercise as written but omit references to the group.

III. **Draw a new narrative timeline.** This can be a very powerful activity, especially when done with an individual client. You may talk through their drawing of their timelines for current and future events, all the while helping them to elaborate and share their thoughts and feelings with regard to these experiences. The guidelines as written should suffice to guide the process.

IV. **What I've learned in the group.** While this activity works best with a group process, you can still use the guidelines to elicit a shorter discussion of what they have gotten out of the program. Make sure you reference their initial goal sheets and praise them for progress made. Ask them "How did you do that?" as you emphasize their role and ownership of positive strides.

V. **Ending in a good way.** The intent here is to accomplish a "soft landing" for the end of the treatment. Use your standard approach towards termination, making sure to acknowledge possible past painful or difficult endings (including deaths and separations, placements, etc.) and highlight how this ending is different. Adapt the content provided.

VI. **Appreciation activity.** In individual sessions this is an opportunity to express your admiration for the work they have done while sharing specific comments about what you appreciated about them. This may be the ending point for the individual program.

VII. **Celebration.** Depending on your preference you may simply omit this activity.

MODULE 4 HANDOUTS

HANDOUT 4.01

Feeling Thermometer

Sometimes we feel a feeling *just a little bit*, and other times we feel a feeling so strongly that we feel like we might *burst* with that feeling! You can rate or measure your feelings, just like a thermometer measures temperature. The number tells how intense the feeling is.

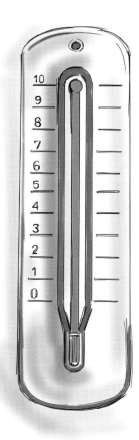

What distressful feelings are you having right now? How would you rate each of these feelings (on a scale of 0 to 10)?

HANDOUT 4.02

What are things you would like to do or have in your life over the next five years?

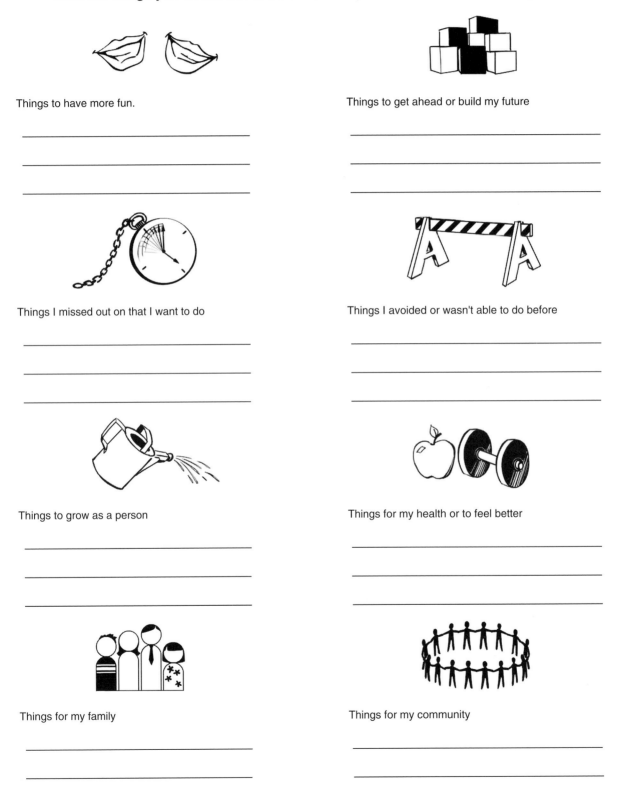

Things to have more fun.

_____

_____

_____

Things to get ahead or build my future

_____

_____

_____

Things I missed out on that I want to do

_____

_____

_____

Things I avoided or wasn't able to do before

_____

_____

_____

Things to grow as a person

_____

_____

_____

Things for my health or to feel better

_____

_____

_____

Things for my family

_____

_____

_____

Things for my community

_____

_____

_____

HANDOUT 4.03

Personal Development Goals: *Stop* Goals

Part I: Stop goal (something that is negative or unproductive that I want to stop doing)

_____

_____

Why is my stop goal important to me?

_____

Part II: What steps do I need to take to achieve this goal?

- Step 1 _____
- Step 2 _____
- Step 3 _____

PART III: What barriers do I need to address?

Look outside of me: What situations will make stopping more difficult?

_____

_____

Look inside of me: What discouraging thoughts or feelings are getting in the way of stopping this behavior?

_____

_____

Part IV: *Brainstorm* what are all my options for dealing with the barriers?

(Write down as many as you can.)

_____

_____

Part V: *Choose* the best option

Which options are "do-able" and which are not? (Which do you have the time, strength, know-how, support, and other resources to carry out?)

_____

_____

_____

What is the best option? (Which option looks best in terms of its "do-ability" and likelihood of success?)

_____

HANDOUT 4.04

Personal Development Goals: *Start* Goals

Part I: *Start* goal (a positive change that will help me make a step forward in my life)

_____

_____

Why is my start goal important to me?

_____

Part II: What steps do I need to take to achieve this goal?

- Step 1 _____
- Step 2 _____
- Step 3 _____

Part III: What barriers do I need to address?

Look outside of me: What situations will make stopping more difficult?

_____

_____

Look inside of me: What discouraging thoughts or feelings are getting in the way of stopping this behavior?

_____

_____

Part IV: Brainstorm *what* are all my options for dealing with the barriers?

(Write down as many as you can.)

_____

_____

_____

Part V: *Choose* the best option

Which options are "do-able" and which are not? (Which do you have the time, strength, know-how, support, and other resources to carry out?)

_____

_____

_____

What is the best option? (Which option looks best in terms of its "do-ability" and likelihood of success?)

_____

HANDOUT 4.05

Check-Out Feedback Form

Session topic: Next Steps

Your date of birth: _____

Today's date: _____

Facility: _____

What about today's session was most useful to you? Which activities and materials were the most helpful?

_____

_____

_____

What specific suggestions do you have for how to make the group better?

_____

_____

_____

How comfortable were you about today's topic? (Please circle a number.)

1	2	3	4	5
Extremely uncomfortable	Fairly uncomfortable	Somewhat comfortable	Fairly comfortable	Very comfortable

What were you thinking and feeling during today's group?

_____

_____

_____

_____

How are you feeling now?

_____

_____

_____

_____

HANDOUT 4.06

"I Can See My Future More Clearly Now, So I Can Make Better Plans for How to Live My Life"

HANDOUT 4.07

Secondary Adversities Following a Natural Disaster, War, or Inner-City Violence

HANDOUT 4.08

Getting Pressured to Do Something I Don't Want to Do

HANDOUT 4.09

Traumatic Bracing

HANDOUT 4.10

Sharing the Same Sad Fate as the Deceased (Fortune Telling)

HANDOUT 4.11

Reluctance to Form New Relationships for Fear of Suffering Further Losses

HANDOUT 4.12

Anticipating Future Reminders (Sending Out Announcements)

HANDOUT 4.13

Wishing I Could Help When It's Not My Job to Fix

Directions: Young people often run into problems that are happening to someone they care about, where they really wish they could step in and solve it for them. In the space below, please describe a situation faced by someone you care about where you wish you could do more to help. Be careful not to include the person's identifying information (such as their name) to protect their privacy.

_____

_____

_____

_____

_____

_____

_____

_____

_____

_____

_____

_____

_____

_____

_____

_____

HANDOUT 4.14

Check-Out Feedback Form

Session topic: Coping with Difficult Days

Your date of birth: _____

Today's date: _____

Facility: _____

What about today's session was most *useful* to you? Which activities and materials were the most helpful?

_____

_____

_____

_____

What specific suggestions do you have for how to make the group better?

_____

_____

_____

_____

How comfortable were you about today's topic? (Please circle a number.)

1	2	3	4	5
Extremely uncomfortable	Fairly uncomfortable	Somewhat comfortable	Fairly comfortable	Very comfortable

What were you thinking and feeling during today's group?

_____

_____

_____

_____

How are you feeling now?

_____

_____

_____

HANDOUT 4.15

Boy Considers Dropping Out of School So He Can Help Mom Earn Money

HANDOUT 4.16

Girl Looks with Worry at her Grieving Father and Brother

HANDOUT 4.17

Boy Vows That "He's Just Got to" Get his Mom to Stop Drinking

HANDOUT 4.18

Even if Life at Home Gets Crazy, I Still Have my Own Personal Space"

HANDOUT 4.19

How to Tell if a Problem Is my Job to Handle

Ask myself two questions:

- Is the problem happening *to me*, or *between me* and someone else? Or,
- Is the problem happening *to someone else*, or *between other people*?

The problem *is* my job to handle when:

- The problem is happening *between me* and someone else, or

- The problem is happening *to me*

- **The problem is *not* my job to handle when:**

- The problem is happening *between other people*, or

- The problem is happening *to someone else*

  The key: it's not your job to handle if the "problem" arrow isn't pointing at you!

HANDOUT 4.20

How Can I Help When the Problem Is Not My Job to Fix?

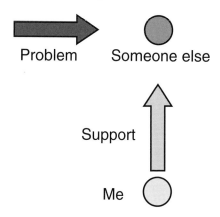

The key: support the person who *has* the job of handling the problem!

Providing support will:

- Show that you care.
- Support the person whose job it is to handle the problem.
- Help you not take on too much responsibility for others' problems.
- Help you create a "safe distance" from the problem so it doesn't feel so overwhelming.

Ideas for supporting someone include:

• Let them get it off their chest by listening.	• Tell them about a time when you went through a similar experience (if you have!).
• Give them a hug or hold their hand.	• Point out what's going well in their life.
• Tell them you hope they feel better.	• Remind them that things will get better.
• Show them you are thinking about them (send them a card, or do something thoughtful for them without being asked).	• Check in with them to see how they're doing.
• Remind them of challenges they've faced before, and reassure them that they can handle this one too.	• If they need professional help, help them get it.
• Encourage them to not give up.	• Say a prayer for them.
• Give them a sincere compliment.	• Work on something that *is* your job, like your chores and homework (this will remind them that some things are still going well).
• Keep them company.	• Stay out of trouble, so you don't add to their list of things to worry about.

HANDOUT 4.21

Girl Graduates While Family Celebrates

HANDOUT 4.22

Three, Two, One Questions

To prepare for the discussions in our last session, write some brief answers to the following questions:

What are **three** positive or difficult things you have experienced in the past month?

1. _____

2. _____

3. _____

What are **two** things you would like to make happen in your life over the next few years?

1. _____

2. _____

What is **one** way you would like to live your life as an answer to what happened to you?

1. _____

HANDOUT 4.23

Check-Out Feedback Form

Session topic: What *Is* and What *Is Not* your Job?

Your date of birth: _____

Today's date: _____

Facility: _____

What about today's session was most useful to you? Which activities and materials were the most helpful?

_____

_____

_____

_____

What specific suggestions do you have for how to make the group better?

_____

_____

_____

_____

How comfortable were you about today's topic? (Please circle a number.)

1	2	3	4	5
Extremely uncomfortable	Fairly uncomfortable	Somewhat comfortable	Fairly comfortable	Very comfortable

What were you thinking and feeling during today's group?

_____

_____

_____

_____

How are you feeling now?

_____

_____

_____

HANDOUT 4.24

My New Narrative Timeline

The past month   The next five years

Appendix 1

Guide for Streamlined Implementation of Module 1

Certain treatment settings, such as schools, have significant limitations on how long sessions may be and how many sessions overall are possible. In these circumstances sessions may be limited to 50–60 minutes and, perhaps, only 15–20 sessions overall are possible. Since a number of the sessions in Module 1 require approximately 75 minutes to complete, this appendix was designed to provide a guide to how you may select the most important activities in each session and thereby move through the material in a timely manner. The key is to be very clear on the one to two concepts and activities that are most central to each session and focus on these. The guide below will highlight those core components. And rather than spending time going through multi-step handouts, you may save time by converting these into more interactive discussions. Preparation prior to conducting the session is essential.

Session 1.1: The primary tasks in this session involve introducing the program and structure to the youth, developing a customized contract or agreement, and eliciting current coping strategies. The primary activities on which to focus are the *group contract* and the *sharing of current coping strategies.*

Session 1.2: The key and central activity in this session is to help the participants recognize their personal posttraumatic stress and grief reactions. The bulk of the time should be spent on using the handouts to accomplish this in the form of a very interactive discussion.

Session 1.3: The central task here is to introduce the Three-Step Model and select only one to two of the emotion awareness activities that are most suitable to your group members.

Session 1.4: The central task here is to help group members recognize their personal trauma and loss reminders and how they elicit distress or prompt problematic behaviors and reactions.

Session 1.5: The central task here is to help group members understand the functionality of their current reactions and coping strategies. Even problematic responses to stress, such as drug or alcohol use, have very clear payoffs. That is why they persist. The concept of getting stuck in "alarm mode" is important and the bulk of the time should be spent on the activity in which group members review the short- and long-term consequences of their coping strategies.

Session 1.6: The central task in this session is to make the case that how you think about things and what you "say to yourself" is a critical factor in how you will end up feeling and acting. The illustrated handouts are very useful in this regard. Use them to introduce and get a little practice using the "Sizing Up a Situation" model.

Session 1.7: The central task here is to practice identifying and "gently updating" hurtful thoughts and beliefs that are often inaccurate. You may do this in a very simple way by simply identifying the thought and evaluating facts that support or do not support the interpretation and then find a more accurate and helpful way of thinking. Or you may layer on the training on common "thinking errors." The bulk of the time should be spent first practicing this on one or two of the skit examples and then having them practice on a situation in their own life that elicited feelings or behaviors that they did not like.

Session 1.8: The heart of this session is to have group members reflect on what kinds of support and engagement they would like to have more of in their life and then practice a specific skill designed to help them obtain this. The bulk of the session should be focused on the activity Five Steps to Getting Support.

Appendix 2

Dissemination, Implementation, and Sustainability Guidelines

There is an established literature and an emerging evidence base for successful implementation of new practices in child-serving systems (see, for example, Meyers et al., 2012). The following guidelines offer a brief overview of steps to consider, based primarily on our experience.

In Juvenile Justice Residential and Probation Settings

TGCTA focuses on reducing posttraumatic stress disorder and other posttraumatic symptoms and behaviors, and these goals are consistent with those of child-serving clinical settings. Juvenile justice facilities have different primary goals. Their mandate is to ensure community and facility safety, reduce youth recidivism, and address and correct criminogenic thinking and behavior in youth who are in trouble with the law. Mental health treatment is not central to their mission. Unless trauma-focused treatment helps them meet their correctional goals, it will likely not be successfully implemented and sustained in juvenile justice systems.

Guidelines

Senior leaders: Work collaboratively with senior leaders to invite their commitment to this new project. Share outcome data that trauma-focused treatment, combined with trauma-informed staff training, can make facilities safer and reduce incidents and incident reports. Remind leaders that TGCTA does not replace the correctional work essential to their mandate but adds another tool to their toolkit of effective practices.

Staff: Combine the treatment groups in residential facilities with trauma-informed practices for staff, so that the facility is permeated with trauma-informed awareness and practices. To facilitate staff training, go to the National Child Traumatic Stress Network website (nctsn.org) and access *Think Trauma*, a staff training manual available at no cost. *Think Trauma* has been implemented throughout the United States and in some

Canadian juvenile justice facilities and should be used as a complement to TGCTA. Staff in residential facilities function in "parental" roles for incarcerated youth, so including them in trauma awareness and treatment parallels the parent and caregiver involvement found essential for other evidence-based trauma treatments such as trauma-focused cognitive behavioral therapy. To the extent possible, include trauma-informed training and skills building for juvenile probation officers and parents of youth receiving TGCTA who still live in the community while on probation or parole. If youth are returning to foster care placements, access the trauma-informed foster-parent training at nctsn.org entitled *Caring for Children Who Have Experienced Trauma: A Guide for Resource Parents.*

Youth selection: Even after careful individual selection, it can happen that some youth cannot function in a trauma treatment group. Youth from rival gangs may need to be separated, for example, or the primary trauma issue may be one, such as child sexual abuse, that is not appropriate to share with peers. We have found that it works well to transition the youth to individual work by explaining that they are better suited for individual sessions and they generally accept and are even relieved to leave the group.

Manual: It is not essential to complete every exercise of every session with every group. Use your clinical judgment about how to proceed. This is a modularized manual intended for flexible use in response to the needs of each group. The TGCTA manual is not a cookbook. It is a treatment guided by a manual. Some sessions can last more than one week with one group and be easily completed in a single hour during the next group sequence. Sessions can last 45, 60, 75, or 90 minutes, but whatever length is chosen, it should be the same every week.

Voluntary: Some facilities implement only Modules 1 and 4, and because these two modules focus on foundational coping skills and future orientation, they can be required parts of the curriculum in correctional facilities. However, *facilities must never require that youth participate in trauma treatments that include the sharing of their own trauma and grief histories.* Therefore, facilities that implement TGCTA using Modules 1, 2, and 4; 1, 2, 3, and 4; or 1, 3, and 4 should never require youth to take part in these groups. Staff and clinicians who work with residents and have some knowledge of their trauma histories and the impact of them can recommend individuals for groups, and selection for participation is covered in detail in the pre-session chapter of the manual.

Confidentiality: Because a residential treatment center or a school can be like a small village, it can be tempting for youth to use the confidences shared during groups as gossip back on the units. The group contract that youth develop in Session 1.1 has been generally effective in blocking this behavior, but we have found that backing it up with institutional sanctions for youth who violate group confidentiality ensures adherence.

Alerting staff, caregivers, and parents: Youth who are working with trauma reminders or sharing their trauma and grief histories can become temporarily reactive or experience some sleep disturbances. Although this is not very common, it can happen, so it is wise to alert caregivers, staff, or probation officers that this can be a predictable and temporary byproduct of trauma treatment and can be managed on the units or at home with the coping strategies taught and practiced in Module 1.

Outcome data: In addition to collecting standard outcome data about symptom reduction, we suggest that including data more consistent with the mission of correctional facilities, such as incident report data, may support sustainability and convince administrators and funders that trauma treatment is useful to fulfill their mission.

In Outpatient and Community-Based Settings

Many of the guidelines given above are also relevant for implementing TGCT-A in community-based settings. In addition, there are some specific challenges to consider. Below are suggestions from community providers who have successfully used the intervention.

Recruitment and retention: Recruit more participants than you think you want. Daily stressors will interfere with attendance, so attrition may occur at a greater rate than in residential or school settings. Partnering with another agency, especially Juvenile Probation Services, can be an effective way to encourage and reinforce attendance. Partnering with parents and guardians is also highly recommended to help sustain youth investment in the intervention. It is important that parents understand the benefits of the intervention for both their children and themselves. Some settings run a parallel parenting group, especially for foster and adoptive parents. Location and transportation issues will need to be addressed during planning sessions. Be realistic about how many sessions you can conduct. Completing Modules 1 and 4 may be all you can accomplish.

Promoting group cohesion: Because participants may be less likely to know each other than those who do TGCTA in residential settings, consider expanding Session 1 into two sessions and developing additional creative ways to help them become comfortable with each other. Getting-acquainted games and activities as well as food offerings can be very helpful. Conducting a 90–120 minute group with a substantial snack or meal provided at break has been effective in sustaining attendance in some settings. Youth often like to call the group a "club" and give it a special name.

In Schools

Although the guidelines about youth selection, confidentiality, voluntary participation, and modularized implementation also apply to groups run in schools, this setting poses unique challenges. School administrators measure success as higher rates of graduation, better report cards and test scores, fewer students who are suspended or who drop out, and the establishment of a safe environment. The daily schedule is very full, and class periods are briefer than the standard session length for TGCT-A. Time is at a premium; so is space. In addition, school districts have many levels of hierarchical leadership, and programmatic interventions and changes can be lost without clear support from top leadership. As a result, it can be helpful to begin with meetings at the district level with clear buy-in from senior leadership. Target schools are then identified and school leadership brought in with a clear understanding that the program is a district priority. And while this level of support is not essential it is extremely helpful.

Senior leaders: In school settings, it is essential to work with school administrators and teachers from the outset to plan the logistics of implementing TGCTA and *Think Trauma* and to garner their support. This requires time, many conversations, and the ability to translate your program goals into changes that benefit their bottom line. Ideally, plan on school level meetings before the summer of the academic year you wish to implement. This will ensure time to meet with administrators and key stakeholders within the school that include counseling staff, nurses, security, and the general faculty. Have all of your logistics, referral systems, and meeting times and places worked out through careful negotiation. Become a part of the school team with a very visible presence. During the summer in-service training sessions, provide presentations on the program and enlist faculty as partners in this work that will result in changes they care about.

Class periods are often as short as 45 minutes, and private, quiet settings can be hard to find. We have learned that without full support and commitment from leadership, this group treatment does not succeed in the schools. If the group is scheduled during the school day, visiting clinicians need support from staff to assist with scheduling and attendance. Some schools have found it preferable to schedule groups (with healthy snacks) after school, and as with community dissemination, youth often like to call the group a "club." An after-school group also allows for more time than one conducted during the school day. After-school sessions can allow for more intense and sustained work with traumatic memories and trauma reminders, and members will not have to transition from intensive trauma memory work back into classes when groups take place after school.

Trauma-informed schools: It is more challenging to make a school "trauma-informed" than it is to do so in a home or a residential treatment center. The role of a teacher is not primarily to act as a parent or caregiver to a child but to teach a skill or a subject, so trauma-informed manuals such as the staff training, *Think Trauma*, or the foster-parent training, *Caring for Children Who Have Experienced Trauma*, are not directly applicable to teachers. There is, however, a guide developed by the National Child Traumatic Stress Network that may be useful in this regard (NCTSN, 2016).

Selecting participants: Participants can be identified by referrals from school staff and faculty as well as by screening. For school personnel, it is helpful to develop a one-page flyer that provides a paragraph describing the program and a simple form for referring a student. You should also reach out to parent–teacher associations and provide information on the program. In this way, parents can also refer their children. For screening, you can use any of a number of trauma- and loss-screening instruments that may be administered to students with parent consent. Once you have parental consent and have selected youth based on the screening interview, you will conduct a full pre-session interview with each youth being considered for group

participation to explain the purpose of the group and determine whether that adolescent is interested and would be able to participate in a school-based trauma treatment group. For more detailed information about screening and selection for school-based TGCTA groups, see Saltzman et al. (2006) and Saltzman et al. (2001).

Scheduling: By the time that students are identified and you have obtained parent permission for them to participate in the program, you may well be two months into the semester. For this reason, we recommend that the groups meet for the entire school year. Even then, with holidays, you may only have 18–24 sessions. With the modular structure of the program, however, you can adjust the length of the program and find a way to do good work even in a foreshortened amount of time. You can even try and conduct a trauma-grief group within a single semester though this will probably entail only using Modules 1 and 4.

References

Meyers, D. C., Durlak, J. A., & Wandersman, A. (2012). The quality implementation framework: A synthesis of critical steps in the implementation process. *American Journal of Community Psychology*, 50, 462–480.

NCTSN Schools Committee (in press). *Creating, Supporting, and Sustaining Trauma-Informed Schools: A System Framework*. Los Angeles, CA, and Durham, NC: National Center for Child Traumatic Stress.

Saltzman, W. R., Layne, C. M., Pynoos, R. S., Steinberg, A. M., & Aisenberg, E. (2001). Trauma-and grief-focused intervention for adolescents exposed to community violence: Results of a school-based screening and group treatment protocol. *Group Dynamics: Theory, Research, and Practice*, 5, 291–303.

Saltzman, W. R., Layne, C. M., Steinberg, A. M., & Pynoos, R. S. (2006). Trauma/grief-focused group psychotherapy with adolescents. In J. Rose, H. I. Spitz, L. Schein, G. Burlingame, & P. Muskin (eds.), *Psychological Effects of Catastrophic Disasters: Group Approaches to Treatment*. Binghamton, NY: Haworth Press, pp. 669–730.

Appendix 3

Working with Parents and Caregivers In TGCTA

Caregiver Engagement

TGCTA can be implemented for incarcerated adolescents in the juvenile justice system, for justice-involved youth in diversion or probation programs, for youth in residential treatment programs, in schools, and in community clinics. Caregivers range from a biological parent or parents living together or separately, foster parents, older siblings, grandparents, aunts, uncles, and family friends. Caregiver attitudes range widely, from those who may be afraid of their aggressive offspring and wish they would never return home, to those who are devoted and make the effort to participate in treatment and faithfully visit youth who are in residential treatment. Trauma and loss know no boundaries, so that families vary as well by income, race, ethnicity, vocational status, age, sexual orientation, and religious affiliation.

Practical obstacles to participation include caregiver poverty, mental illness, substance misuse, need for childcare, scheduling, and the availability and affordability of transportation. In cases where families cannot be seen in person, phone or Skype consultation is recommended, but many families move often and have no regular telephone service. The first step to parent/caregiver participation involves a joint discussion during which these obstacles are identified and realistically addressed. Some facilities offer bus or taxi vouchers for caregivers to attend as many sessions as possible; some offer group treatment sessions during which healthy snacks are provided; and some residential centers use Sunday caregiver visiting days to connect with caregivers. When in-person contact is not possible, try to send trauma-informed parenting handouts to caregivers either by mail or with the youth who is in treatment.

For those parents and caregivers who are willing and able to participate, the following principles can enhance engagement.

1. Work with caregivers to articulate their goals for themselves and their children and explain how TGCTA can help achieve these goals. The principles of *motivational interviewing* are effective for this step,

especially in cases where caregivers have given up hope that anything can change.

2. Level the playing field by working collaboratively with caregivers rather than establishing a hierarchical structure with you as the expert who is remedying family deficiencies. Instead, listen as they identify not only the challenges they and their children encounter, but also their strengths and resiliencies. You are not "pretending" to be collaborative – caregivers have expertise about their children and the circumstances of their lives that more than matches your expertise about the impact of trauma and treatments for it.

3. As part of your collaborative listening, ask parents and caregivers to describe their past experiences with the mental health and/or juvenile justice systems and show that you hear them by repeating to them what you understand them to be saying. Do not agree or disagree; just listen.

4. Following this listening, explain to caregivers how TGCTA works with traumatized families to reduce children's behavior problems and prevent family conflicts by describing how we all can become stressed or triggered by trauma reminders. When triggered, we can all act impulsively and often destructively in negative interpersonal reactions that too often escalate. For this psychoeducation piece, the youth handouts from Module 1, Session 1.4, should be shared with parents, along with the coping strategy handouts from Module 1, Session 1.5. Share these with the parents and go over them in detail, and ask parents to offer examples in their family experience where they felt they or their children were triggered and handled it well, and other instances where they felt they had not done well and the interaction may have escalated into reactive aggression. If it would be helpful, you can share the data from TGCTA implementation in juvenile justice residential treatment programs that show how incident reports reduced dramatically as staff and youth practiced new coping skills in response to trauma reminders.

5. In joint parent sessions, prepare and coach the parents to notice and comment positively on the concrete positive steps their children are making for trauma recovery and behavioral stabilization. We have too often observed parents wishing to use these visits to give their offspring advice, to scold, and to criticize. Praising their progress will be far more effective in helping youth sustain their treatment progress, so the clinician needs to prepare caregivers with guidelines about the effectiveness of praise before the joint session, and be watchful, directive, and even a little bossy during the joint parent–child session. When we have been able to get parents and caregivers to do this, we have seen this interactive shift transform family relationships. Youth begin to look forward to family visits rather than dreading them.

6. Assist those parents that need it with case management resources and community services about which many of them may be unaware. Access will be greater for urban families than for impoverished families in rural and small town areas, but do all you can to identify supports.

Index

abdominal breathing, 80

adaptive grieving, 6

adolescence, 1, 5
    aspects of development, 1–2

adolescent expert reframe, 27–28

adversities, coping with, 273–275, *See also* secondary adversities

alarm mode, 52–53
    distraction through positive activities, 56

alternative interpretations, generation of, 66, 67–68

anger, 43
    about a death, 200–201
    at people responsible, 201–202
    facts about angry feelings, 202–203

appreciation activity, 292

Armenian earthquake, 1988, 4

avoidance reactions, 37, 83

belief problem statement, 161

bereavement. *See also* grief reactions; life changes following a death; loss reminders; Module 3
    adaptive grieving, 6
    feeling alienated/ostracized, 221–222
    how to talk about the death, 219
    other people's expectations, 223
    primary bereavement, 18
    rumors about the death, 221
    situations that usually involve the deceased, 221
    staying connected after a loss, 212–213, 248
    stigmatized deaths, 222
    trauma interactions, 6
    who to tell about the death, 219

bereavement-related distress, 18

blame for not preventing death, 202

Bosnian civil war, 4

breathing, 35

deep (abdominal) breathing, 35
    stress reduction exercise, 35

calming activity, 49
    calming exercises, 56
    calming self-talk, 55, 103

Can't Stop Thinking About the Way He Died handout, 194–195

caregiver engagement, 321–322

causal reasoning ability development, 1

Check-In procedure, 25, 33

Child and Adolescent Trauma Treatments and Services Consortium (CATTS), New York, 4

circumstance-related distress, 176, 184, 264
    anger at people responsible, 201–202
    blame for not preventing death, 202
    guilty thoughts related to a death, 199–200
    risk factors, 176
    shame over circumstances of death, 194
    unable to stop thinking about the manner of death, 194–195

cognitive triangle for situation–thought–feeling–behavior link, 60

communication, 71
    aids and barriers to, 71
    "I" messages, 72–73
    purpose of communication focus, 71

community-based settings, 319

complexity of the traumatic experience, 133–134

coping strategies. *See also* positive personal coping toolkit
    development, 1, 27
    positive and negative strategies, 53
    sharing within group, 32

counterfactual reasoning, 1

daily occurrences, dealing with, 219

death. *See* bereavement; grief reactions; loss reminders; Module 3

deep (abdominal) breathing, 80

developmental adversities, 8

developmental derailment, 263

developmental disruptions, 262–264

developmental themes, 135

difficult days
    anticipating, 218
    dealing with, 218–219

emotions
    color of, 43
    locating in the body, 43
    monitoring changes exercise, 44–45
    reading emotional expressions in others, 43

engagement with adolescent, 14–15

existential distress, 176, 183, 264
    feeling nothing matters anymore, 192–193
    giving up on future plans, 192
    reunification fantasies, 191
    thinking they will never love again, 193–194

externalizing symptoms, 4

Fear of Getting Close handout, 191–192

Feeling Thermometer, 35, 47, 79, 162, 224

Feelings Selfie, 42–43, 90

fight response, 53

fixing other people's problems, 280–285

flight response, 53

freeze response, 53

gender differences, 5

Giving Up on Future Plans handout, 192

goals, 18–19
    goal statement, 19